Shojo Beat

OTOMEN

Story & Art by
Aya Kanno

Volume
TEN

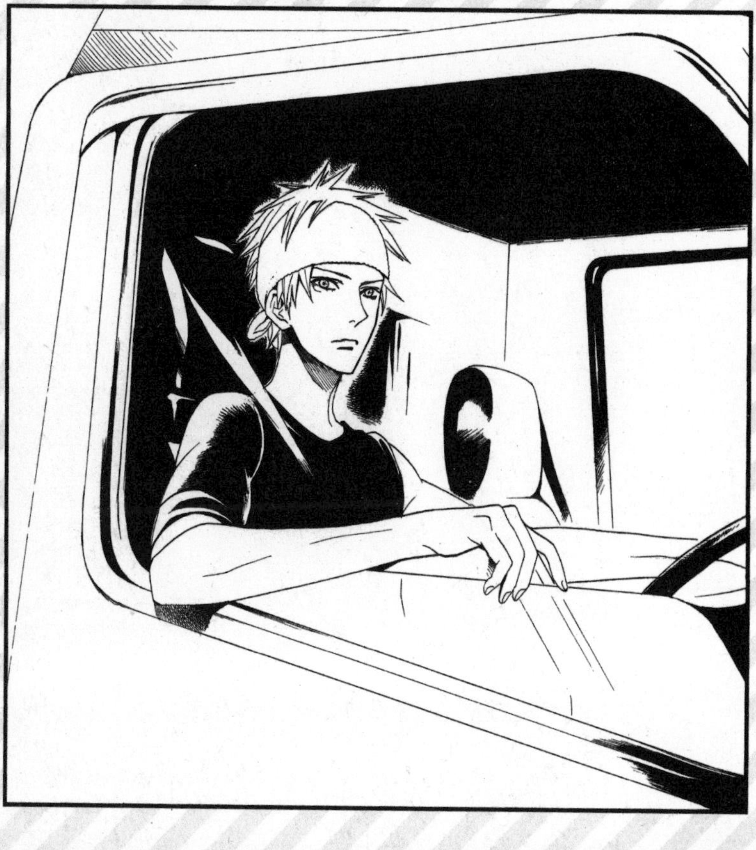

·OTOMEN *volume 10* CONTENTS

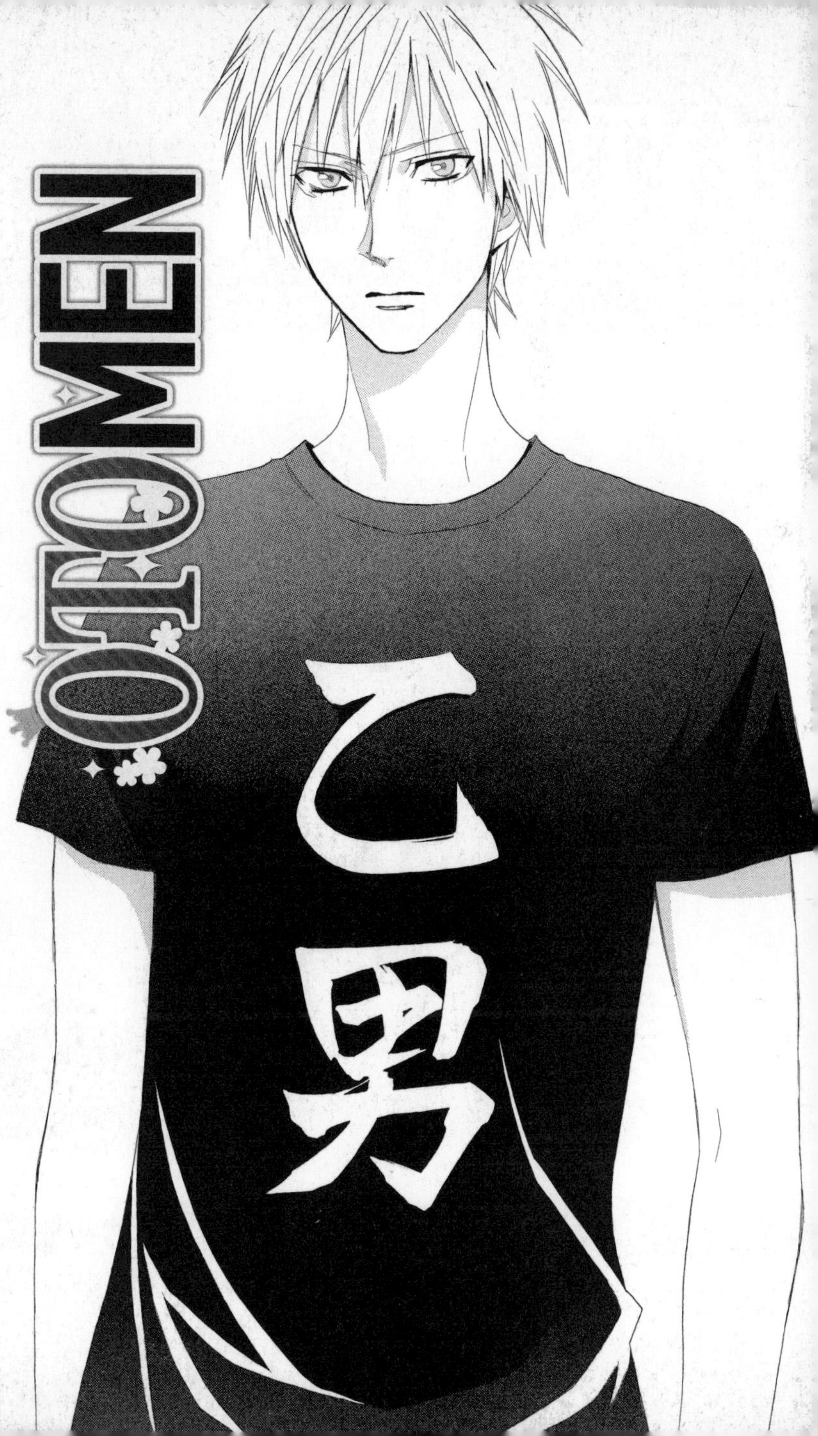
OTOMEN
乙男

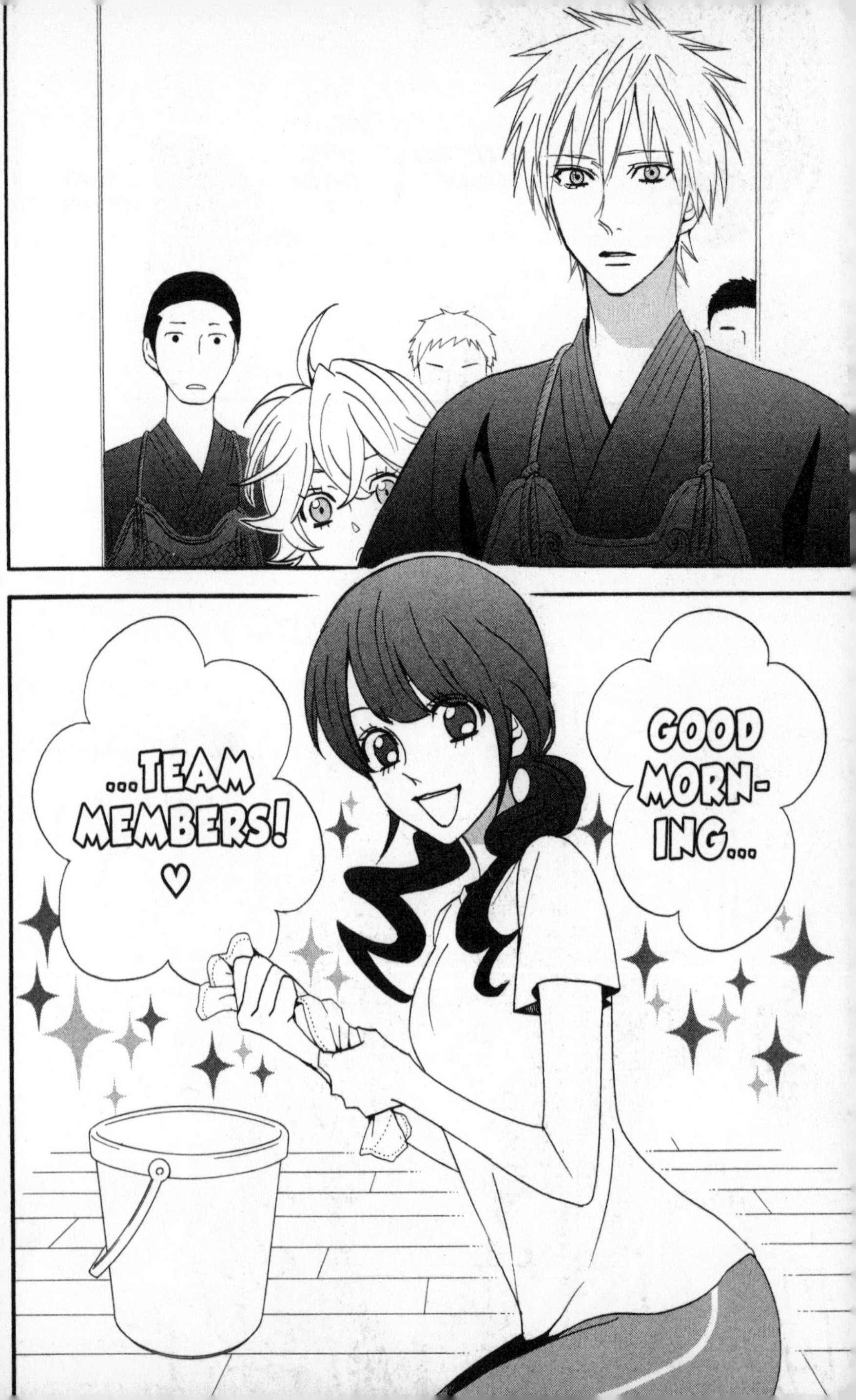
GOOD MORN-ING...
...TEAM MEMBERS! ♥

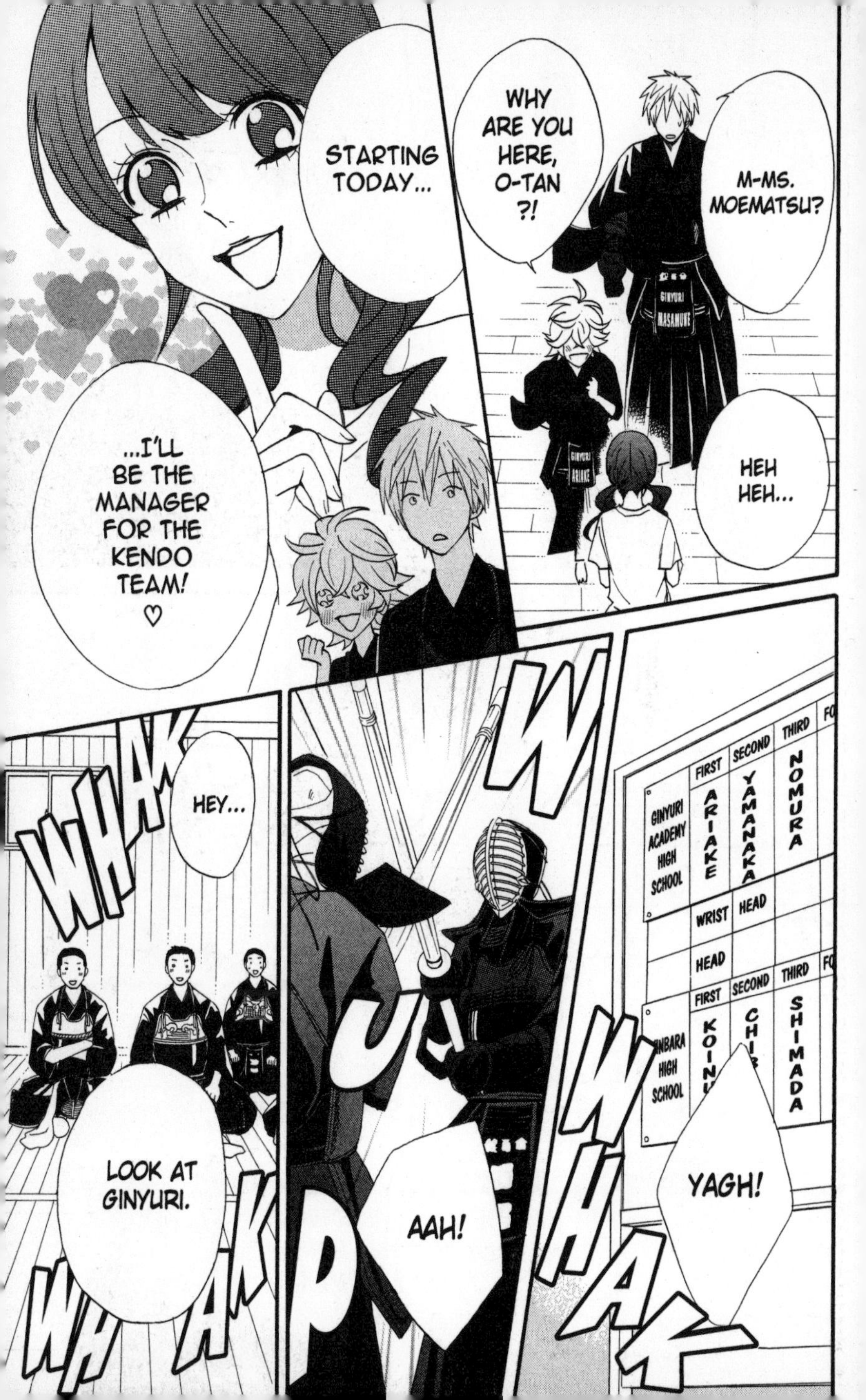
M-MS. MOEMATSU?
WHY ARE YOU HERE, O-TAN?!
GINYURI MASAMUNE
GINYURI ARIAKE
HEH HEH...
STARTING TODAY...
...I'LL BE THE MANAGER FOR THE KENDO TEAM! ♡
FIRST SECOND THIRD
GINYURI ACADEMY HIGH SCHOOL
ARIAKE
YAMANAKA
NOMURA
WRIST HEAD
HEAD
FIRST SECOND THIRD
HIGH SCHOOL
SHIMADA
WHAK
YAGH!
AAH!
WHAK
HEY...
LOOK AT GINYURI.
WHAK

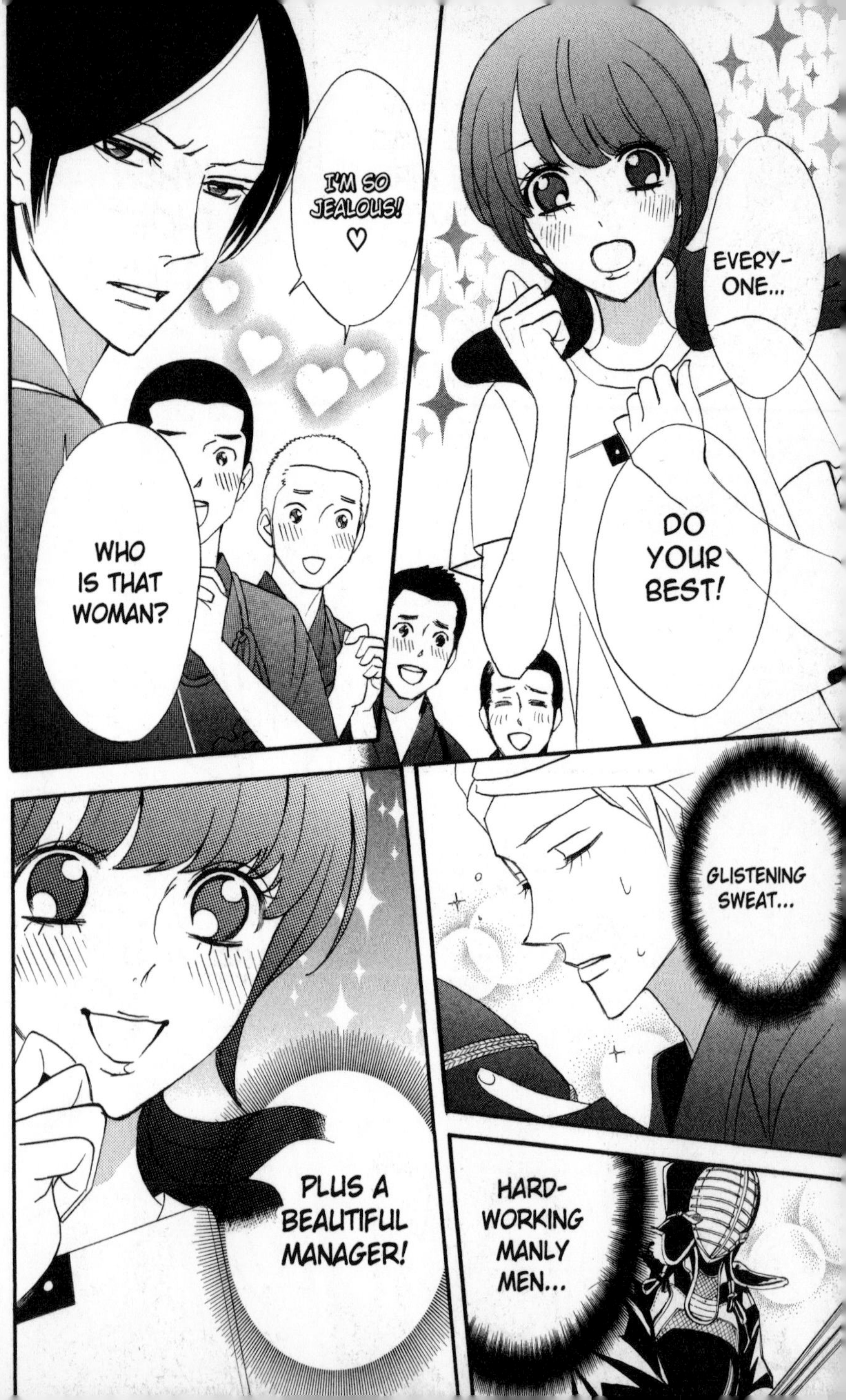
EVERY-ONE...
DO YOUR BEST!
I'M SO JEALOUS! ♡
WHO IS THAT WOMAN?
GLISTENING SWEAT...
HARD-WORKING MANLY MEN...
PLUS A BEAUTIFUL MANAGER!

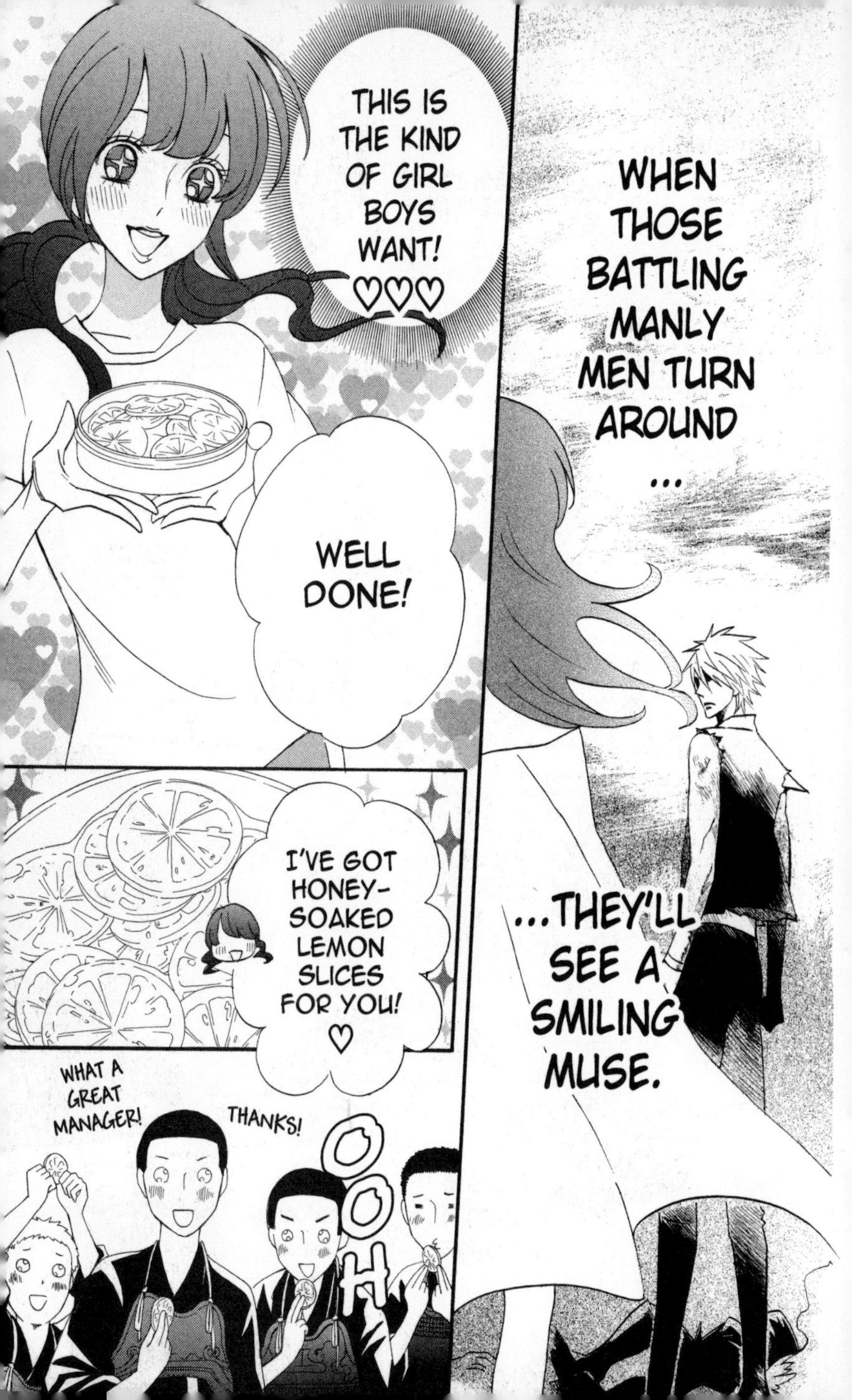
WHEN THOSE BATTLING MANLY MEN TURN AROUND ...
...THEY'LL SEE A SMILING MUSE.
THIS IS THE KIND OF GIRL BOYS WANT! ♡♡♡
WELL DONE!
I'VE GOT HONEY-SOAKED LEMON SLICES FOR YOU! ♡
OOH
THANKS!
WHAT A GREAT MANAGER!

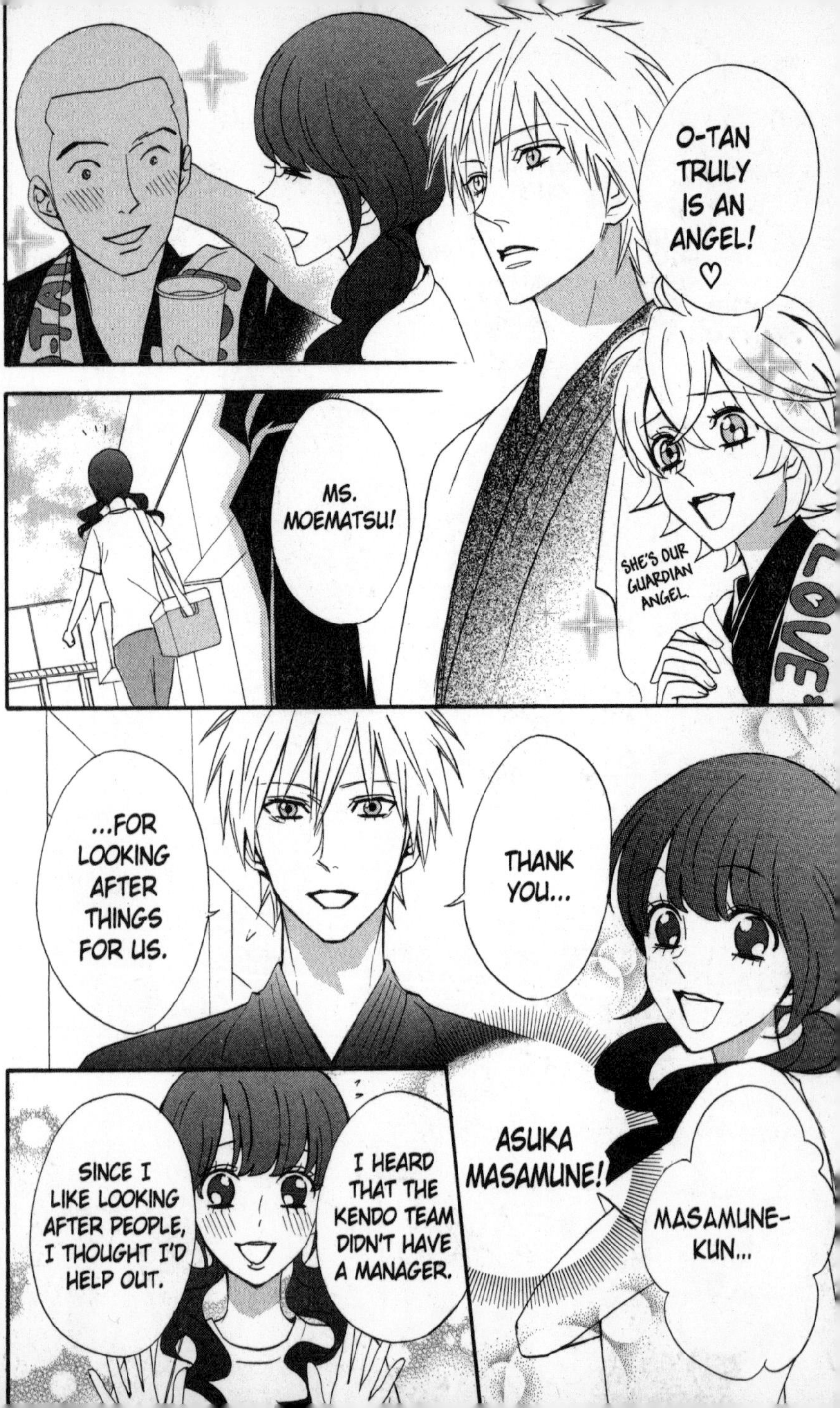
O-TAN TRULY IS AN ANGEL! ♡
SHE'S OUR GUARDIAN ANGEL.
MS. MOEMATSU!
THANK YOU...
...FOR LOOKING AFTER THINGS FOR US.
MASAMUNE-KUN...
ASUKA MASAMUNE!
I HEARD THAT THE KENDO TEAM DIDN'T HAVE A MANAGER.
SINCE I LIKE LOOKING AFTER PEOPLE, I THOUGHT I'D HELP OUT.
LOVE

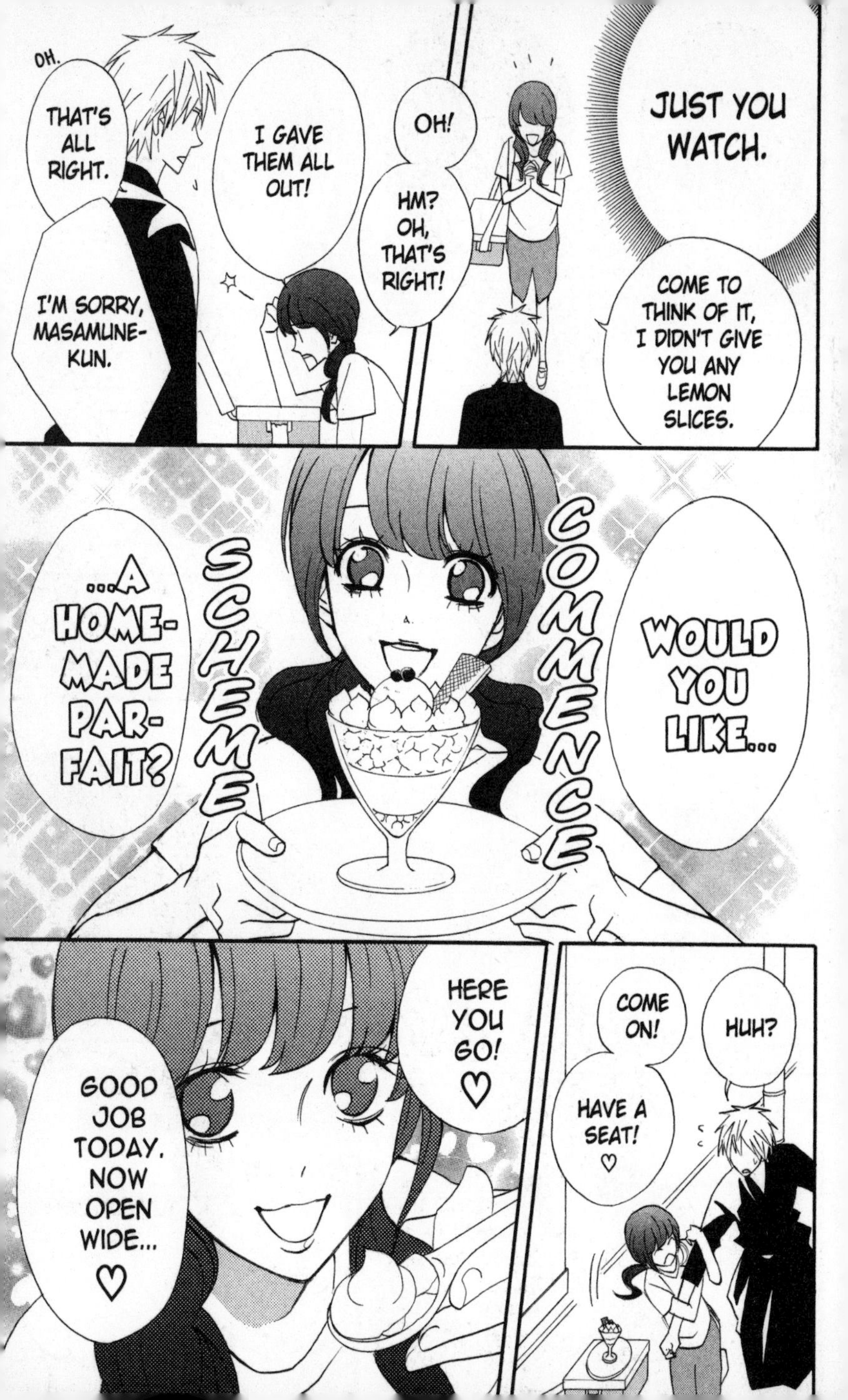
JUST YOU WATCH.
COME TO THINK OF IT, I DIDN'T GIVE YOU ANY LEMON SLICES.
OH!
HM? OH, THAT'S RIGHT!
I GAVE THEM ALL OUT!
OH.
THAT'S ALL RIGHT.
I'M SORRY, MASAMUNE-KUN.
WOULD YOU LIKE...
COMMENCE
SCHEME
...A HOME-MADE PAR-FAIT?
HUH?
COME ON!
HAVE A SEAT! ♡
HERE YOU GO! ♡
GOOD JOB TODAY. NOW OPEN WIDE... ♡

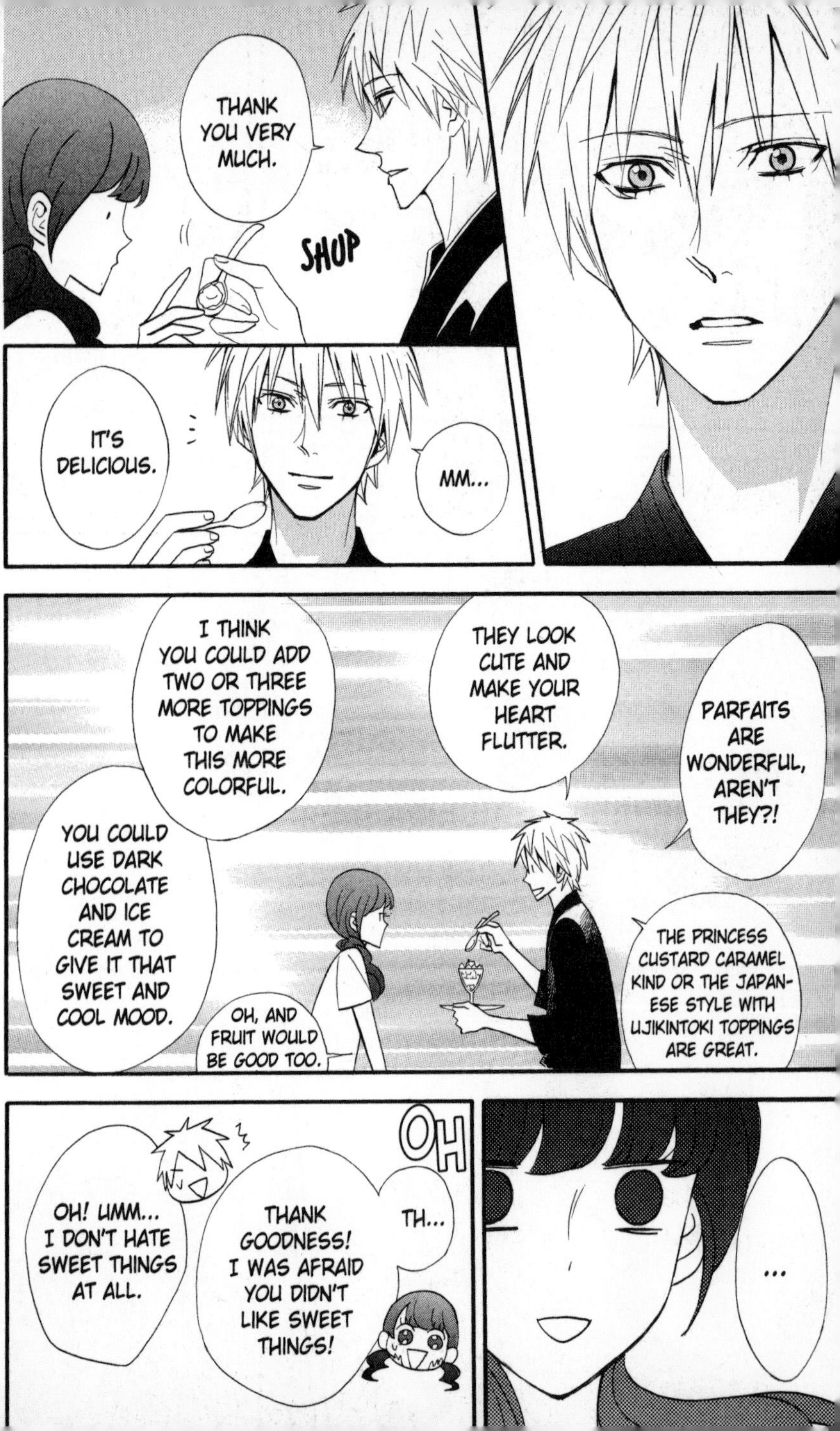
THANK YOU VERY MUCH.
SHUP
MM...
IT'S DELICIOUS.
PARFAITS ARE WONDERFUL, AREN'T THEY?!
THEY LOOK CUTE AND MAKE YOUR HEART FLUTTER.
I THINK YOU COULD ADD TWO OR THREE MORE TOPPINGS TO MAKE THIS MORE COLORFUL.
THE PRINCESS CUSTARD CARAMEL KIND OR THE JAPAN-ESE STYLE WITH UJIKINTOKI TOPPINGS ARE GREAT.
YOU COULD USE DARK CHOCOLATE AND ICE CREAM TO GIVE IT THAT SWEET AND COOL MOOD.
OH, AND FRUIT WOULD BE GOOD TOO.
...
OH
TH...
THANK GOODNESS! I WAS AFRAID YOU DIDN'T LIKE SWEET THINGS!
OH! UMM... I DON'T HATE SWEET THINGS AT ALL.

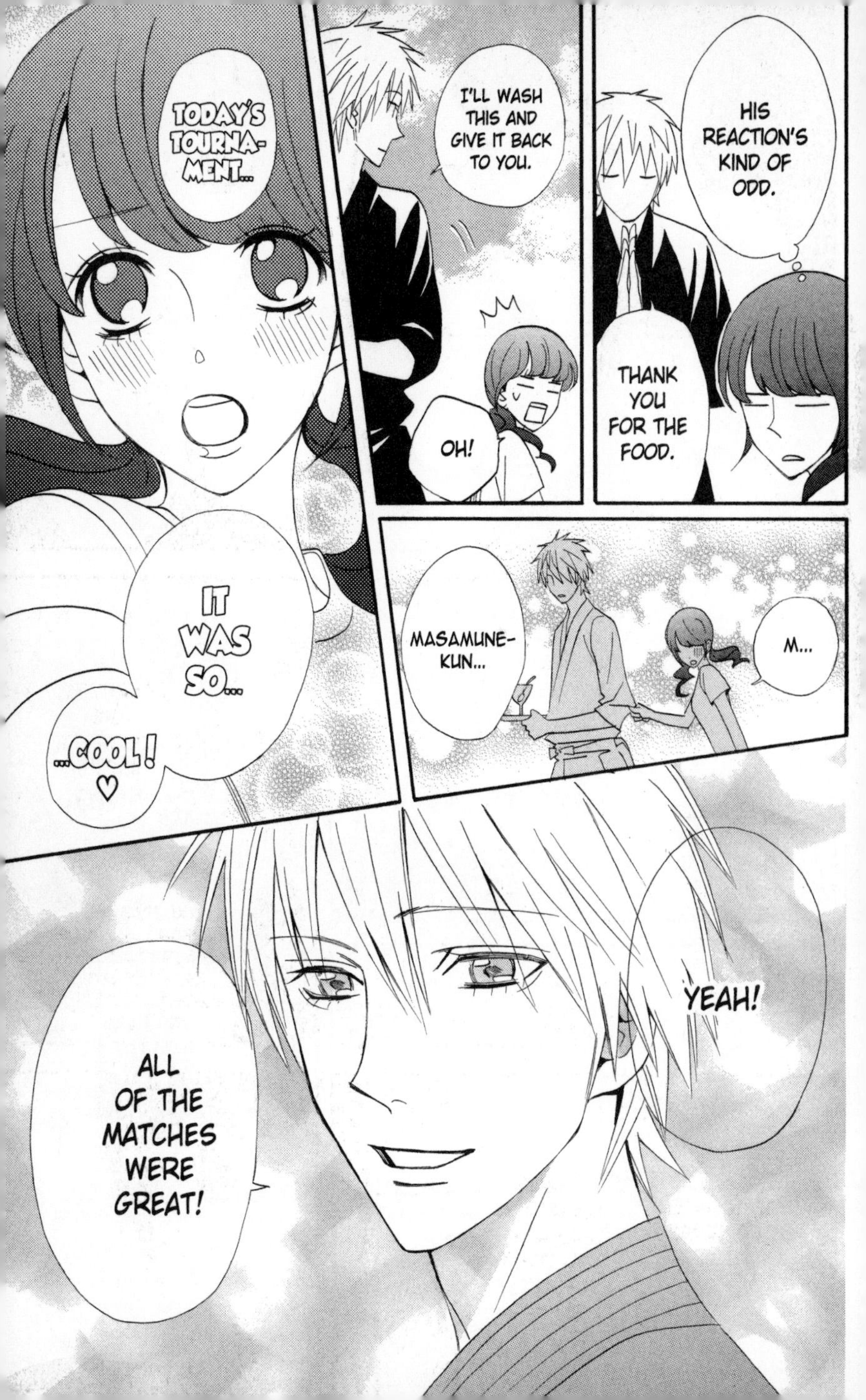
HIS REACTION'S KIND OF ODD.
THANK YOU FOR THE FOOD.
I'LL WASH THIS AND GIVE IT BACK TO YOU.
OH!
M...
MASAMUNE-KUN...
TODAY'S TOURNAMENT...
IT WAS SO...
...COOL! ♥
YEAH!
ALL OF THE MATCHES WERE GREAT!

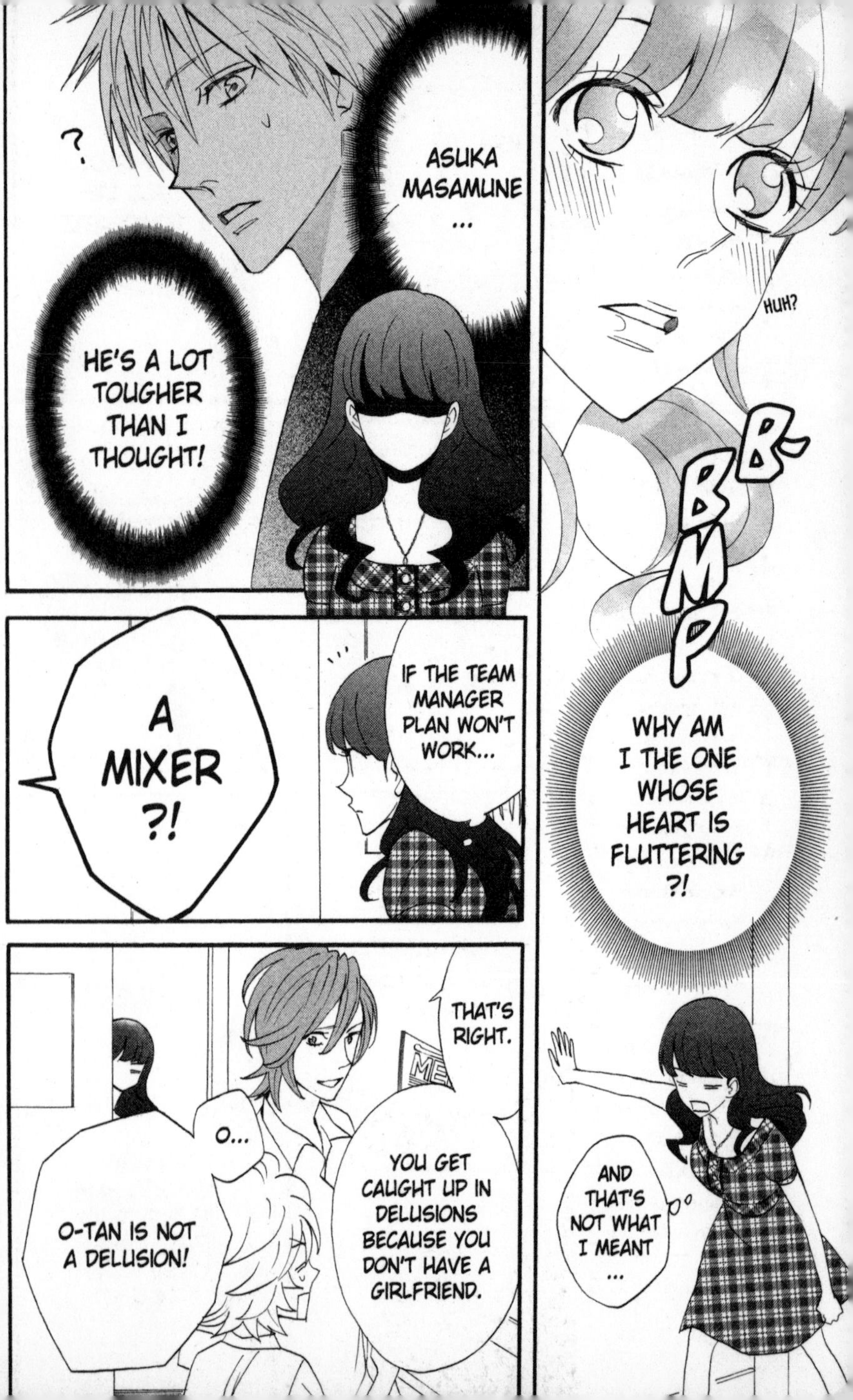
HUH?
B-BMP
WHY AM I THE ONE WHOSE HEART IS FLUTTERING?!
AND THAT'S NOT WHAT I MEANT...
?
ASUKA MASAMUNE...
HE'S A LOT TOUGHER THAN I THOUGHT!
IF THE TEAM MANAGER PLAN WON'T WORK...
A MIXER?!
THAT'S RIGHT.
YOU GET CAUGHT UP IN DELUSIONS BECAUSE YOU DON'T HAVE A GIRLFRIEND.
O...
O-TAN IS NOT A DELUSION!

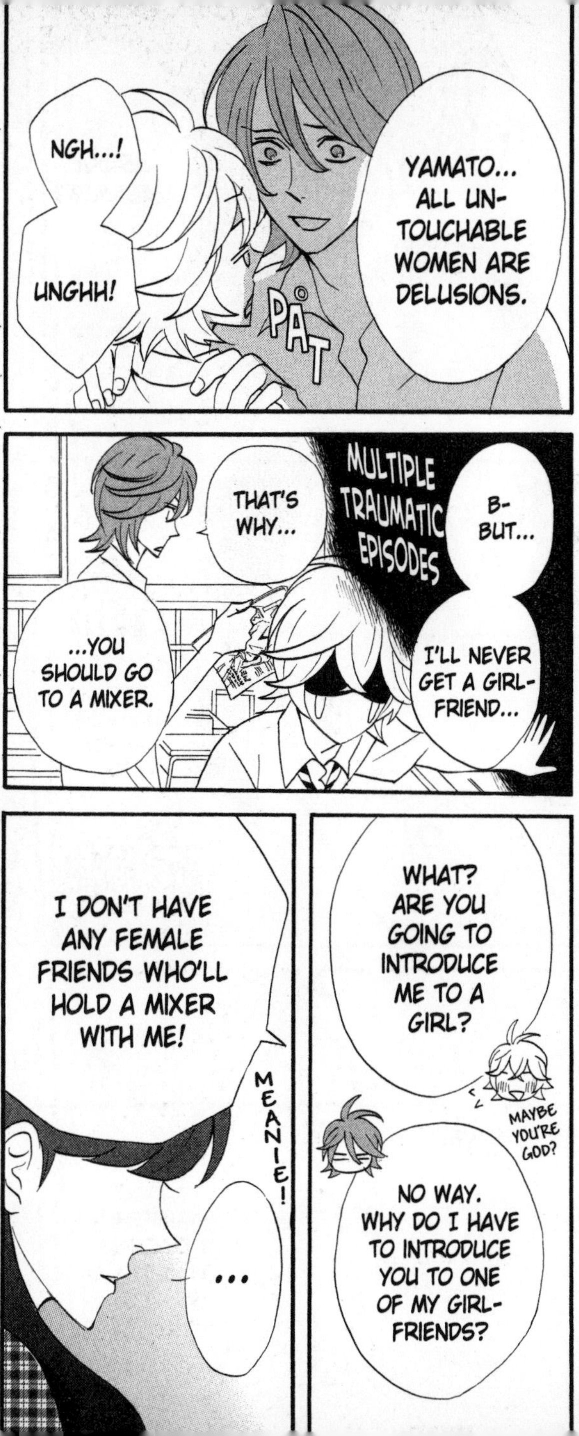
YAMATO... ALL UNTOUCHABLE WOMEN ARE DELUSIONS.
NGH...!
UNGHH!
PAT
B- BUT...
I'LL NEVER GET A GIRLFRIEND...
MULTIPLE TRAUMATIC EPISODES
THAT'S WHY...
...YOU SHOULD GO TO A MIXER.
WHAT? ARE YOU GOING TO INTRODUCE ME TO A GIRL?
MAYBE YOU'RE GOD?
NO WAY. WHY DO I HAVE TO INTRODUCE YOU TO ONE OF MY GIRLFRIENDS?
I DON'T HAVE ANY FEMALE FRIENDS WHO'LL HOLD A MIXER WITH ME!
MEANIE!
...

Volume 10!

We're finally at volume 10... I've been able to continue writing *Otomen* this far because of all you readers. I'm really pleased. Thank you. I'll continue to do my best! I have an extra chapter at the back of this volume called "Glass Otomen." I don't think this needs explaining, but it's a parody of Suzue Miuchi's great masterpiece, *Glass Mask*. I wrote it as a part of *Bessatsu Hana to Yume*'s tribute to *Glass Mask*. I had a lot of fun writing it since I'm a fan of the series. If you're familiar with *Glass Mask*, I think you'll enjoy the small details. Those of you who haven't read the series, please do!

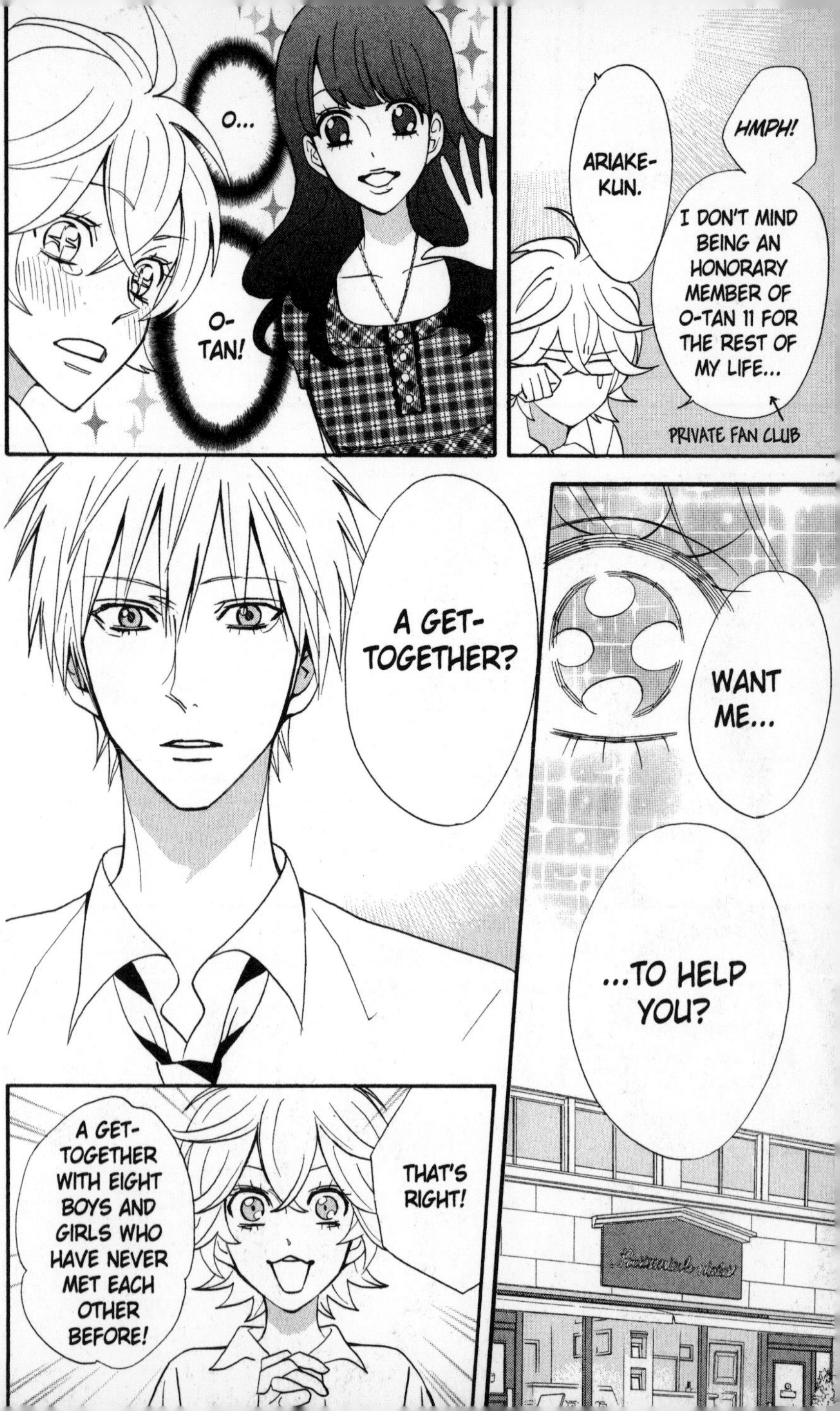
HMPH!
ARIAKE-KUN.
I DON'T MIND BEING AN HONORARY MEMBER OF O-TAN 11 FOR THE REST OF MY LIFE...
PRIVATE FAN CLUB
O...
O-TAN!
WANT ME...
...TO HELP YOU?
A GET-TOGETHER?
THAT'S RIGHT!
A GET-TOGETHER WITH EIGHT BOYS AND GIRLS WHO HAVE NEVER MET EACH OTHER BEFORE!

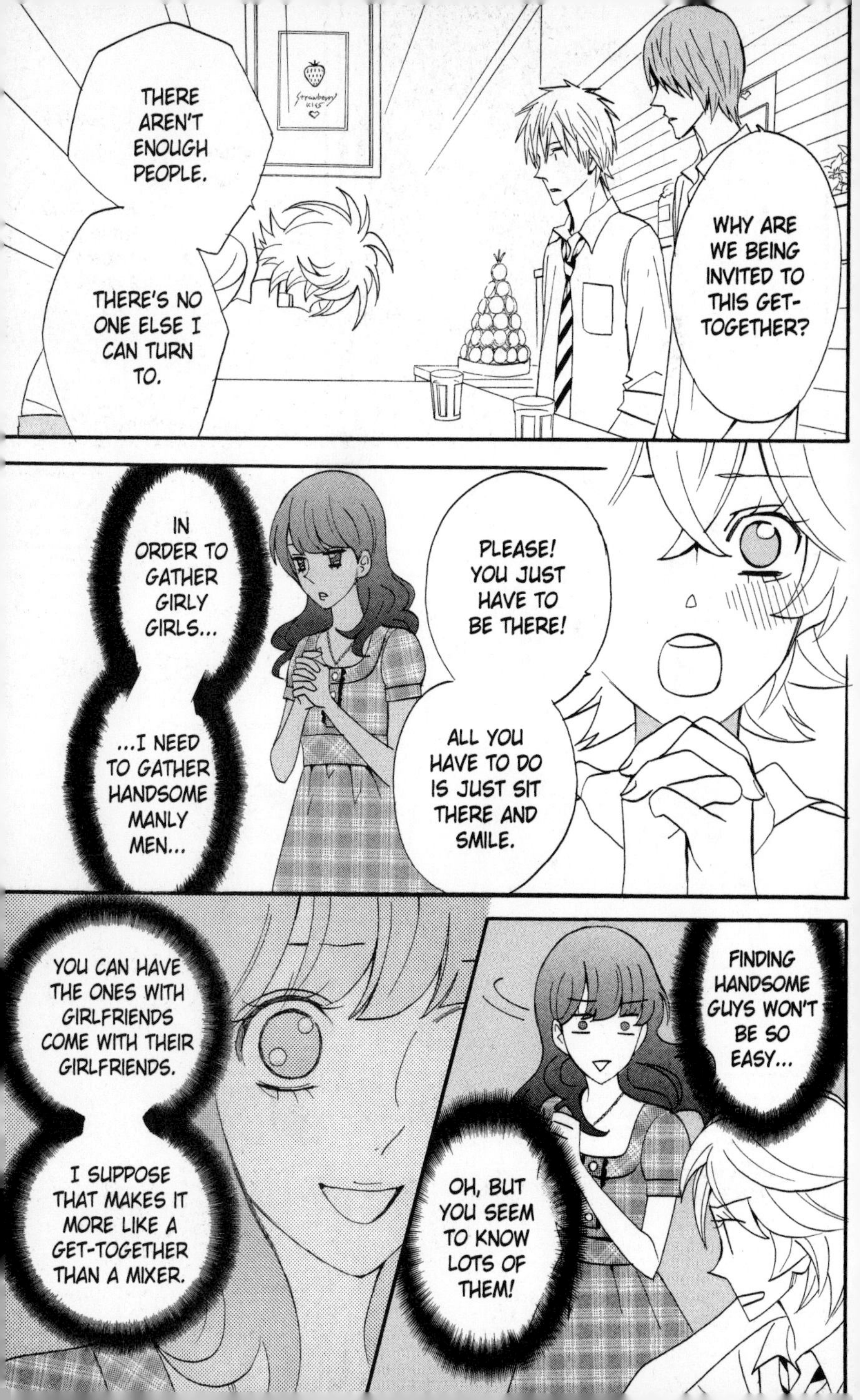
WHY ARE WE BEING INVITED TO THIS GET-TOGETHER?
THERE AREN'T ENOUGH PEOPLE.
THERE'S NO ONE ELSE I CAN TURN TO.
PLEASE! YOU JUST HAVE TO BE THERE!
ALL YOU HAVE TO DO IS JUST SIT THERE AND SMILE.
IN ORDER TO GATHER GIRLY GIRLS...
...I NEED TO GATHER HANDSOME MANLY MEN...
FINDING HANDSOME GUYS WON'T BE SO EASY...
OH, BUT YOU SEEM TO KNOW LOTS OF THEM!
YOU CAN HAVE THE ONES WITH GIRLFRIENDS COME WITH THEIR GIRLFRIENDS.
I SUPPOSE THAT MAKES IT MORE LIKE A GET-TOGETHER THAN A MIXER.

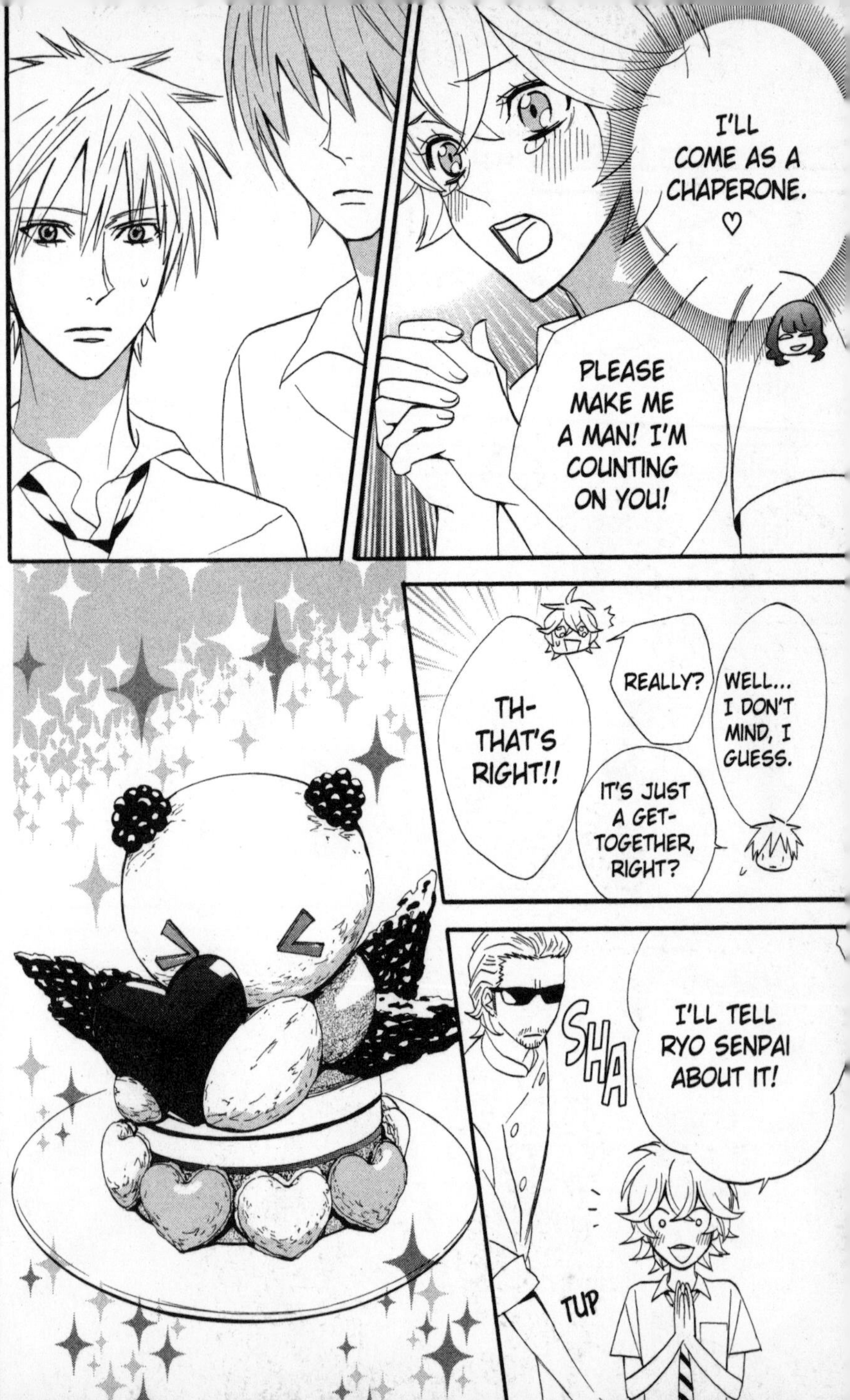
I'LL COME AS A CHAPERONE. ♡
PLEASE MAKE ME A MAN! I'M COUNTING ON YOU!
WELL... I DON'T MIND, I GUESS.
REALLY?
IT'S JUST A GET-TOGETHER, RIGHT?
TH-THAT'S RIGHT!!
I'LL TELL RYO SENPAI ABOUT IT!
SHA
TUP

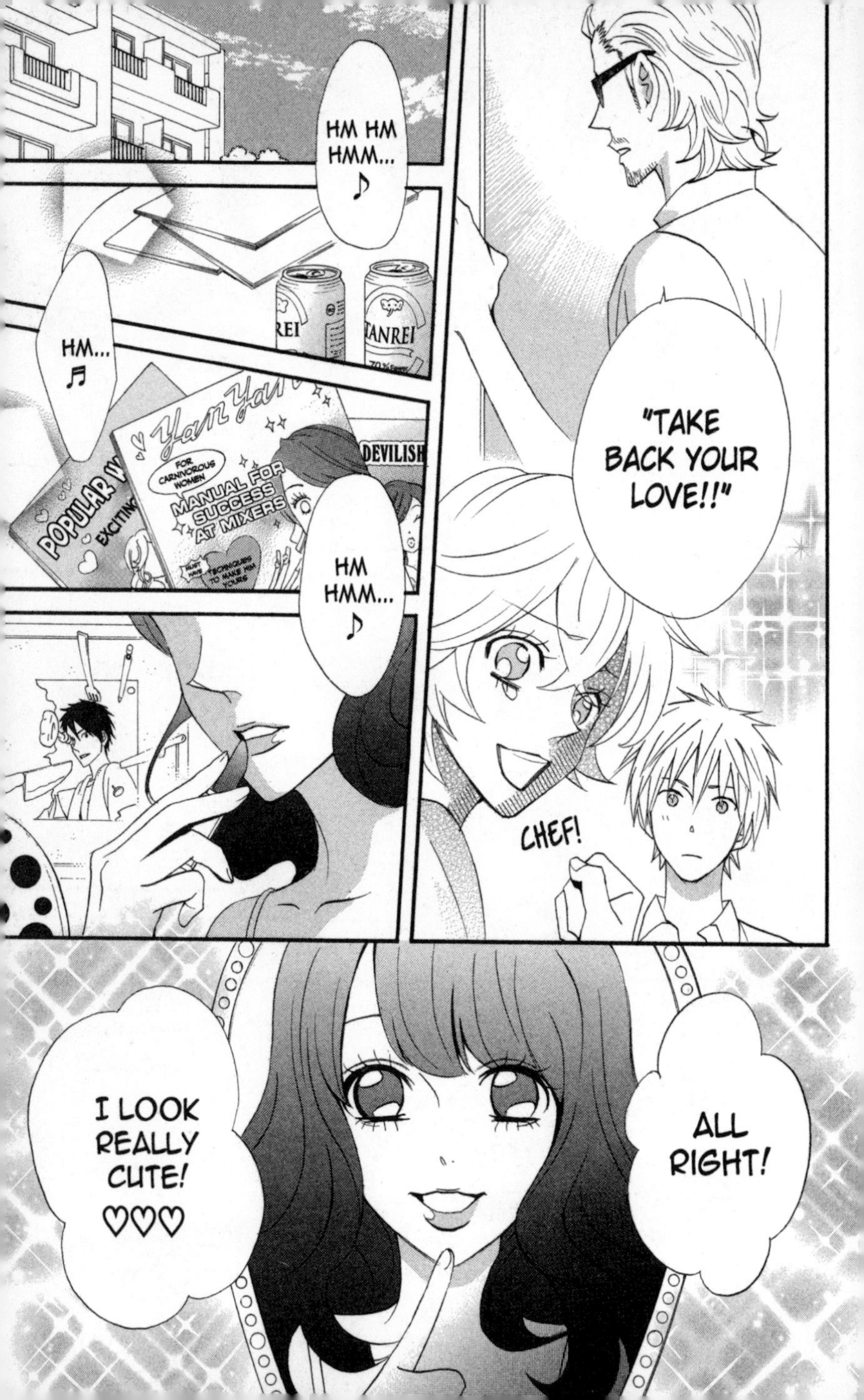
"TAKE BACK YOUR LOVE!!"
CHEF!
HM HM HMM... ♪
TANREI
HM... ♫
FOR CARNIVOROUS WOMEN
MANUAL FOR SUCCESS AT MIXERS
MUST HAVE TECHNIQUES TO MAKE HIM YOURS
POPULAR W
EXCITING
DEVILISH
HM HMM... ♪
ALL RIGHT!
I LOOK REALLY CUTE! ♡♡♡

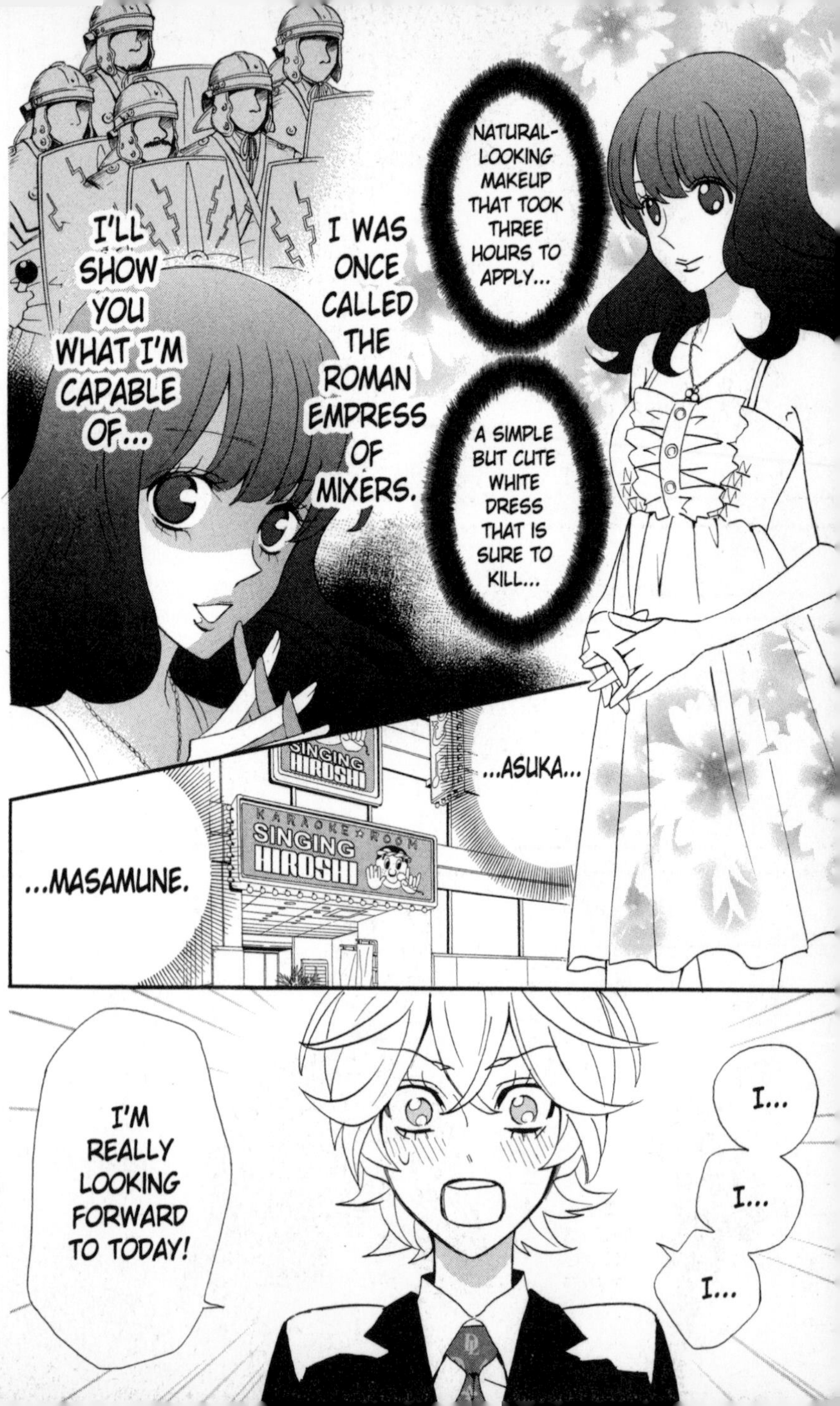
NATURAL-LOOKING MAKEUP THAT TOOK THREE HOURS TO APPLY...
A SIMPLE BUT CUTE WHITE DRESS THAT IS SURE TO KILL...
I WAS ONCE CALLED THE ROMAN EMPRESS OF MIXERS.
I'LL SHOW YOU WHAT I'M CAPABLE OF...
SINGING HIROSHI
KARAOKE☆ROOM
SINGING HIROSHI
...ASUKA...
...MASAMUNE.
I...
I...
I...
I'M REALLY LOOKING FORWARD TO TODAY!

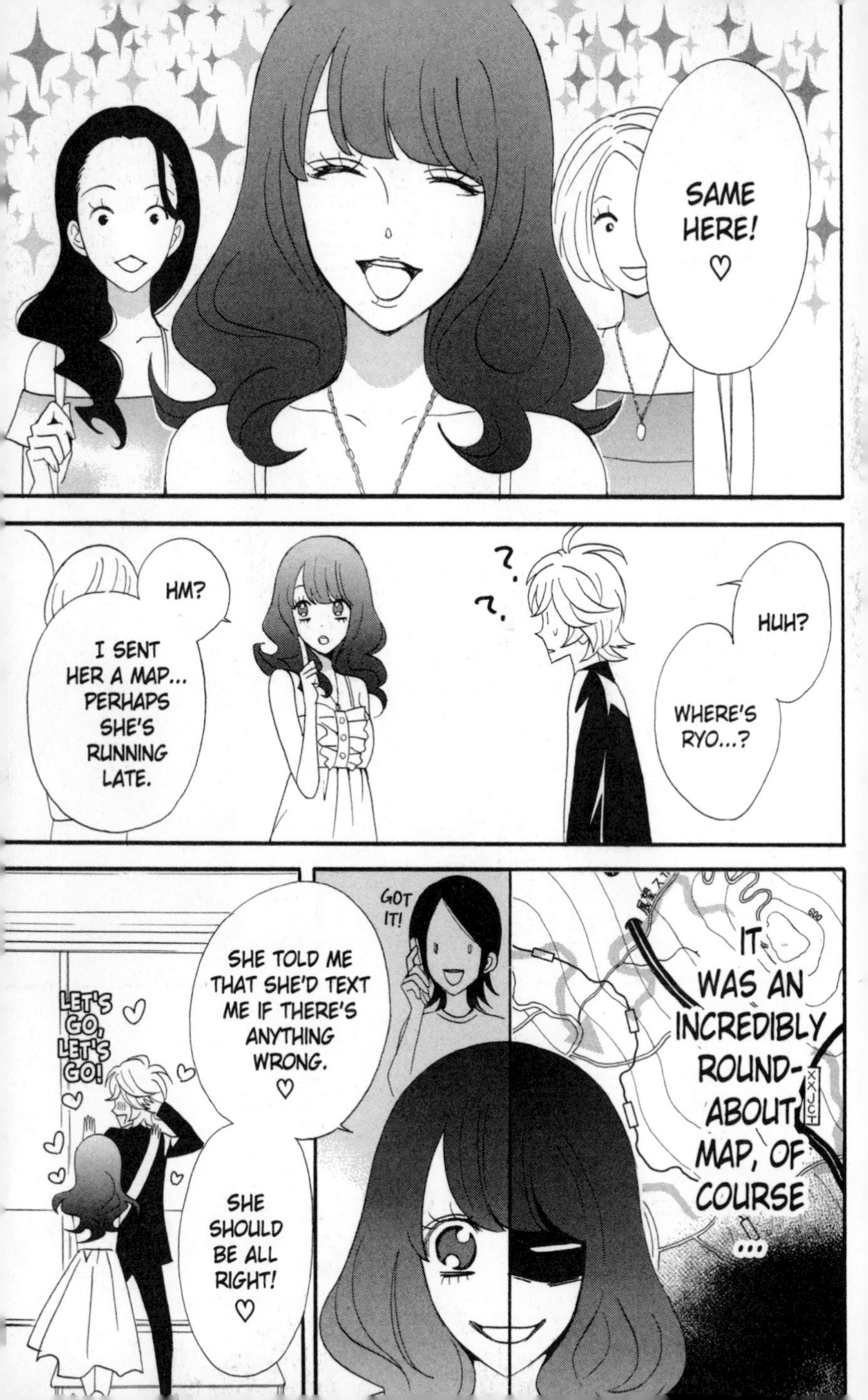
SAME HERE! ♡
HUH?
WHERE'S RYO...?
HM?
I SENT HER A MAP... PERHAPS SHE'S RUNNING LATE.
IT WAS AN INCREDIBLY ROUND-ABOUT MAP, OF COURSE...
GOT IT!
SHE TOLD ME THAT SHE'D TEXT ME IF THERE'S ANYTHING WRONG. ♡
SHE SHOULD BE ALL RIGHT! ♡
LET'S GO, LET'S GO!

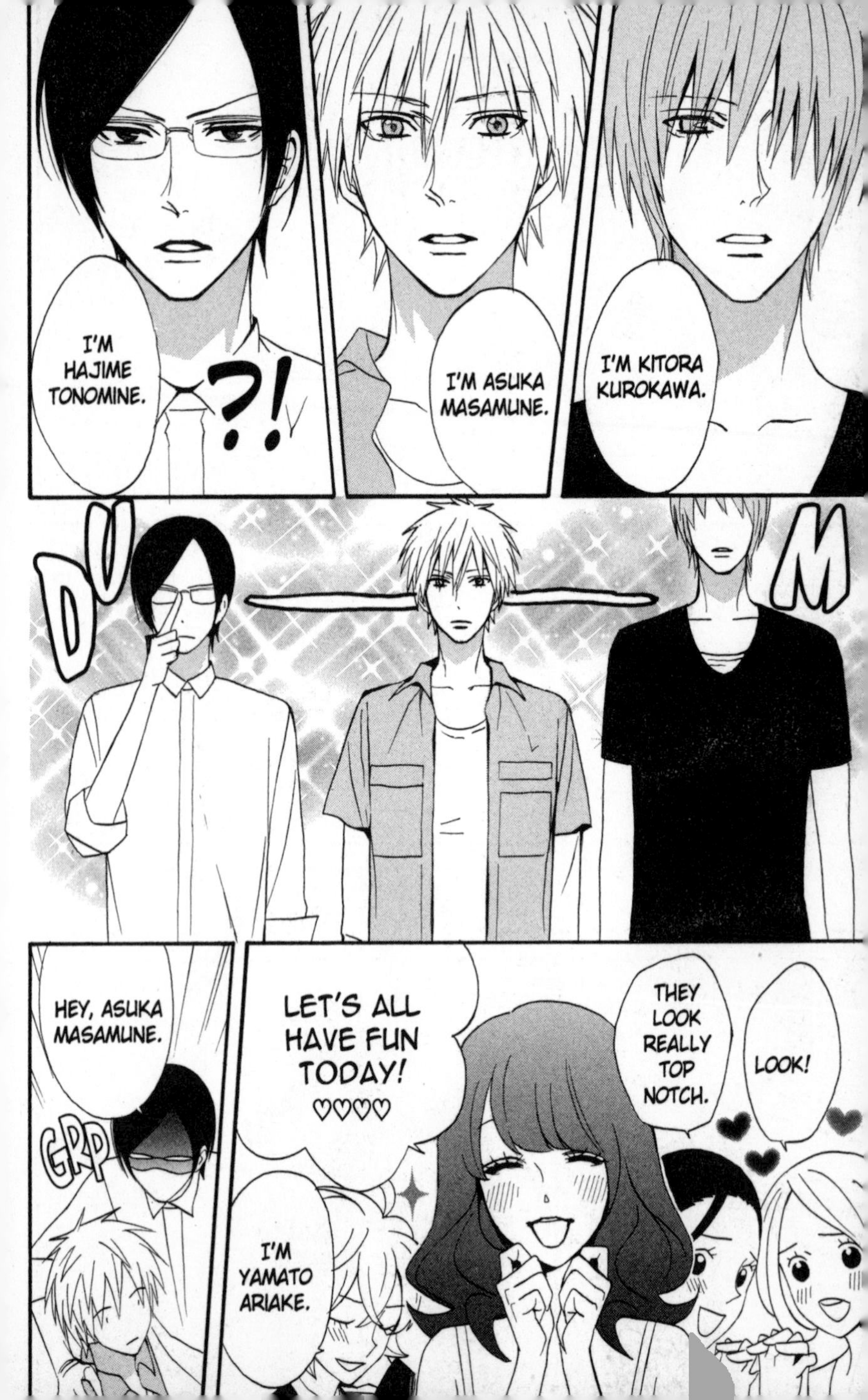
I'M KITORA KUROKAWA.
I'M ASUKA MASAMUNE.
I'M HAJIME TONOMINE.
?!
DUM
LOOK!
THEY LOOK REALLY TOP NOTCH.
LET'S ALL HAVE FUN TODAY! ♡♡♡♡
I'M YAMATO ARIAKE.
HEY, ASUKA MASAMUNE.
GRP

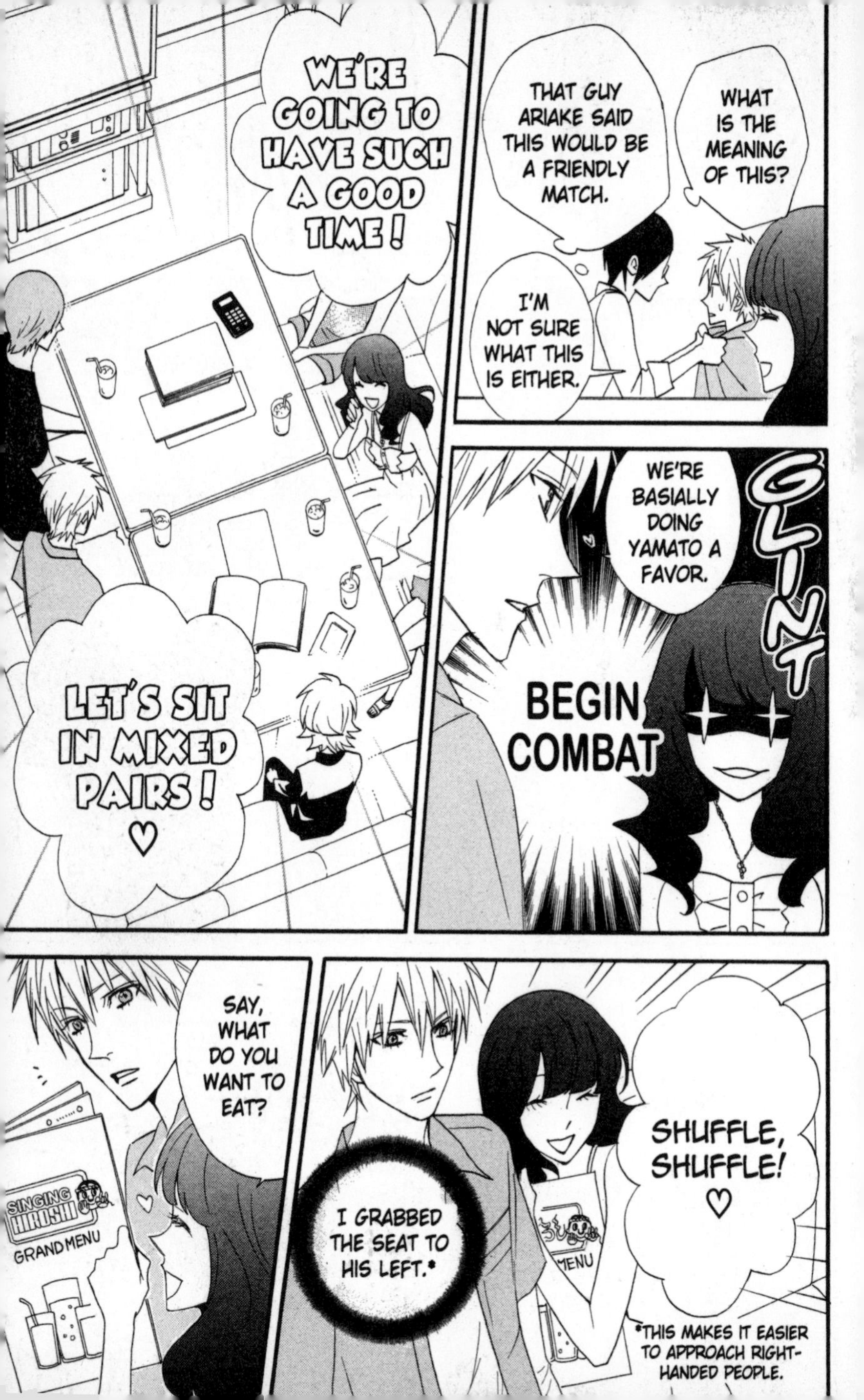
WHAT IS THE MEANING OF THIS?
THAT GUY ARIAKE SAID THIS WOULD BE A FRIENDLY MATCH.
I'M NOT SURE WHAT THIS IS EITHER.
GLINT
WE'RE BASIALLY DOING YAMATO A FAVOR.
BEGIN COMBAT
WE'RE GOING TO HAVE SUCH A GOOD TIME!
LET'S SIT IN MIXED PAIRS! ♡
SHUFFLE, SHUFFLE! ♡
I GRABBED THE SEAT TO HIS LEFT.*
MENU
*THIS MAKES IT EASIER TO APPROACH RIGHT-HANDED PEOPLE.
SAY, WHAT DO YOU WANT TO EAT?
SINGING HIROSHI
GRAND MENU

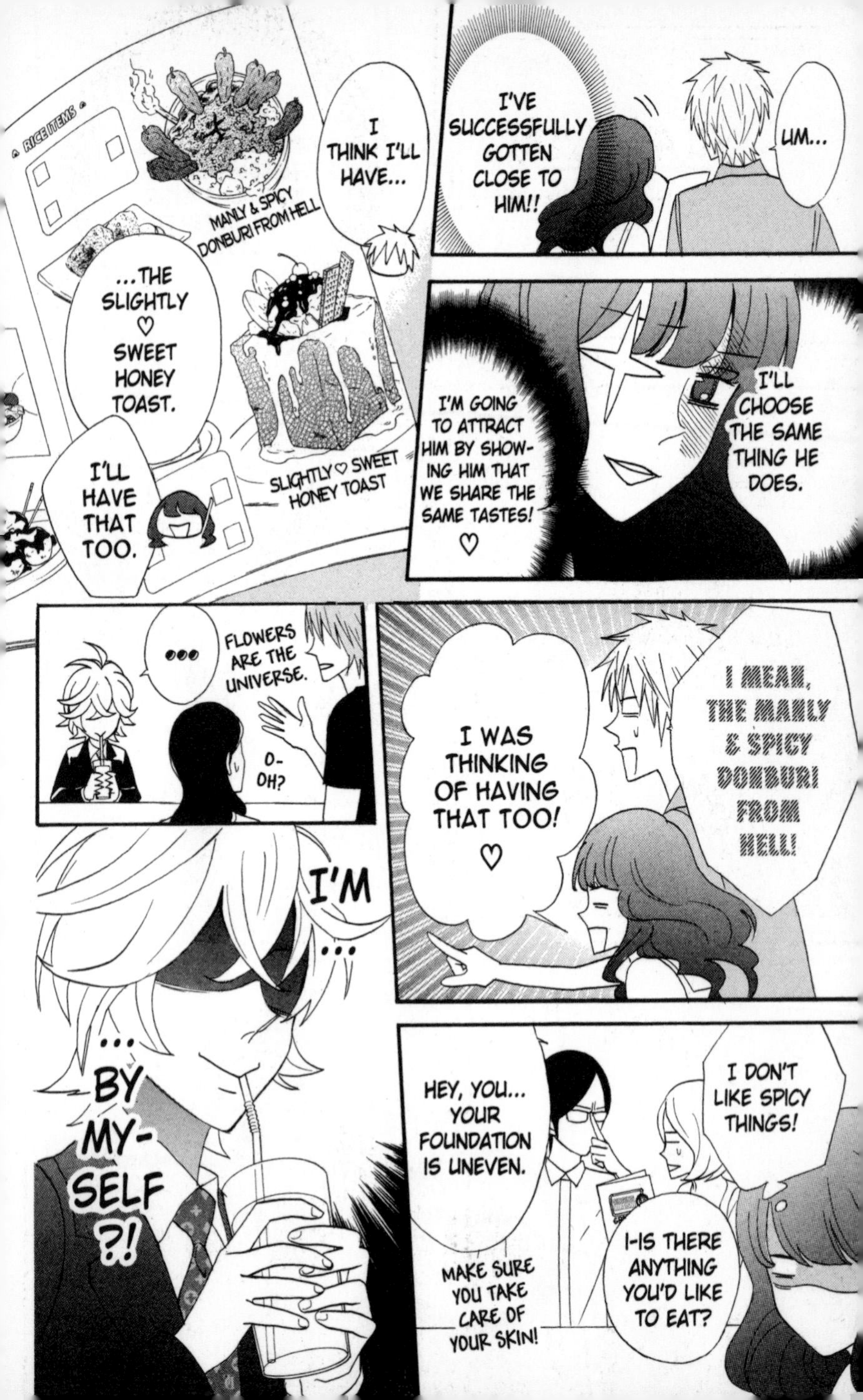
UM...
I'VE SUCCESSFULLY GOTTEN CLOSE TO HIM!!
I'LL CHOOSE THE SAME THING HE DOES.
I'M GOING TO ATTRACT HIM BY SHOWING HIM THAT WE SHARE THE SAME TASTES! ♡
I THINK I'LL HAVE...
RICE ITEMS
MANLY & SPICY DONBURI FROM HELL
...THE SLIGHTLY ♡ SWEET HONEY TOAST.
SLIGHTLY ♡ SWEET HONEY TOAST
I'LL HAVE THAT TOO.
I MEAN, THE MANLY & SPICY DONBURI FROM HELL!
I WAS THINKING OF HAVING THAT TOO! ♡
FLOWERS ARE THE UNIVERSE.
O-OH?
●●●
I DON'T LIKE SPICY THINGS!
HEY, YOU... YOUR FOUNDATION IS UNEVEN.
I-IS THERE ANYTHING YOU'D LIKE TO EAT?
MAKE SURE YOU TAKE CARE OF YOUR SKIN!
I'M...
...BY MYSELF?!

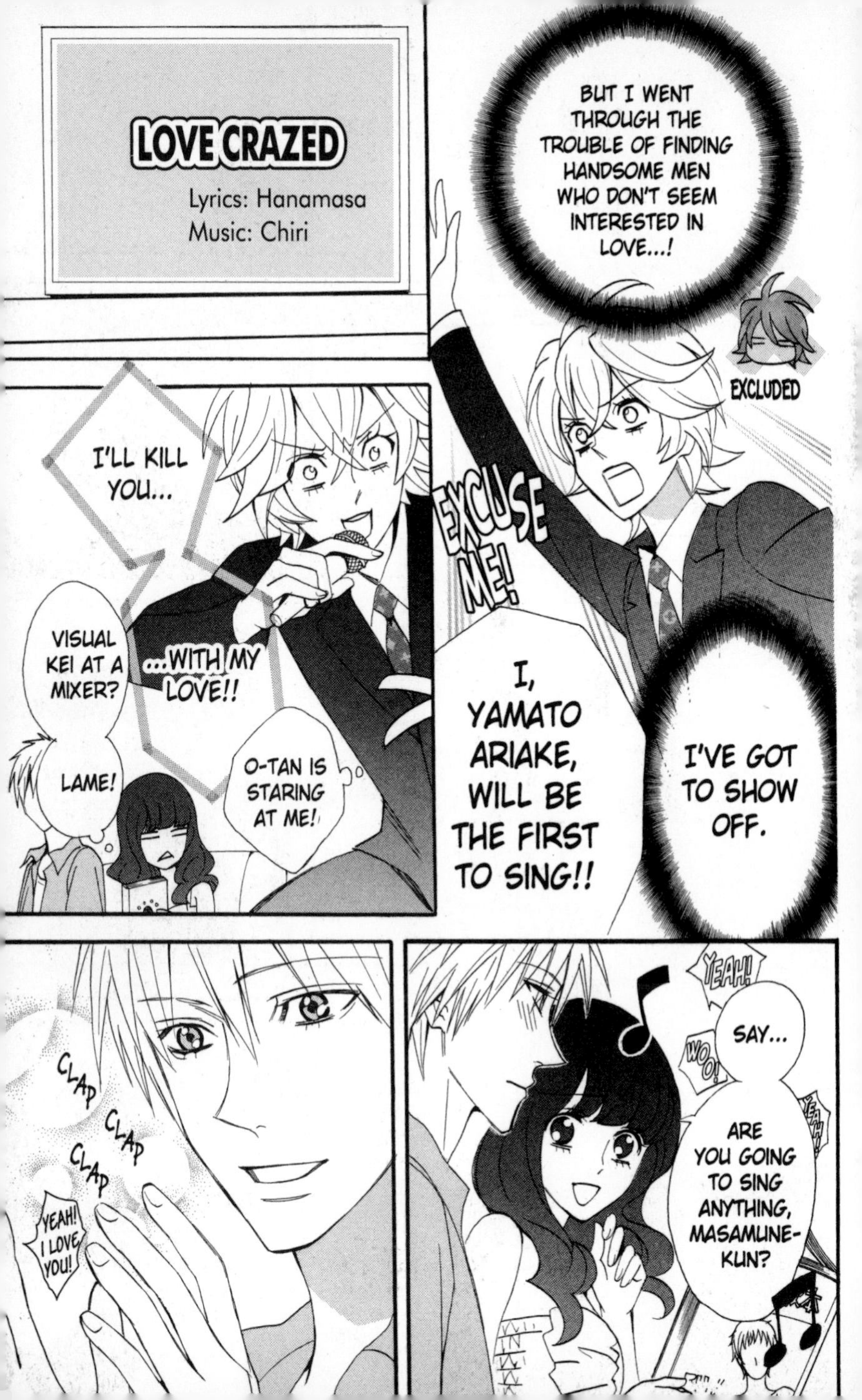

BUT I WENT THROUGH THE TROUBLE OF FINDING HANDSOME MEN WHO DON'T SEEM INTERESTED IN LOVE...!
EXCLUDED
EXCUSE ME!
I'VE GOT TO SHOW OFF.
I, YAMATO ARIAKE, WILL BE THE FIRST TO SING!!
LOVE CRAZED
Lyrics: Hanamasa
Music: Chiri
I'LL KILL YOU...
...WITH MY LOVE!!
O-TAN IS STARING AT ME!
VISUAL KEI AT A MIXER?
LAME!
YEAH!
SAY...
WOO!
YEAH!
ARE YOU GOING TO SING ANYTHING, MASAMUNE-KUN?
CLAP
CLAP
CLAP
YEAH! I LOVE YOU!

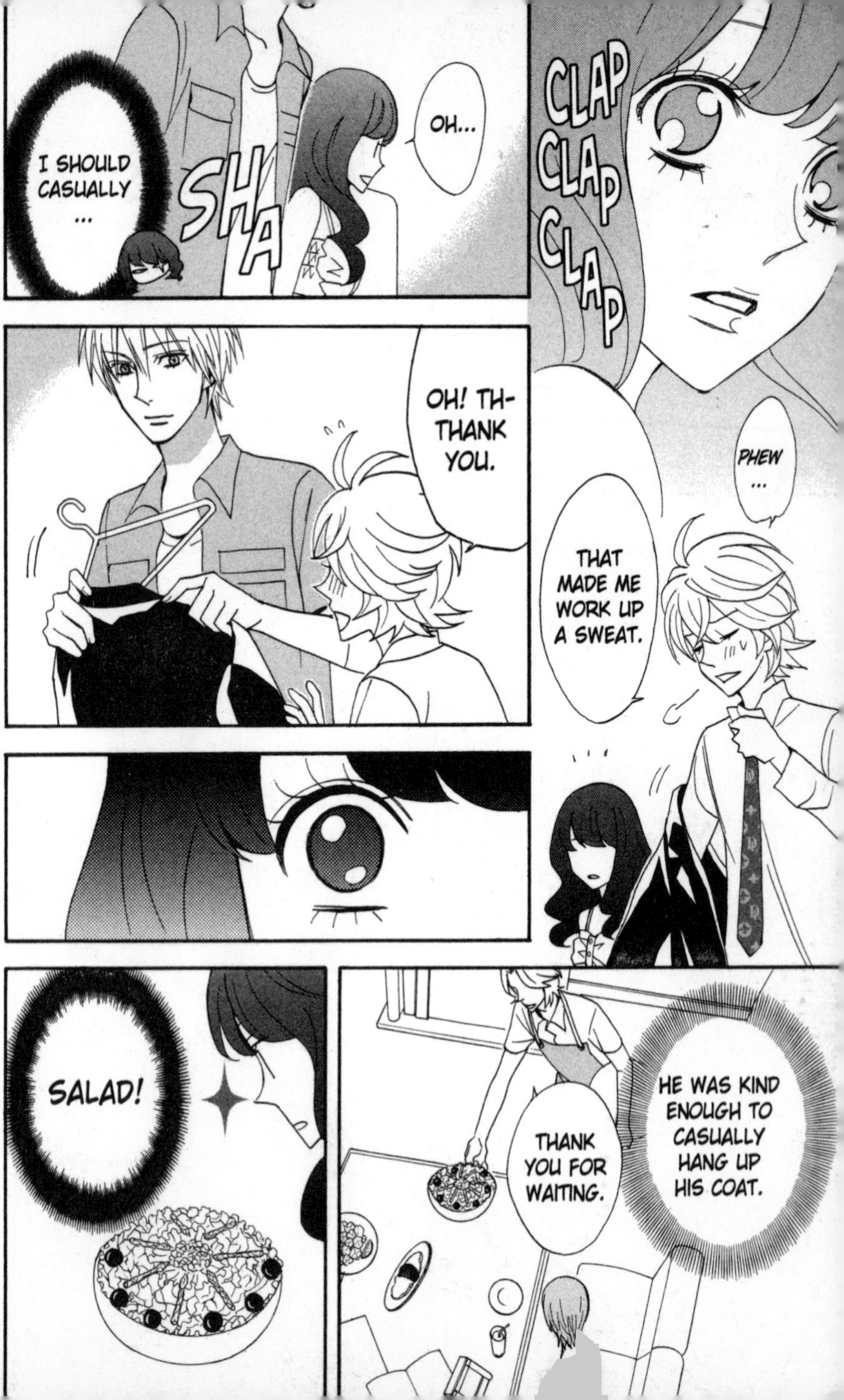
CLAP CLAP CLAP CLAP
PHEW ...
THAT MADE ME WORK UP A SWEAT.
OH...
SHA
I SHOULD CASUALLY ...
OH! TH-THANK YOU.
HE WAS KIND ENOUGH TO CASUALLY HANG UP HIS COAT.
THANK YOU FOR WAITING.
SALAD!

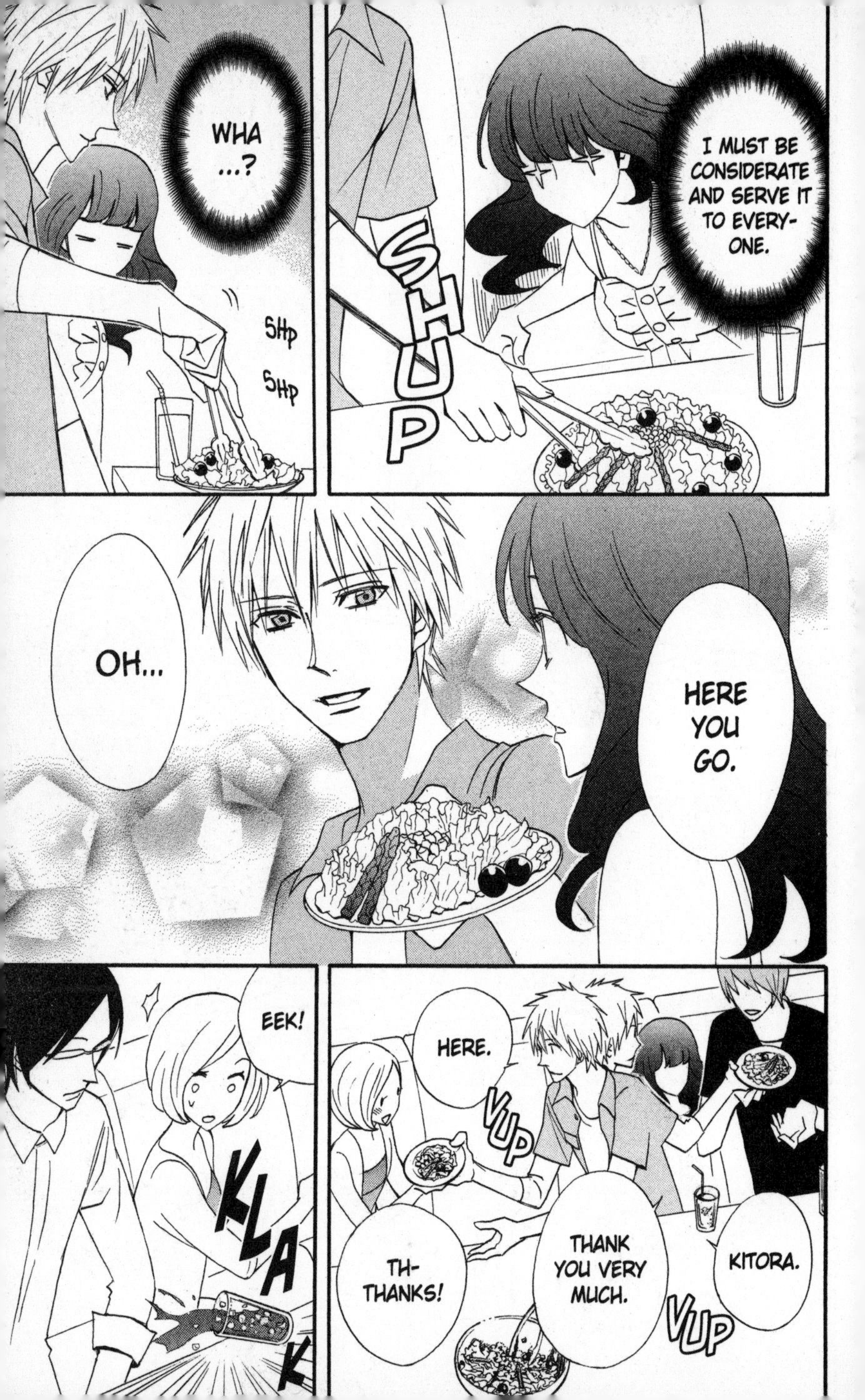
I MUST BE CONSIDERATE AND SERVE IT TO EVERY-ONE.
SHUP
WHA ...?
SHp
SHp
HERE YOU GO.
OH...
HERE.
VUP
TH-THANKS!
KITORA.
THANK YOU VERY MUCH.
VUP
EEK!
KLAK

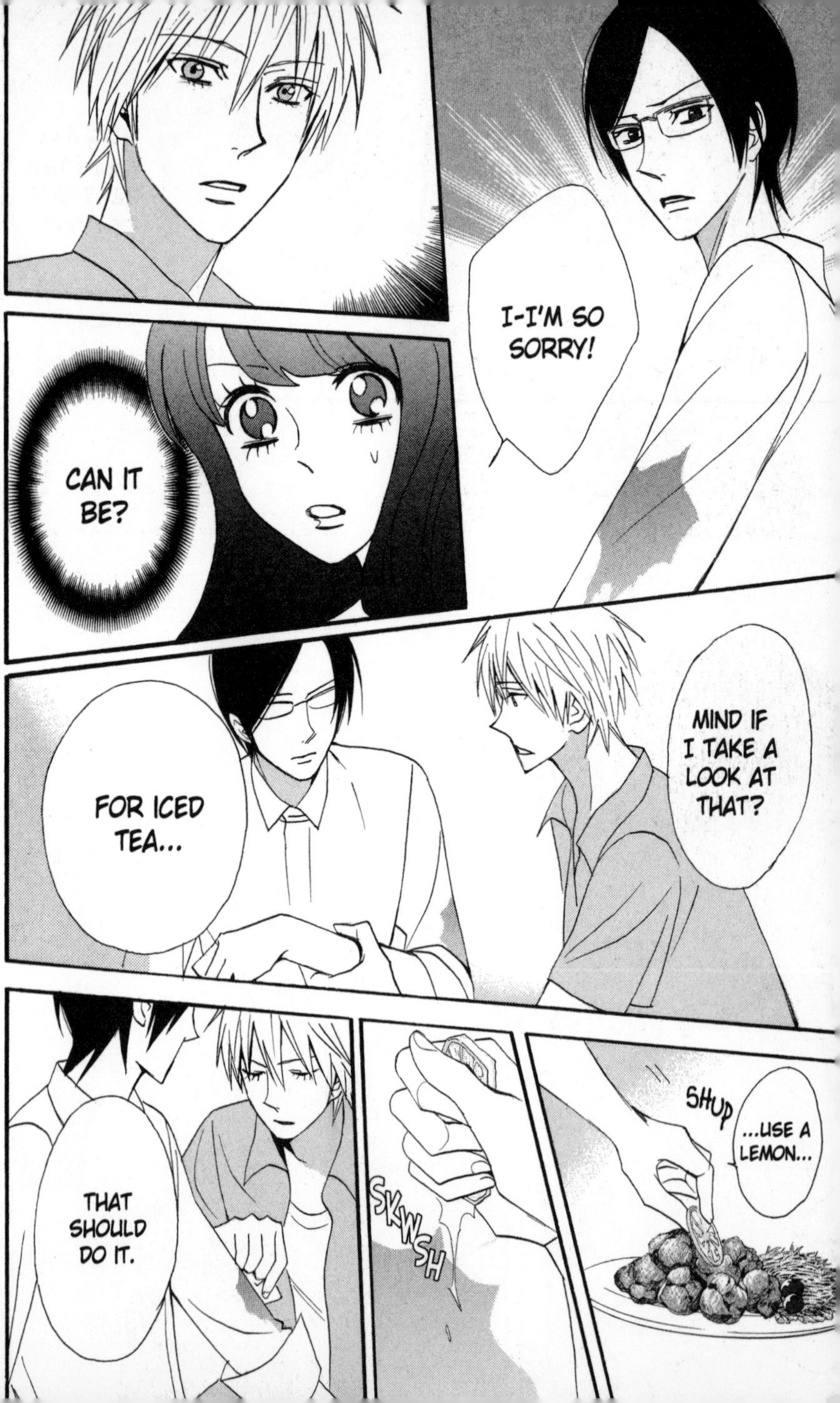
I-I'M SO SORRY!
CAN IT BE?
MIND IF I TAKE A LOOK AT THAT?
FOR ICED TEA...
SHUP
...USE A LEMON...
SKWSH
THAT SHOULD DO IT.

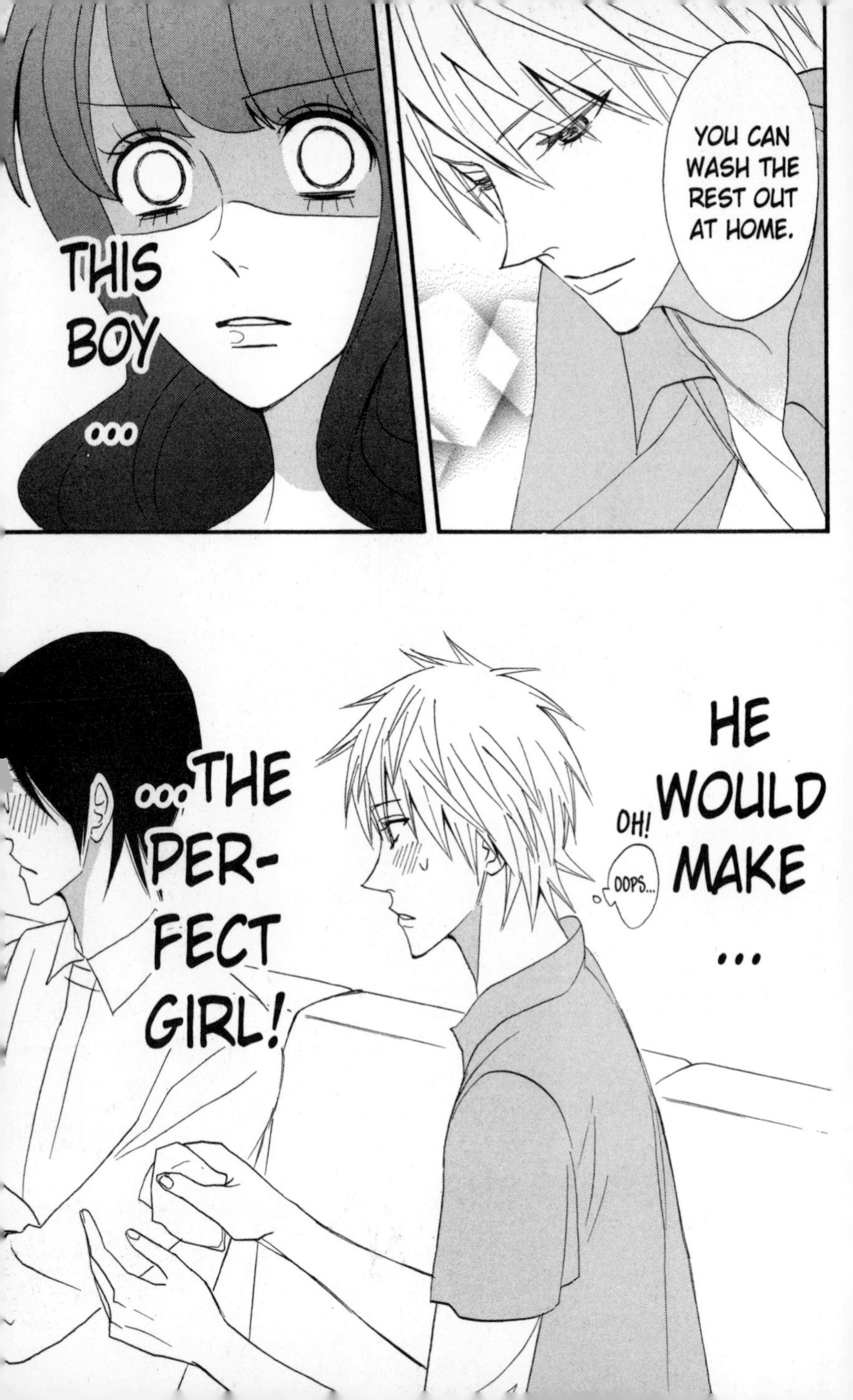
YOU CAN WASH THE REST OUT AT HOME.
THIS BOY...
HE WOULD MAKE...
OH!
OOPS...
...THE PER-FECT GIRL!

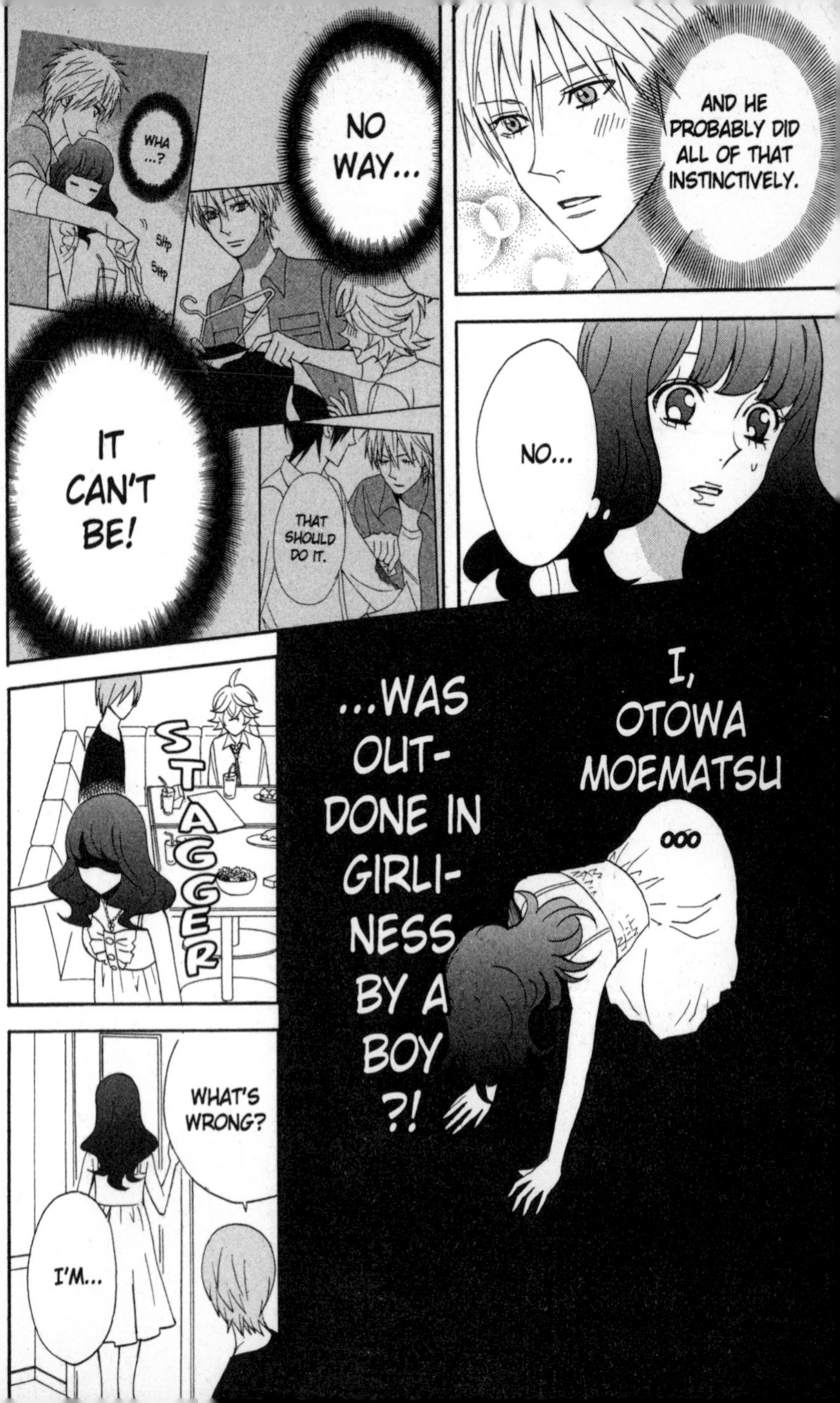
AND HE PROBABLY DID ALL OF THAT INSTINCTIVELY.
NO...
NO WAY...
WHA ...?
SHP
SHP
IT CAN'T BE!
THAT SHOULD DO IT.
I, OTOWA MOEMATSU
...WAS OUT-DONE IN GIRLI-NESS BY A BOY ?!
ooo
STAGGER
WHAT'S WRONG?
I'M...

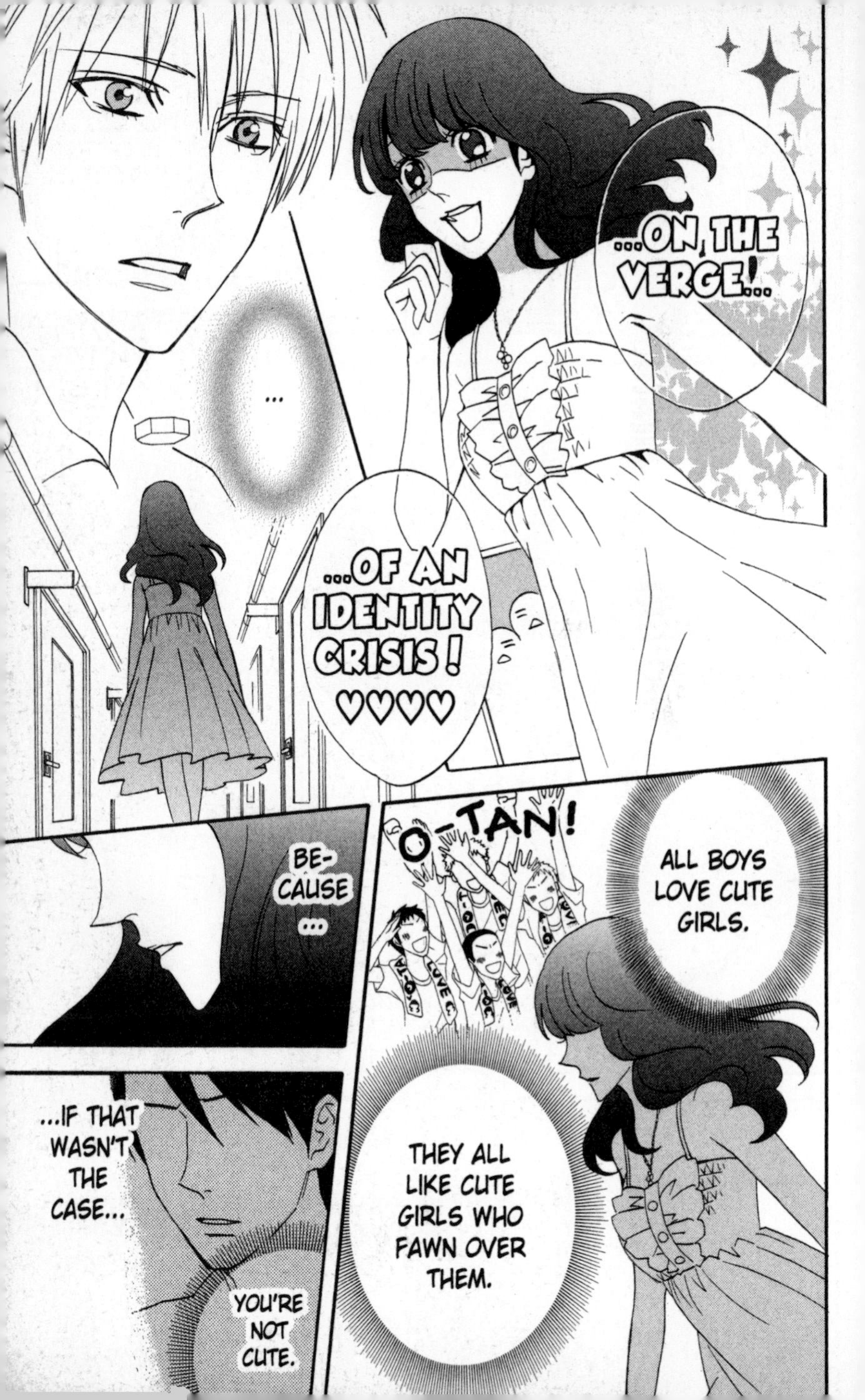
...ON THE VERGE!...
...OF AN IDENTITY CRISIS! ♥♥♥♥
...
O-TAN!
ALL BOYS LOVE CUTE GIRLS.
THEY ALL LIKE CUTE GIRLS WHO FAWN OVER THEM.
BE-CAUSE...
...IF THAT WASN'T THE CASE...
YOU'RE NOT CUTE.

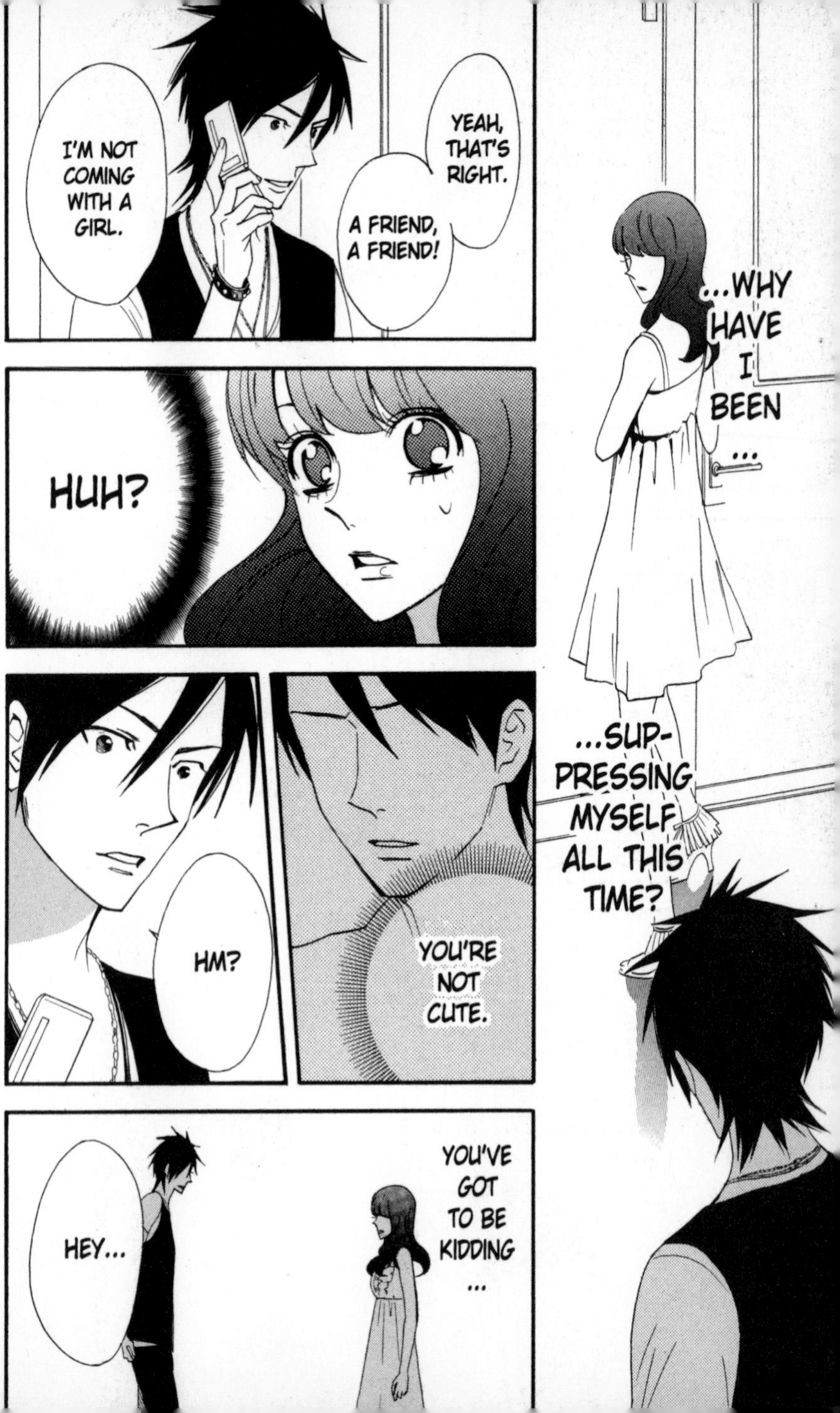
...WHY HAVE I BEEN ...
...SUP-PRESSING MYSELF ALL THIS TIME?
YEAH, THAT'S RIGHT.
A FRIEND, A FRIEND!
I'M NOT COMING WITH A GIRL.
HUH?
YOU'RE NOT CUTE.
HM?
YOU'VE GOT TO BE KIDDING ...
HEY...

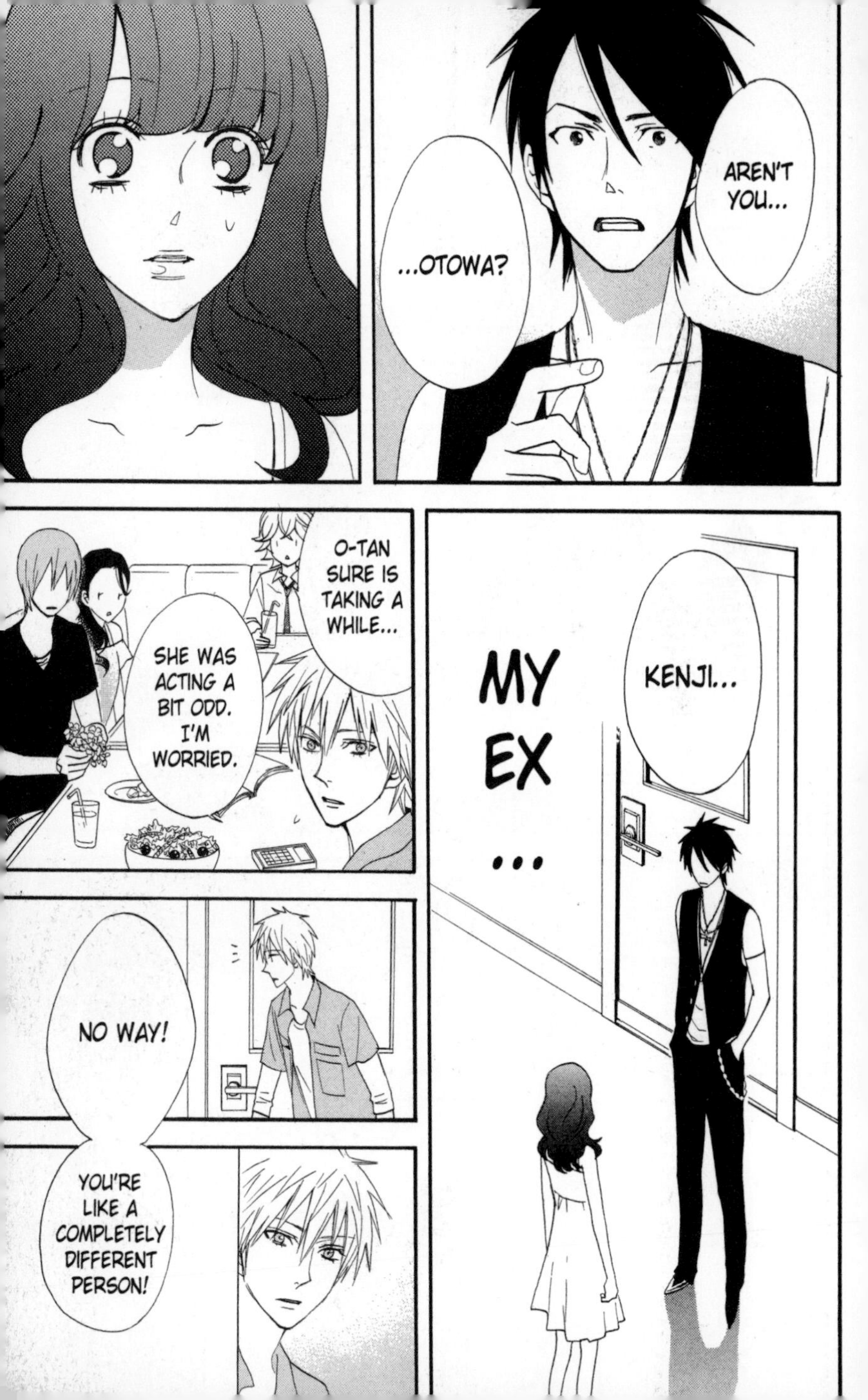
AREN'T YOU...
...OTOWA?
KENJI...
MY EX ...
O-TAN SURE IS TAKING A WHILE...
SHE WAS ACTING A BIT ODD. I'M WORRIED.
NO WAY!
YOU'RE LIKE A COMPLETELY DIFFERENT PERSON!

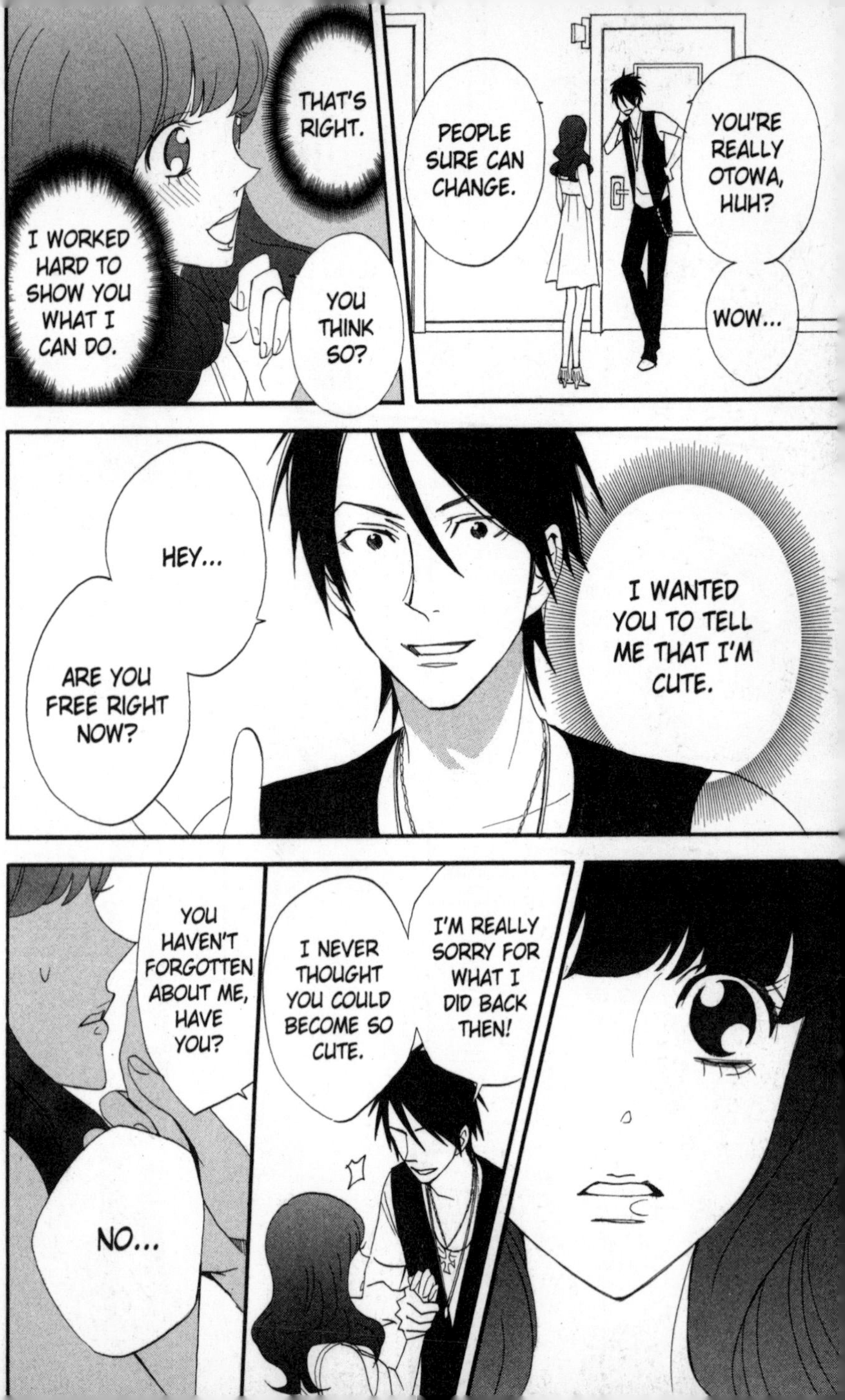
YOU'RE REALLY OTOWA, HUH?
WOW...
PEOPLE SURE CAN CHANGE.
YOU THINK SO?
THAT'S RIGHT.
I WORKED HARD TO SHOW YOU WHAT I CAN DO.
I WANTED YOU TO TELL ME THAT I'M CUTE.
HEY...
ARE YOU FREE RIGHT NOW?
I'M REALLY SORRY FOR WHAT I DID BACK THEN!
I NEVER THOUGHT YOU COULD BECOME SO CUTE.
YOU HAVEN'T FORGOTTEN ABOUT ME, HAVE YOU?
NO...

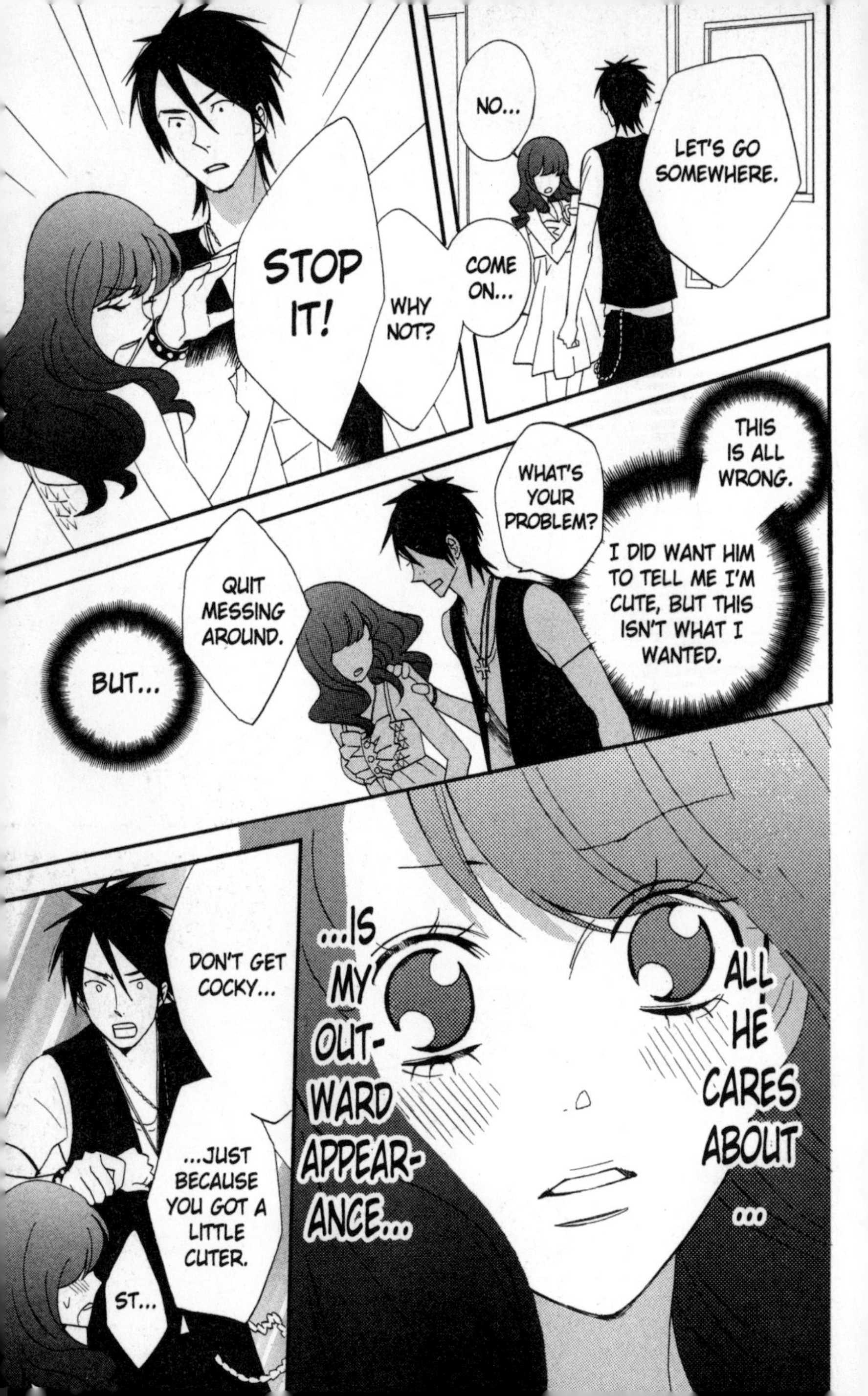
LET'S GO SOMEWHERE.
NO...
COME ON...
WHY NOT?
STOP IT!
THIS IS ALL WRONG.
WHAT'S YOUR PROBLEM?
I DID WANT HIM TO TELL ME I'M CUTE, BUT THIS ISN'T WHAT I WANTED.
QUIT MESSING AROUND.
BUT...
ALL HE CARES ABOUT...
...IS MY OUT-WARD APPEAR-ANCE...
DON'T GET COCKY...
...JUST BECAUSE YOU GOT A LITTLE CUTER.
ST...

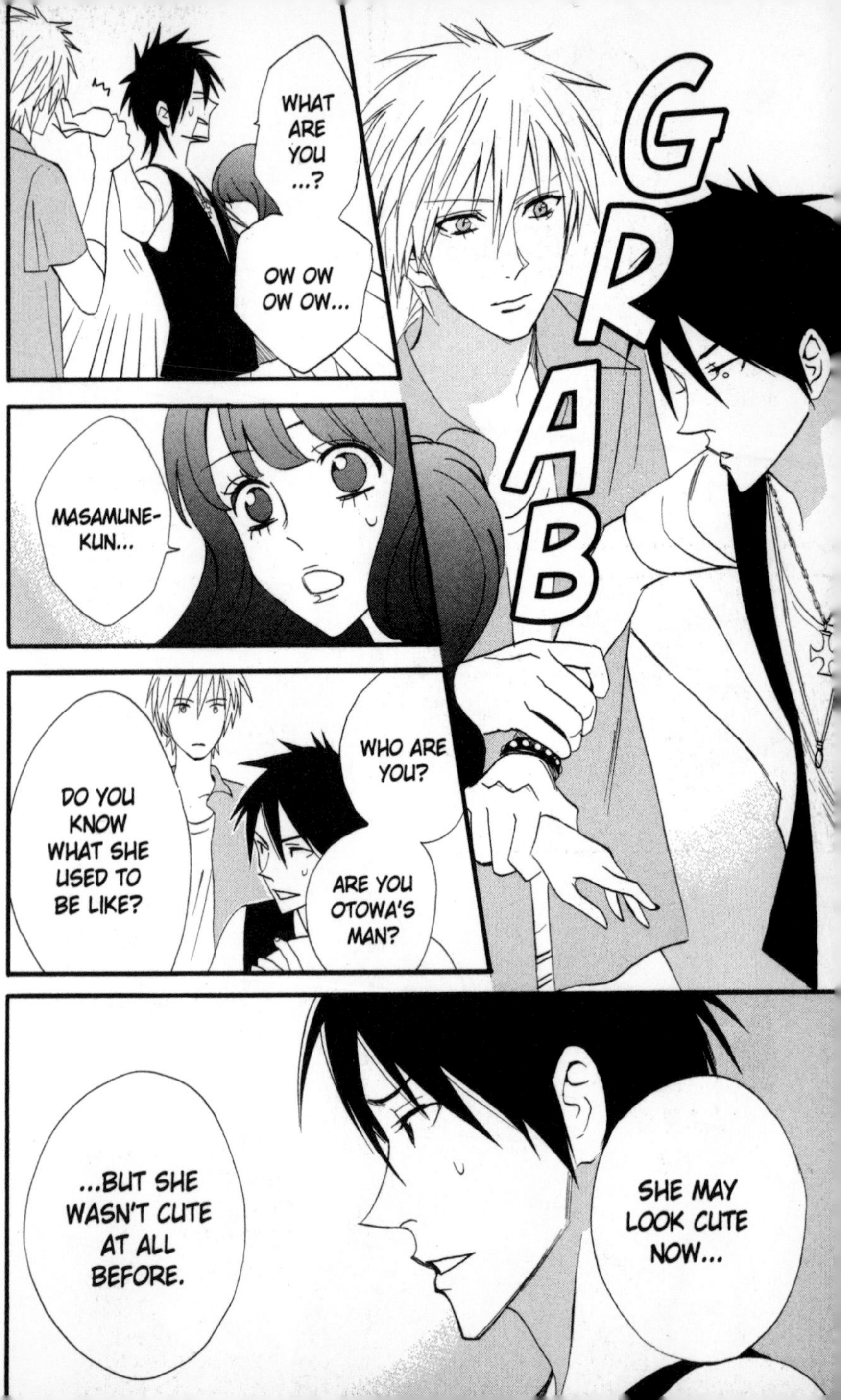
GRAB
WHAT ARE YOU ...?
OW OW OW OW...
MASAMUNE-KUN...
WHO ARE YOU?
ARE YOU OTOWA'S MAN?
DO YOU KNOW WHAT SHE USED TO BE LIKE?
SHE MAY LOOK CUTE NOW...
...BUT SHE WASN'T CUTE AT ALL BEFORE.

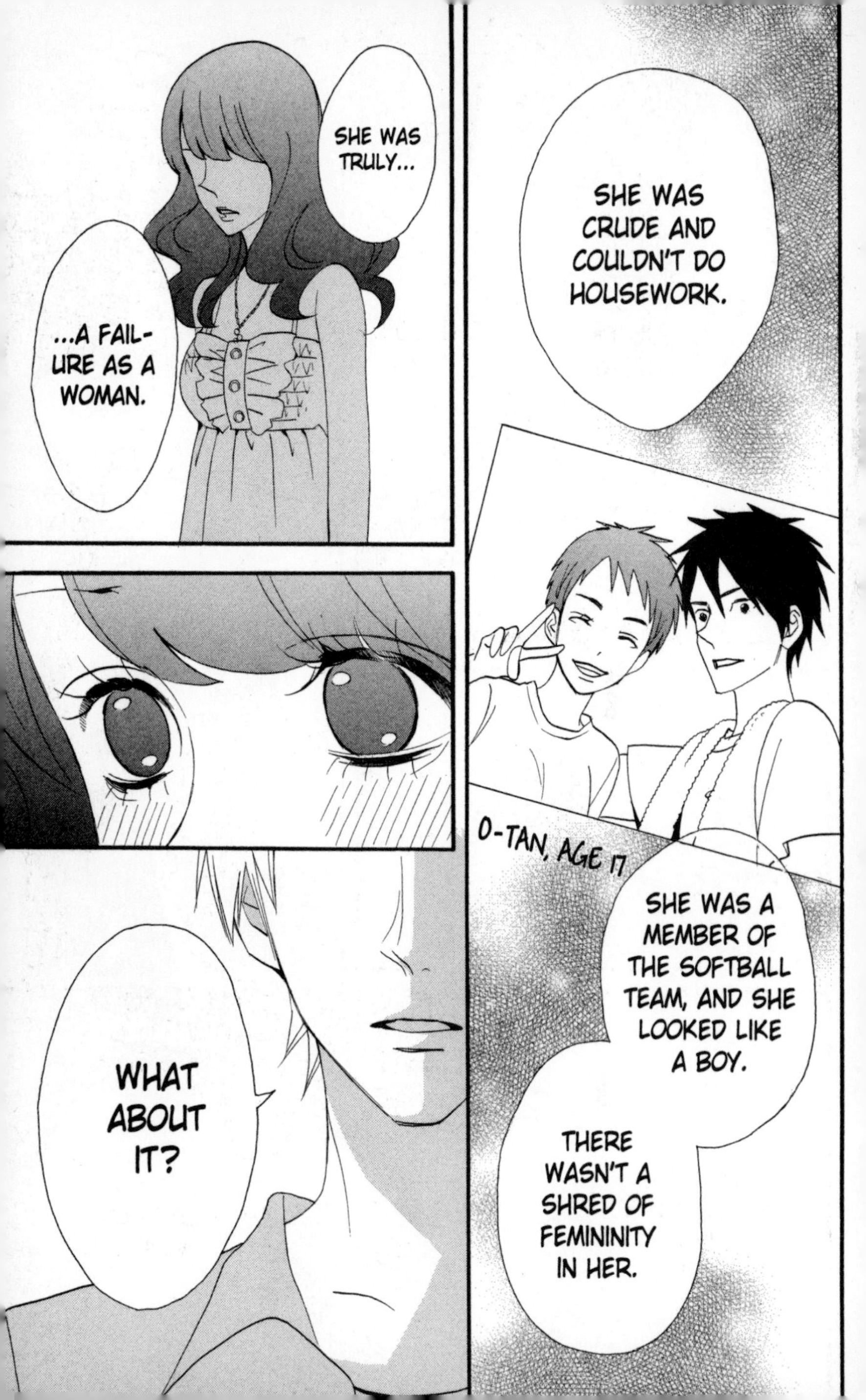

SHE WAS CRUDE AND COULDN'T DO HOUSEWORK.
O-TAN, AGE 17
SHE WAS A MEMBER OF THE SOFTBALL TEAM, AND SHE LOOKED LIKE A BOY.
THERE WASN'T A SHRED OF FEMININITY IN HER.
SHE WAS TRULY...
...A FAIL-URE AS A WOMAN.
WHAT ABOUT IT?

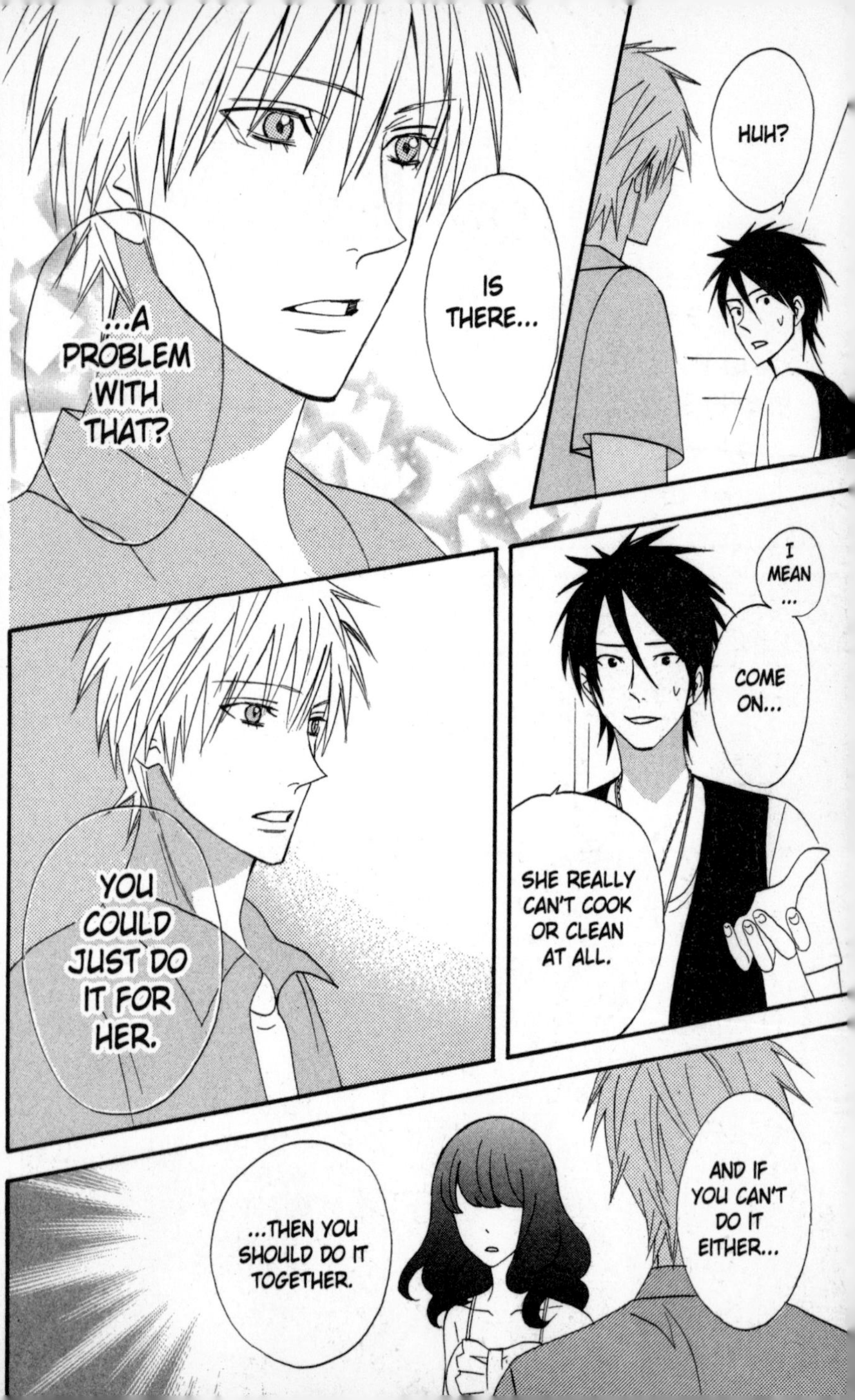
HUH?
IS THERE...
...A PROBLEM WITH THAT?
I MEAN...
COME ON...
SHE REALLY CAN'T COOK OR CLEAN AT ALL.
YOU COULD JUST DO IT FOR HER.
AND IF YOU CAN'T DO IT EITHER...
...THEN YOU SHOULD DO IT TOGETHER.

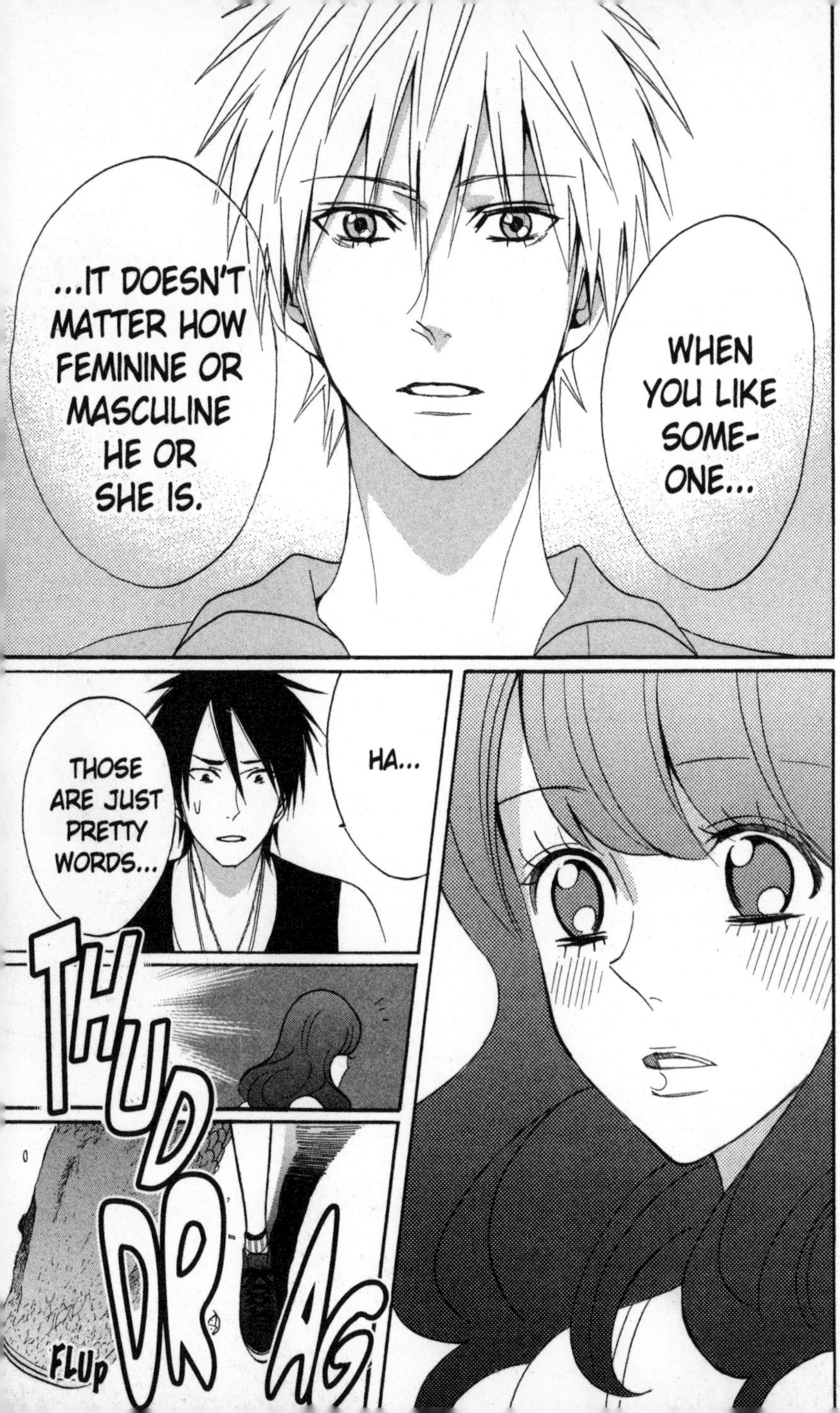
WHEN YOU LIKE SOME-ONE...
...IT DOESN'T MATTER HOW FEMININE OR MASCULINE HE OR SHE IS.
HA...
THOSE ARE JUST PRETTY WORDS...
THUD
DRAG
FLUP

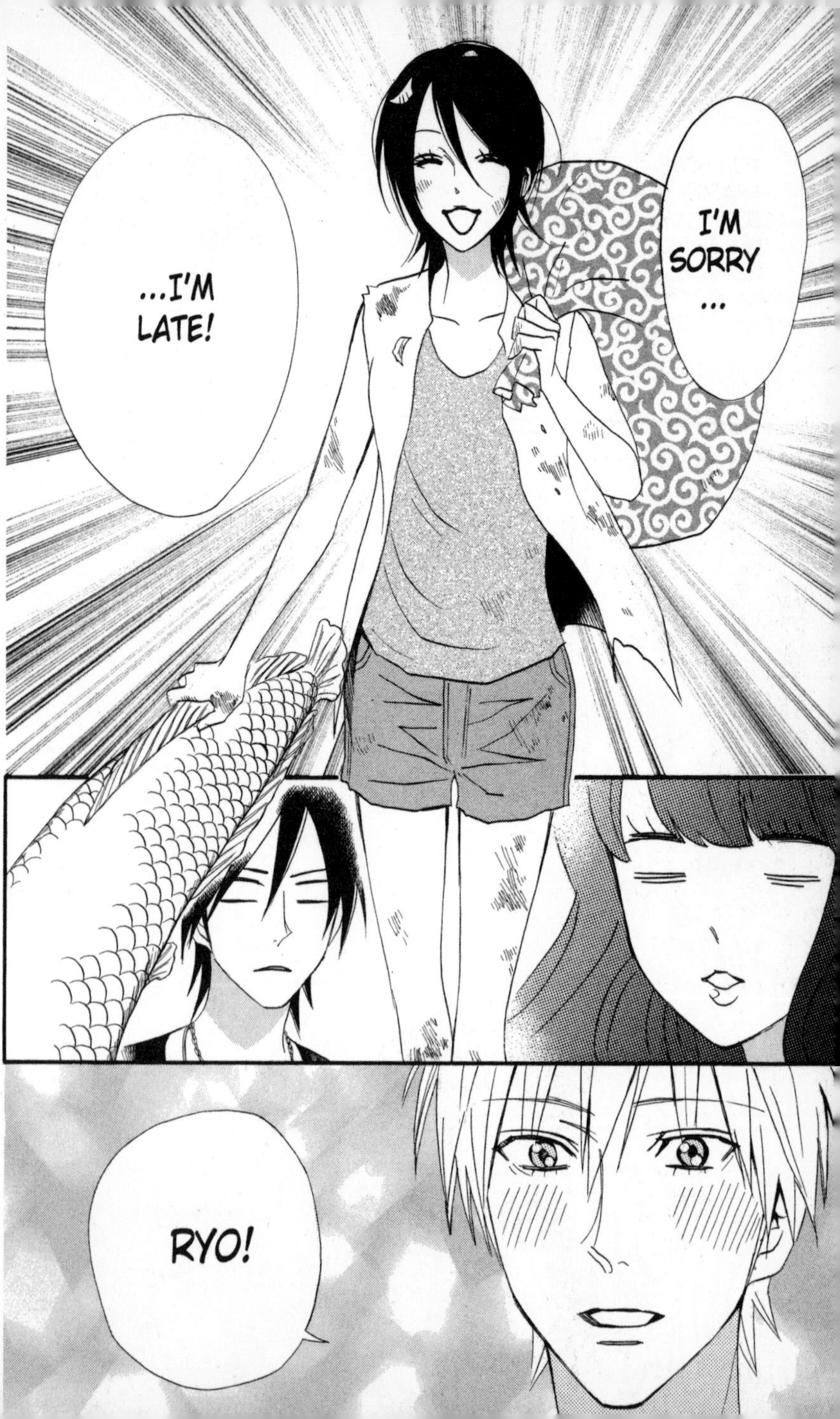
I'M SORRY ...
...I'M LATE!
RYO!

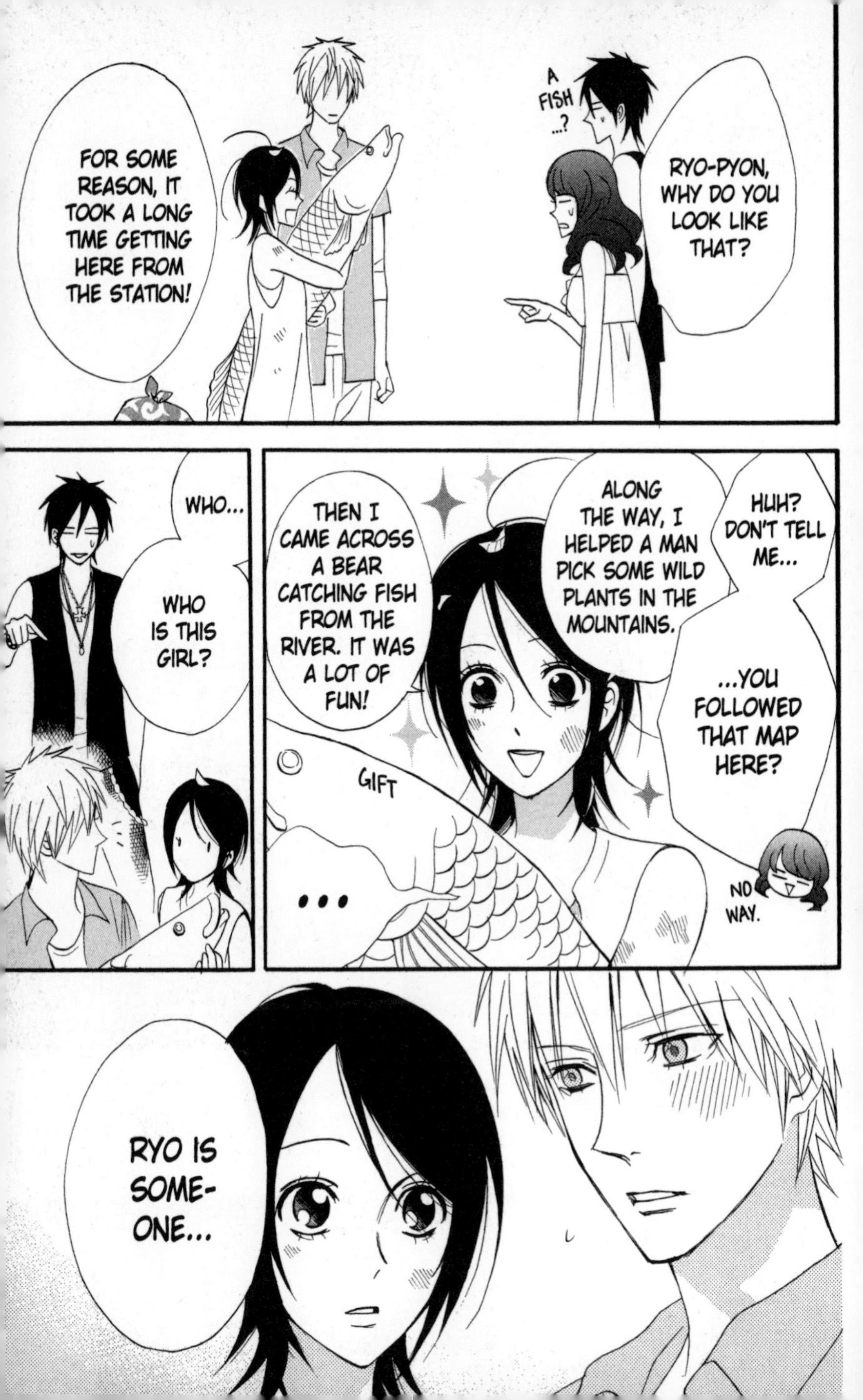
A FISH ...?
RYO-PYON, WHY DO YOU LOOK LIKE THAT?
FOR SOME REASON, IT TOOK A LONG TIME GETTING HERE FROM THE STATION!
HUH? DON'T TELL ME...
...YOU FOLLOWED THAT MAP HERE?
ALONG THE WAY, I HELPED A MAN PICK SOME WILD PLANTS IN THE MOUNTAINS.
THEN I CAME ACROSS A BEAR CATCHING FISH FROM THE RIVER. IT WAS A LOT OF FUN!
NO WAY.
GIFT
...
WHO...
WHO IS THIS GIRL?
RYO IS SOME-ONE...

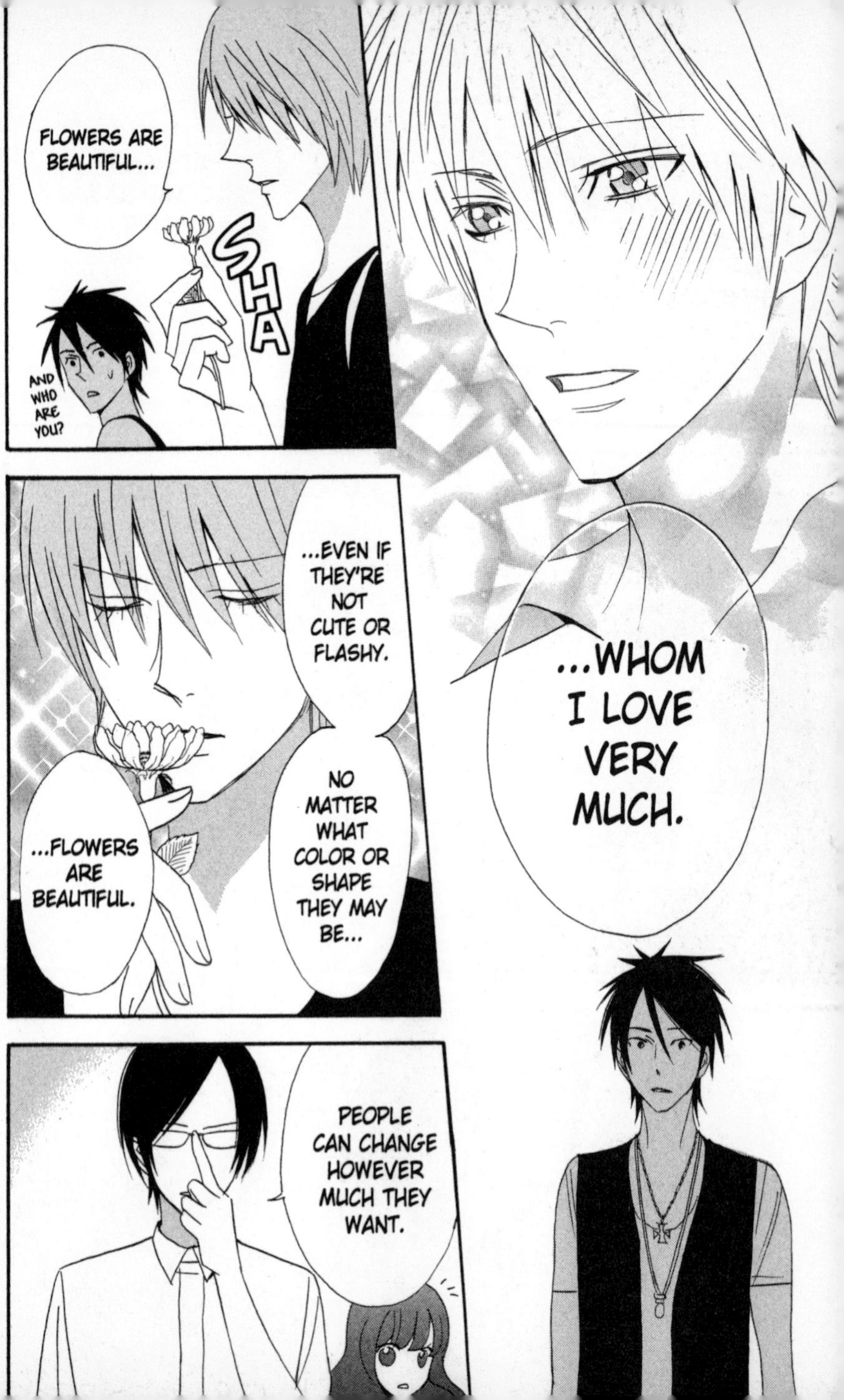
...WHOM I LOVE VERY MUCH.
FLOWERS ARE BEAUTIFUL...
SHA
AND WHO ARE YOU?
...EVEN IF THEY'RE NOT CUTE OR FLASHY.
NO MATTER WHAT COLOR OR SHAPE THEY MAY BE...
...FLOWERS ARE BEAUTIFUL.
PEOPLE CAN CHANGE HOWEVER MUCH THEY WANT.

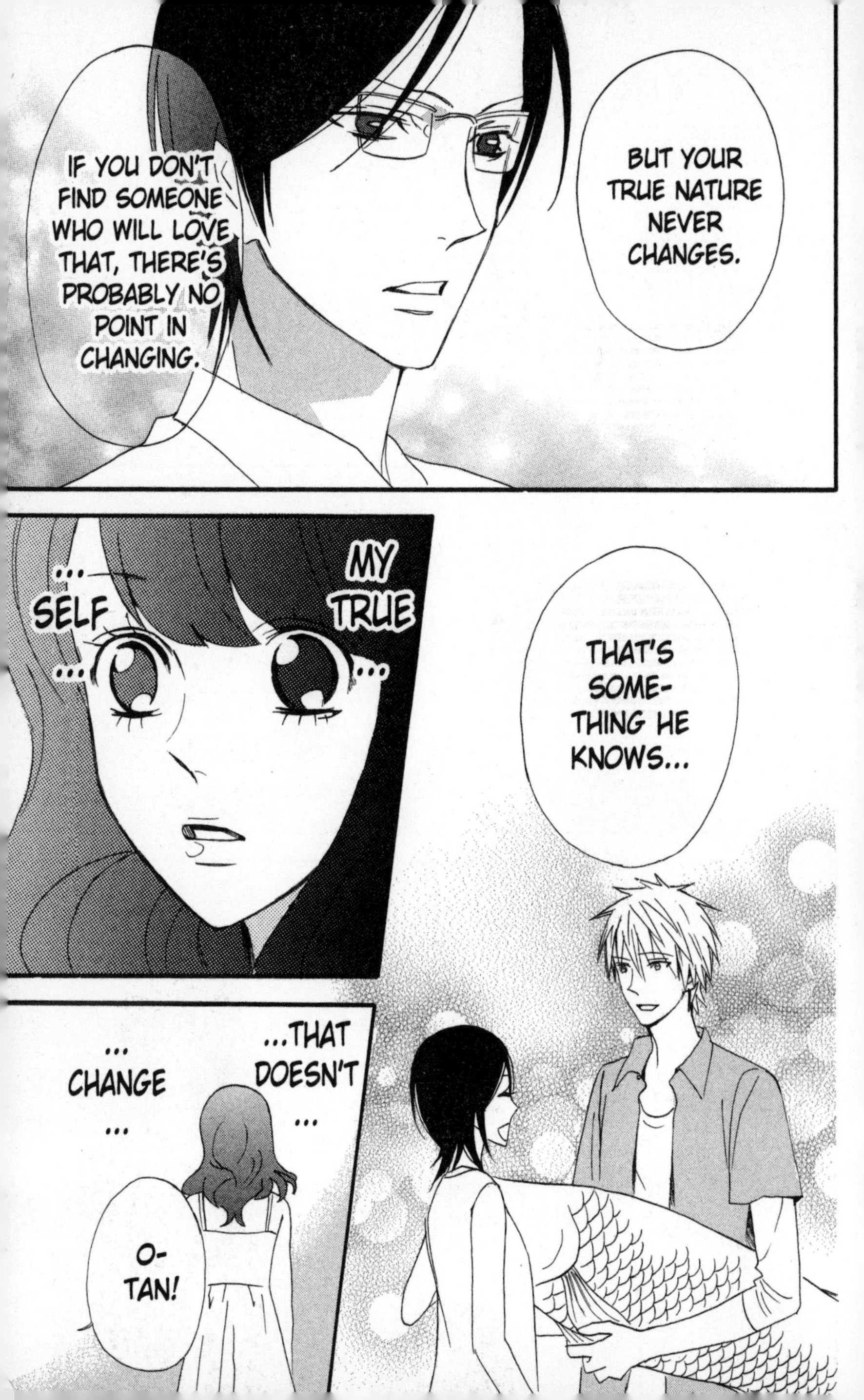
BUT YOUR TRUE NATURE NEVER CHANGES.
IF YOU DON'T FIND SOMEONE WHO WILL LOVE THAT, THERE'S PROBABLY NO POINT IN CHANGING.
THAT'S SOME-THING HE KNOWS...
MY TRUE ...
... SELF ...
...THAT DOESN'T ...
... CHANGE ...
O-TAN!

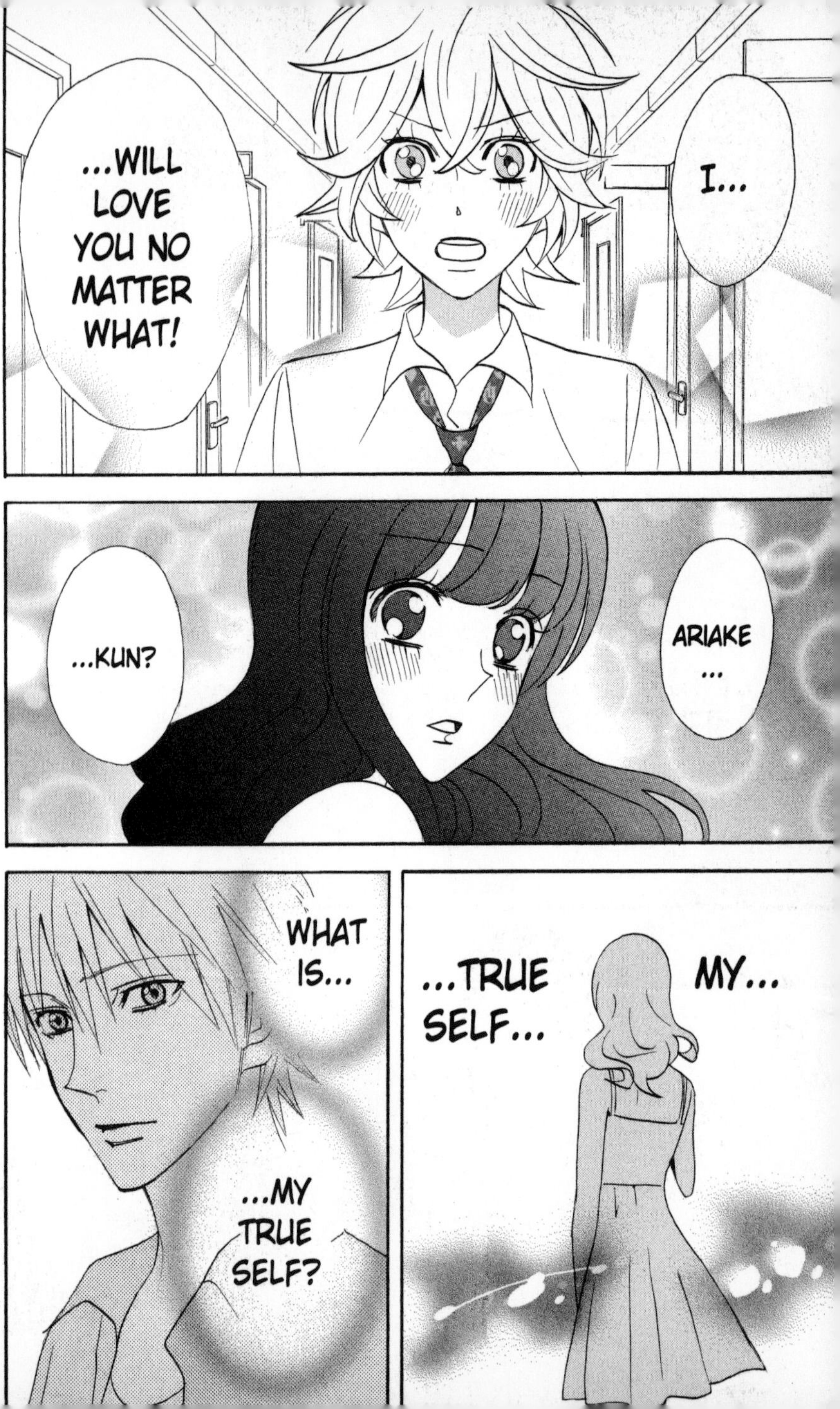
I...
...WILL LOVE YOU NO MATTER WHAT!
ARIAKE...
...KUN?
MY...
...TRUE SELF...
WHAT IS...
...MY TRUE SELF?

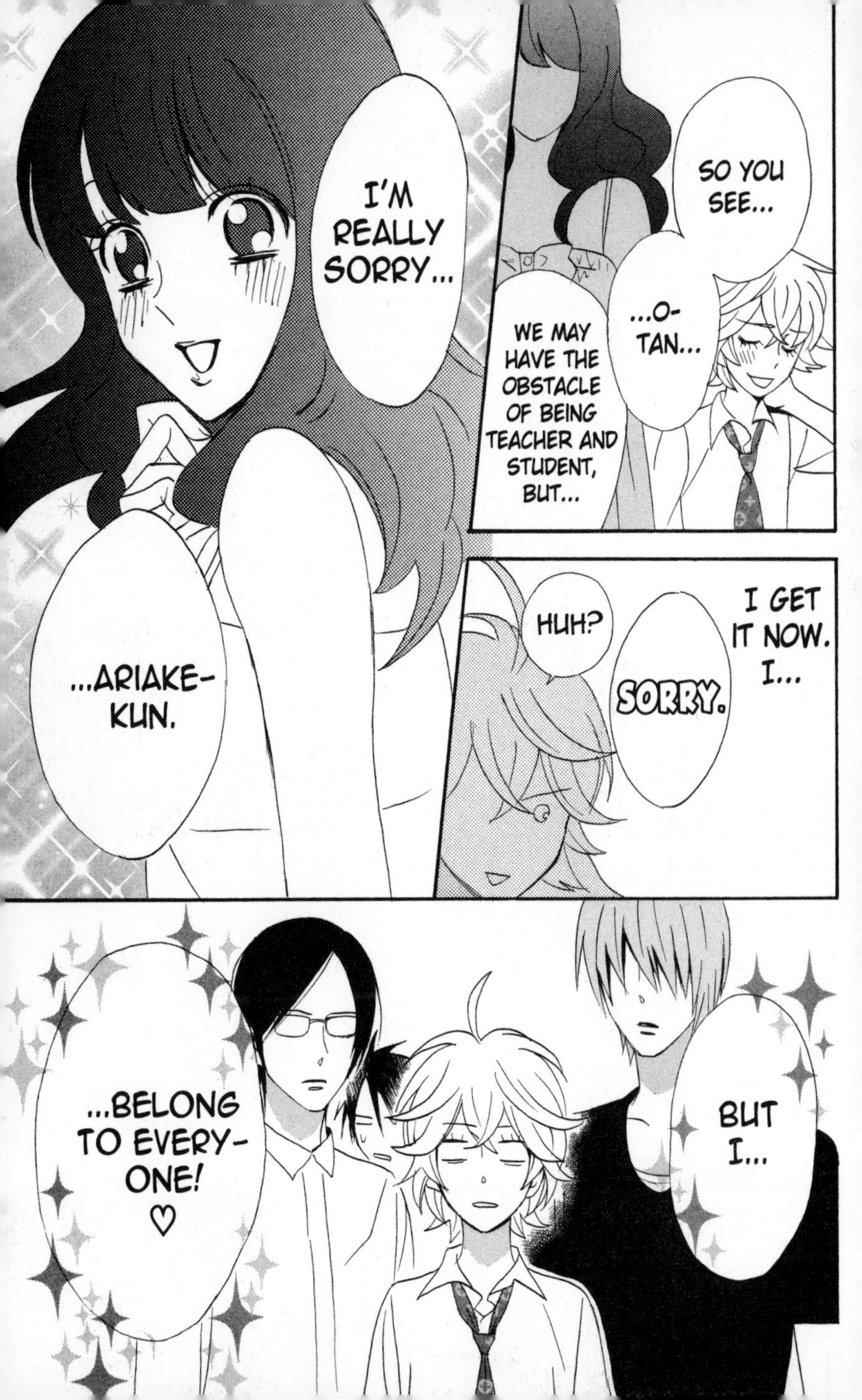
SO YOU SEE...
...O-TAN...
WE MAY HAVE THE OBSTACLE OF BEING TEACHER AND STUDENT, BUT...
I GET IT NOW. I...
SORRY.
HUH?
I'M REALLY SORRY...
...ARIAKE-KUN.
BUT I...
...BELONG TO EVERY-ONE! ♡

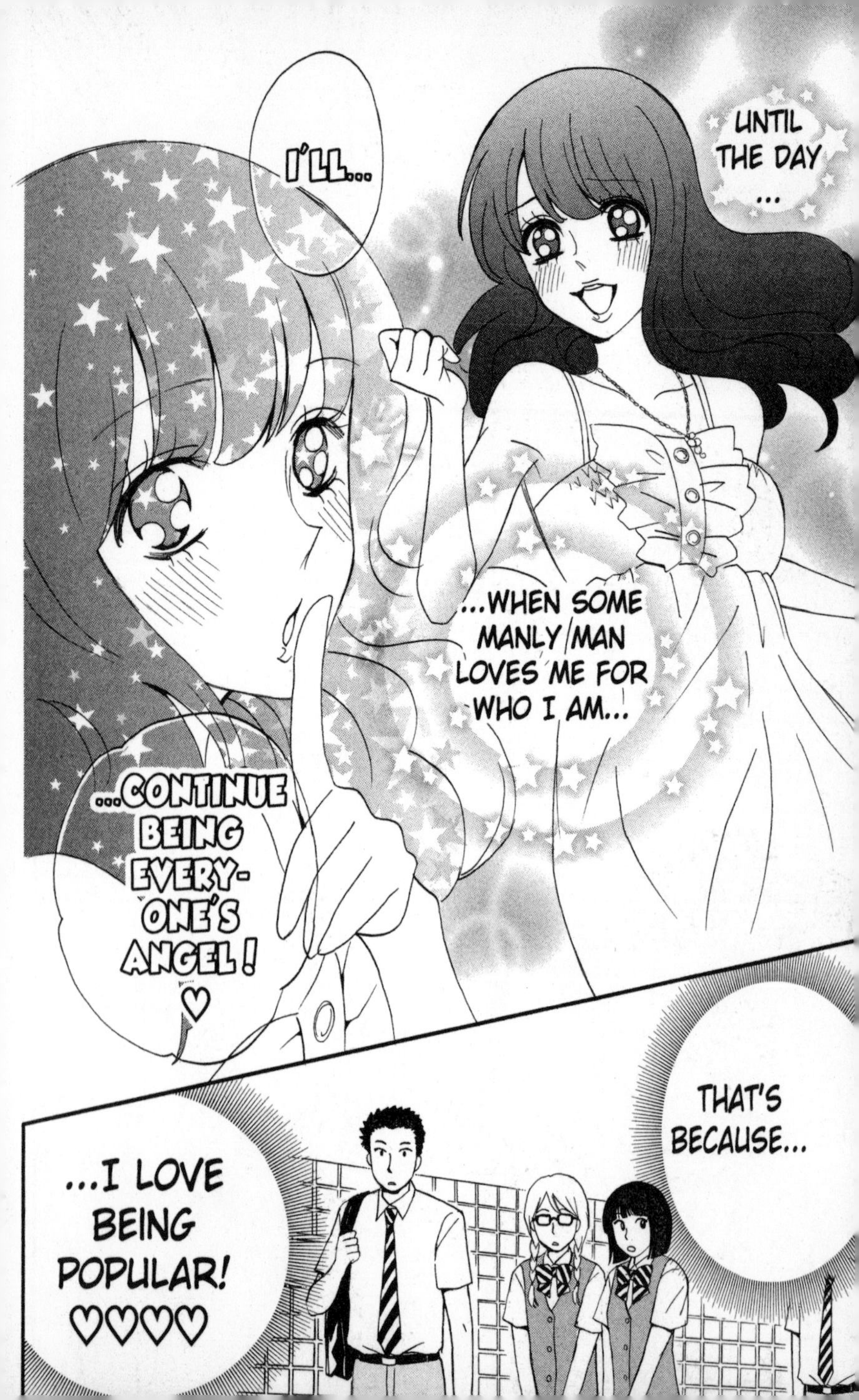
UNTIL THE DAY ...
...WHEN SOME MANLY MAN LOVES ME FOR WHO I AM...
I'LL...
...CONTINUE BEING EVERY-ONE'S ANGEL! ♡
THAT'S BECAUSE...
...I LOVE BEING POPULAR! ♡♡♡♡

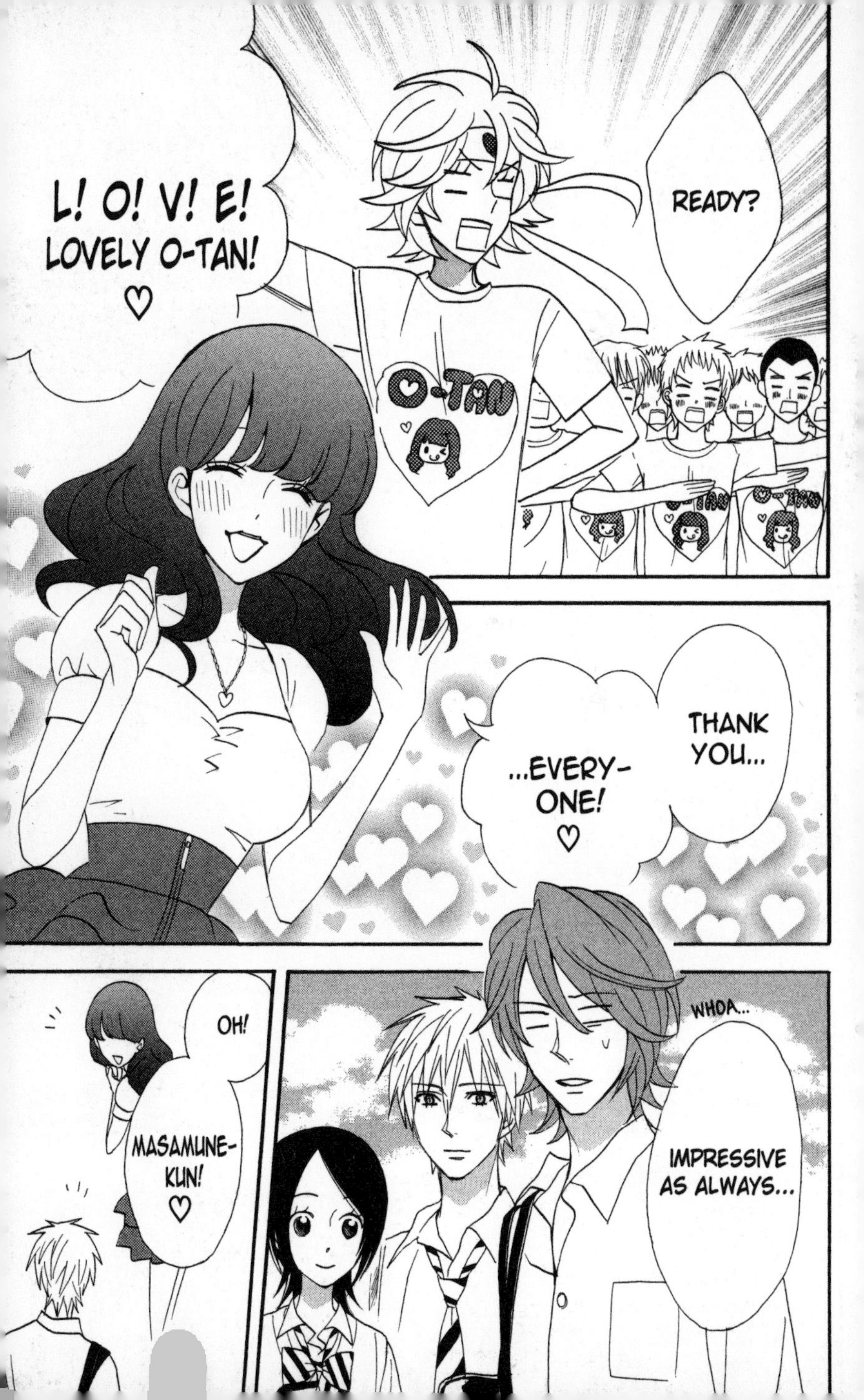
READY?
L! O! V! E! LOVELY O-TAN! ♡
O-TAN
THANK YOU...
...EVERY-ONE! ♡
WHOA...
IMPRESSIVE AS ALWAYS...
OH!
MASAMUNE-KUN! ♡

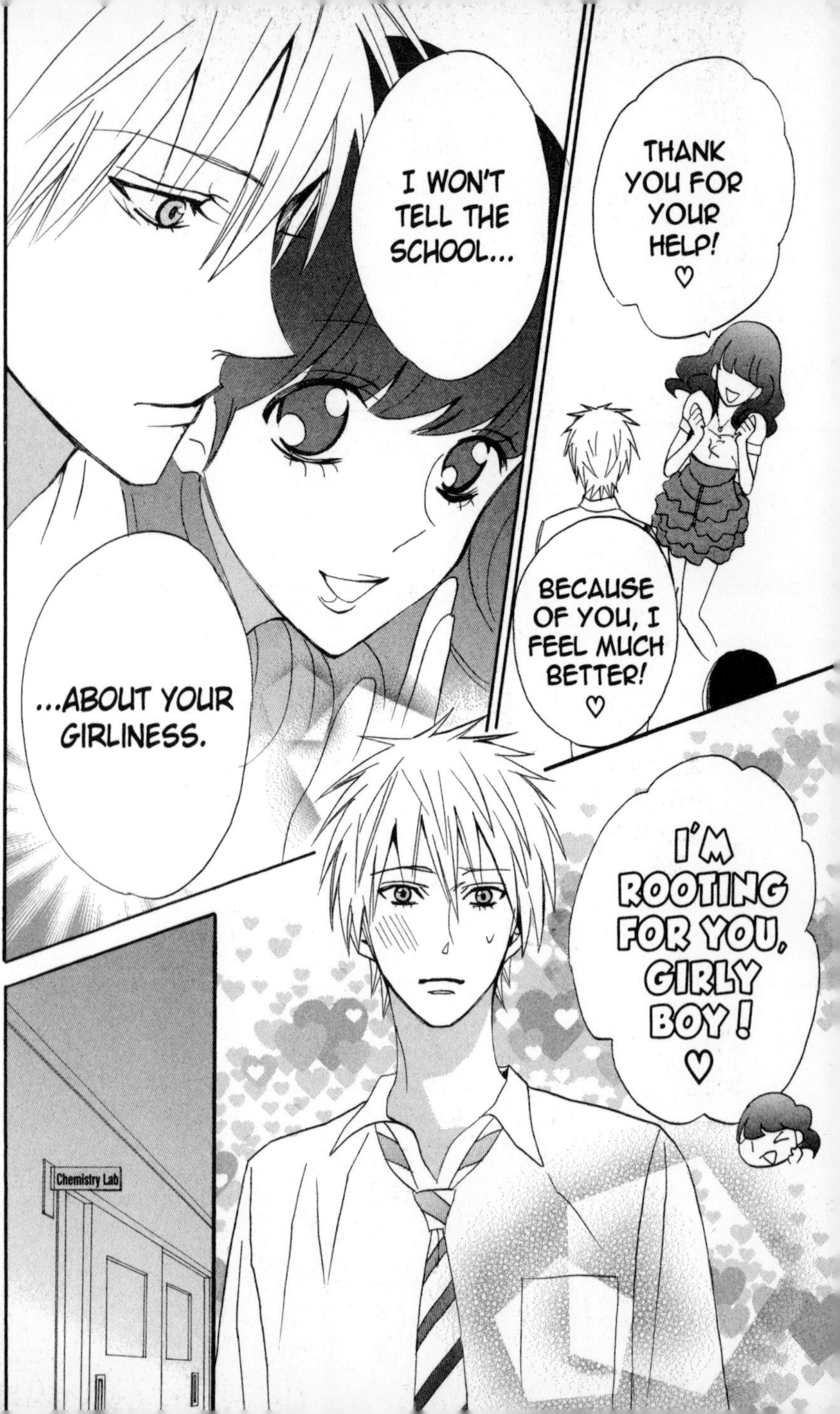
THANK YOU FOR YOUR HELP! ♡
BECAUSE OF YOU, I FEEL MUCH BETTER! ♡
I WON'T TELL THE SCHOOL...
...ABOUT YOUR GIRLINESS.
I'M ROOTING FOR YOU, GIRLY BOY! ♡
Chemistry Lab

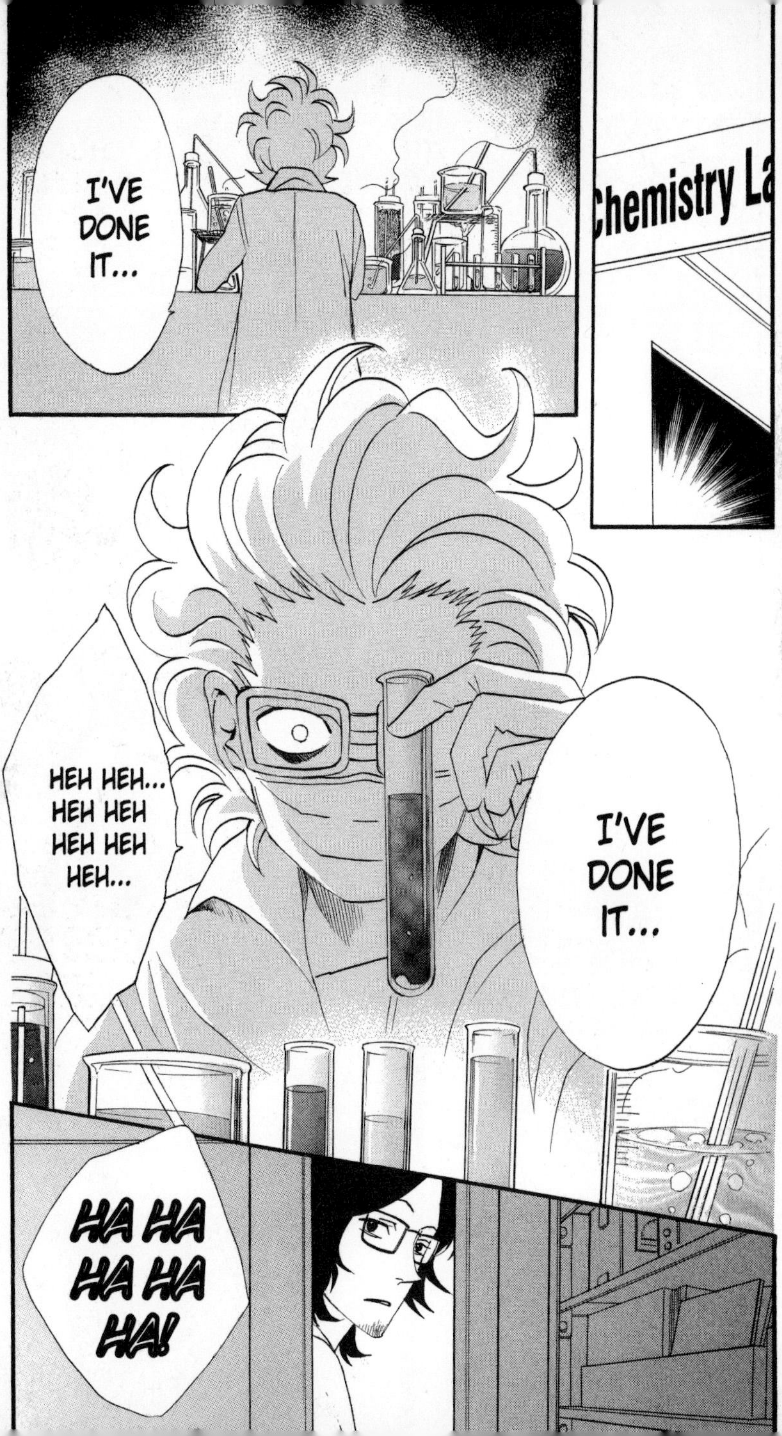
Chemistry La
I'VE DONE IT...
I'VE DONE IT...
HEH HEH... HEH HEH HEH HEH HEH...
HA HA HA HA HA!

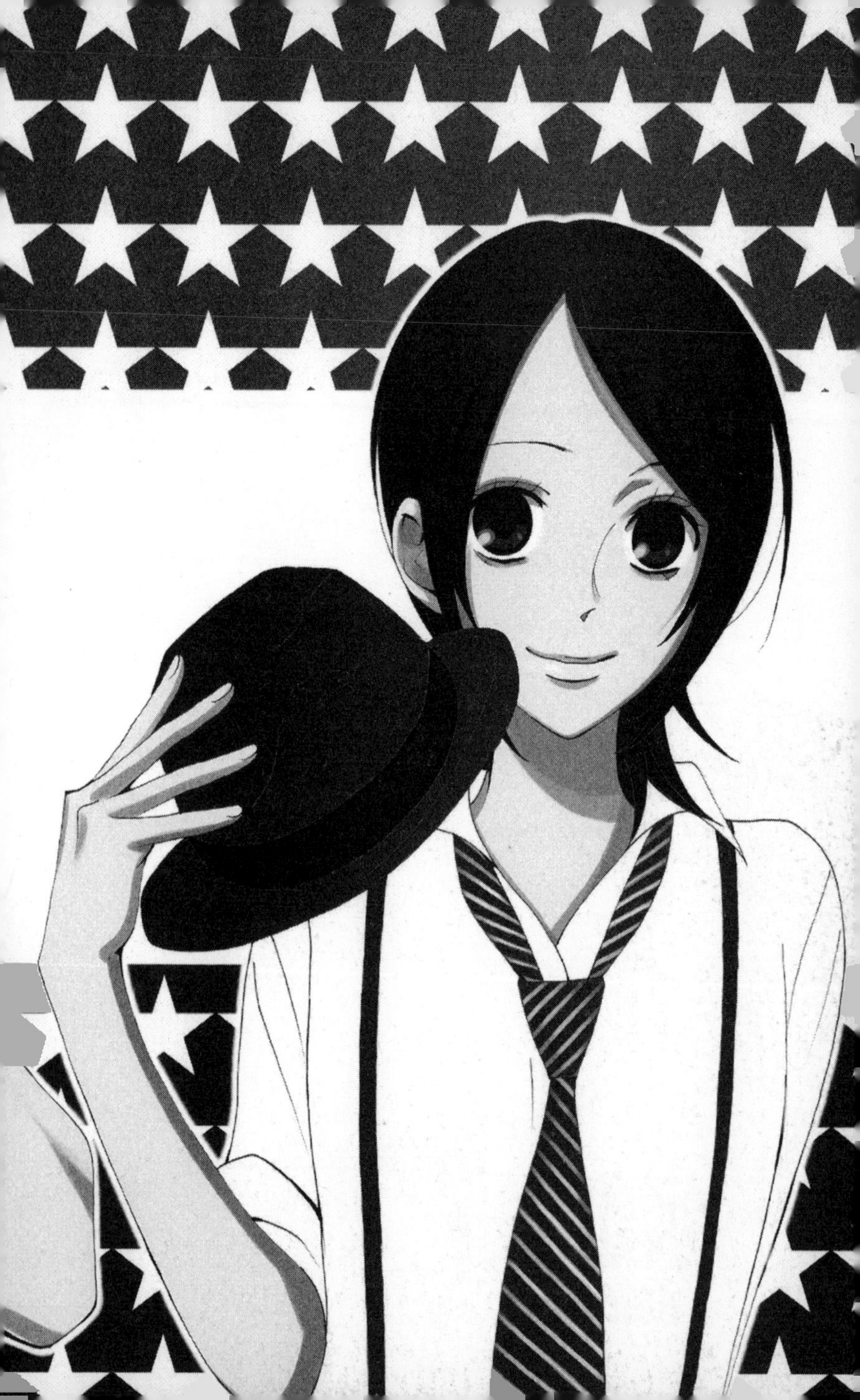

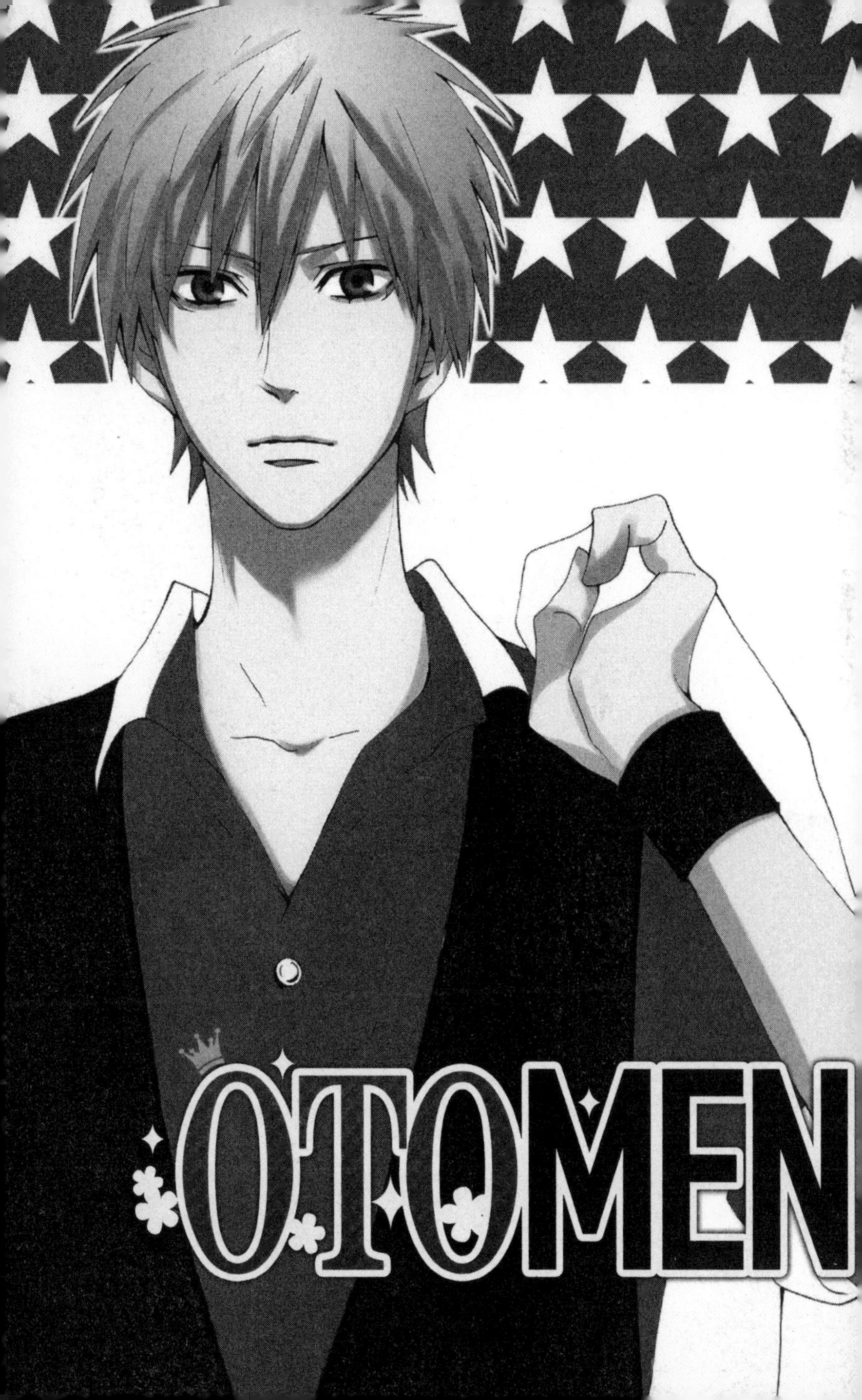
OTOMEN

OTOMEN

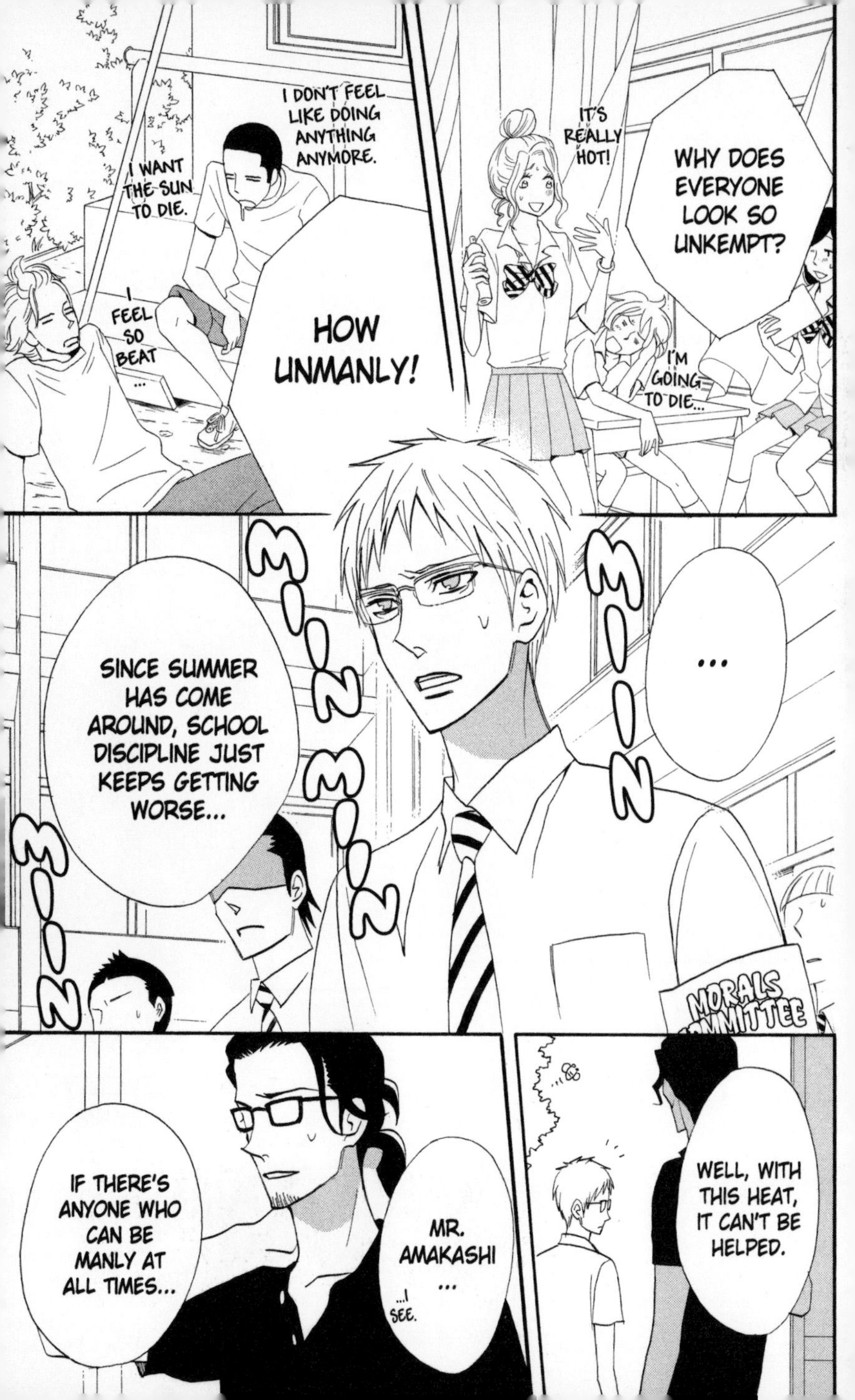
WHY DOES EVERYONE LOOK SO UNKEMPT?
IT'S REALLY HOT!
I'M GOING TO DIE...
I DON'T FEEL LIKE DOING ANYTHING ANYMORE.
I WANT THE SUN TO DIE.
I FEEL SO BEAT...
HOW UNMANLY!
...
MI-I-N
MI-I-N
MI-I-N
SINCE SUMMER HAS COME AROUND, SCHOOL DISCIPLINE JUST KEEPS GETTING WORSE...
MI-I-N
MORALS COMMITTEE
WELL, WITH THIS HEAT, IT CAN'T BE HELPED.
MR. AMAKASHI...
...I SEE.
IF THERE'S ANYONE WHO CAN BE MANLY AT ALL TIMES...

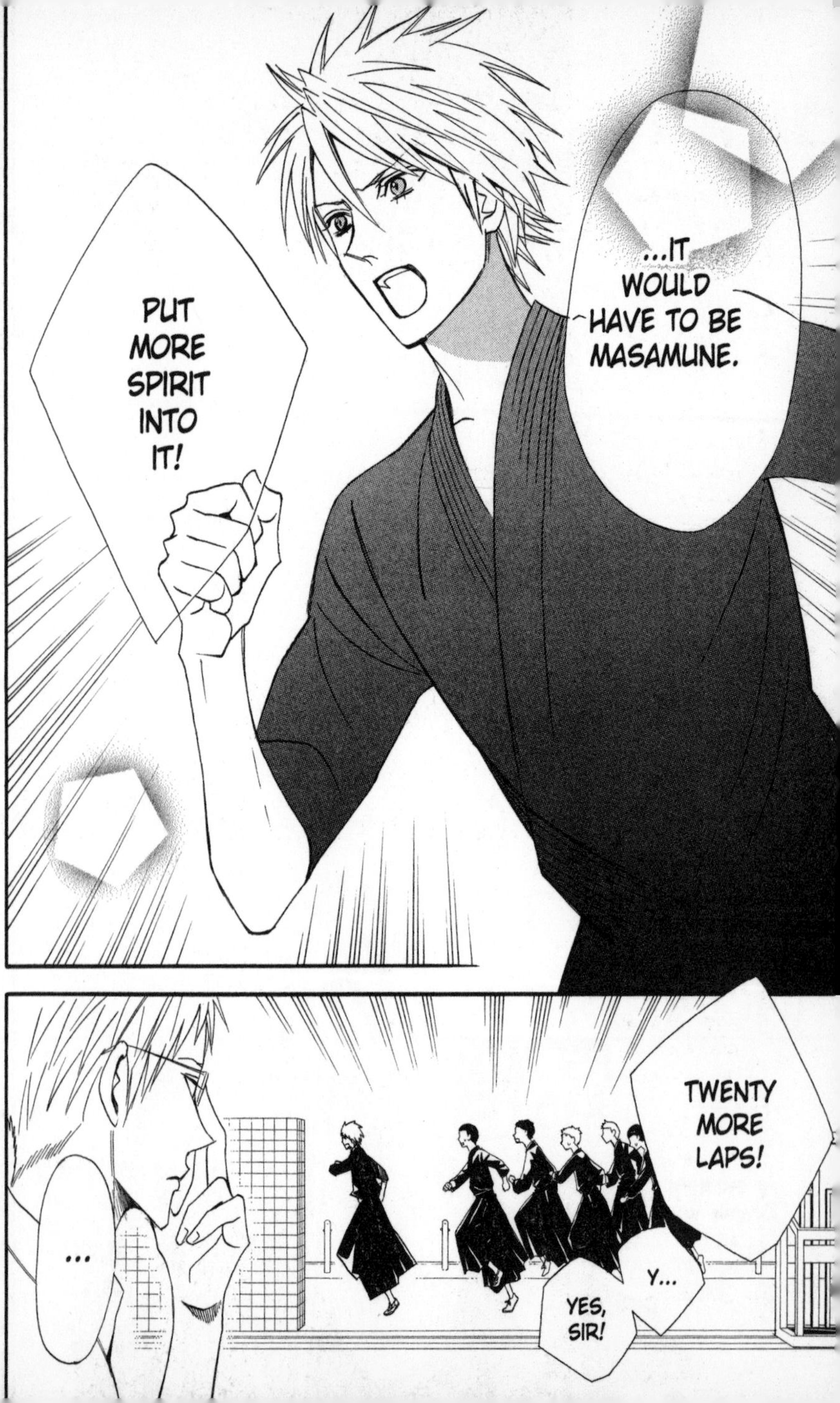
...IT WOULD HAVE TO BE MASAMUNE.
PUT MORE SPIRIT INTO IT!
TWENTY MORE LAPS!
Y...
YES, SIR!
...

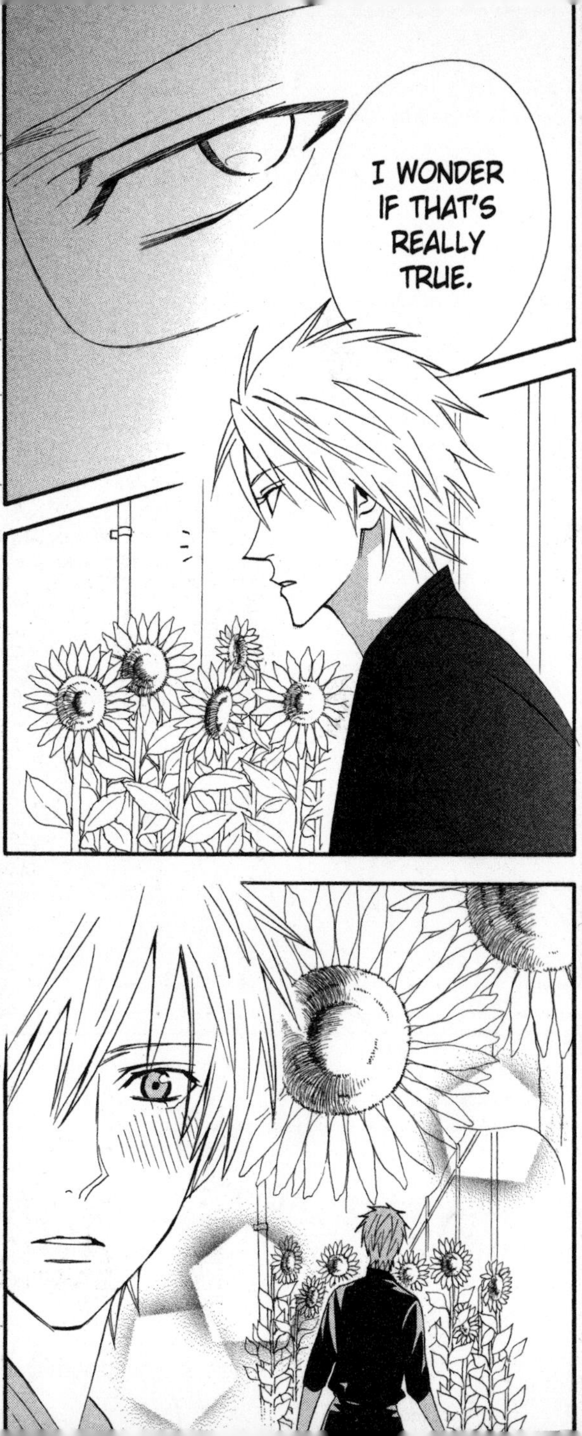
I WONDER IF THAT'S REALLY TRUE.

The episode that I liked the best from the *Otomen* TV series was the one with O-tan in it. O-tan just kept on getting more and more fun to write. Kibino was a character I created because I felt like I should have a character who isn't good-looking. When you draw only good-looking characters, you have to do things like that. I temporarily made Juta's hair short because I got bored with his hairstyle. In real life, people never keep the same hairstyle forever anyway. I'm going to be changing my hairstyle soon too. When I changed Juta's hairstyle back to the way it was, I felt that he looked more natural with his hair messy. Anyway, I don't change the school year every year either.

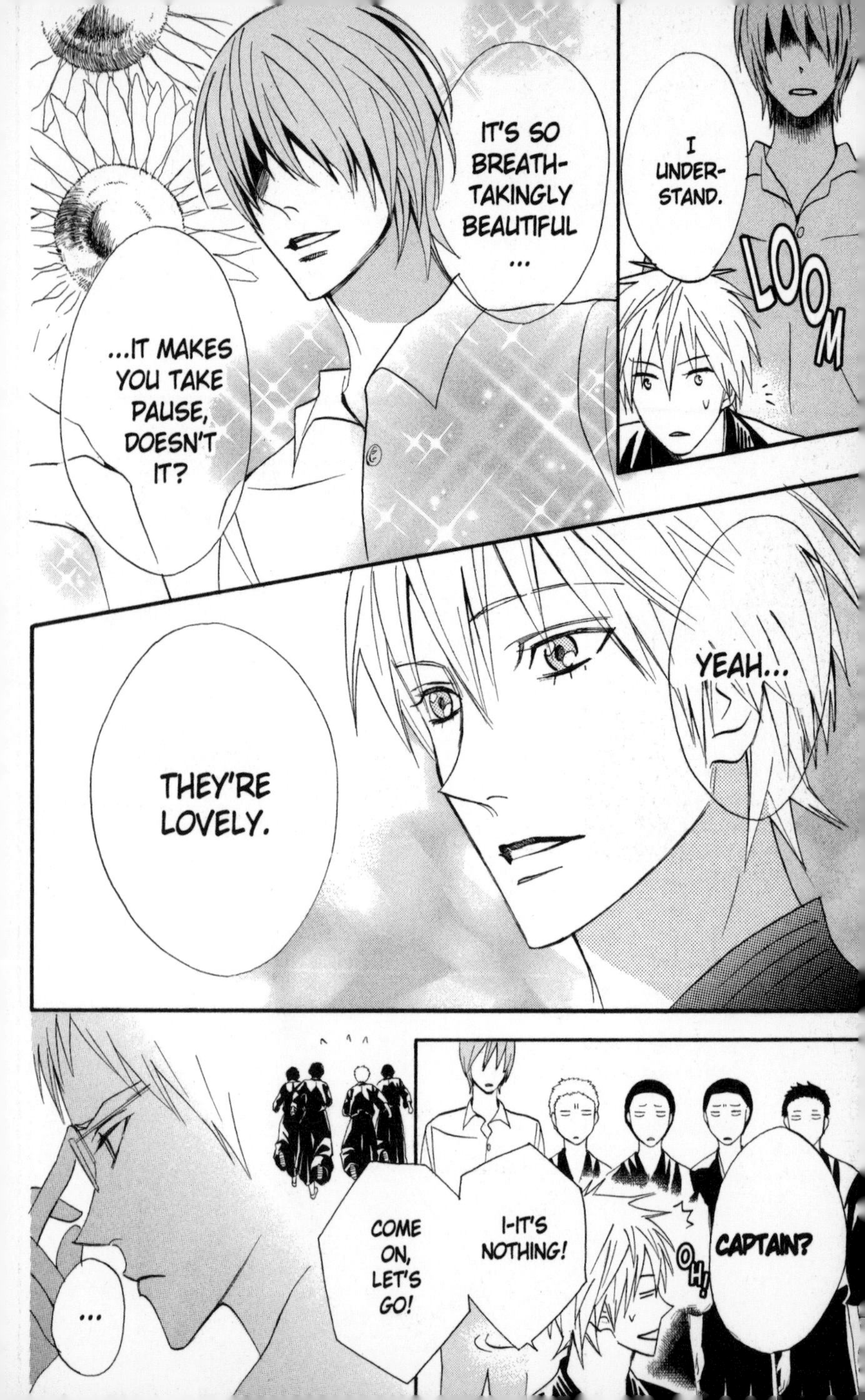
I UNDERSTAND.
LOOM
IT'S SO BREATHTAKINGLY BEAUTIFUL...
...IT MAKES YOU TAKE PAUSE, DOESN'T IT?
YEAH...
THEY'RE LOVELY.
CAPTAIN?
OH!
I-IT'S NOTHING!
COME ON, LET'S GO!
...

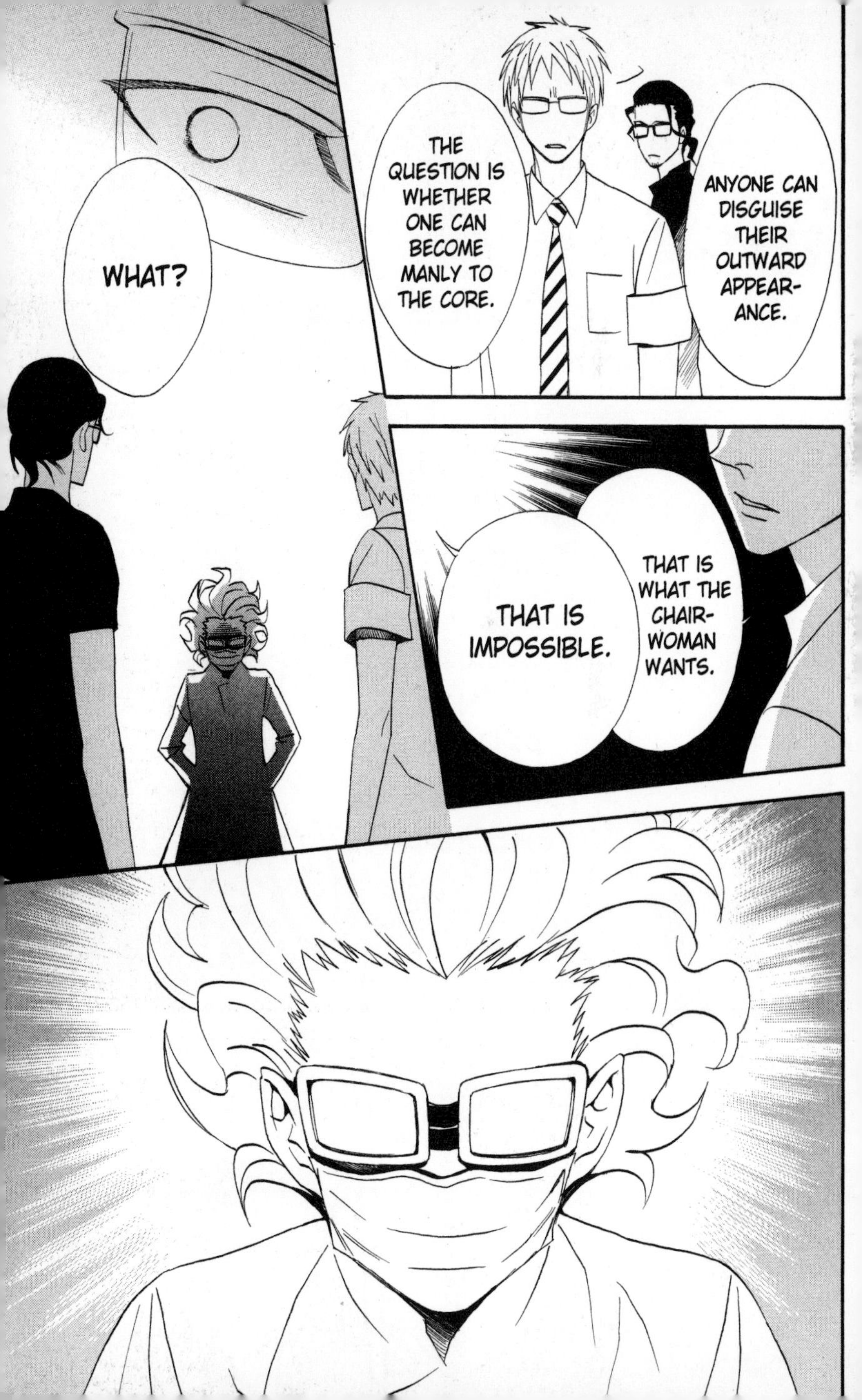

ANYONE CAN DISGUISE THEIR OUTWARD APPEAR-ANCE.
THE QUESTION IS WHETHER ONE CAN BECOME MANLY TO THE CORE.
THAT IS WHAT THE CHAIR-WOMAN WANTS.
THAT IS IMPOSSIBLE.
WHAT?

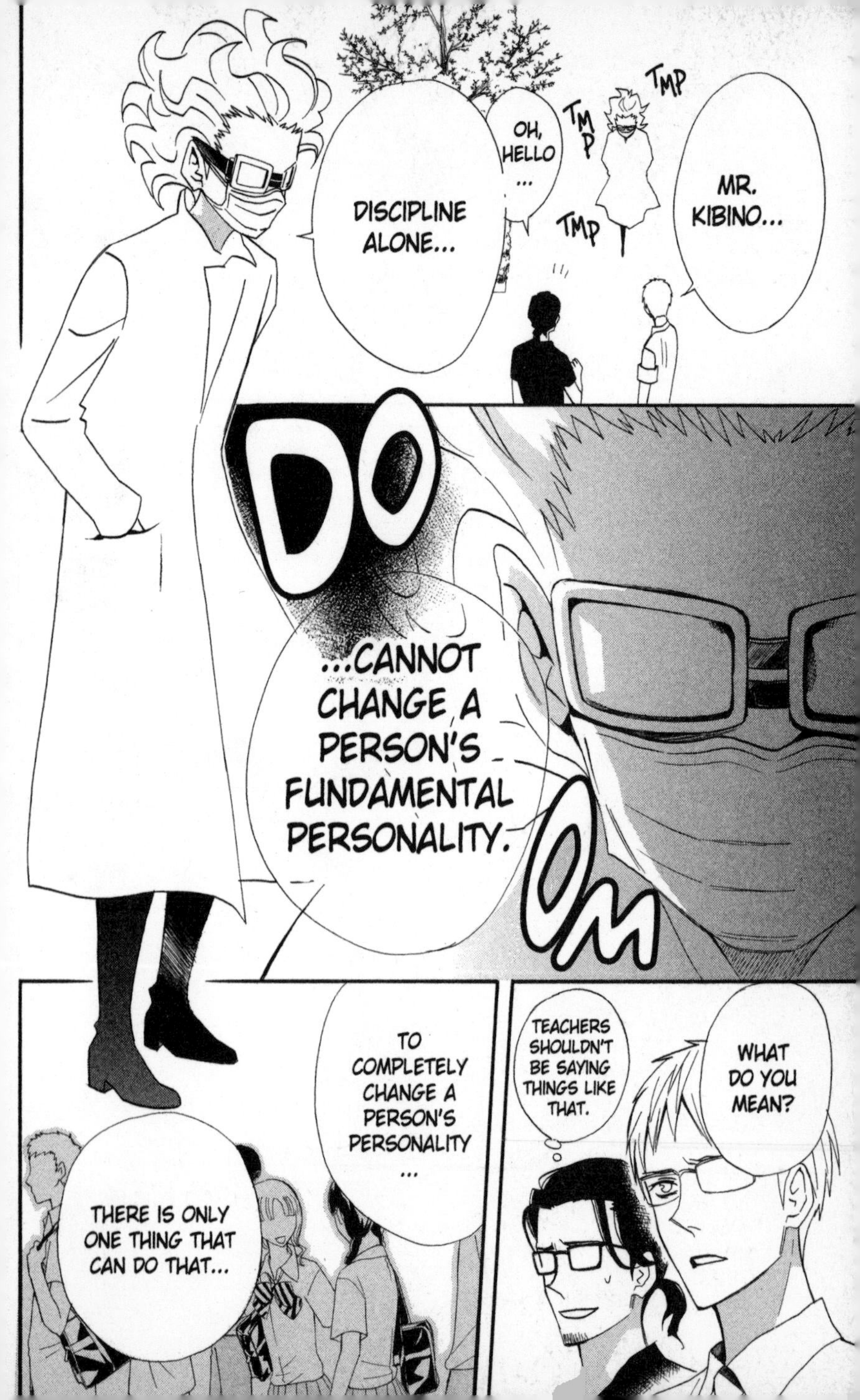
MR. KIBINO...
TMP
TMP
TMP
OH, HELLO ...
DISCIPLINE ALONE...
DOOM
...CANNOT CHANGE A PERSON'S FUNDAMENTAL PERSONALITY.
WHAT DO YOU MEAN?
TEACHERS SHOULDN'T BE SAYING THINGS LIKE THAT.
TO COMPLETELY CHANGE A PERSON'S PERSONALITY ...
THERE IS ONLY ONE THING THAT CAN DO THAT...

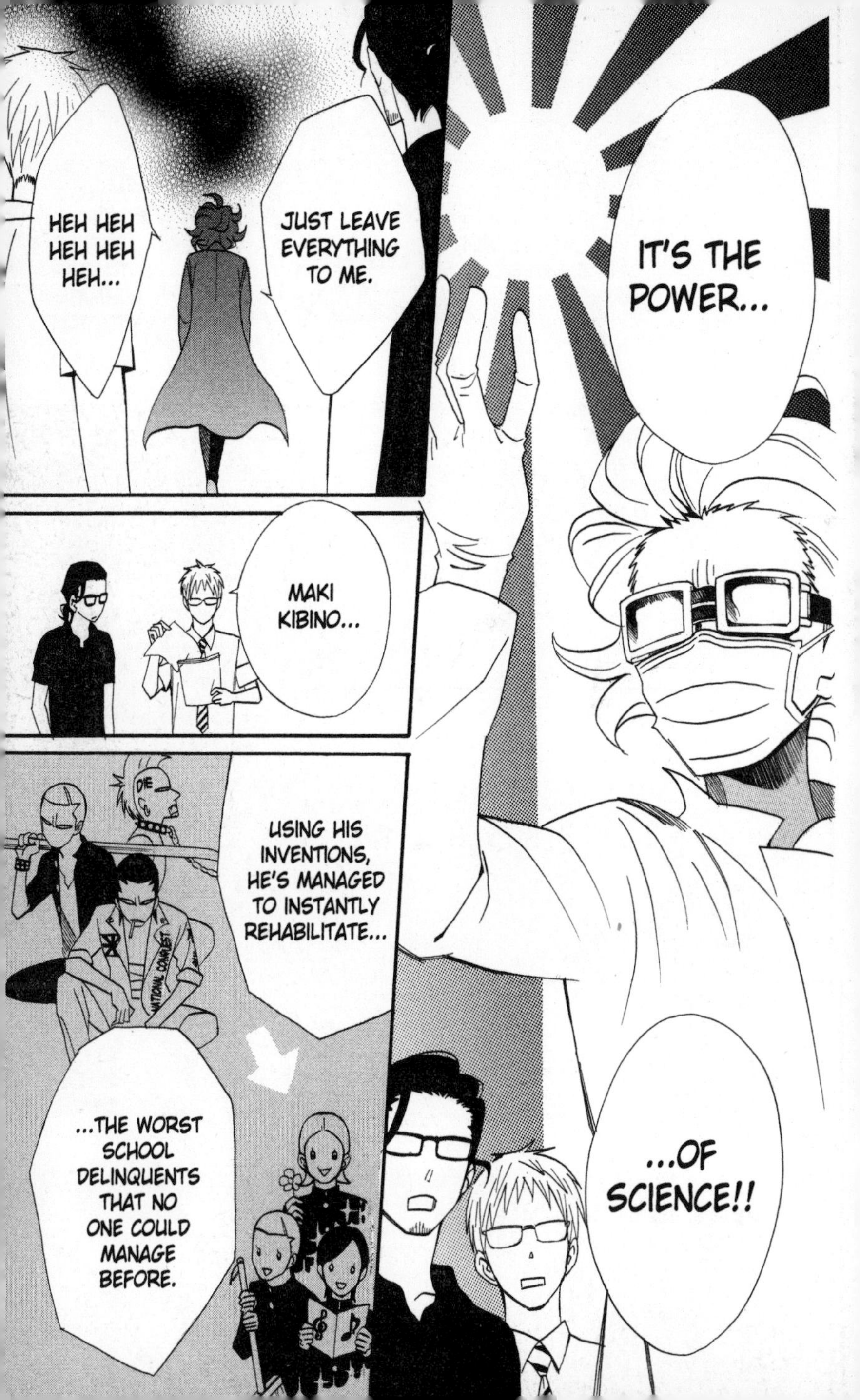
IT'S THE POWER...
...OF SCIENCE!!
JUST LEAVE EVERYTHING TO ME.
HEH HEH HEH HEH HEH...
MAKI KIBINO...
USING HIS INVENTIONS, HE'S MANAGED TO INSTANTLY REHABILITATE...
...THE WORST SCHOOL DELINQUENTS THAT NO ONE COULD MANAGE BEFORE.
DIE
NATIONAL CONQUEST

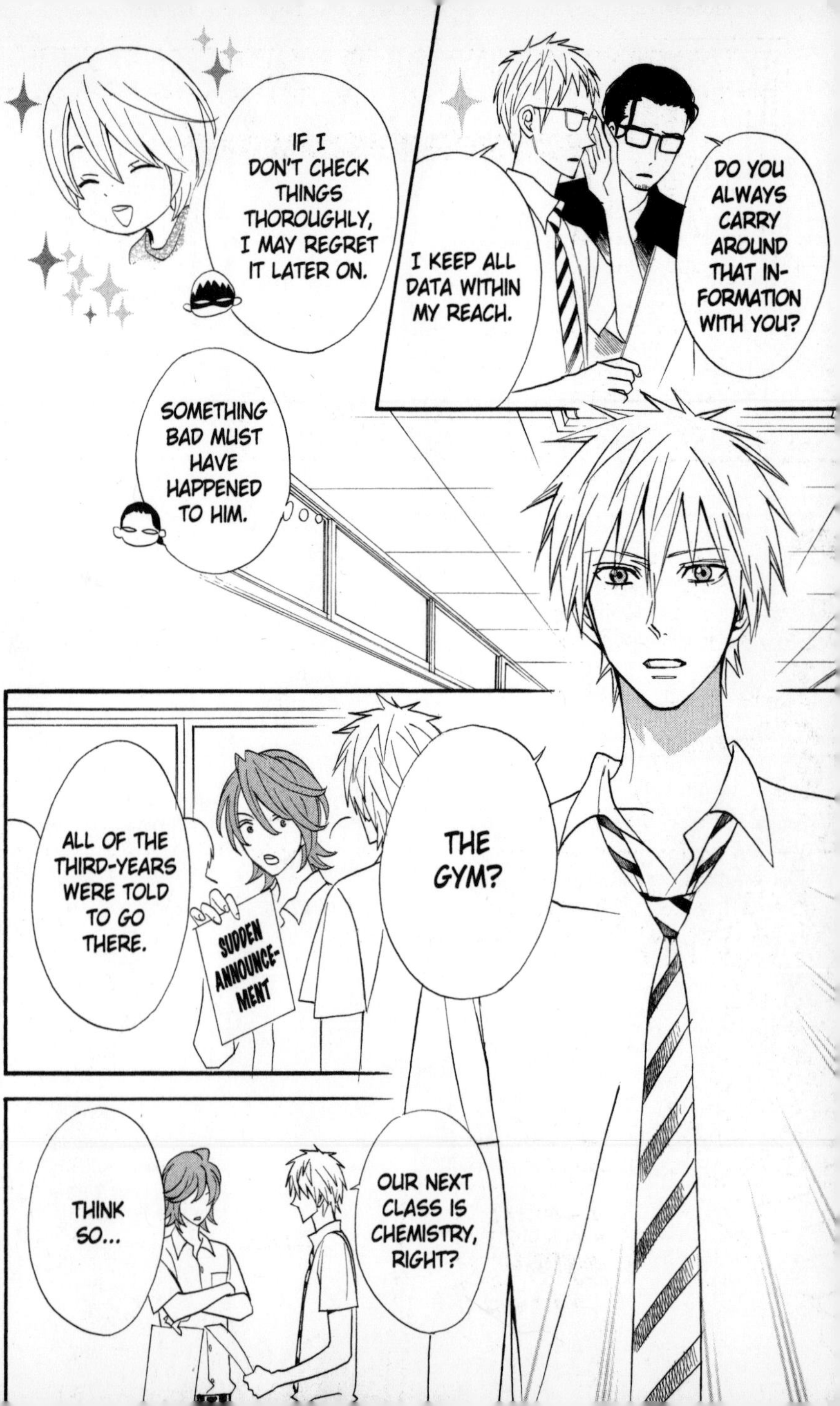
DO YOU ALWAYS CARRY AROUND THAT IN-FORMATION WITH YOU?
I KEEP ALL DATA WITHIN MY REACH.
IF I DON'T CHECK THINGS THOROUGHLY, I MAY REGRET IT LATER ON.
SOMETHING BAD MUST HAVE HAPPENED TO HIM.
THE GYM?
ALL OF THE THIRD-YEARS WERE TOLD TO GO THERE.
SUDDEN ANNOUNCE-MENT
OUR NEXT CLASS IS CHEMISTRY, RIGHT?
THINK SO...

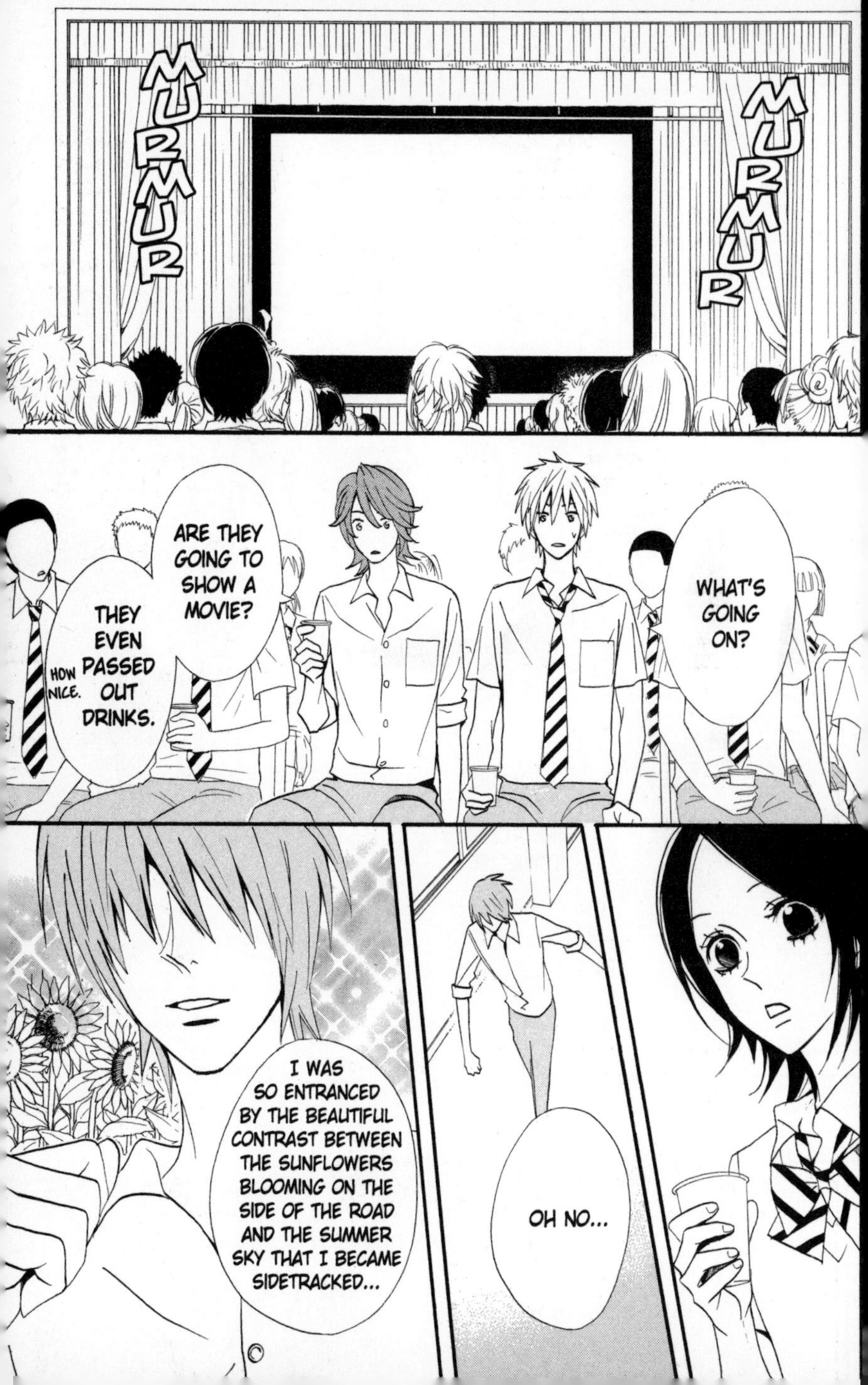
MURMUR
MURMUR
WHAT'S GOING ON?
ARE THEY GOING TO SHOW A MOVIE?
THEY EVEN PASSED OUT DRINKS.
HOW NICE.
OH NO...
I WAS SO ENTRANCED BY THE BEAUTIFUL CONTRAST BETWEEN THE SUNFLOWERS BLOOMING ON THE SIDE OF THE ROAD AND THE SUMMER SKY THAT I BECAME SIDETRACKED...

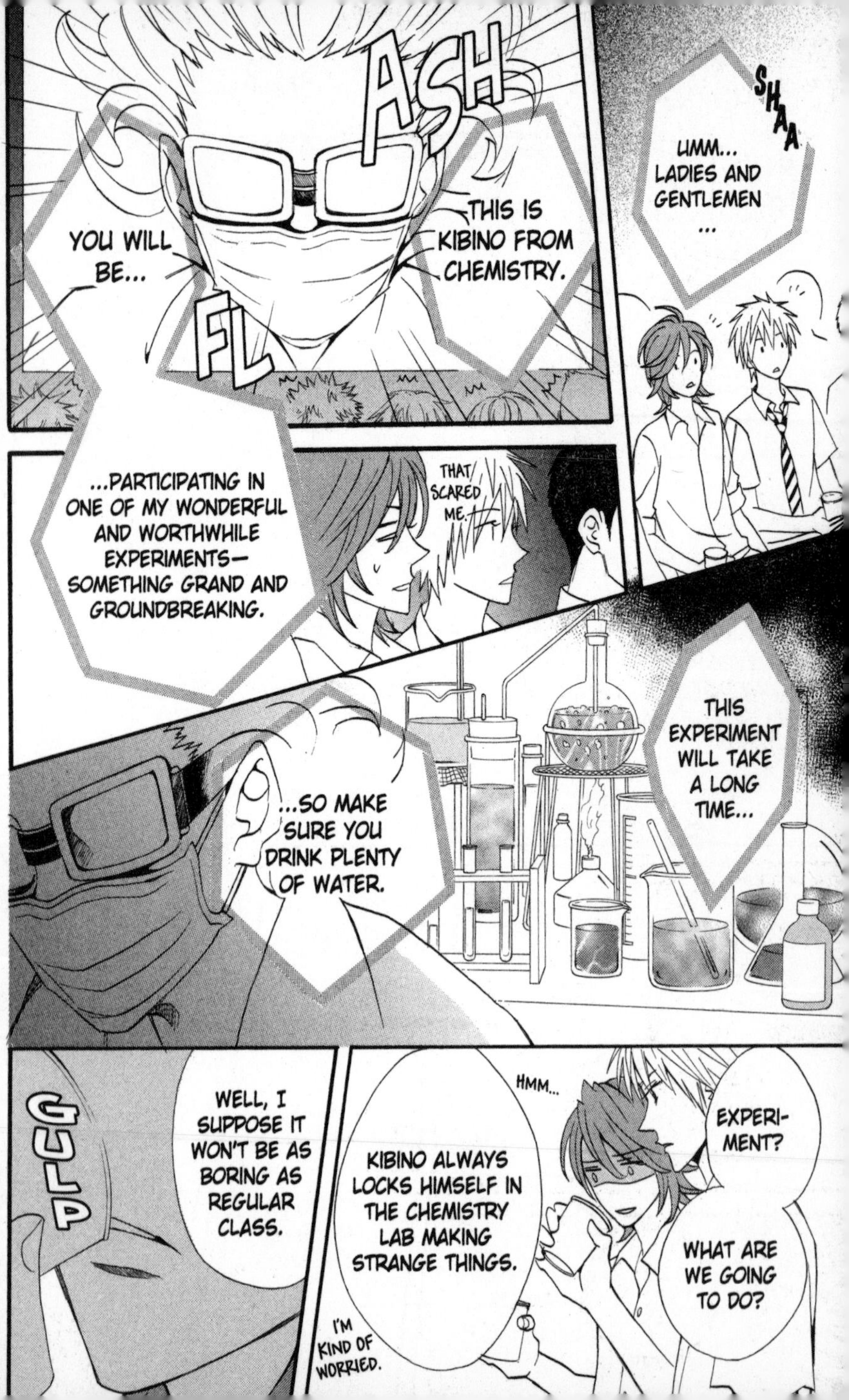
SHAAA
UMM... LADIES AND GENTLEMEN ...
ASH
THIS IS KIBINO FROM CHEMISTRY.
YOU WILL BE...
FL
...PARTICIPATING IN ONE OF MY WONDERFUL AND WORTHWHILE EXPERIMENTS—SOMETHING GRAND AND GROUNDBREAKING.
THAT SCARED ME.
THIS EXPERIMENT WILL TAKE A LONG TIME...
...SO MAKE SURE YOU DRINK PLENTY OF WATER.
EXPERI-MENT?
WHAT ARE WE GOING TO DO?
HMM...
KIBINO ALWAYS LOCKS HIMSELF IN THE CHEMISTRY LAB MAKING STRANGE THINGS.
I'M KIND OF WORRIED.
GULP
WELL, I SUPPOSE IT WON'T BE AS BORING AS REGULAR CLASS.

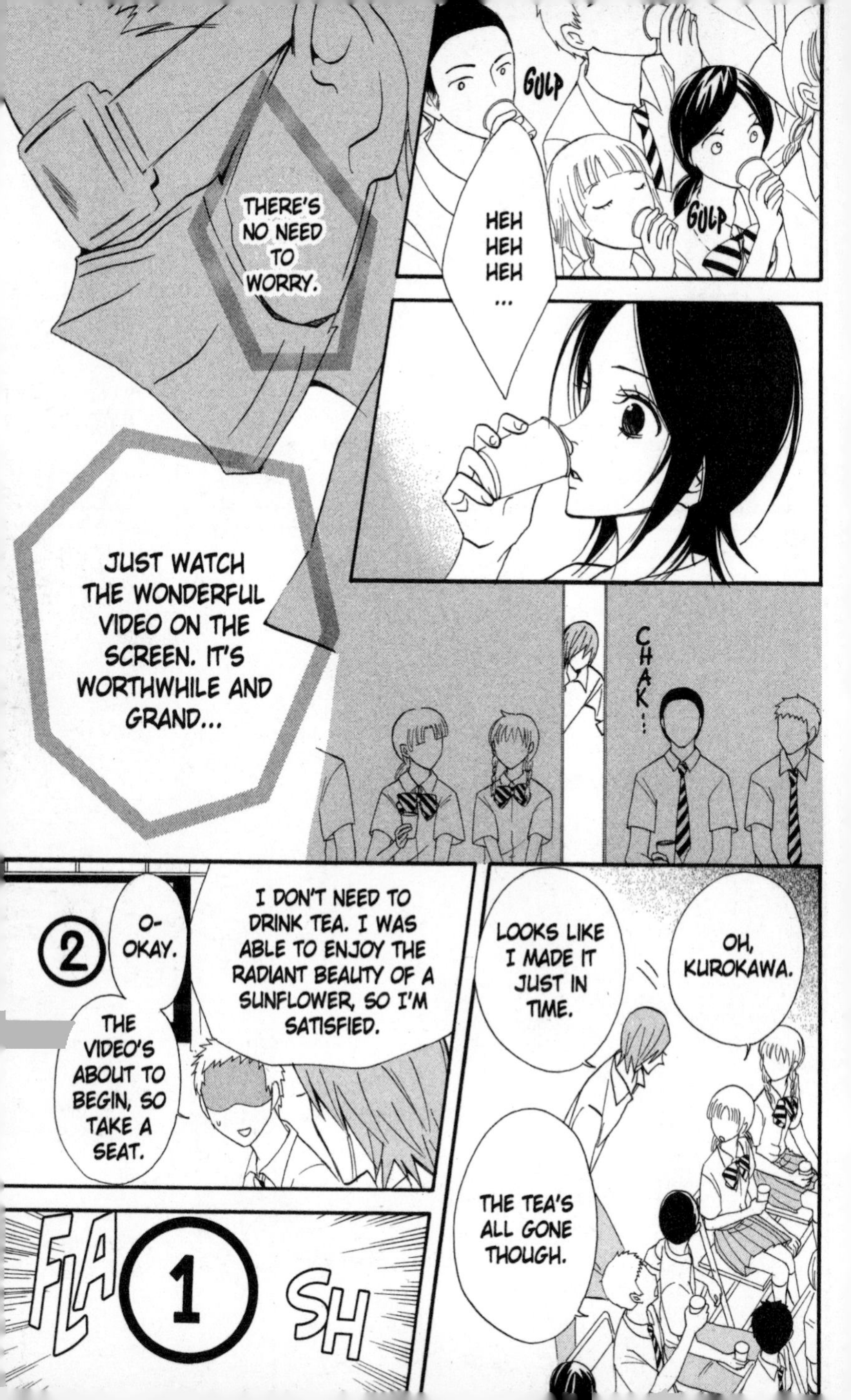
GULP
GULP
HEH HEH HEH ...
THERE'S NO NEED TO WORRY.
JUST WATCH THE WONDERFUL VIDEO ON THE SCREEN. IT'S WORTHWHILE AND GRAND...
CHAK!!
OH, KUROKAWA.
LOOKS LIKE I MADE IT JUST IN TIME.
THE TEA'S ALL GONE THOUGH.
I DON'T NEED TO DRINK TEA. I WAS ABLE TO ENJOY THE RADIANT BEAUTY OF A SUNFLOWER, SO I'M SATISFIED.
O-OKAY.
THE VIDEO'S ABOUT TO BEGIN, SO TAKE A SEAT.
2
FLASH
1

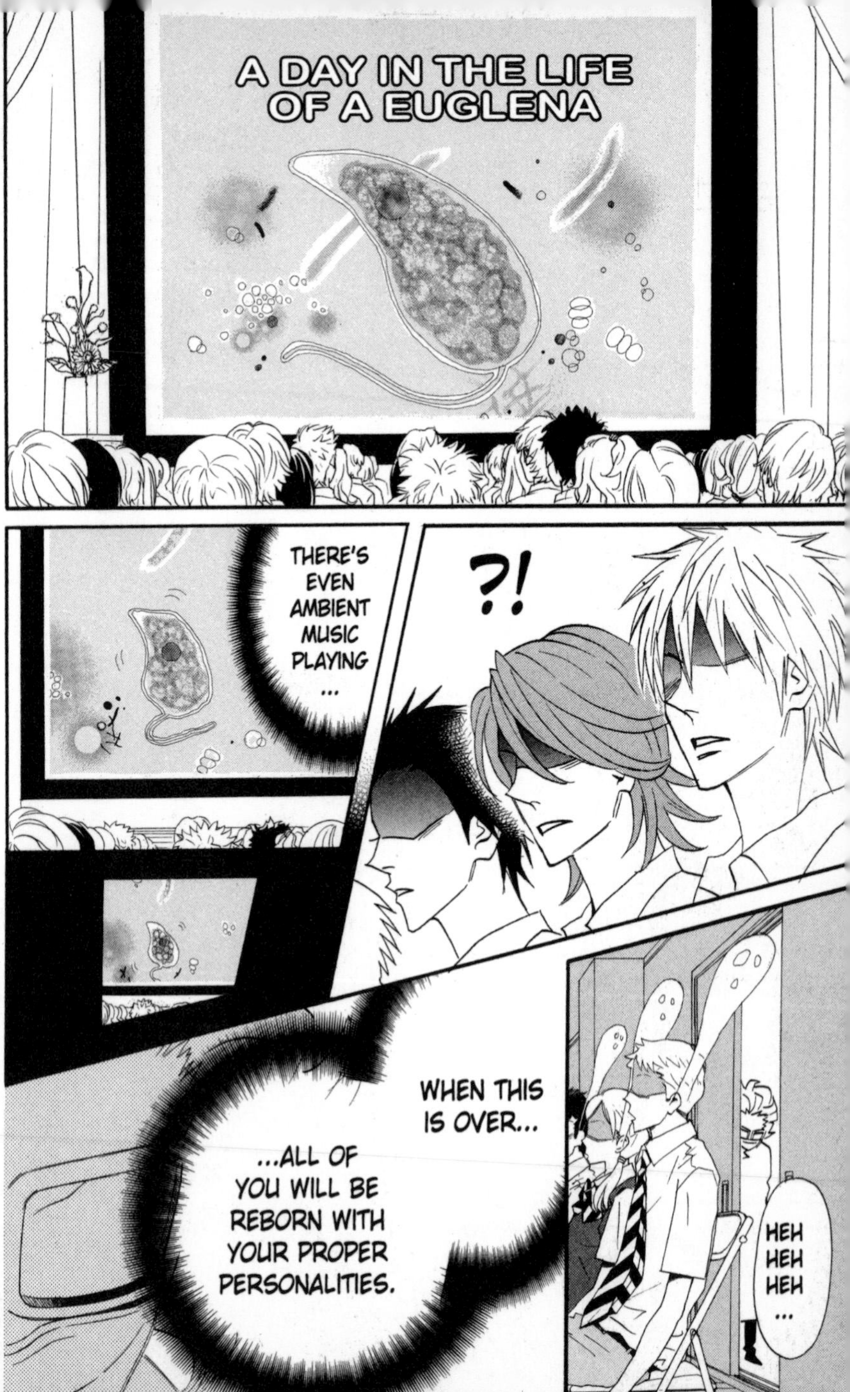
A DAY IN THE LIFE OF A EUGLENA
?!
THERE'S EVEN AMBIENT MUSIC PLAYING ...
HEH HEH HEH ...
WHEN THIS IS OVER...
...ALL OF YOU WILL BE REBORN WITH YOUR PROPER PERSONALITIES.

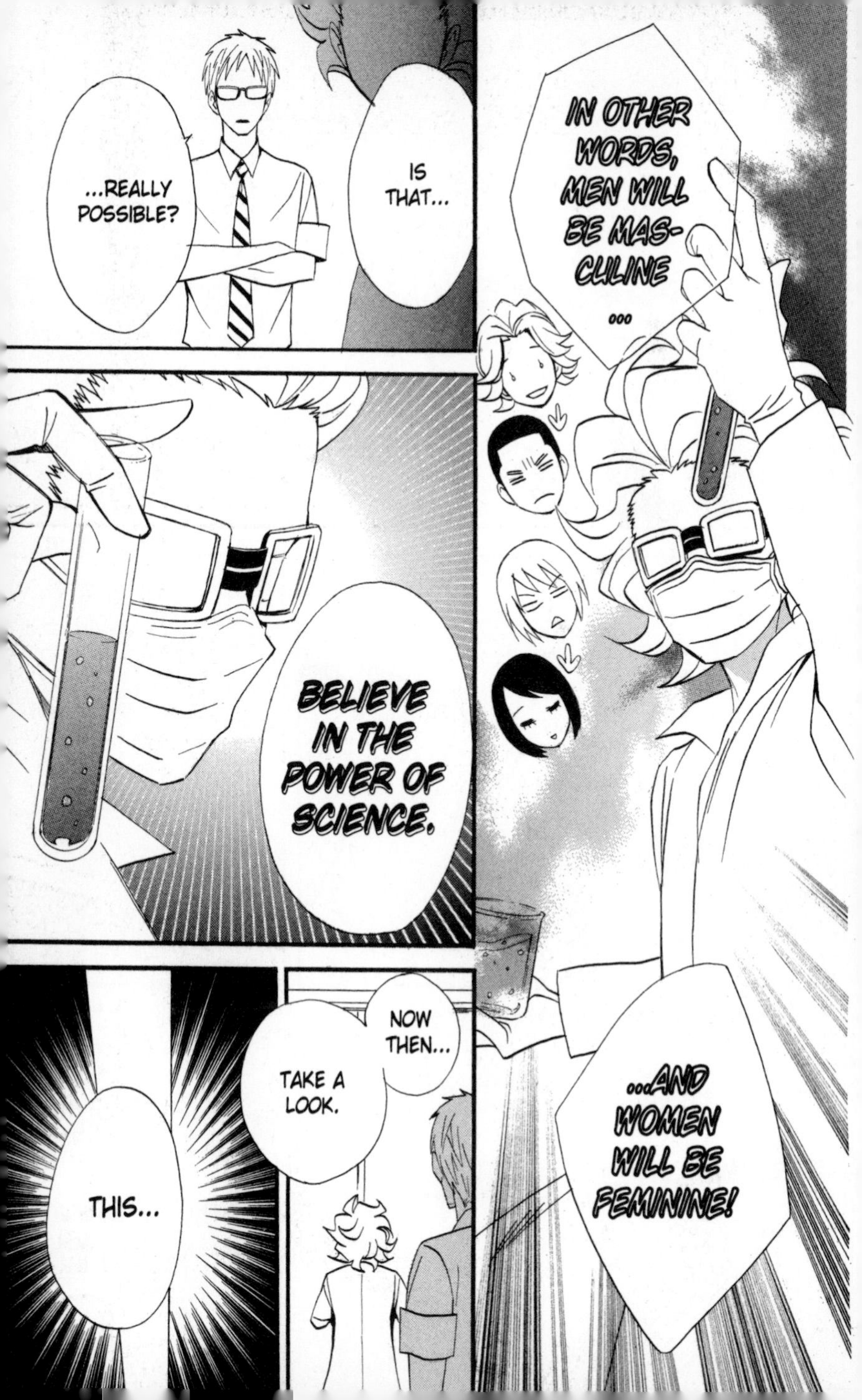
IN OTHER WORDS, MEN WILL BE MAS-CULINE ...
...AND WOMEN WILL BE FEMININE!
IS THAT...
...REALLY POSSIBLE?
BELIEVE IN THE POWER OF SCIENCE.
NOW THEN...
TAKE A LOOK.
THIS...

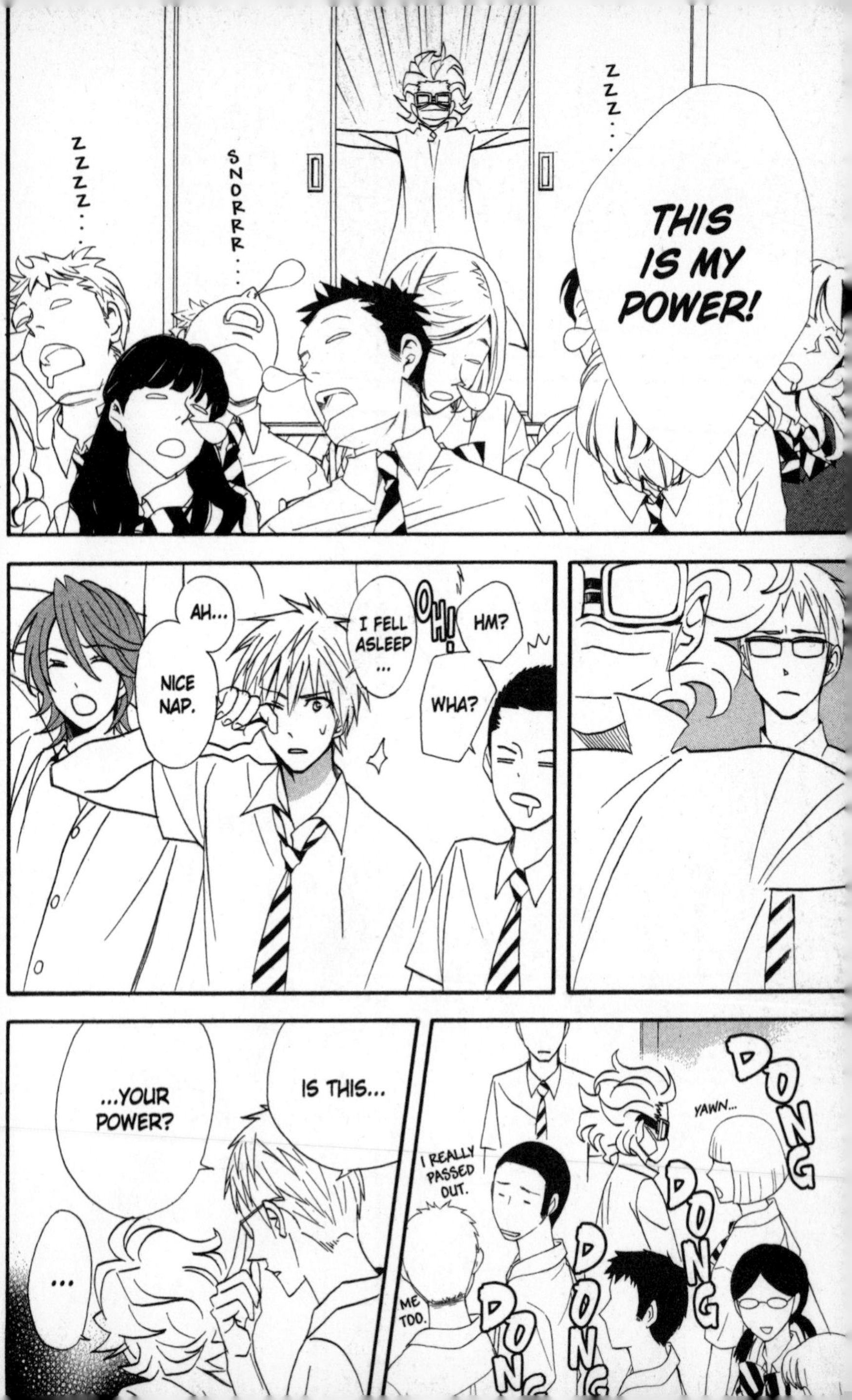
ZZZ...
THIS IS MY POWER!
SNORRR...
ZZZZ...
HM?
WHA?
OH!
I FELL ASLEEP...
AH...
NICE NAP.
DONG
DONG
YAWN...
DONG
DONG
I REALLY PASSED OUT.
ME TOO.
IS THIS...
...YOUR POWER?
...

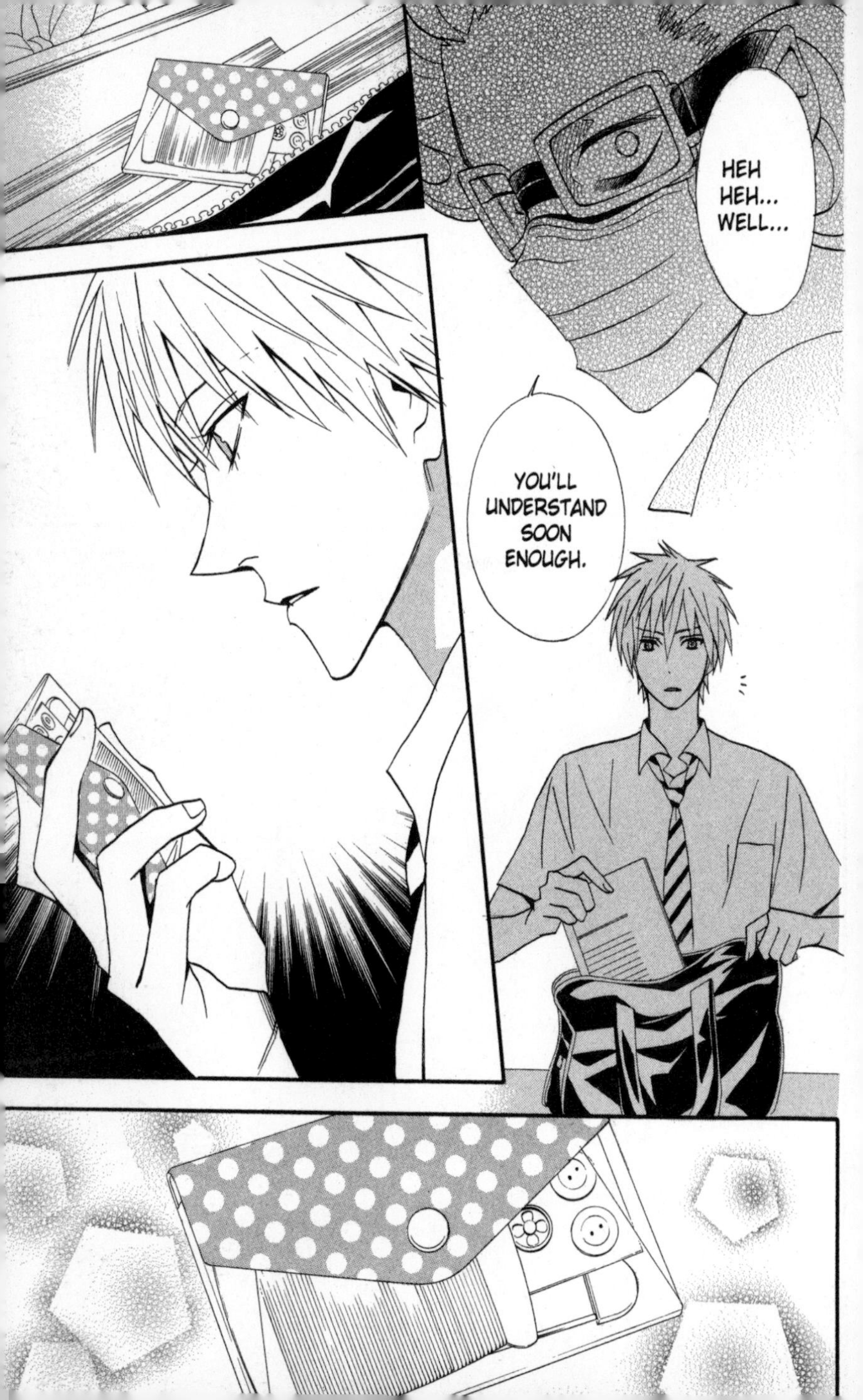
HEH HEH... WELL...
YOU'LL UNDERSTAND SOON ENOUGH.

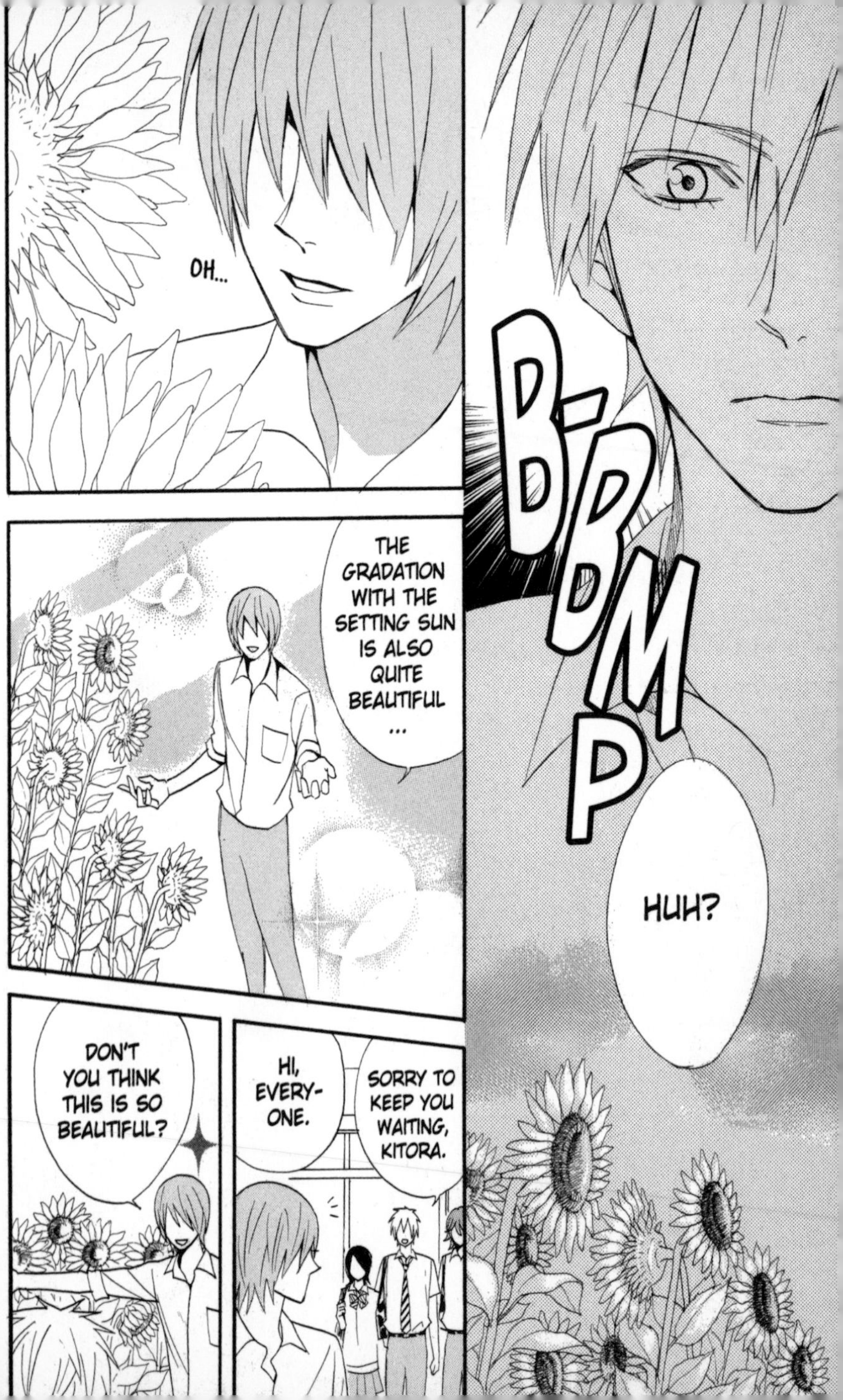
B-BDMP
HUH?
OH...
THE GRADATION WITH THE SETTING SUN IS ALSO QUITE BEAUTIFUL ...
SORRY TO KEEP YOU WAITING, KITORA.
HI, EVERY-ONE.
DON'T YOU THINK THIS IS SO BEAUTIFUL?

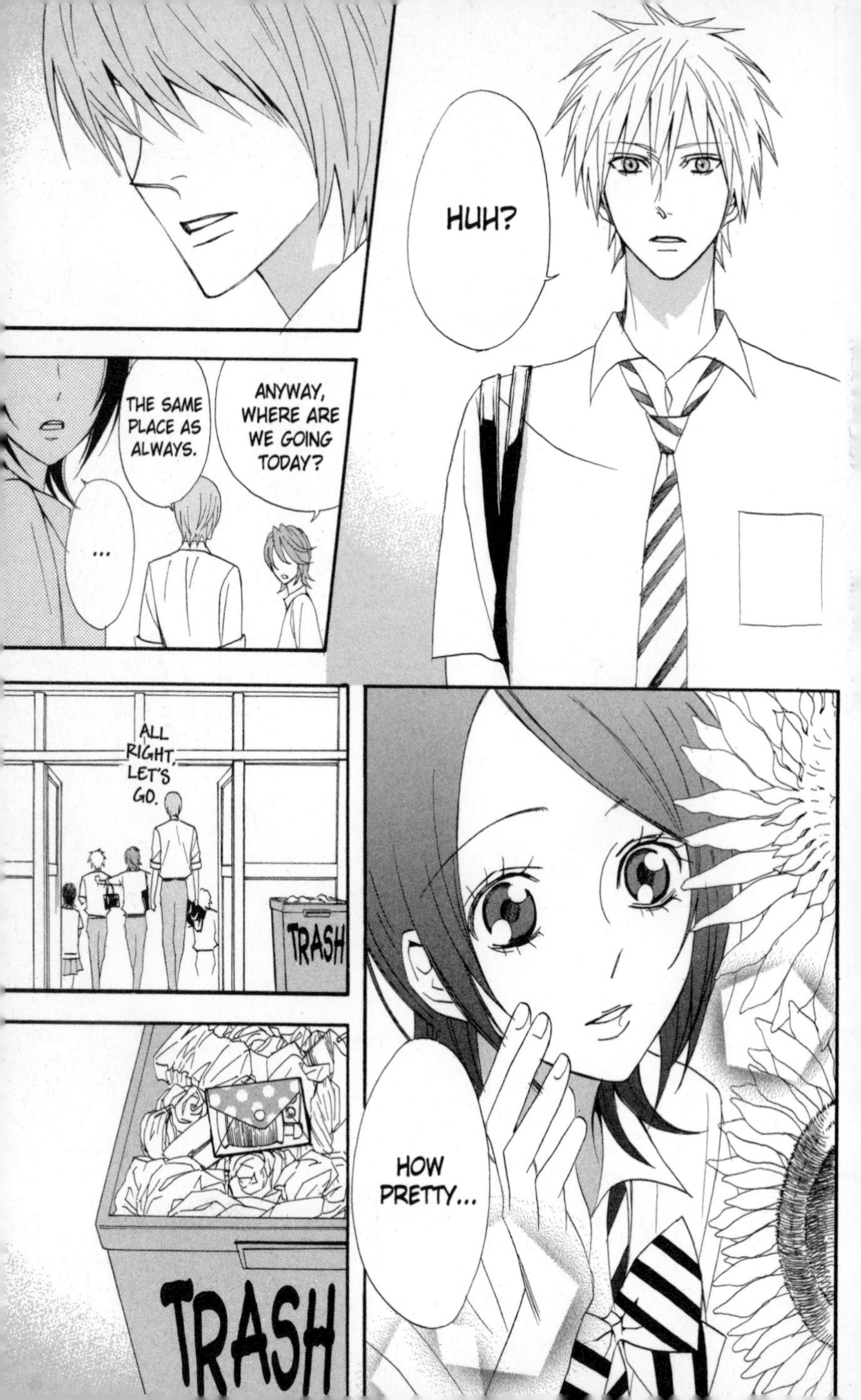
HUH?
ANYWAY, WHERE ARE WE GOING TODAY?
THE SAME PLACE AS ALWAYS.
...
HOW PRETTY...
ALL RIGHT, LET'S GO.
TRASH
TRASH

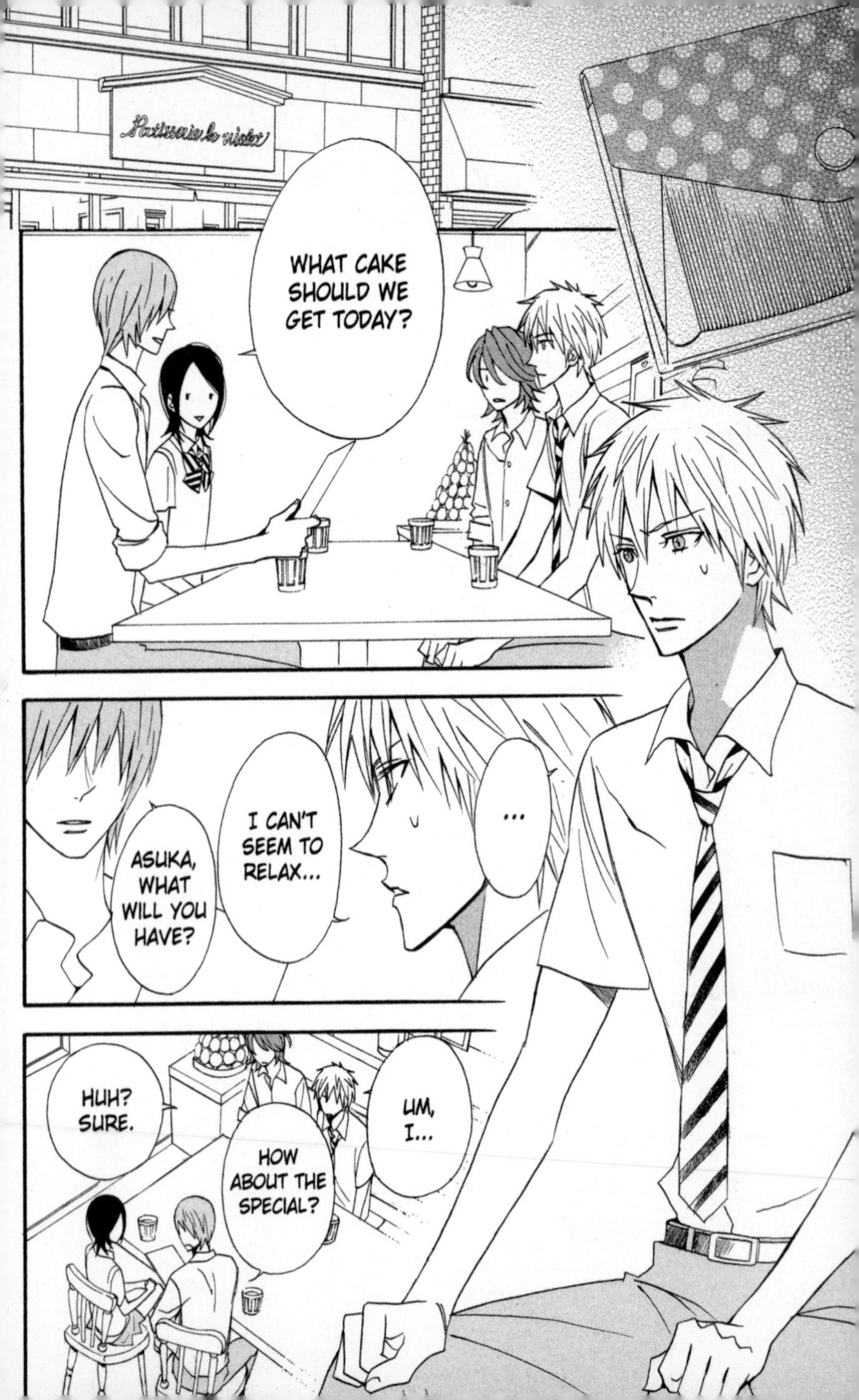
WHAT CAKE SHOULD WE GET TODAY?
...
I CAN'T SEEM TO RELAX...
ASUKA, WHAT WILL YOU HAVE?
UM, I...
HOW ABOUT THE SPECIAL?
HUH? SURE.

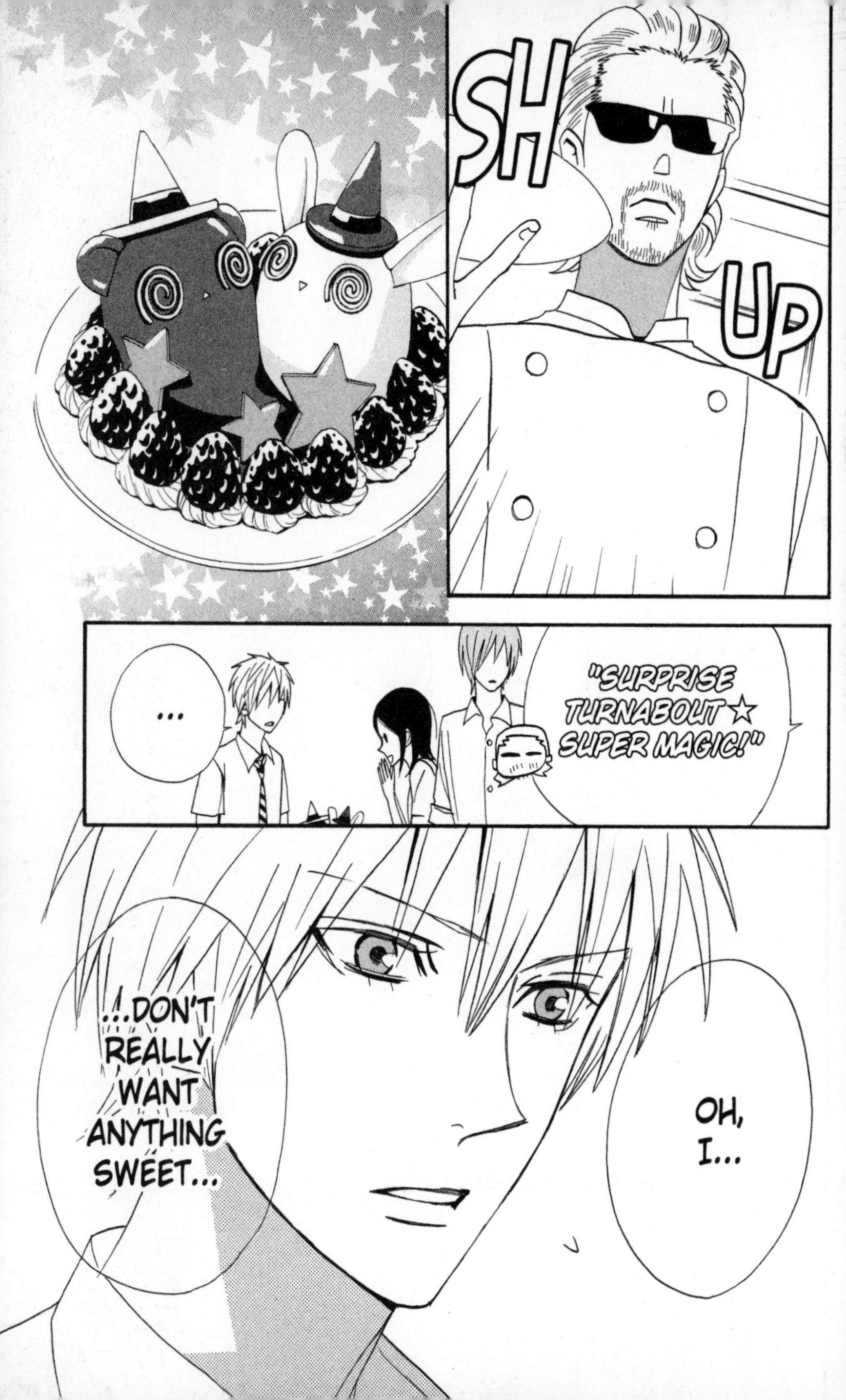
SH
UP
"SURPRISE TURNABOUT☆ SUPER MAGIC!"
...
OH, I...
...DON'T REALLY WANT ANYTHING SWEET...

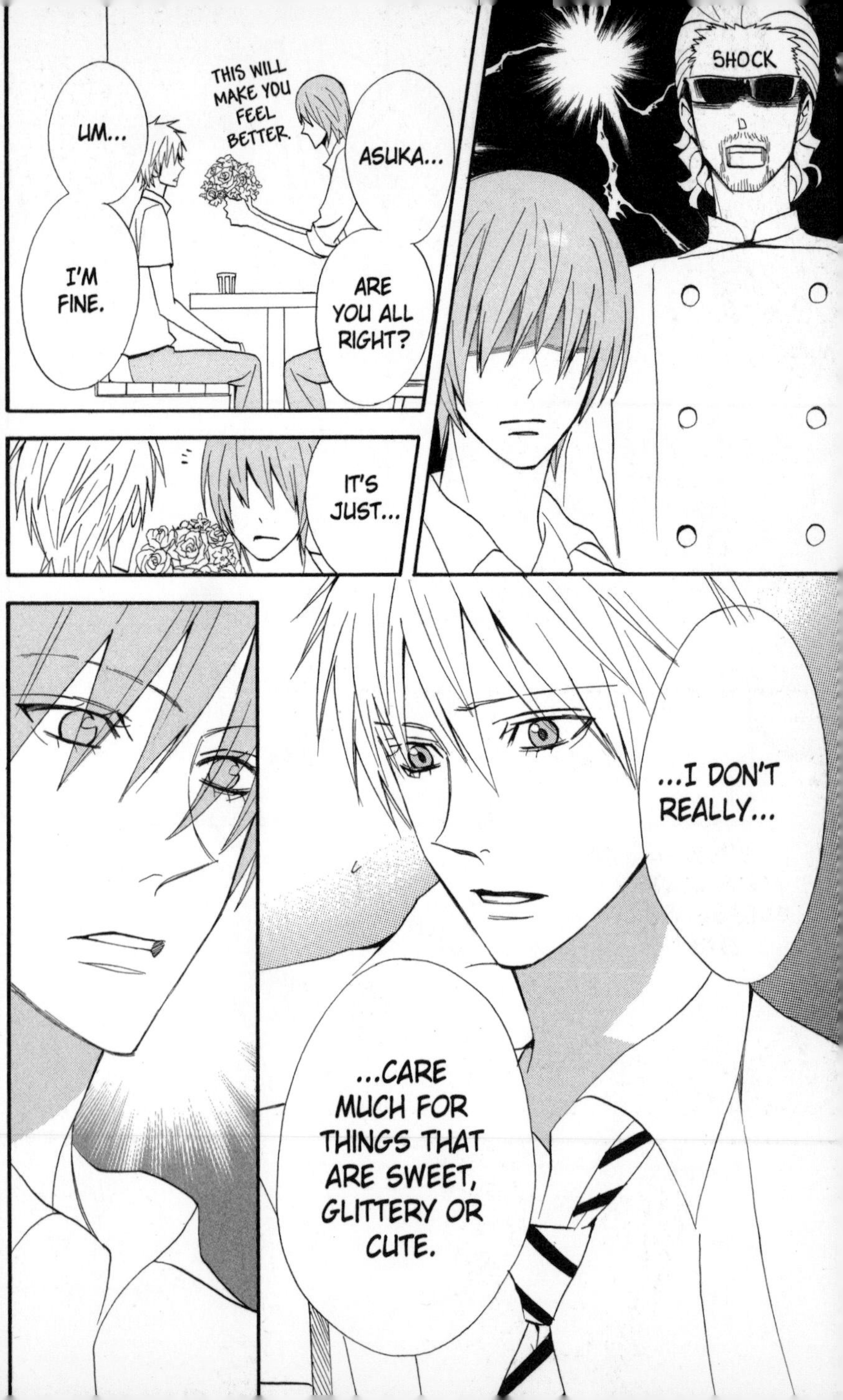
SHOCK
ASUKA...
ARE YOU ALL RIGHT?
THIS WILL MAKE YOU FEEL BETTER.
UM...
I'M FINE.
IT'S JUST...
...I DON'T REALLY...
...CARE MUCH FOR THINGS THAT ARE SWEET, GLITTERY OR CUTE.

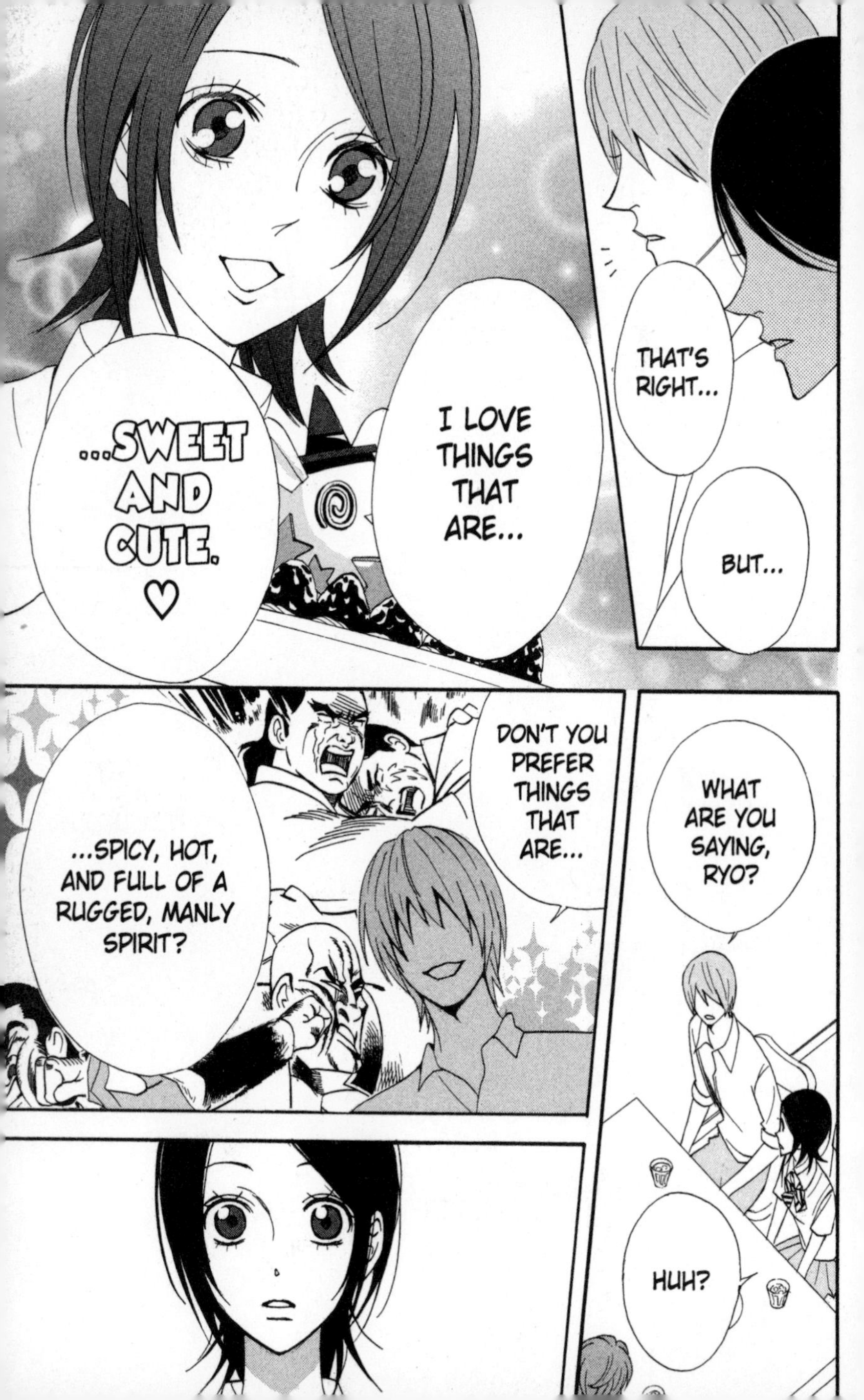
THAT'S RIGHT...
BUT...
I LOVE THINGS THAT ARE...
...SWEET AND CUTE. ♥
WHAT ARE YOU SAYING, RYO?
HUH?
DON'T YOU PREFER THINGS THAT ARE...
...SPICY, HOT, AND FULL OF A RUGGED, MANLY SPIRIT?

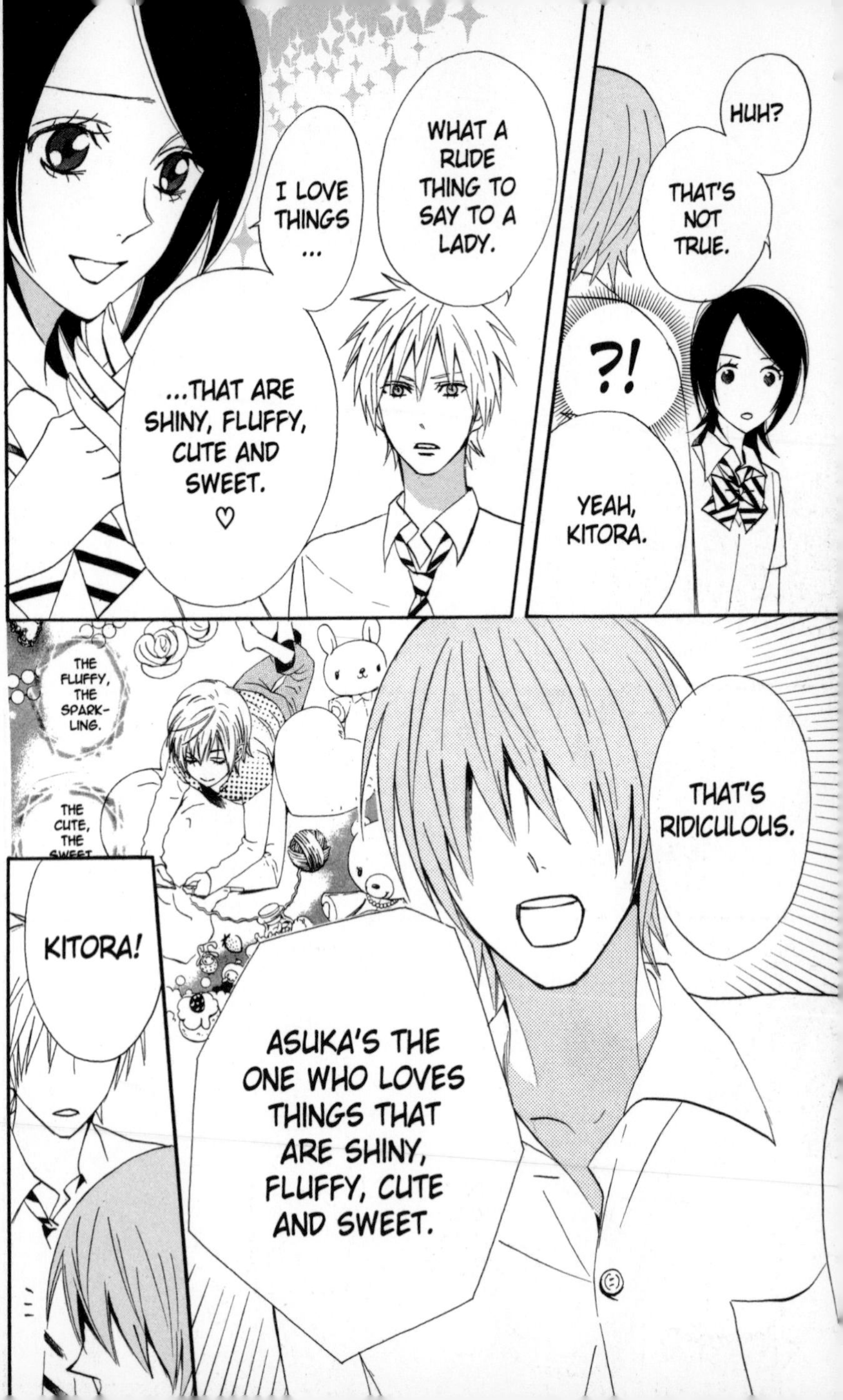
HUH?
THAT'S NOT TRUE.
?!
YEAH, KITORA.
WHAT A RUDE THING TO SAY TO A LADY.
I LOVE THINGS ...
...THAT ARE SHINY, FLUFFY, CUTE AND SWEET. ♡
THAT'S RIDICULOUS.
ASUKA'S THE ONE WHO LOVES THINGS THAT ARE SHINY, FLUFFY, CUTE AND SWEET.
THE FLUFFY, THE SPARK-LING.
THE CUTE, THE
KITORA!

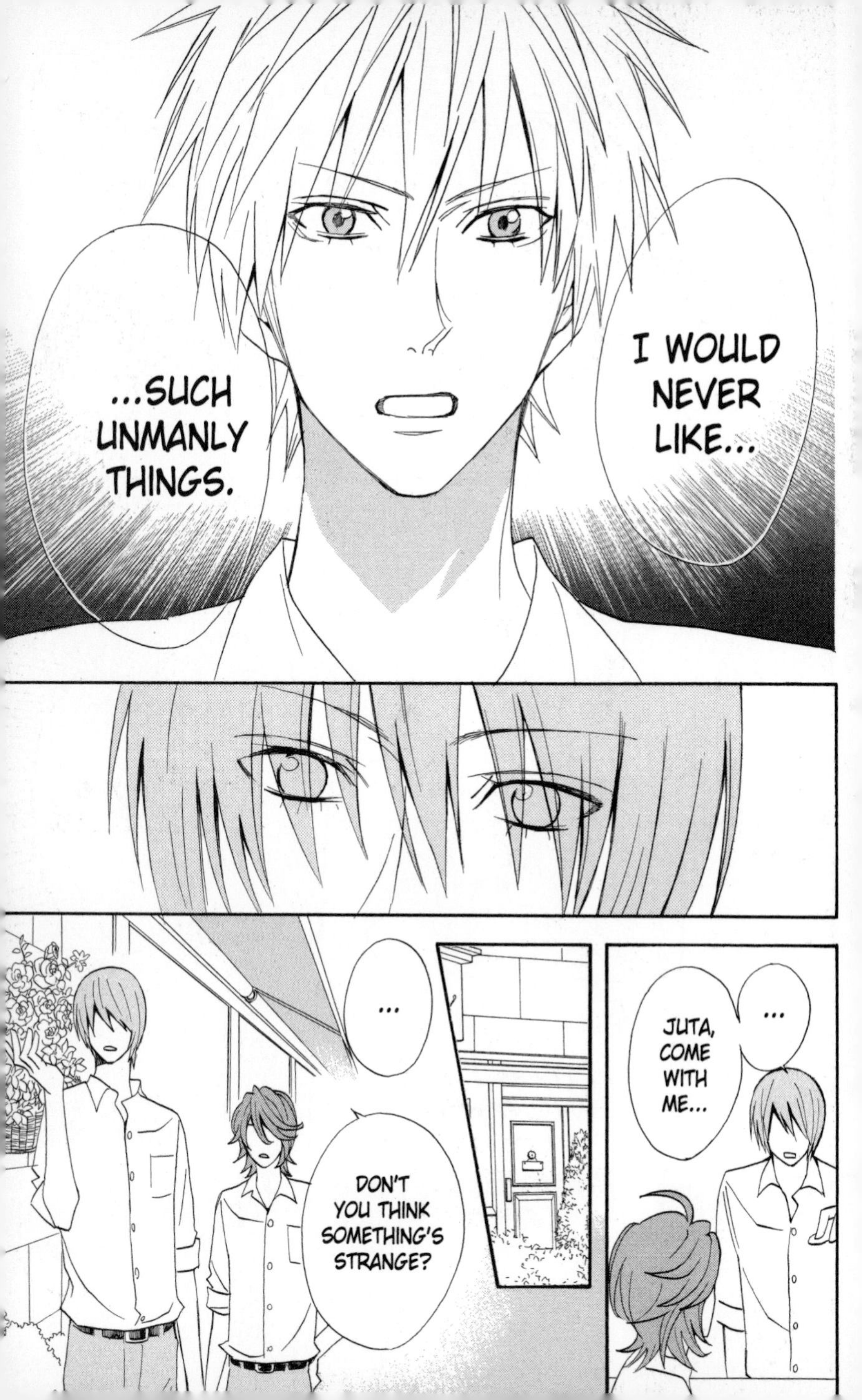
I WOULD NEVER LIKE...
...SUCH UNMANLY THINGS.
...
JUTA, COME WITH ME...
...
DON'T YOU THINK SOMETHING'S STRANGE?

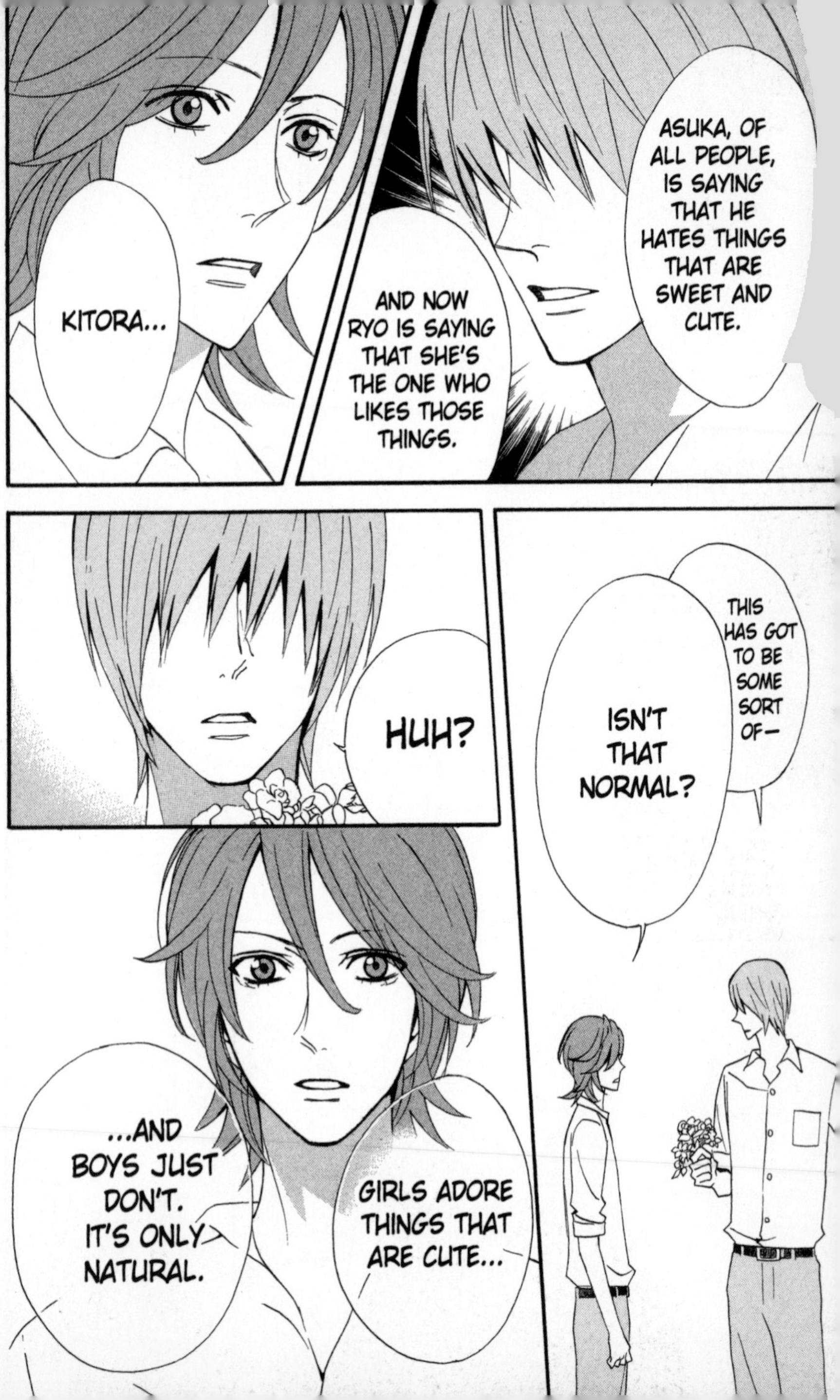
ASUKA, OF ALL PEOPLE, IS SAYING THAT HE HATES THINGS THAT ARE SWEET AND CUTE.
AND NOW RYO IS SAYING THAT SHE'S THE ONE WHO LIKES THOSE THINGS.
KITORA...
THIS HAS GOT TO BE SOME SORT OF—
ISN'T THAT NORMAL?
HUH?
GIRLS ADORE THINGS THAT ARE CUTE...
...AND BOYS JUST DON'T. IT'S ONLY NATURAL.

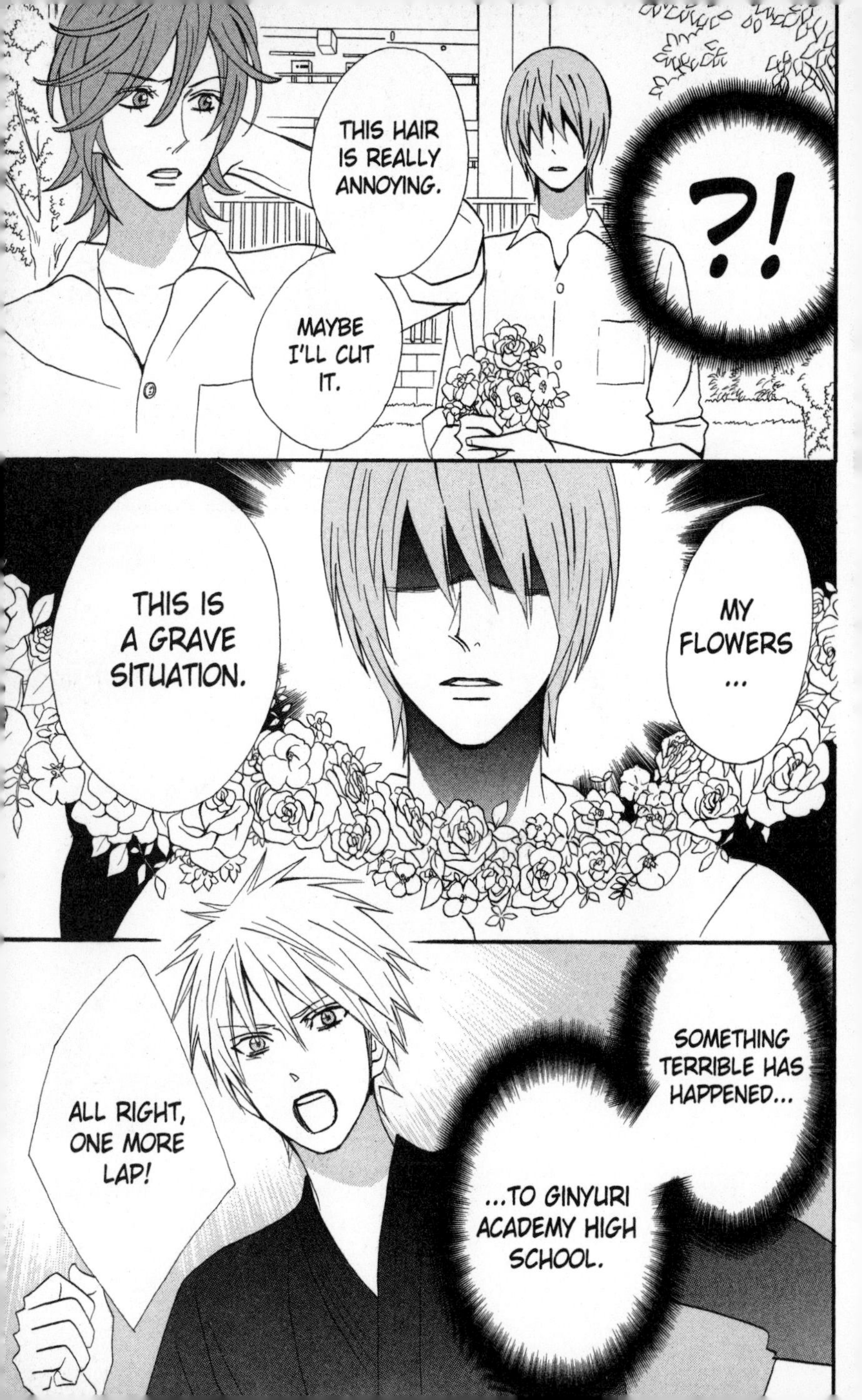
?!
THIS HAIR IS REALLY ANNOYING.
MAYBE I'LL CUT IT.
MY FLOWERS ...
THIS IS A GRAVE SITUATION.
SOMETHING TERRIBLE HAS HAPPENED...
ALL RIGHT, ONE MORE LAP!
...TO GINYURI ACADEMY HIGH SCHOOL.

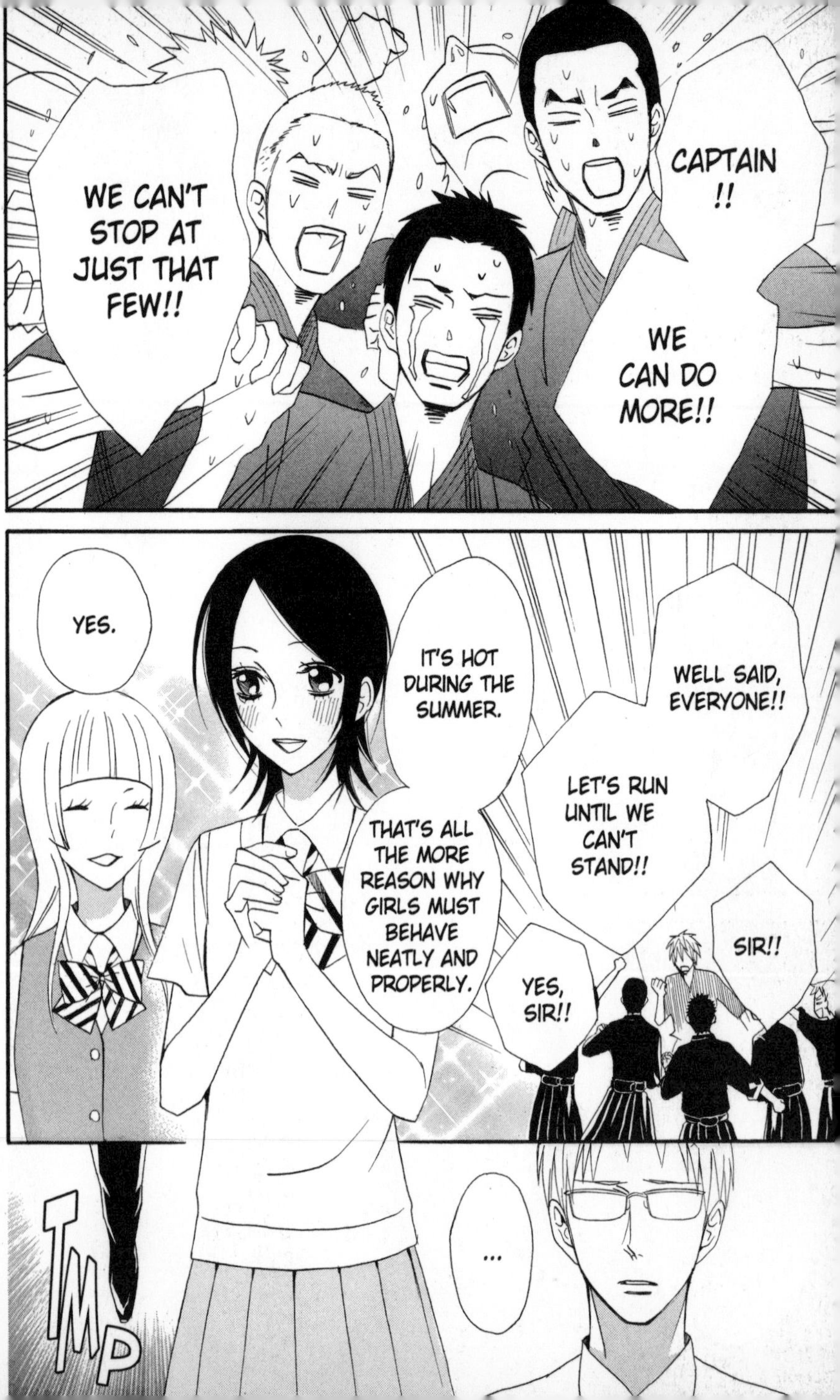
CAPTAIN!!
WE CAN DO MORE!!
WE CAN'T STOP AT JUST THAT FEW!!
WELL SAID, EVERYONE!!
LET'S RUN UNTIL WE CAN'T STAND!!
SIR!!
YES, SIR!!
IT'S HOT DURING THE SUMMER.
THAT'S ALL THE MORE REASON WHY GIRLS MUST BEHAVE NEATLY AND PROPERLY.
YES.
...
TMP

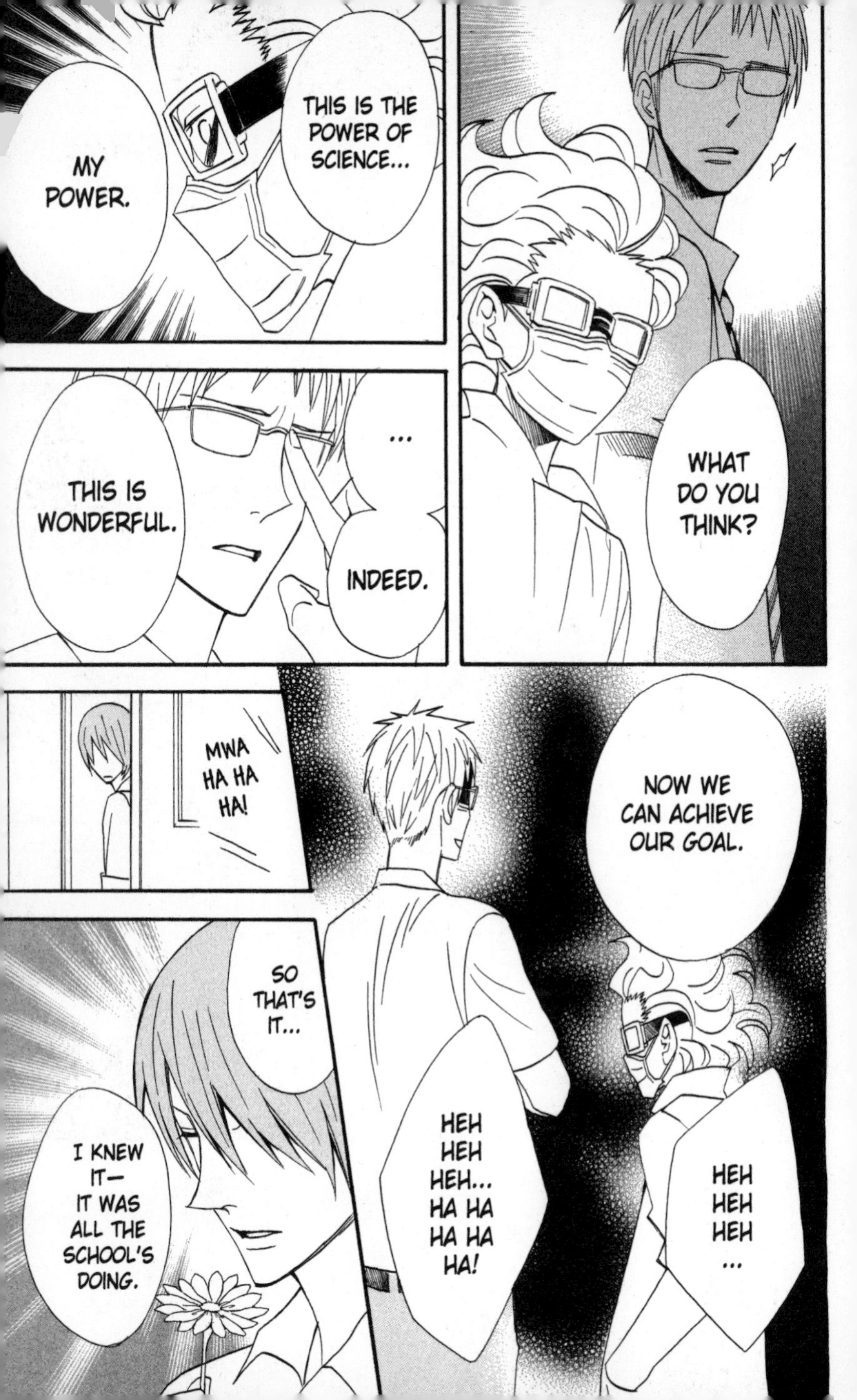
WHAT DO YOU THINK?
THIS IS THE POWER OF SCIENCE...
MY POWER.
...
INDEED.
THIS IS WONDERFUL.
NOW WE CAN ACHIEVE OUR GOAL.
HEH HEH HEH...
HEH HEH HEH... HA HA HA HA HA!
MWA HA HA HA!
SO THAT'S IT...
I KNEW IT— IT WAS ALL THE SCHOOL'S DOING.

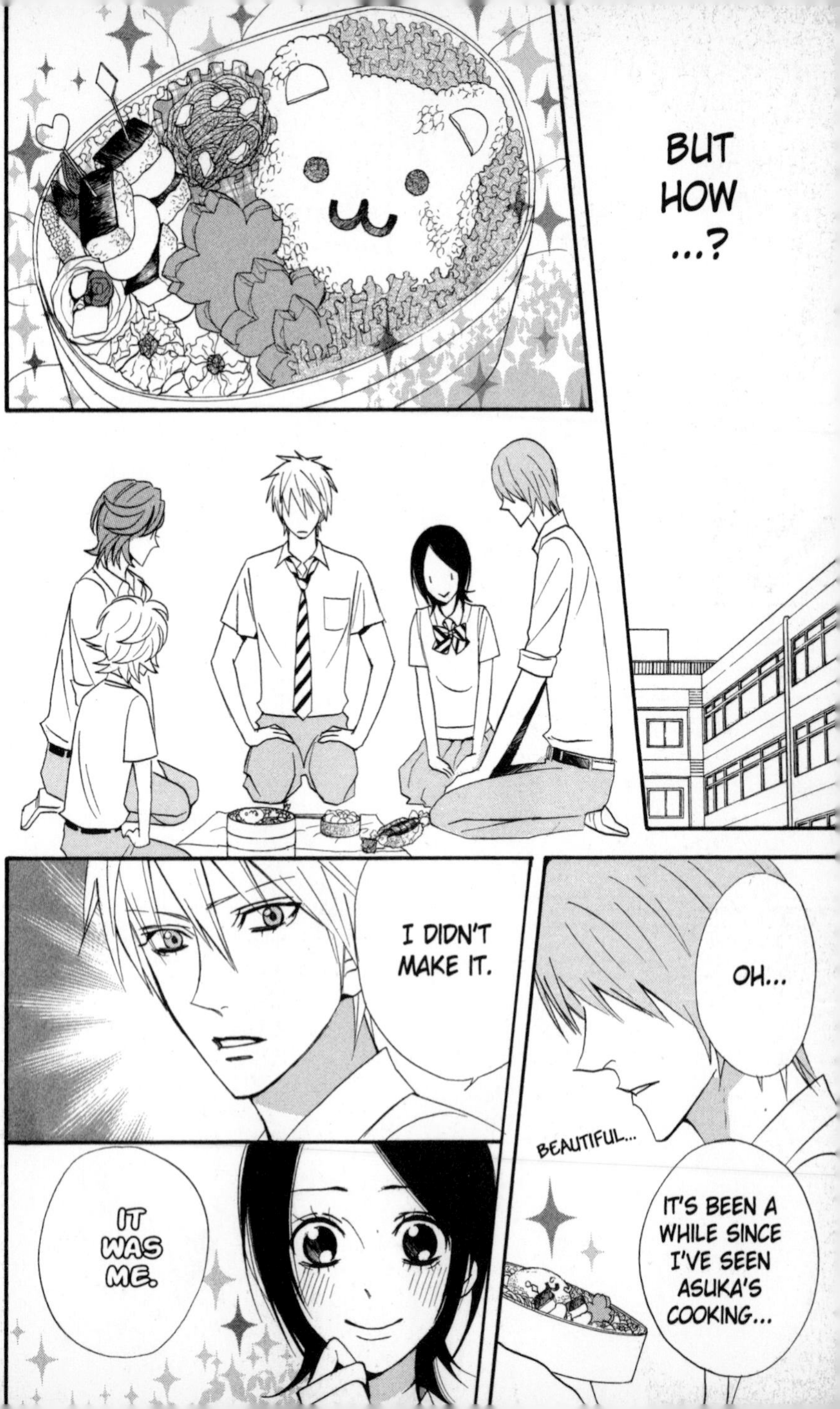
BUT HOW ...?
OH...
BEAUTIFUL...
IT'S BEEN A WHILE SINCE I'VE SEEN ASUKA'S COOKING...
I DIDN'T MAKE IT.
IT WAS ME.

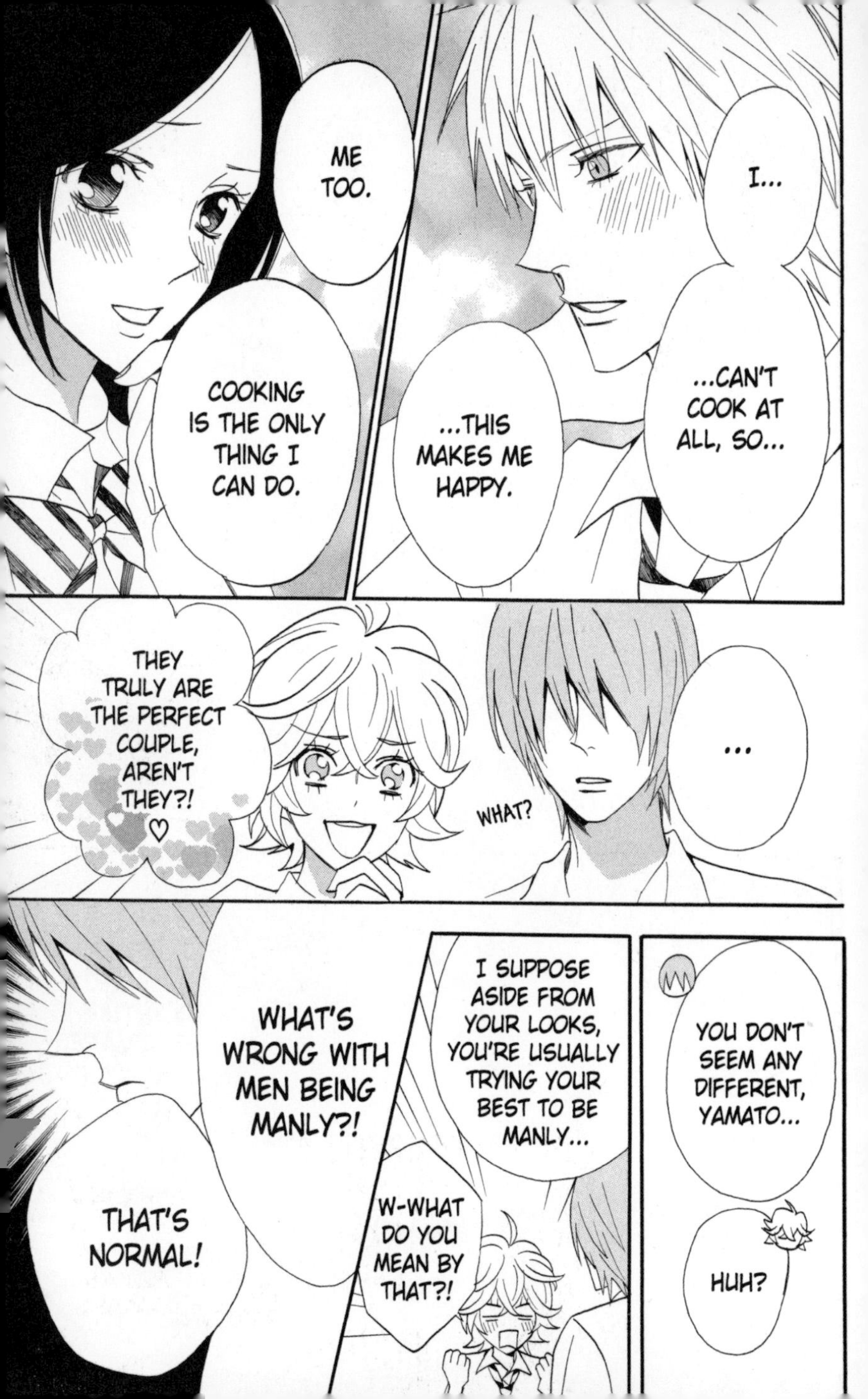
I...
...CAN'T COOK AT ALL, SO...
...THIS MAKES ME HAPPY.
ME TOO.
COOKING IS THE ONLY THING I CAN DO.
...
WHAT?
THEY TRULY ARE THE PERFECT COUPLE, AREN'T THEY?! ♡
YOU DON'T SEEM ANY DIFFERENT, YAMATO...
HUH?
I SUPPOSE ASIDE FROM YOUR LOOKS, YOU'RE USUALLY TRYING YOUR BEST TO BE MANLY...
W-WHAT DO YOU MEAN BY THAT?!
WHAT'S WRONG WITH MEN BEING MANLY?!
THAT'S NORMAL!

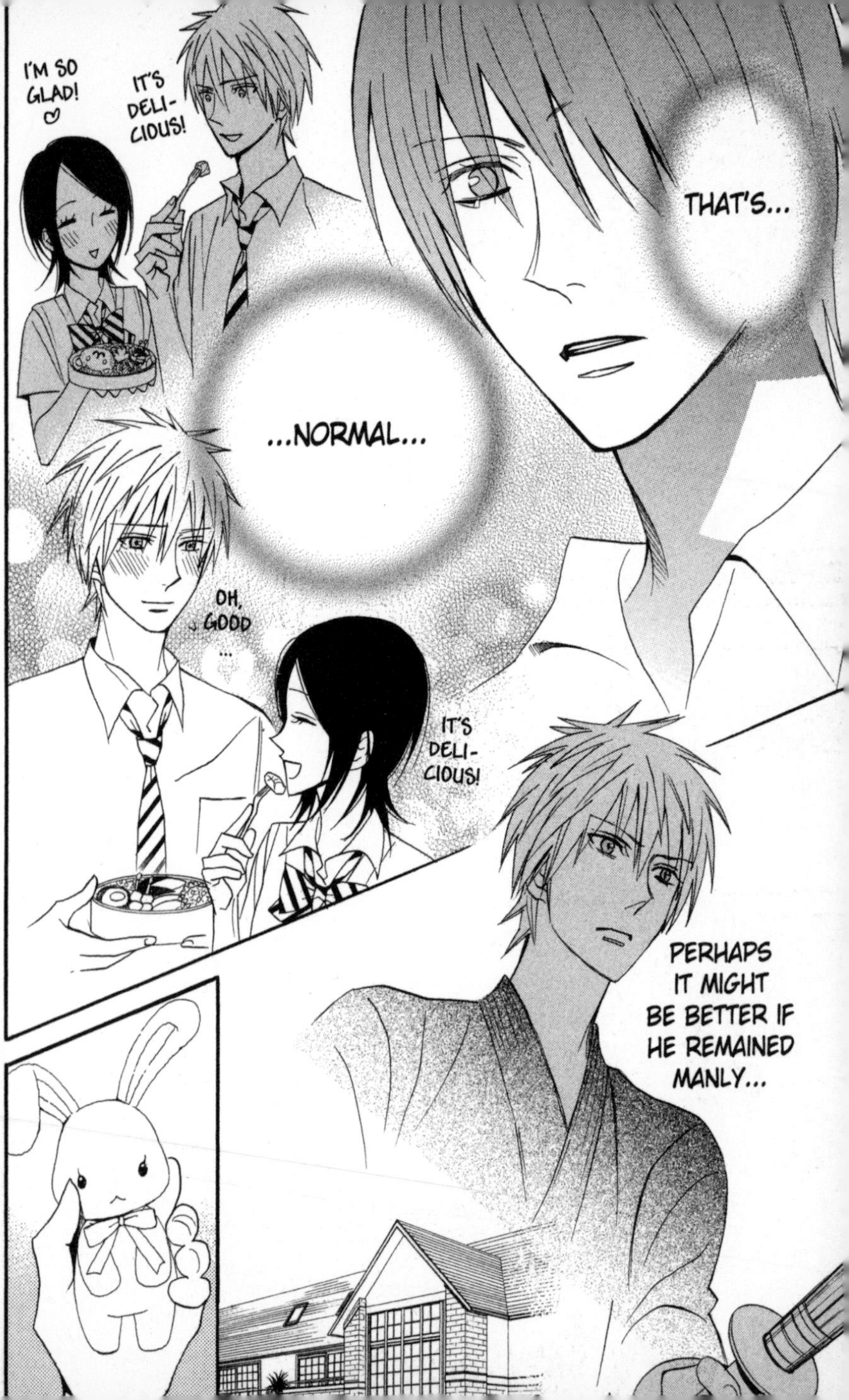
THAT'S...
...NORMAL...
IT'S DELICIOUS!
I'M SO GLAD! ♡
IT'S DELICIOUS!
OH, GOOD...
PERHAPS IT MIGHT BE BETTER IF HE REMAINED MANLY...

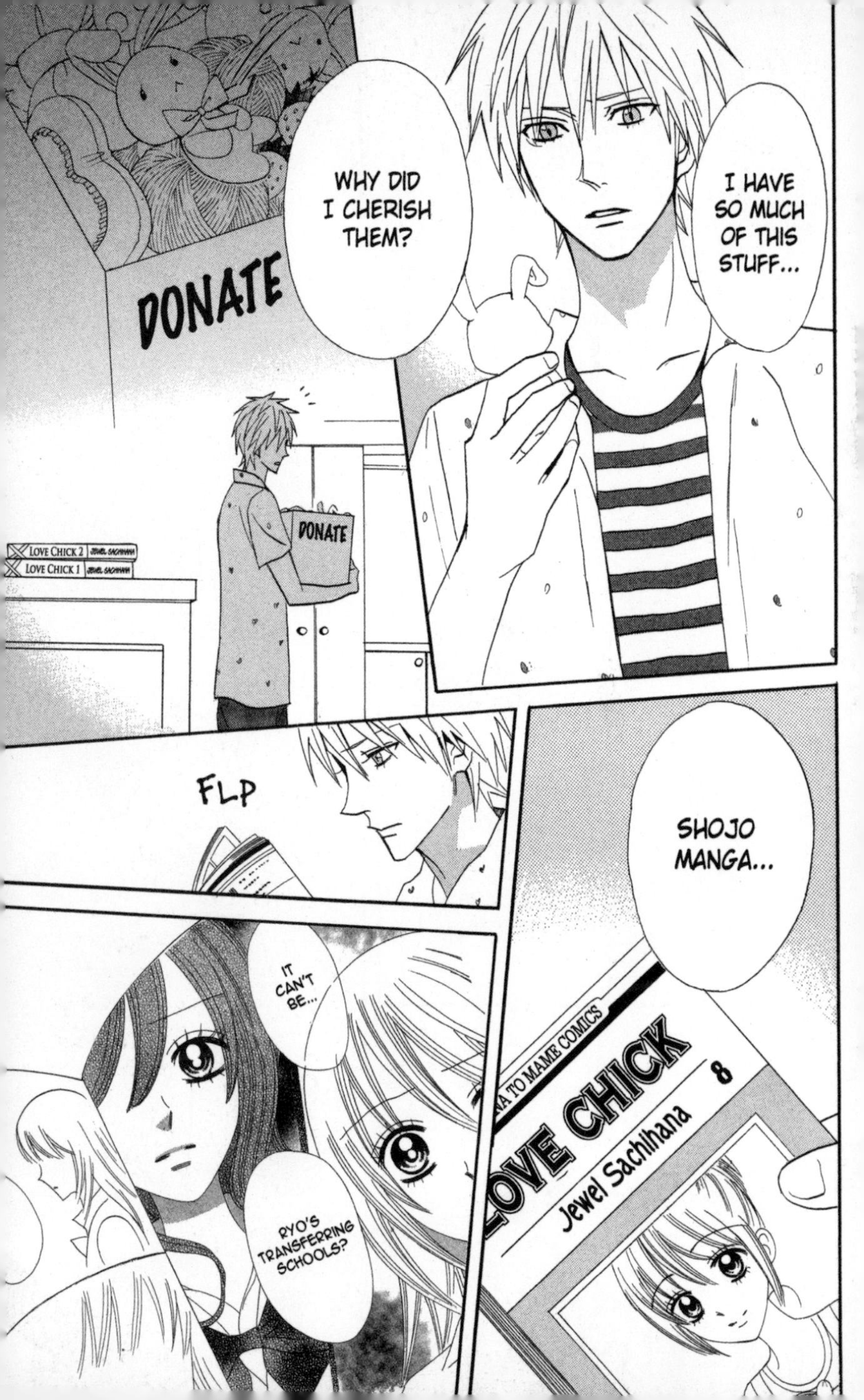
I HAVE SO MUCH OF THIS STUFF...
WHY DID I CHERISH THEM?
DONATE
DONATE
LOVE CHICK 2 JEWEL SACHIHANA
LOVE CHICK 1 JEWEL SACHIHANA
SHOJO MANGA...
NA TO MAME COMICS
LOVE CHICK 8
Jewel Sachihana
FLP
IT CAN'T BE...
RYO'S TRANSFERRING SCHOOLS?

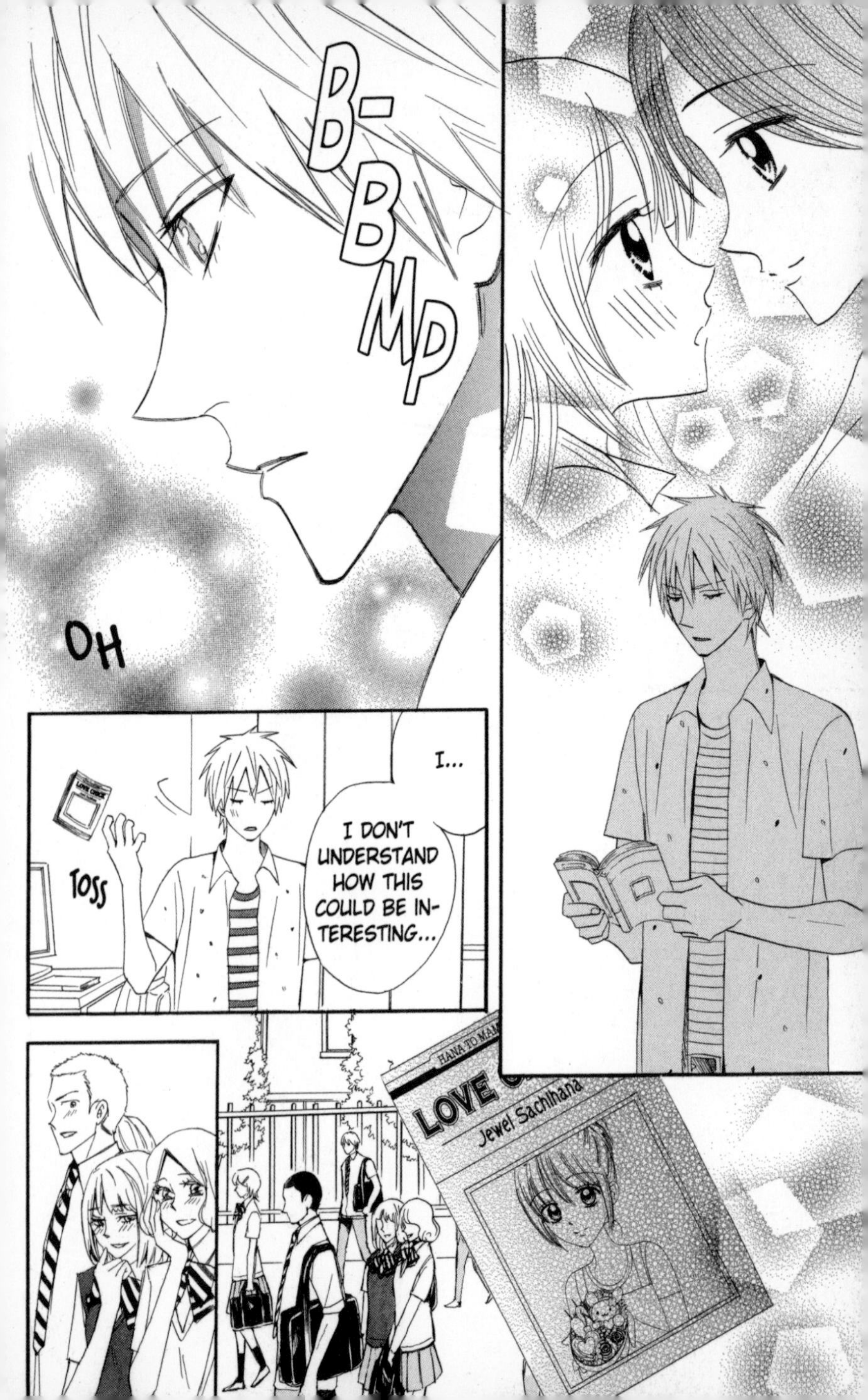
B-BMP
OH
I...
I DON'T UNDERSTAND HOW THIS COULD BE INTERESTING...
TOSS
LOVE
Jewel Sachihana

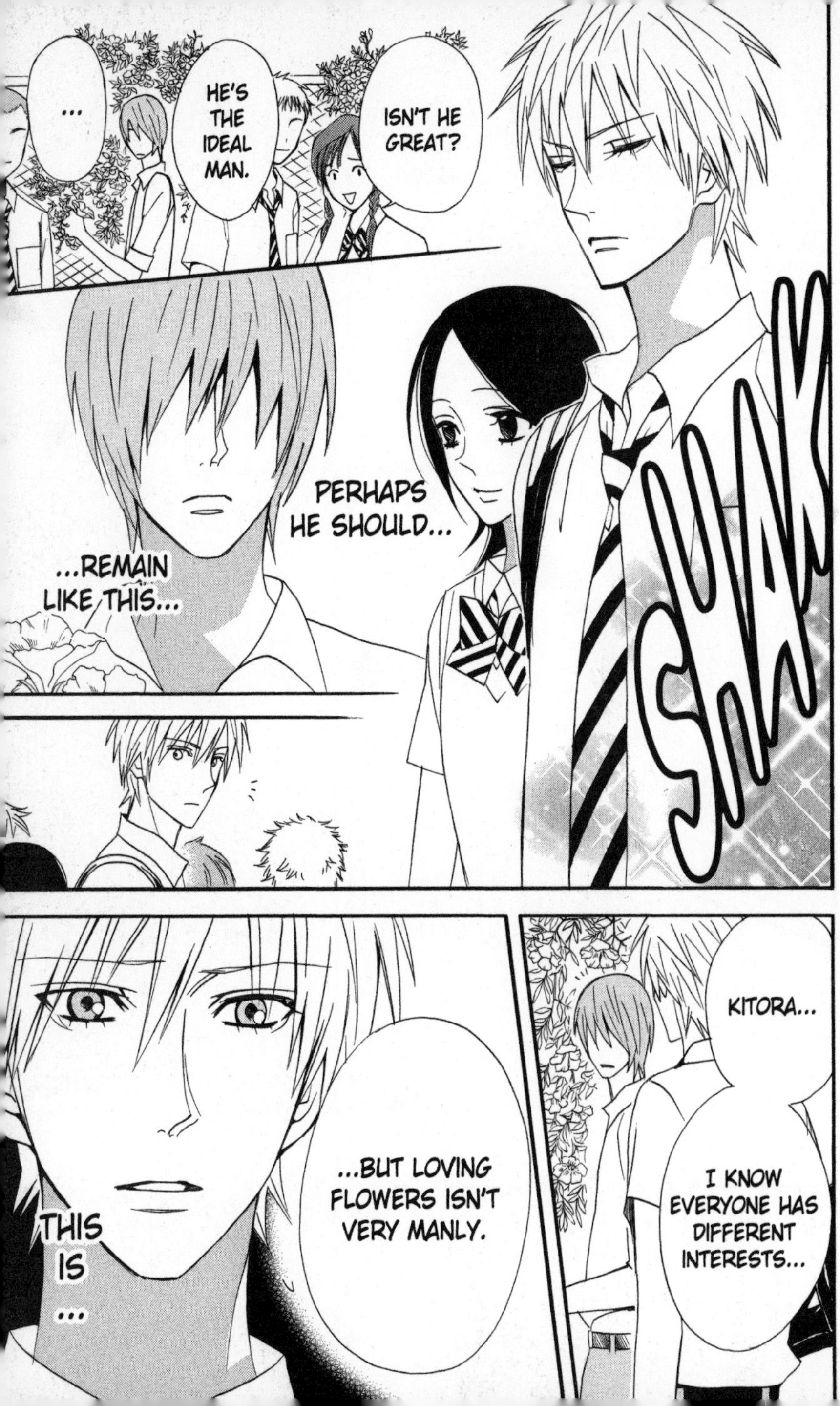
ISN'T HE GREAT?
HE'S THE IDEAL MAN.
...
SHAK
PERHAPS HE SHOULD...
...REMAIN LIKE THIS...
KITORA...
I KNOW EVERYONE HAS DIFFERENT INTERESTS...
...BUT LOVING FLOWERS ISN'T VERY MANLY.
THIS IS ...

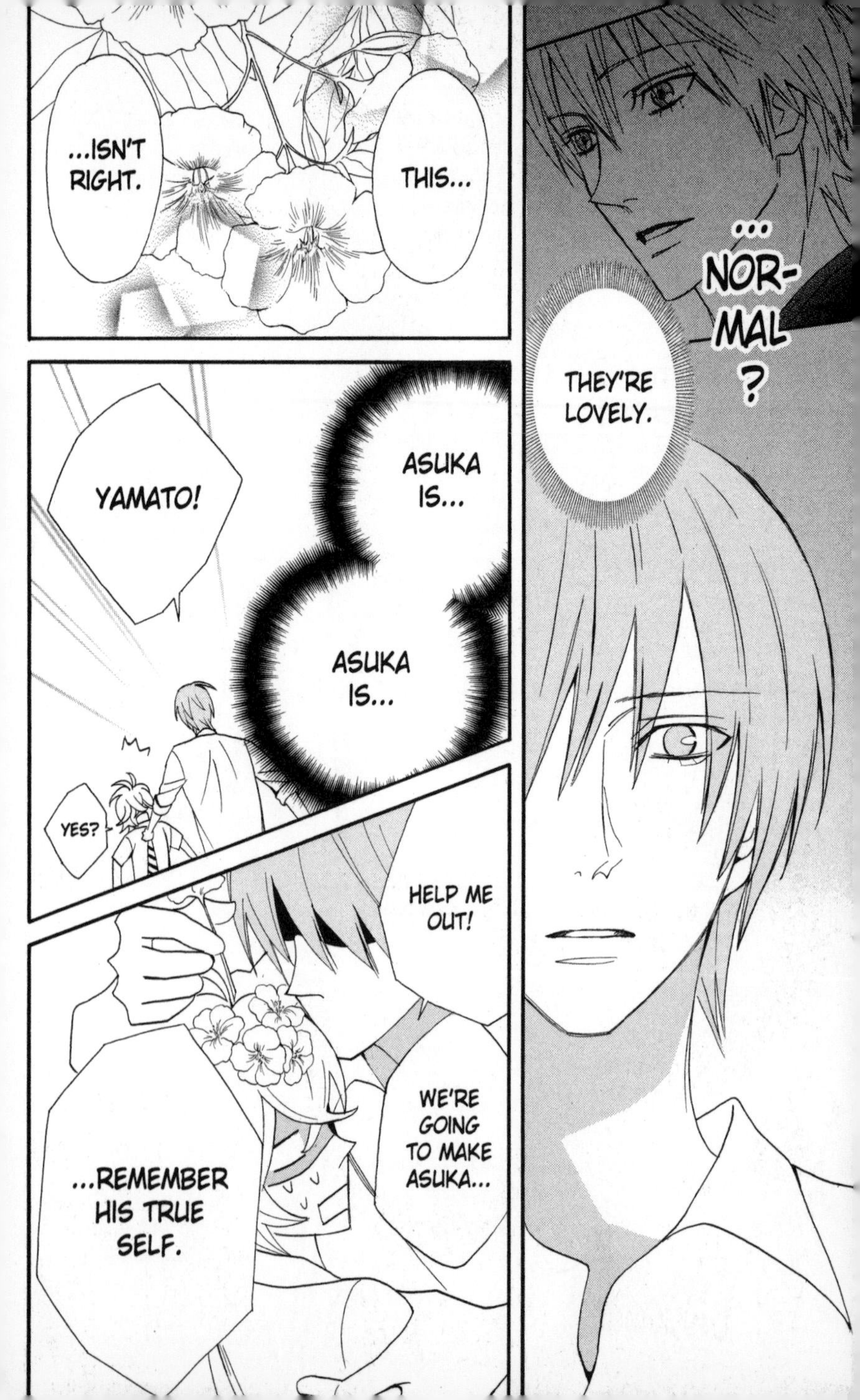
...NOR-MAL?
THEY'RE LOVELY.
THIS...
...ISN'T RIGHT.
ASUKA IS...
ASUKA IS...
YAMATO!
YES?
HELP ME OUT!
WE'RE GOING TO MAKE ASUKA...
...REMEMBER HIS TRUE SELF.

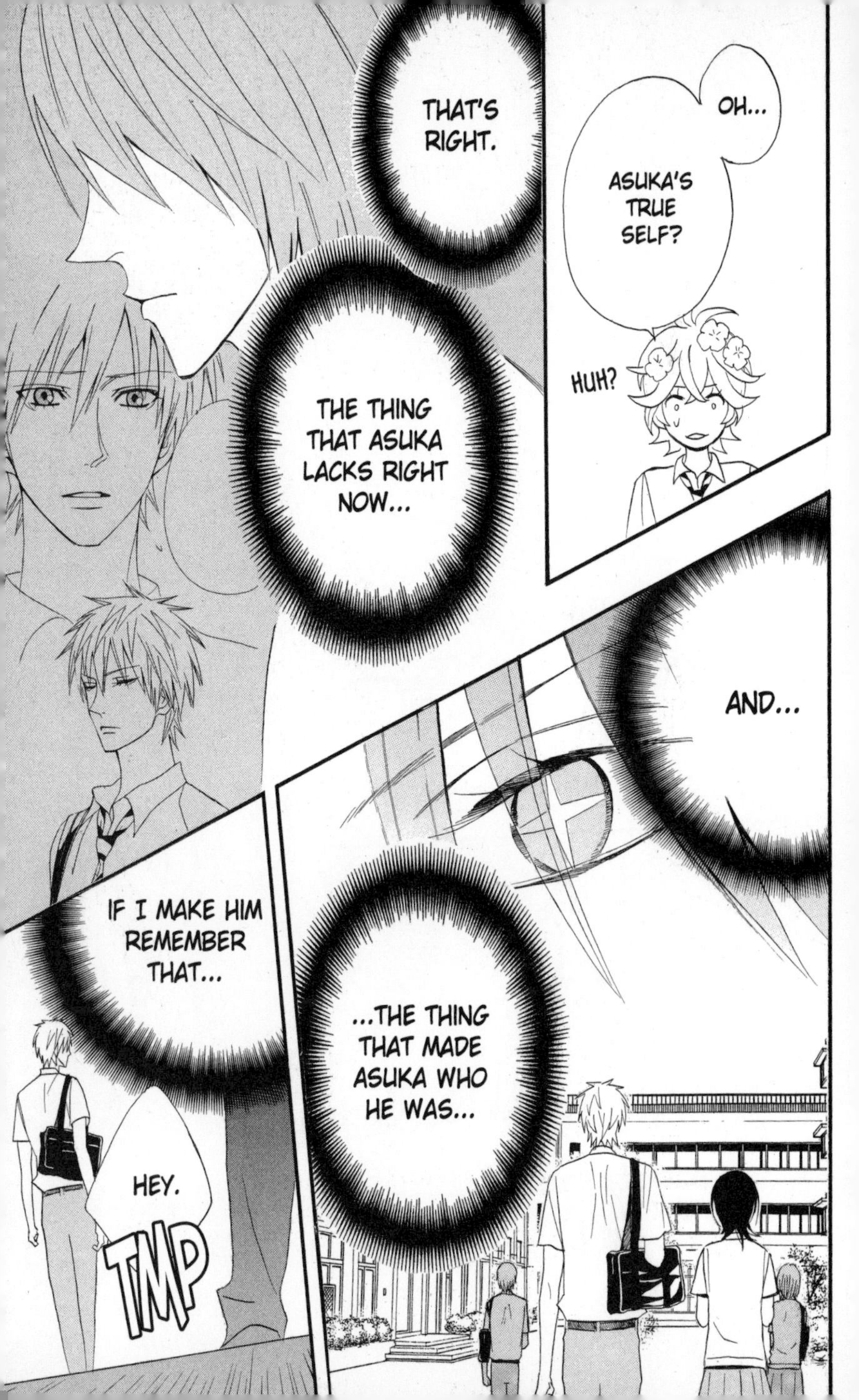

OH...
ASUKA'S TRUE SELF?
HUH?
THAT'S RIGHT.
THE THING THAT ASUKA LACKS RIGHT NOW...
AND...
...THE THING THAT MADE ASUKA WHO HE WAS...
IF I MAKE HIM REMEMBER THAT...
HEY.
TMP

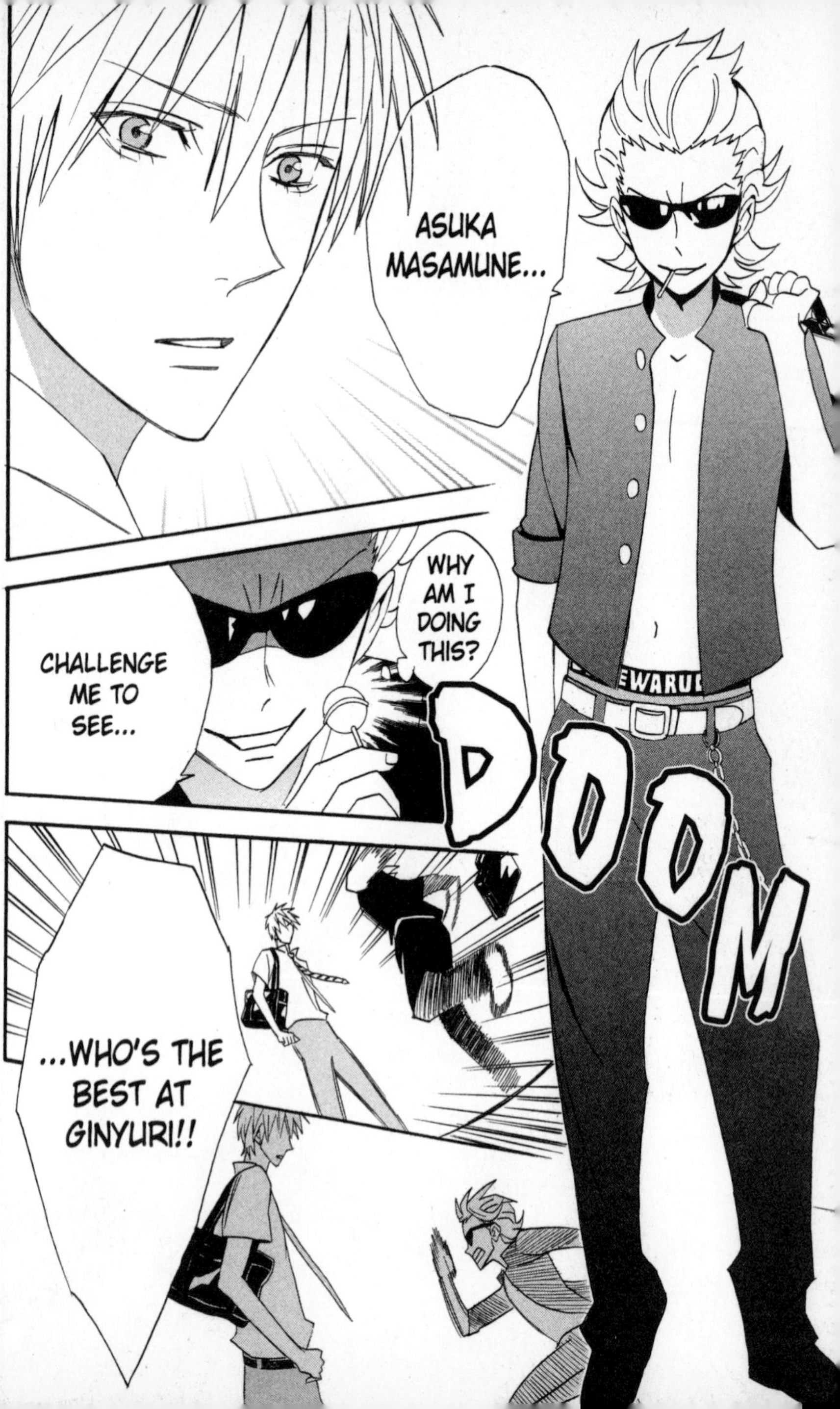
ASUKA MASAMUNE...
WHY AM I DOING THIS?
DOOM
CHALLENGE ME TO SEE...
...WHO'S THE BEST AT GINYURI!!

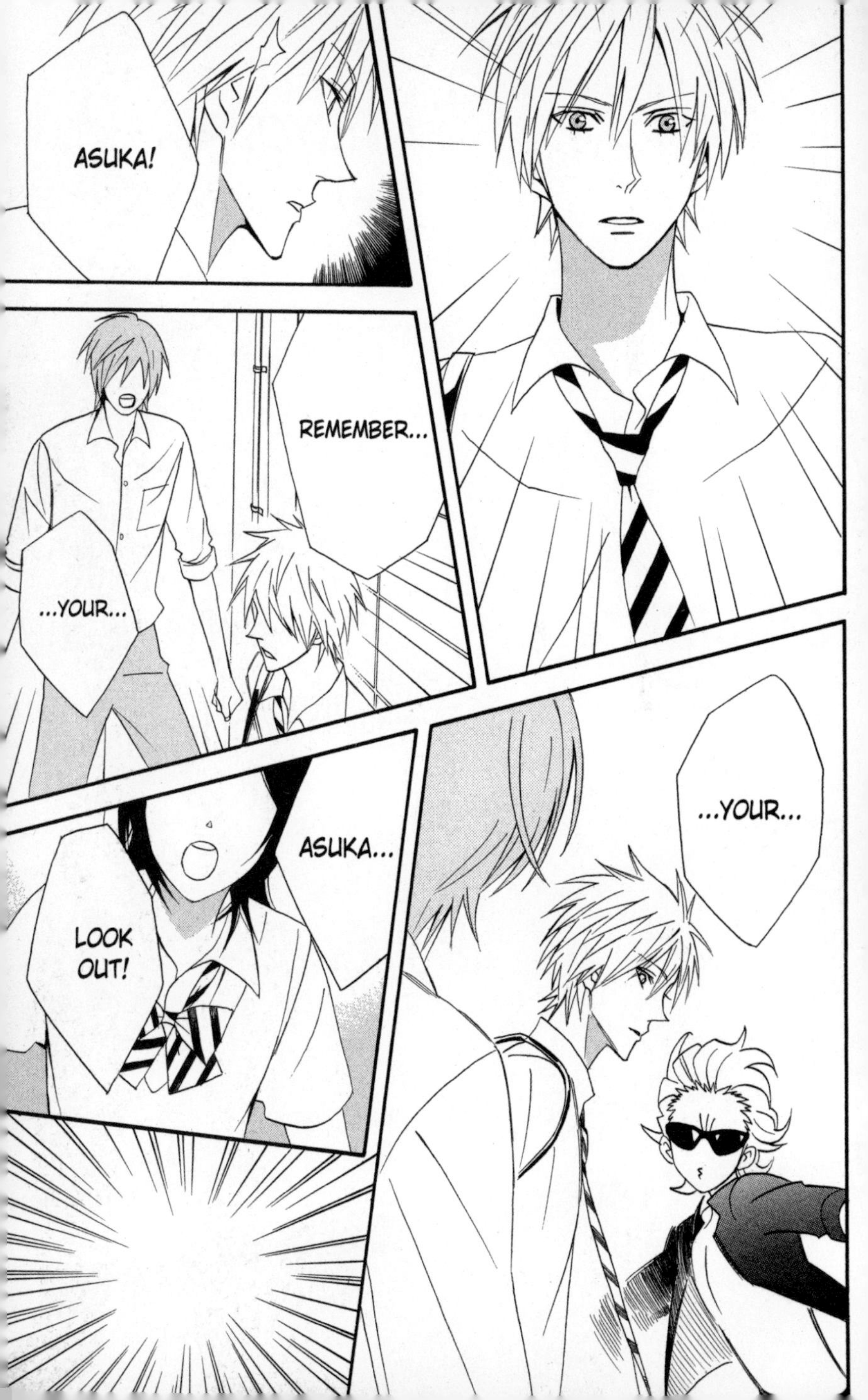
ASUKA!
REMEMBER...
...YOUR...
...YOUR...
ASUKA...
LOOK OUT!

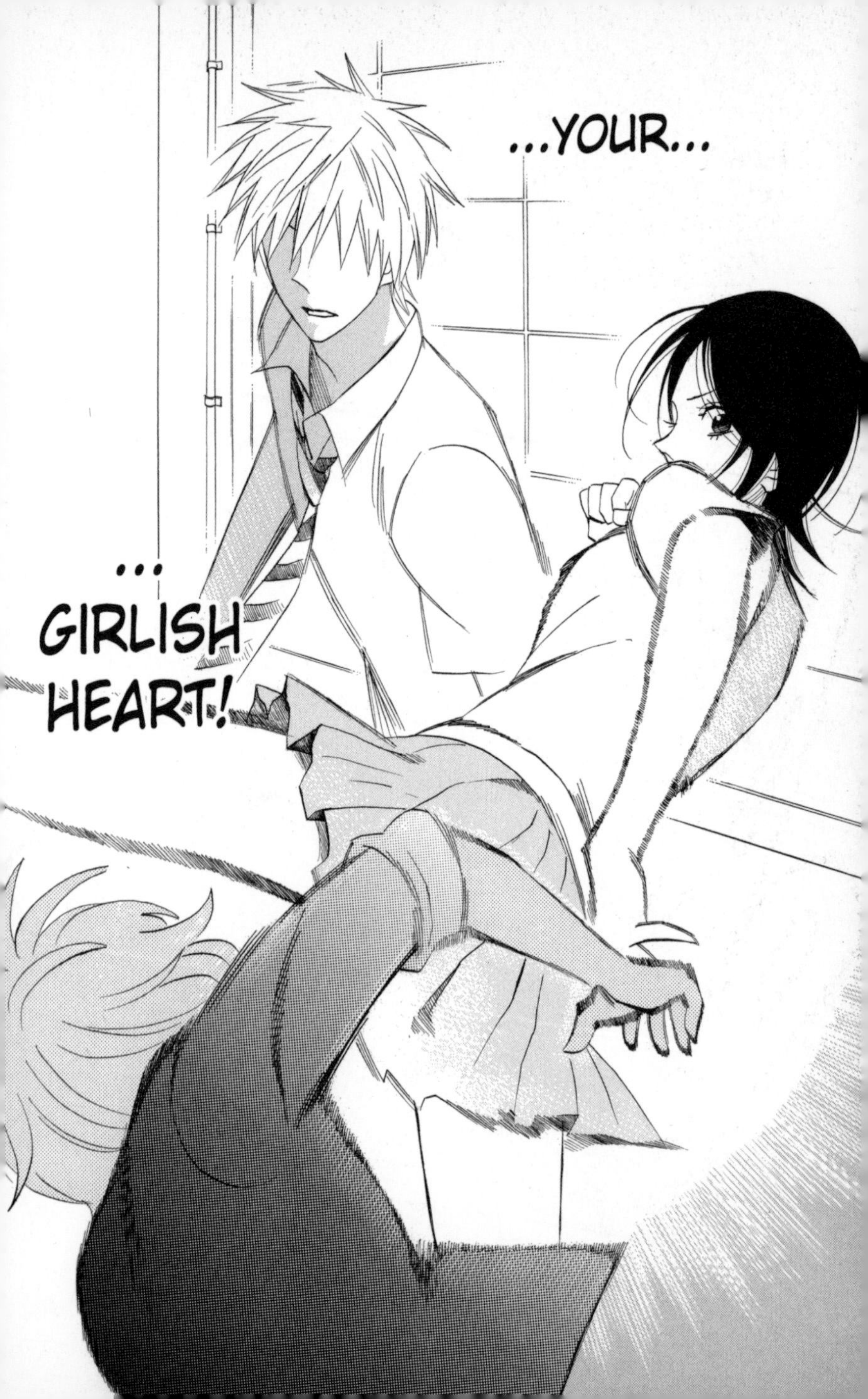
...YOUR...
...GIRLISH HEART!

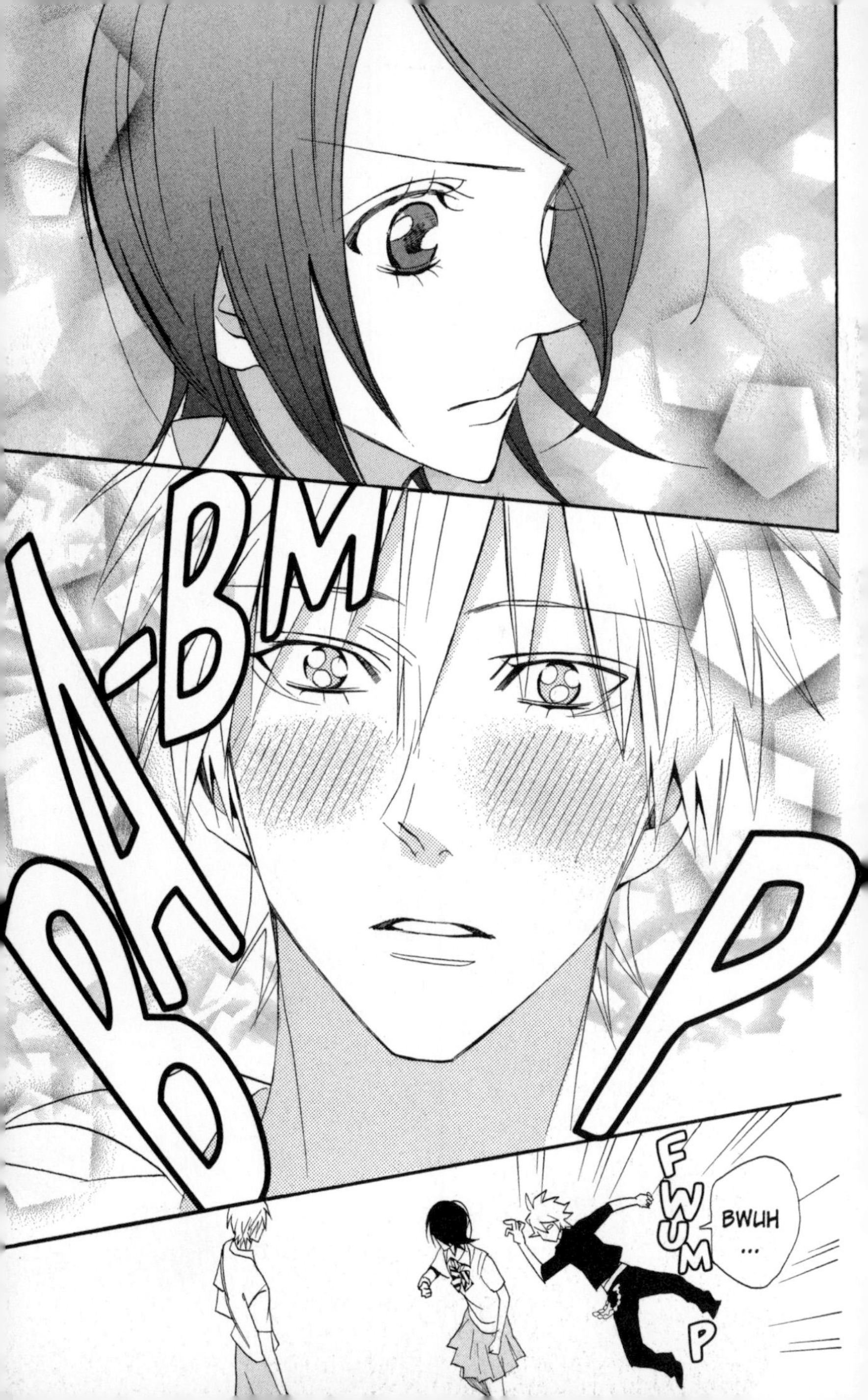
BA-BMP
FWUMP
BWUH ...

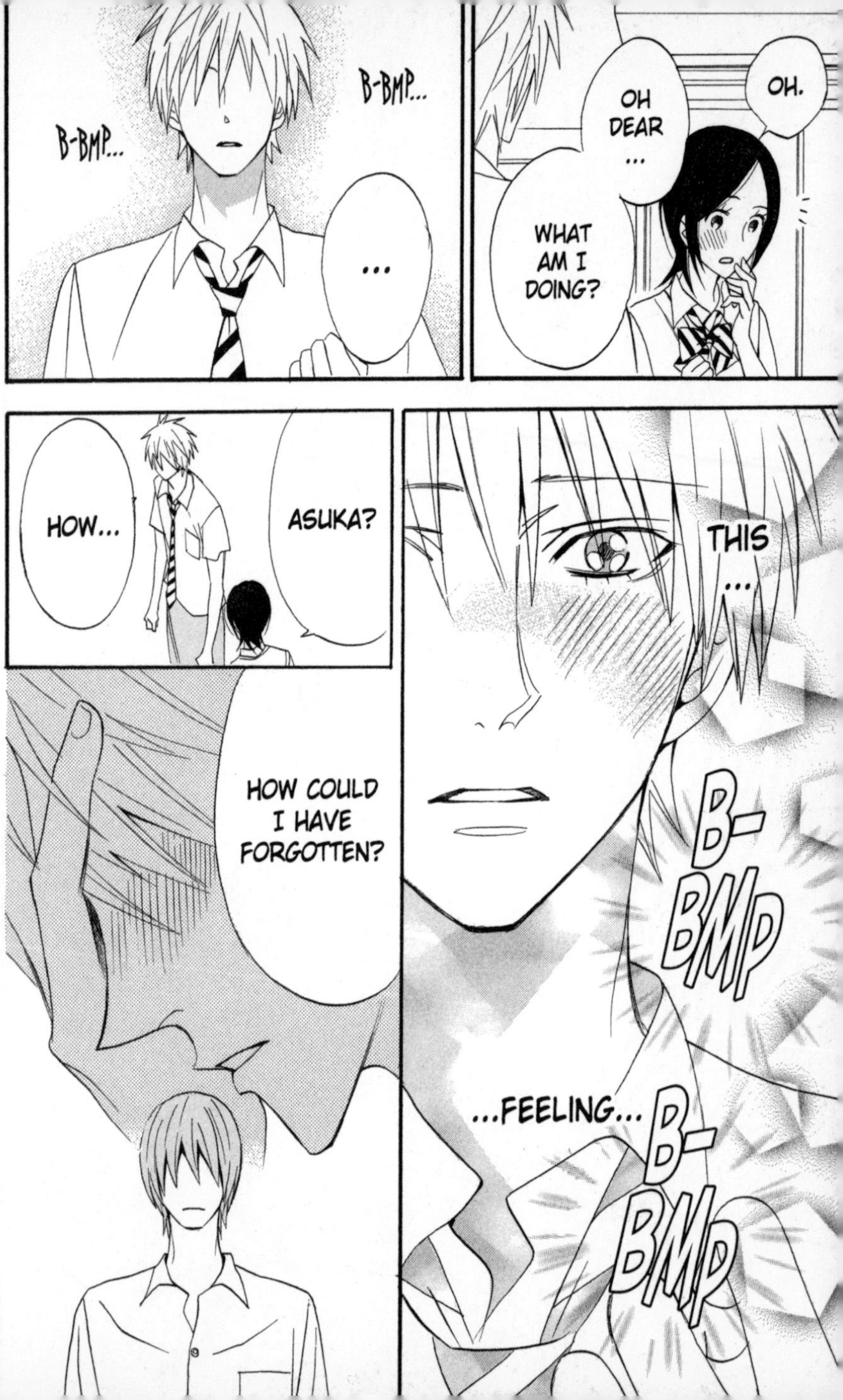
OH.
OH DEAR ...
WHAT AM I DOING?
B-BMP...
B-BMP...
...
THIS ...
B-BMP
...FEELING...
B-BMP
ASUKA?
HOW...
HOW COULD I HAVE FORGOTTEN?

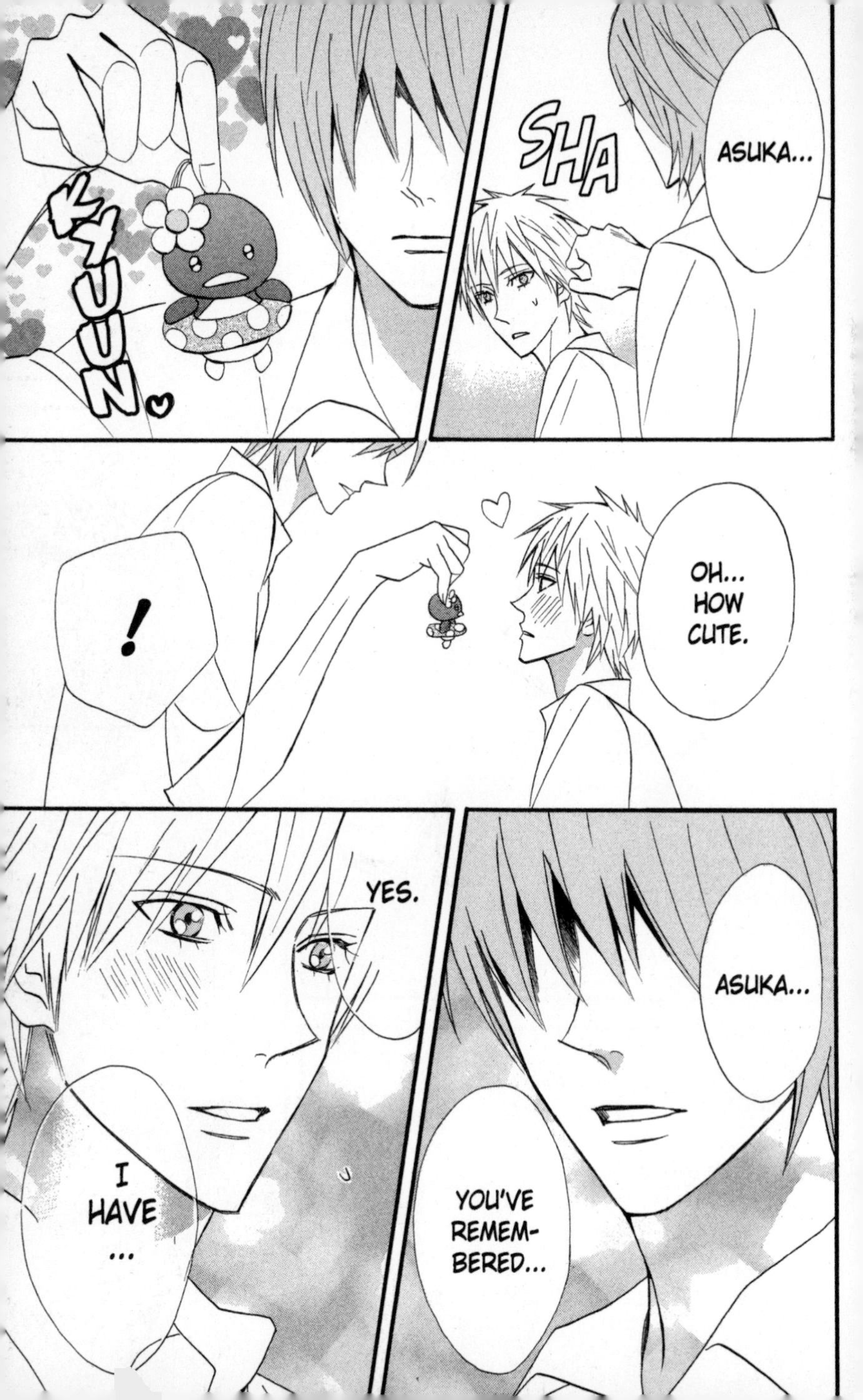
SHA
ASUKA...
KYUUN♡
OH... HOW CUTE.
!
ASUKA...
YOU'VE REMEMBERED...
YES.
I HAVE ...

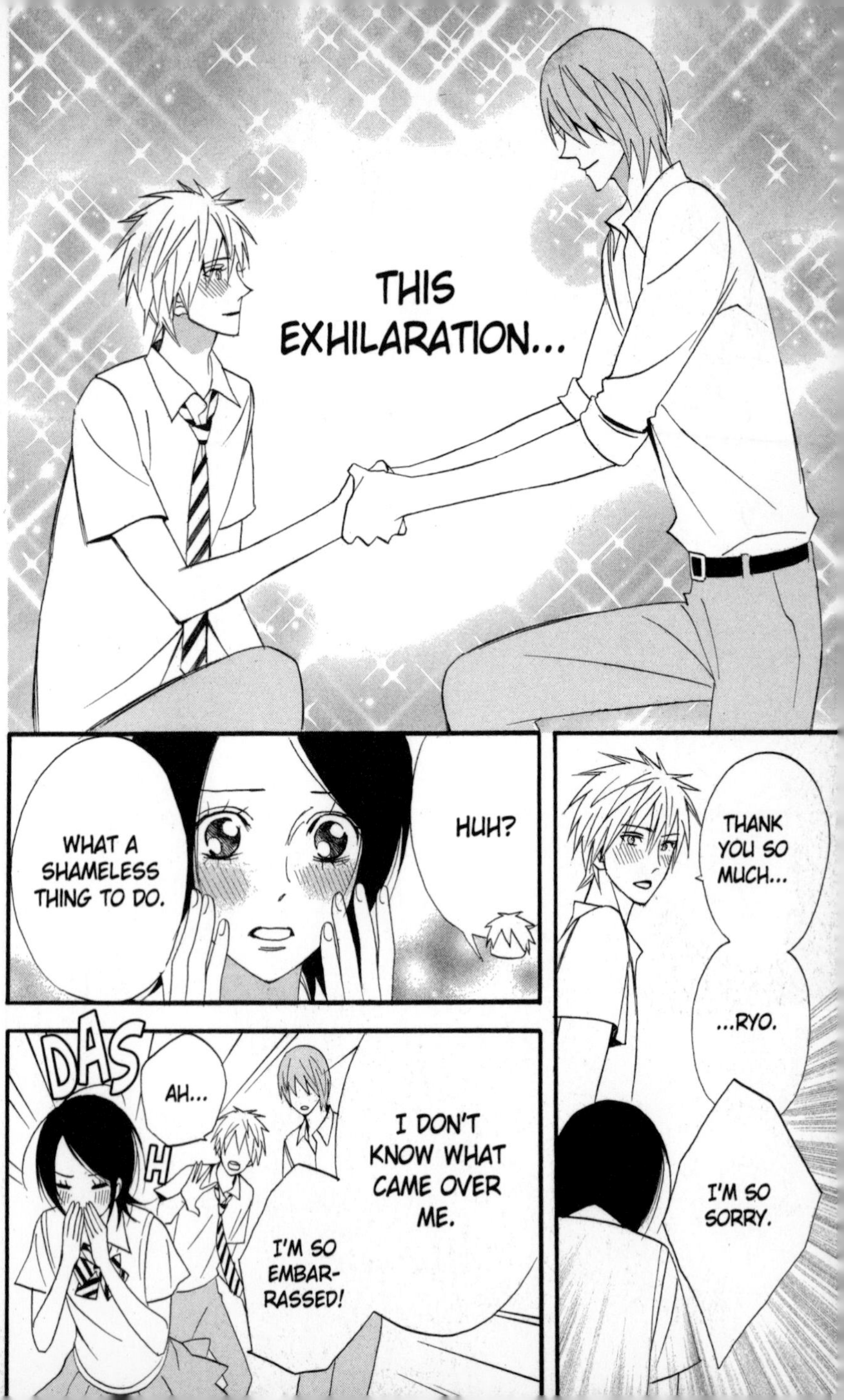
THIS EXHILARATION...
THANK YOU SO MUCH...
...RYO.
I'M SO SORRY.
HUH?
WHAT A SHAMELESS THING TO DO.
I DON'T KNOW WHAT CAME OVER ME.
I'M SO EMBARRASSED!
AH...
DASH

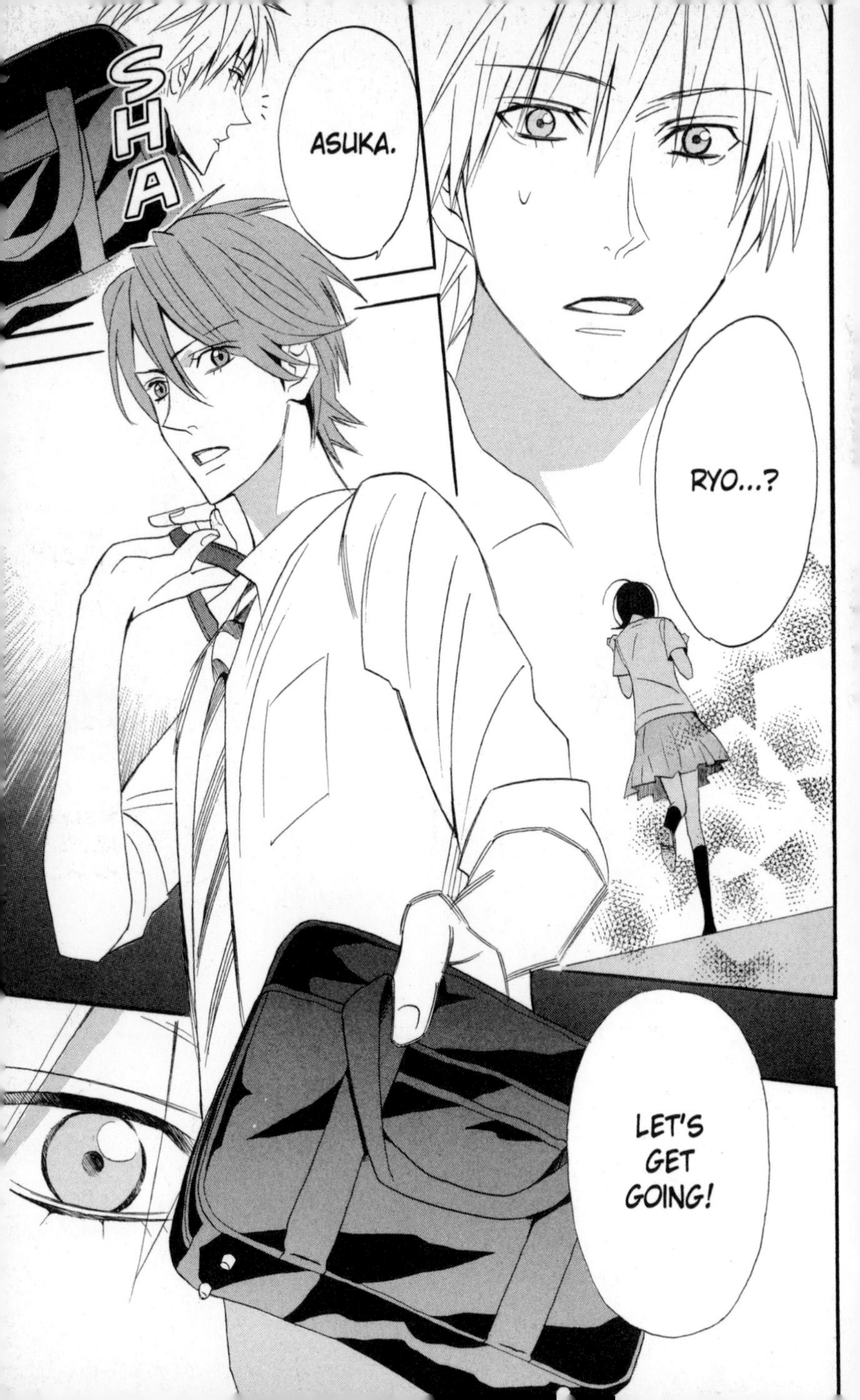
RYO...?
SHA
ASUKA.
LET'S GET GOING!

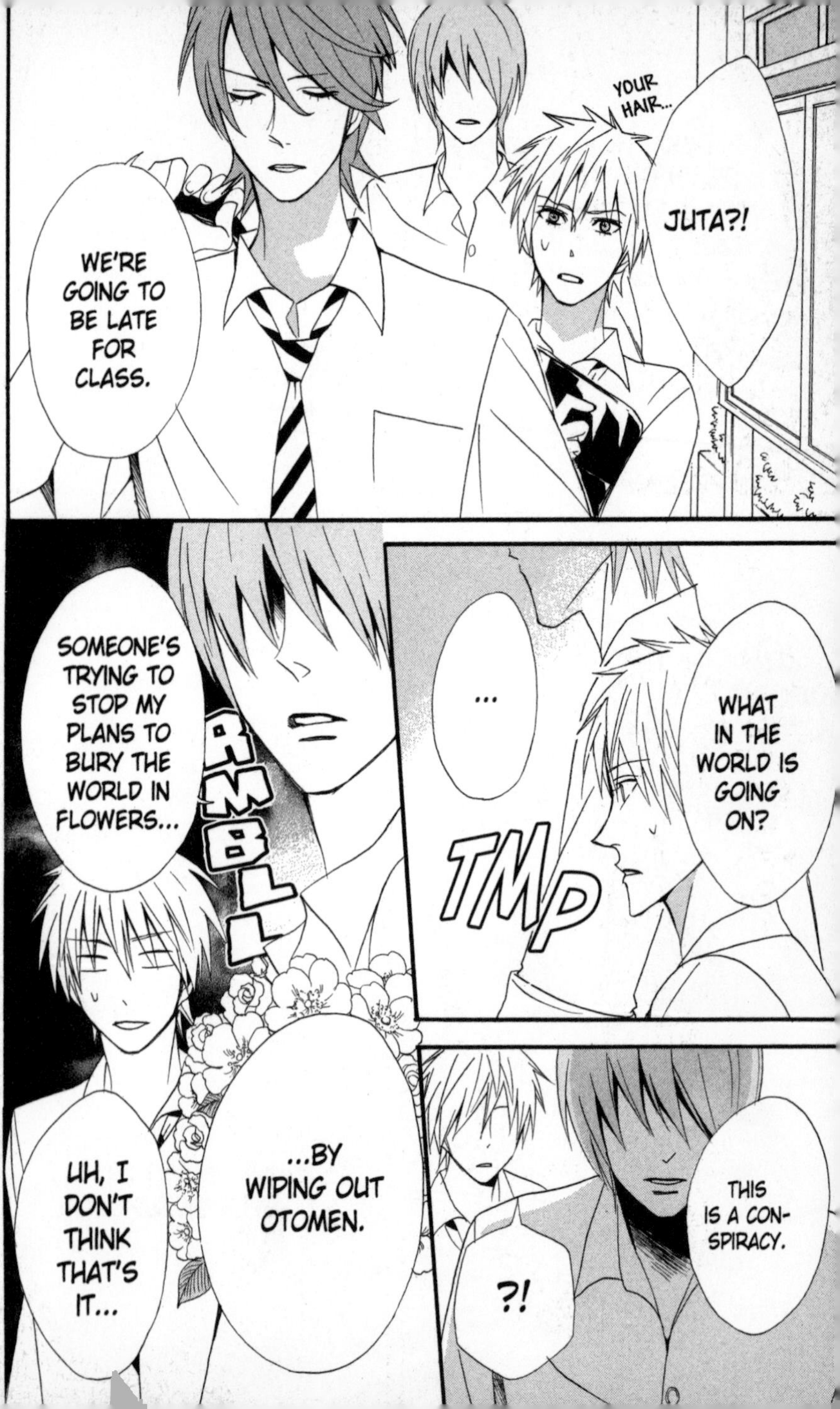
YOUR HAIR...
JUTA?!
WE'RE GOING TO BE LATE FOR CLASS.
WHAT IN THE WORLD IS GOING ON?
...
TMP
THIS IS A CON-SPIRACY.
?!
SOMEONE'S TRYING TO STOP MY PLANS TO BURY THE WORLD IN FLOWERS...
RMBLL
...BY WIPING OUT OTOMEN.
UH, I DON'T THINK THAT'S IT...

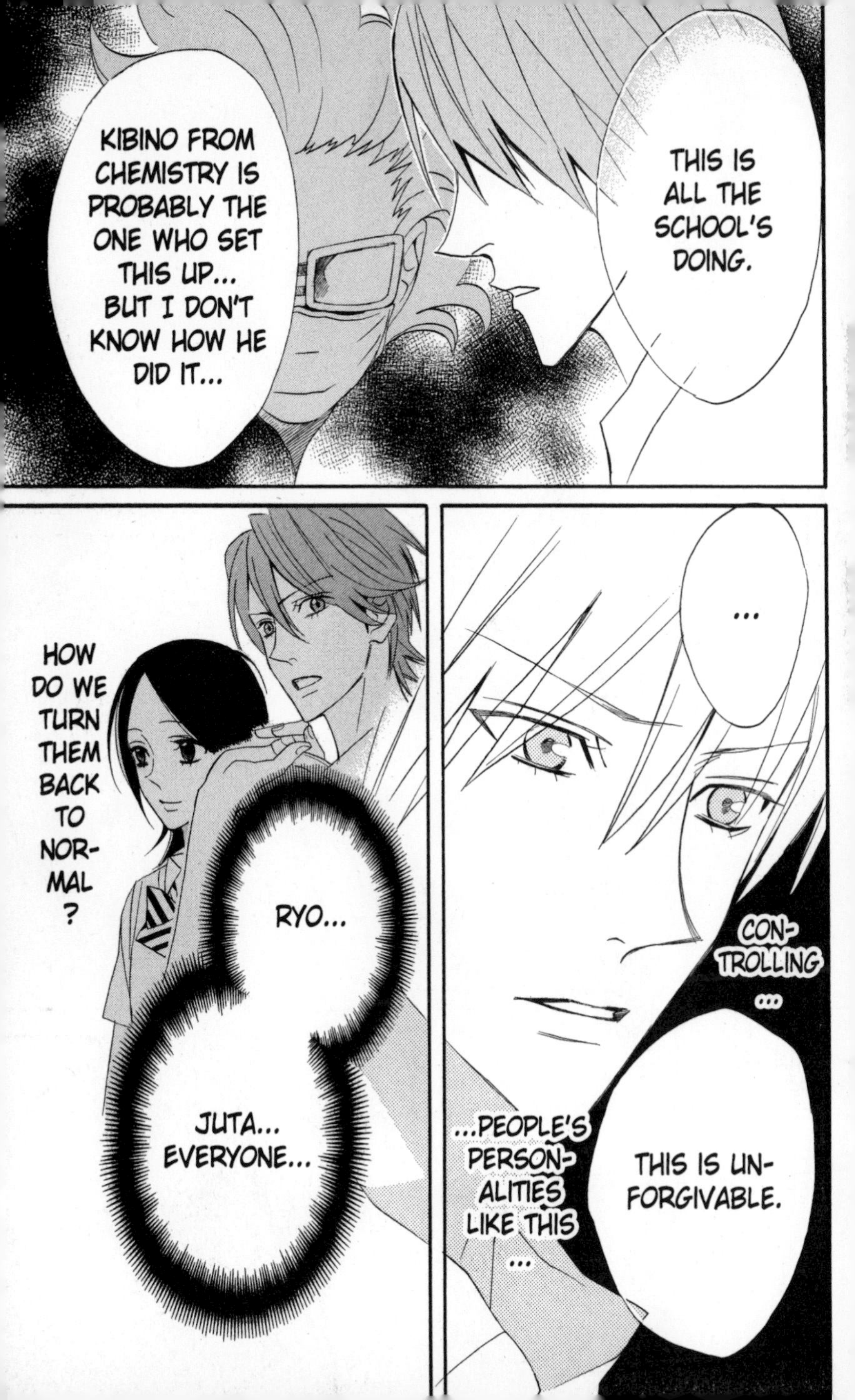
THIS IS ALL THE SCHOOL'S DOING.
KIBINO FROM CHEMISTRY IS PROBABLY THE ONE WHO SET THIS UP... BUT I DON'T KNOW HOW HE DID IT...
...
CON-TROLLING...
...PEOPLE'S PERSON-ALITIES LIKE THIS...
THIS IS UN-FORGIVABLE.
HOW DO WE TURN THEM BACK TO NOR-MAL?
RYO...
JUTA... EVERYONE...

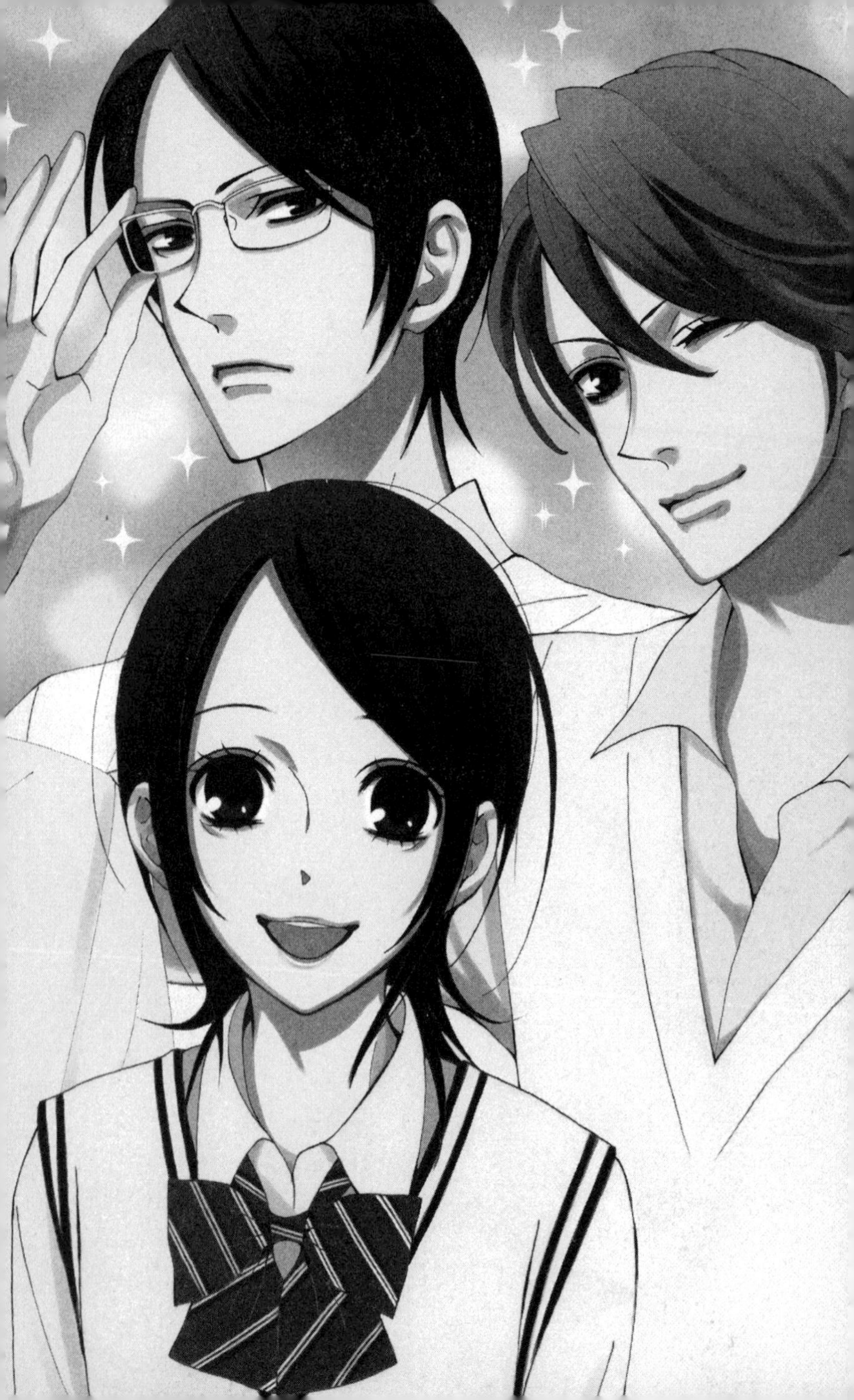

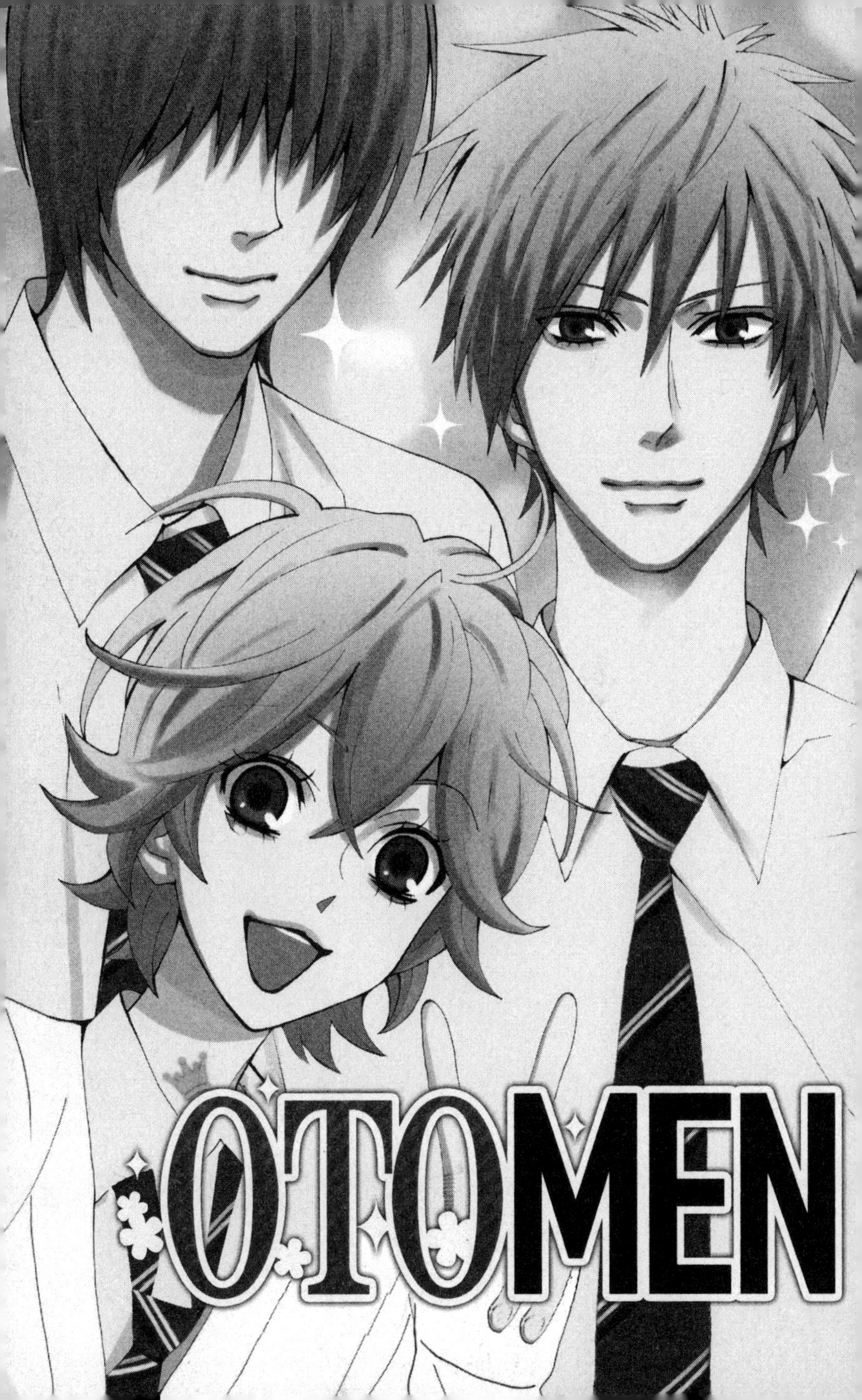
OTOMEN

OTOMEN

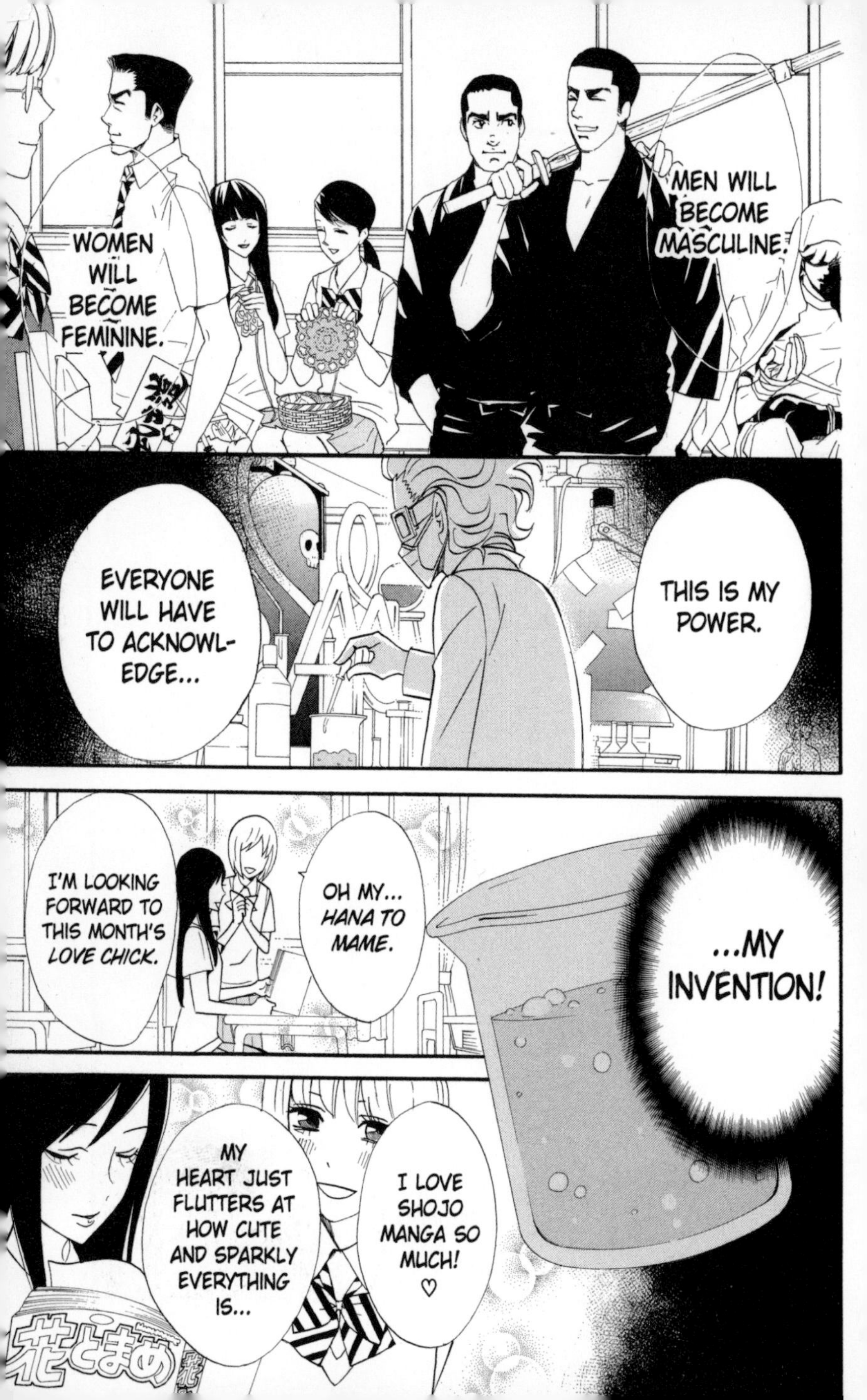
MEN WILL BECOME MASCULINE.
WOMEN WILL BECOME FEMININE.
THIS IS MY POWER.
EVERYONE WILL HAVE TO ACKNOWLEDGE...
...MY INVENTION!
OH MY... *HANA TO MAME.*
I'M LOOKING FORWARD TO THIS MONTH'S *LOVE CHICK.*
I LOVE SHOJO MANGA SO MUCH! ♡
MY HEART JUST FLUTTERS AT HOW CUTE AND SPARKLY EVERYTHING IS...
花とまめ

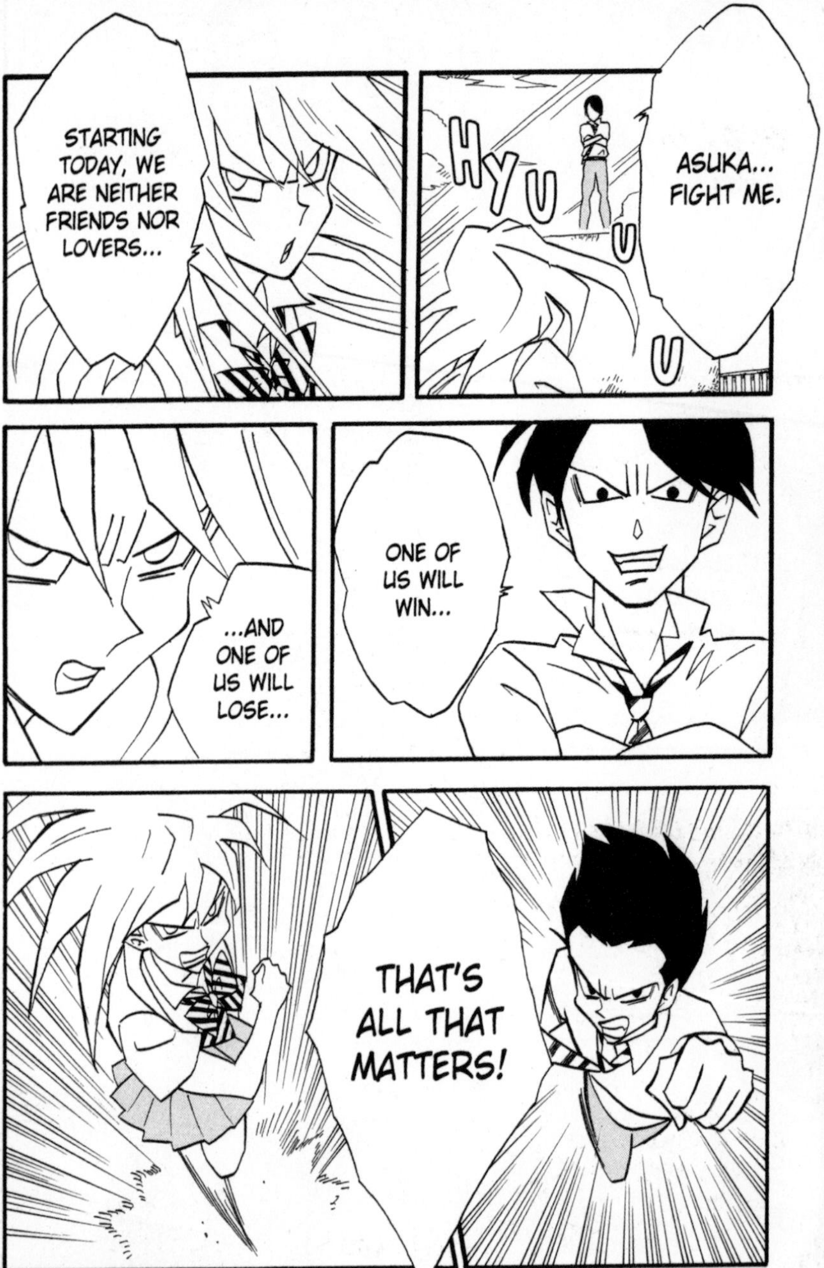
HYUUUU
ASUKA... FIGHT ME.
STARTING TODAY, WE ARE NEITHER FRIENDS NOR LOVERS...
ONE OF US WILL WIN...
...AND ONE OF US WILL LOSE...
THAT'S ALL THAT MATTERS!

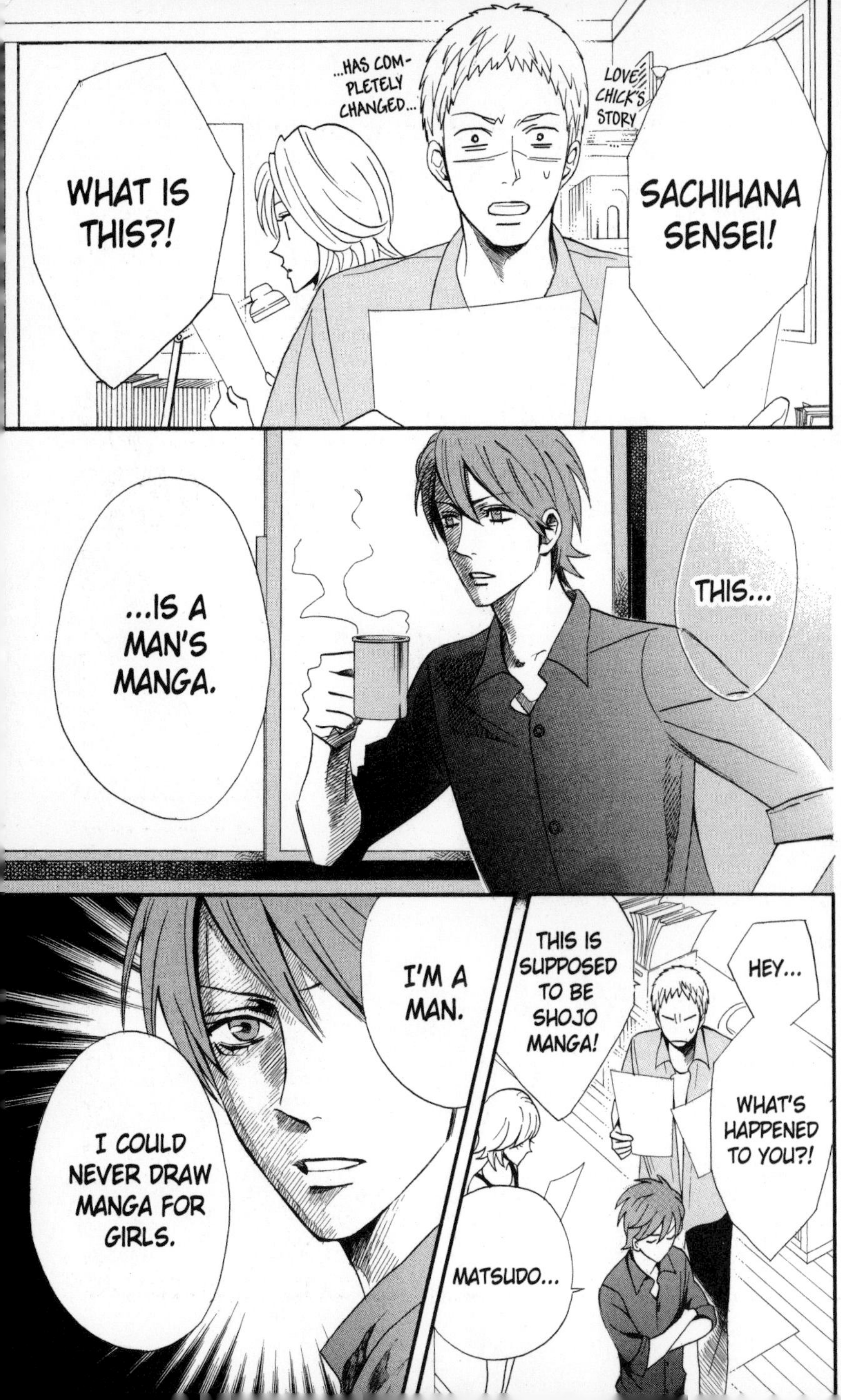
SACHIHANA SENSEI!
LOVE CHICK'S STORY
...HAS COMPLETELY CHANGED...
WHAT IS THIS?!
THIS...
...IS A MAN'S MANGA.
HEY...
WHAT'S HAPPENED TO YOU?!
THIS IS SUPPOSED TO BE SHOJO MANGA!
MATSUDO...
I'M A MAN.
I COULD NEVER DRAW MANGA FOR GIRLS.

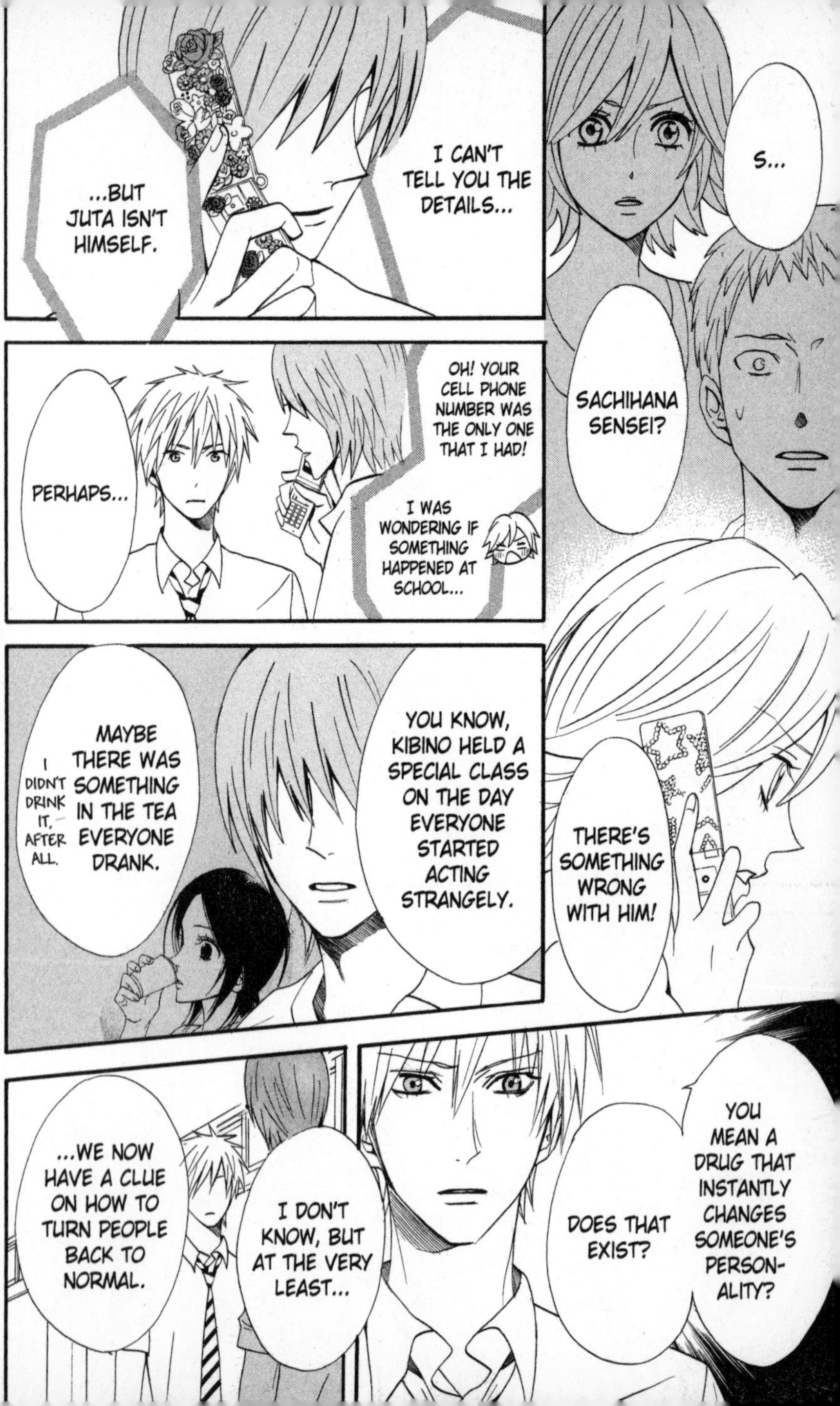
S...
SACHIHANA SENSEI?
THERE'S SOMETHING WRONG WITH HIM!
I CAN'T TELL YOU THE DETAILS...
...BUT JUTA ISN'T HIMSELF.
OH! YOUR CELL PHONE NUMBER WAS THE ONLY ONE THAT I HAD!
I WAS WONDERING IF SOMETHING HAPPENED AT SCHOOL...
PERHAPS...
YOU KNOW, KIBINO HELD A SPECIAL CLASS ON THE DAY EVERYONE STARTED ACTING STRANGELY.
MAYBE THERE WAS SOMETHING IN THE TEA EVERYONE DRANK.
I DIDN'T DRINK IT, AFTER ALL.
YOU MEAN A DRUG THAT INSTANTLY CHANGES SOMEONE'S PERSON-ALITY?
DOES THAT EXIST?
I DON'T KNOW, BUT AT THE VERY LEAST...
...WE NOW HAVE A CLUE ON HOW TO TURN PEOPLE BACK TO NORMAL.

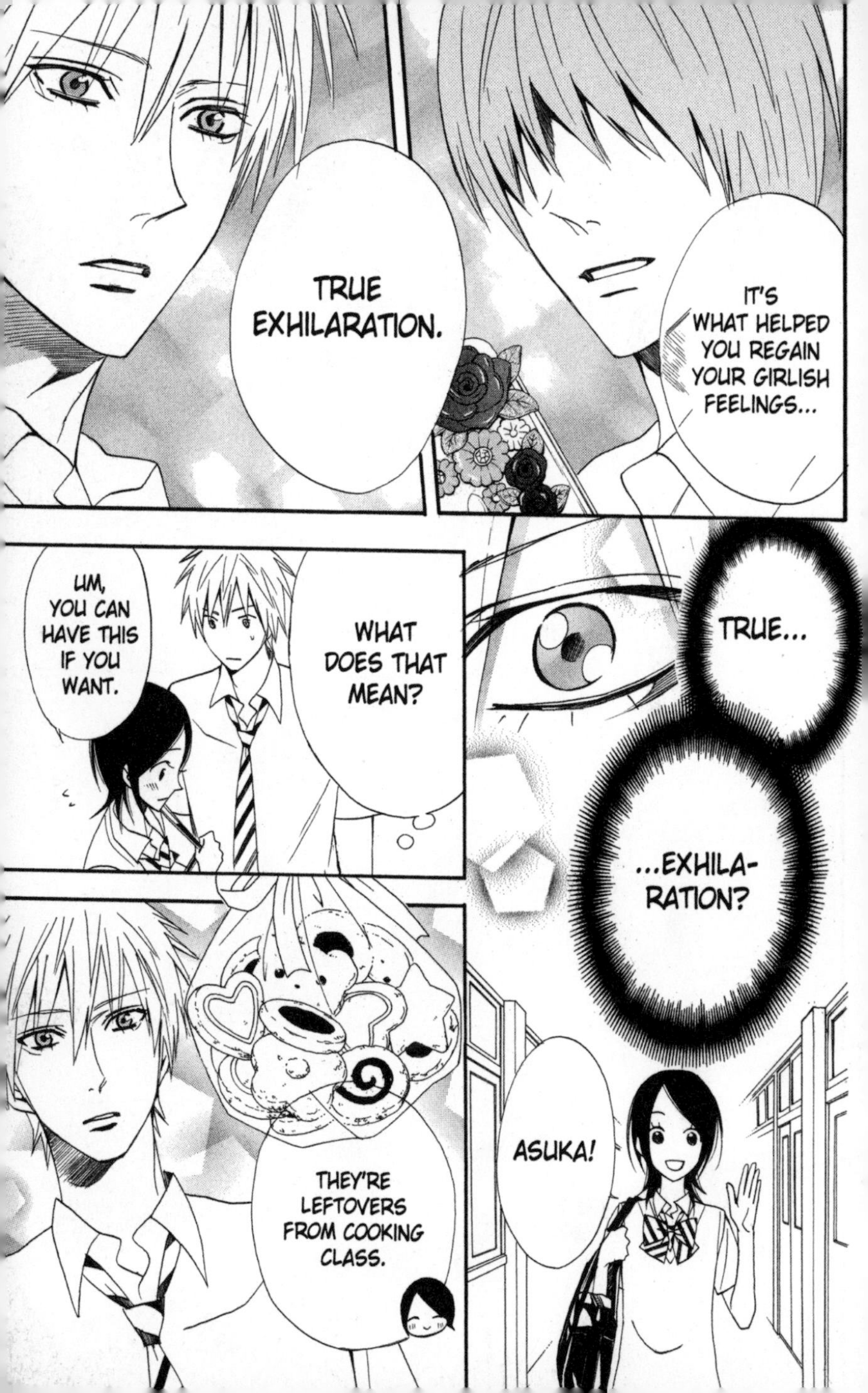
IT'S WHAT HELPED YOU REGAIN YOUR GIRLISH FEELINGS...
TRUE EXHILARATION.
TRUE...
...EXHILA-RATION?
WHAT DOES THAT MEAN?
UM, YOU CAN HAVE THIS IF YOU WANT.
ASUKA!
THEY'RE LEFTOVERS FROM COOKING CLASS.

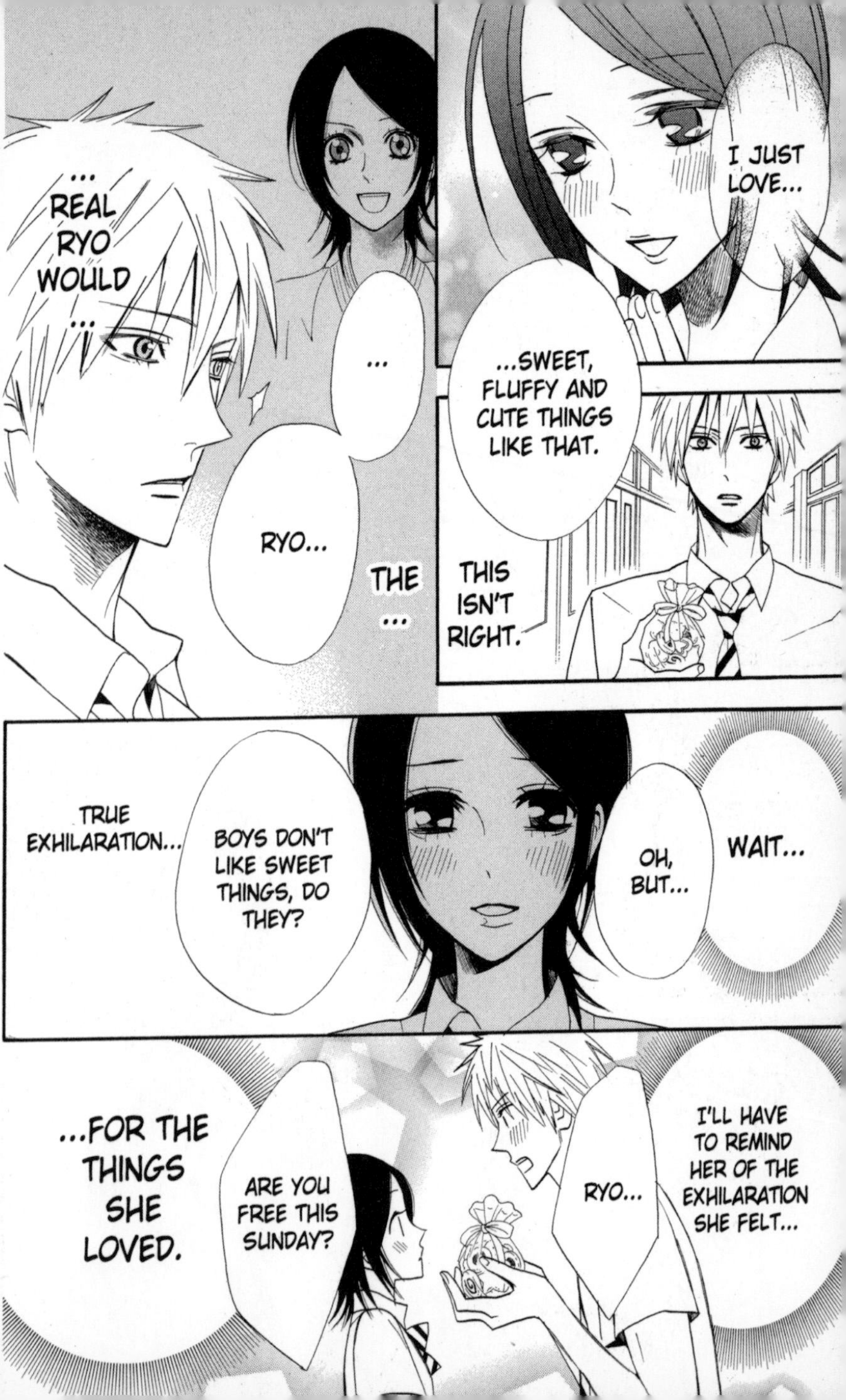
I JUST LOVE...
...SWEET, FLUFFY AND CUTE THINGS LIKE THAT.
THIS ISN'T RIGHT.
...
RYO...
THE ...
... REAL RYO WOULD ...
WAIT...
OH, BUT...
BOYS DON'T LIKE SWEET THINGS, DO THEY?
TRUE EXHILARATION...
I'LL HAVE TO REMIND HER OF THE EXHILARATION SHE FELT...
RYO...
ARE YOU FREE THIS SUNDAY?
...FOR THE THINGS SHE LOVED.

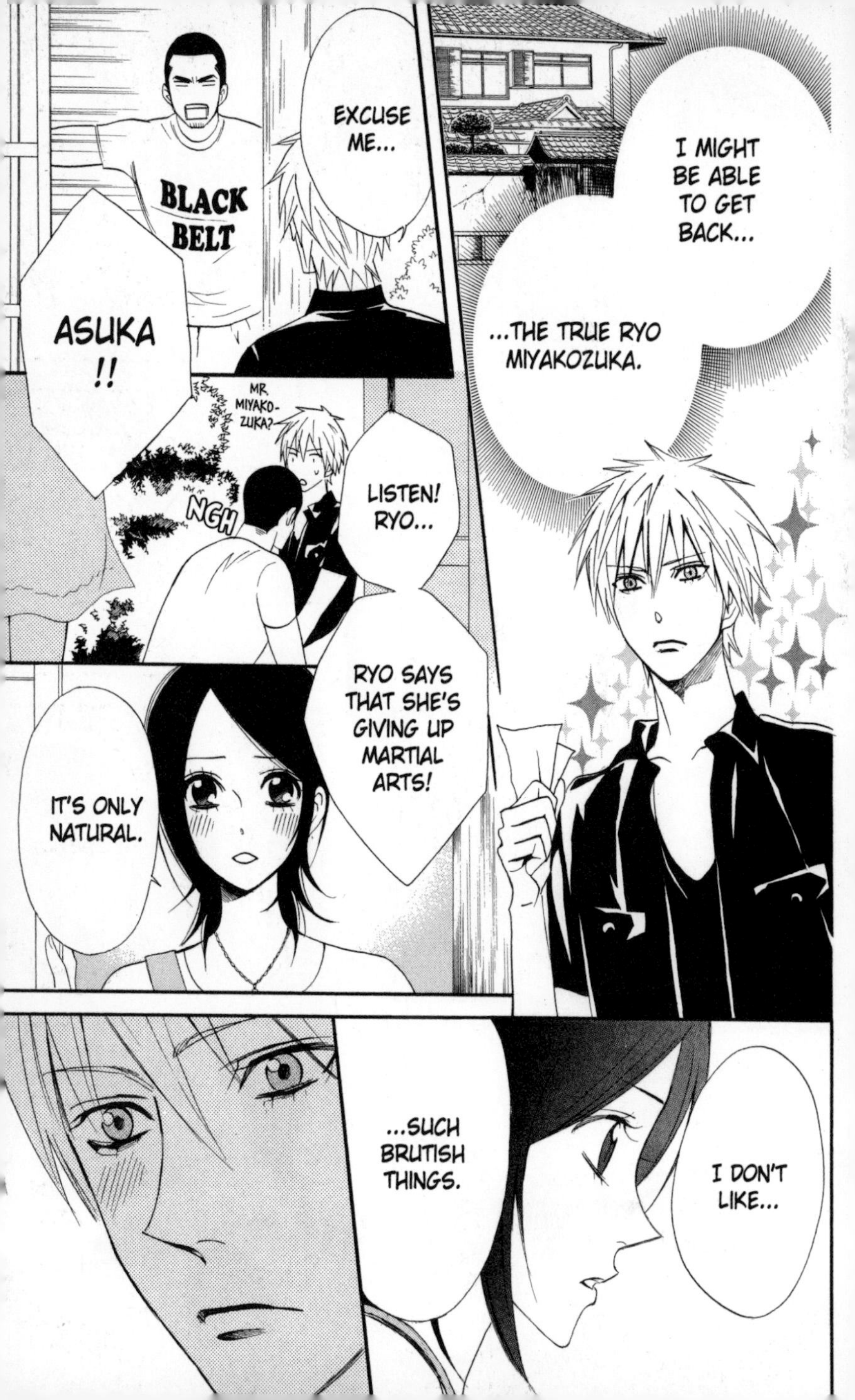
I MIGHT BE ABLE TO GET BACK...
...THE TRUE RYO MIYAKOZUKA.
EXCUSE ME...
BLACK BELT
ASUKA!!
LISTEN! RYO...
MR. MIYAKO-ZUKA?
NGH
RYO SAYS THAT SHE'S GIVING UP MARTIAL ARTS!
IT'S ONLY NATURAL.
I DON'T LIKE...
...SUCH BRUTISH THINGS.

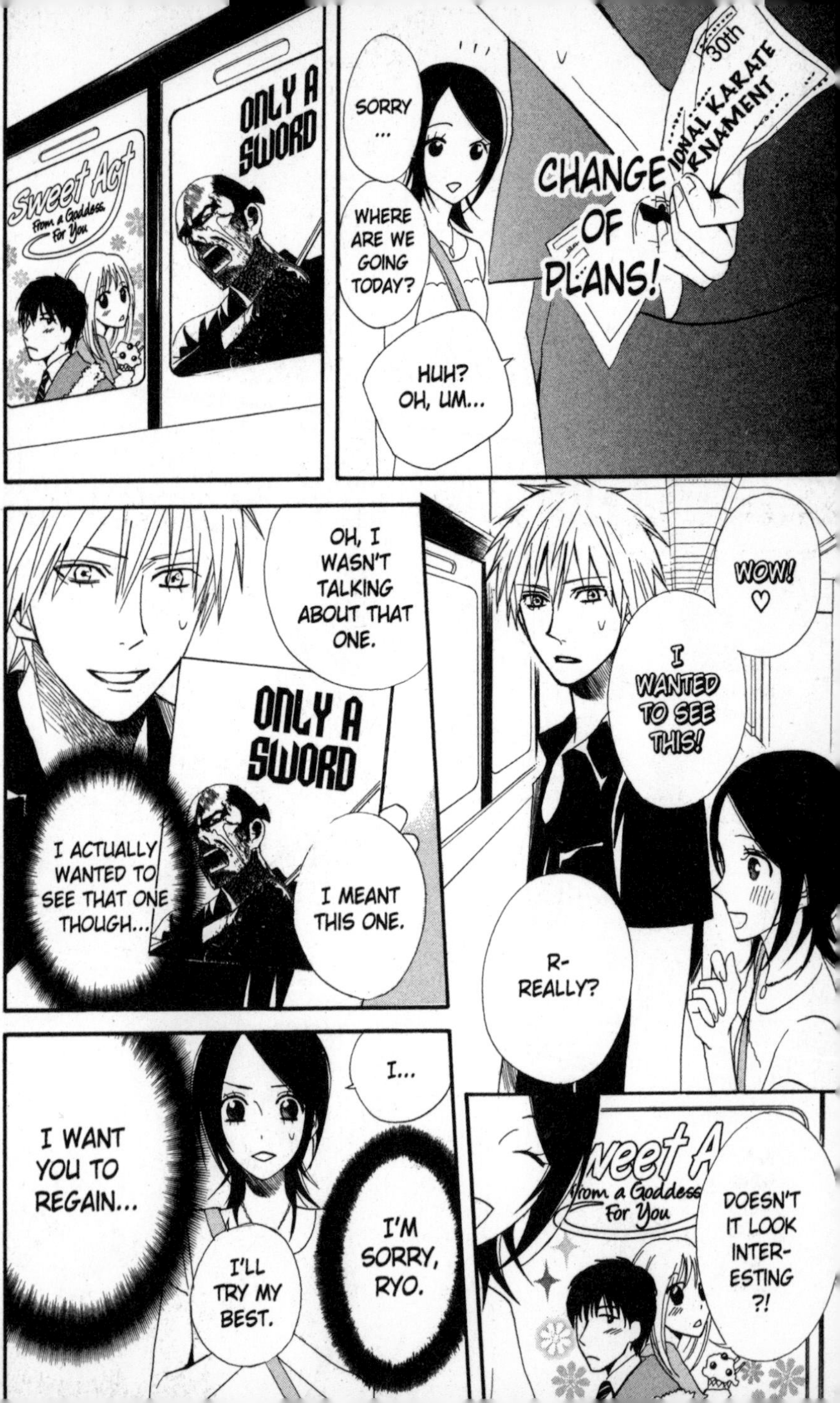
30th
IONAL KARATE
RNAMENT
CHANGE OF PLANS!
SORRY ...
WHERE ARE WE GOING TODAY?
HUH? OH, UM...
ONLY A SWORD
Sweet Act
From a Goddess For You
WOW! ♡
I WANTED TO SEE THIS!
R-REALLY?
OH, I WASN'T TALKING ABOUT THAT ONE.
ONLY A SWORD
I MEANT THIS ONE.
I ACTUALLY WANTED TO SEE THAT ONE THOUGH...
Sweet A
From a Goddess For You
DOESN'T IT LOOK INTER-ESTING?!
I...
I WANT YOU TO REGAIN...
I'M SORRY, RYO.
I'LL TRY MY BEST.

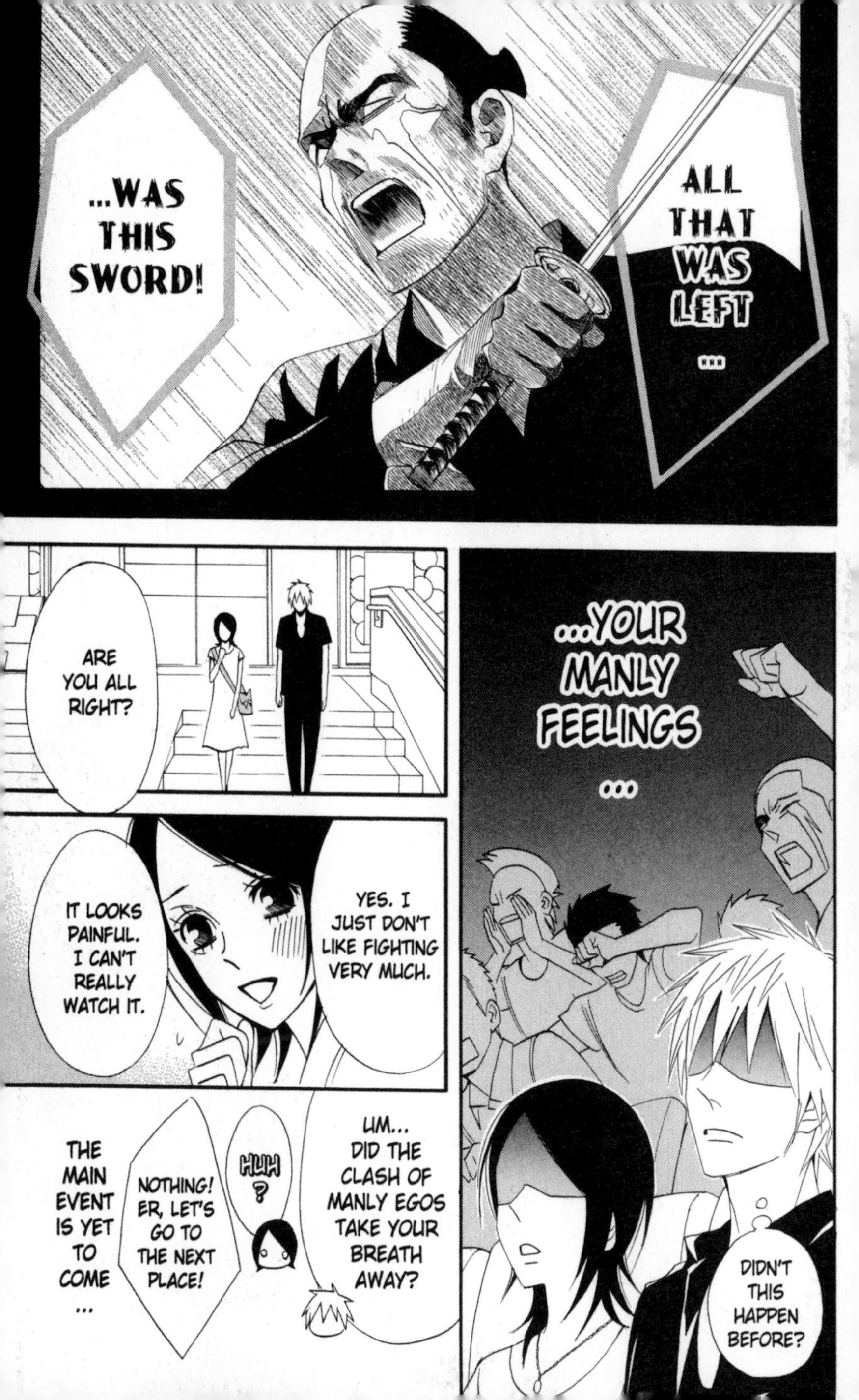
ALL THAT WAS LEFT...
...WAS THIS SWORD!
...YOUR MANLY FEELINGS...
DIDN'T THIS HAPPEN BEFORE?
ARE YOU ALL RIGHT?
YES. I JUST DON'T LIKE FIGHTING VERY MUCH.
IT LOOKS PAINFUL. I CAN'T REALLY WATCH IT.
UM... DID THE CLASH OF MANLY EGOS TAKE YOUR BREATH AWAY?
HUH?
NOTHING! ER, LET'S GO TO THE NEXT PLACE!
THE MAIN EVENT IS YET TO COME...

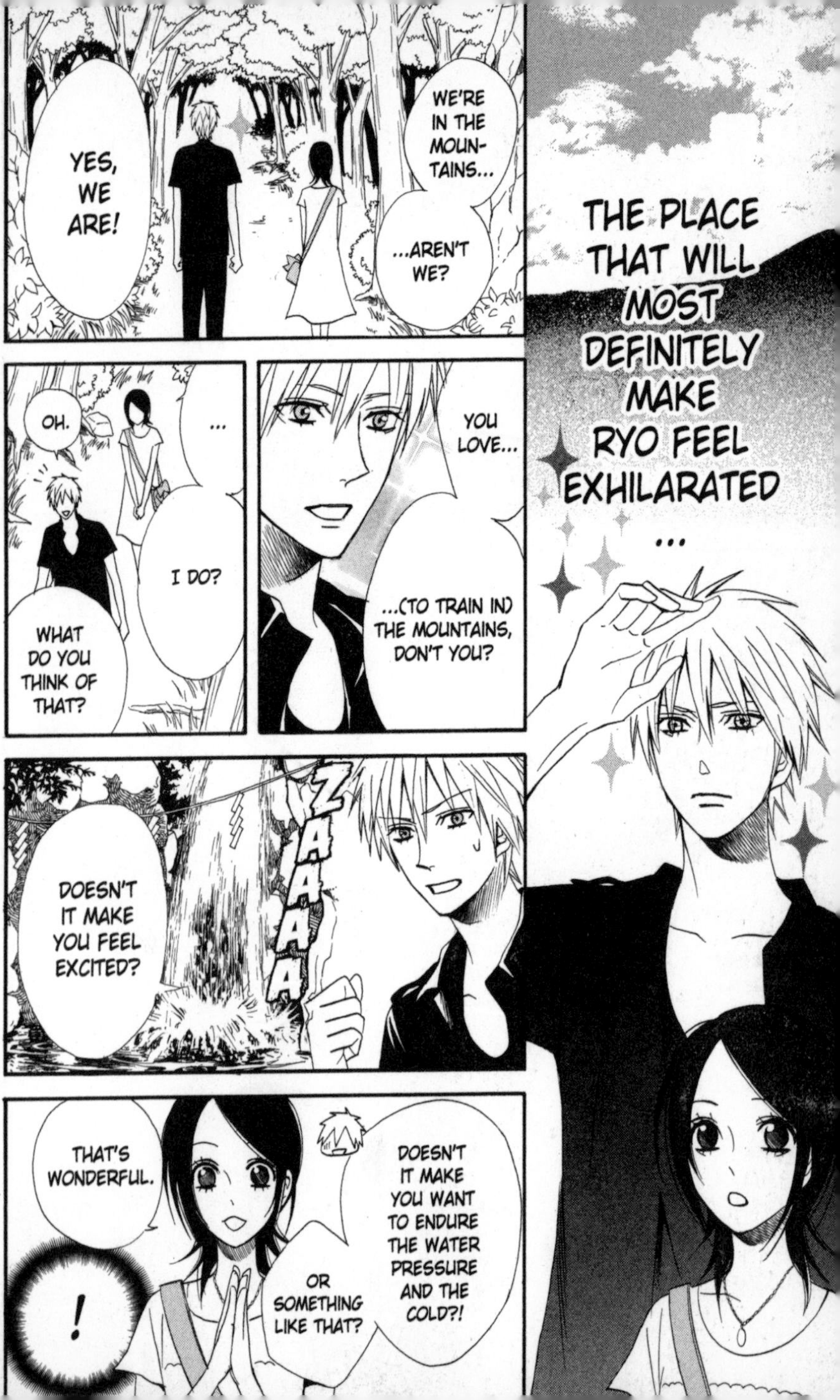
THE PLACE THAT WILL MOST DEFINITELY MAKE RYO FEEL EXHILARATED ...
WE'RE IN THE MOUN-TAINS...
...AREN'T WE?
YES, WE ARE!
YOU LOVE...
...(TO TRAIN IN) THE MOUNTAINS, DON'T YOU?
...
OH.
I DO?
WHAT DO YOU THINK OF THAT?
ZAAAAA
DOESN'T IT MAKE YOU FEEL EXCITED?
DOESN'T IT MAKE YOU WANT TO ENDURE THE WATER PRESSURE AND THE COLD?!
OR SOMETHING LIKE THAT?
THAT'S WONDERFUL.
!

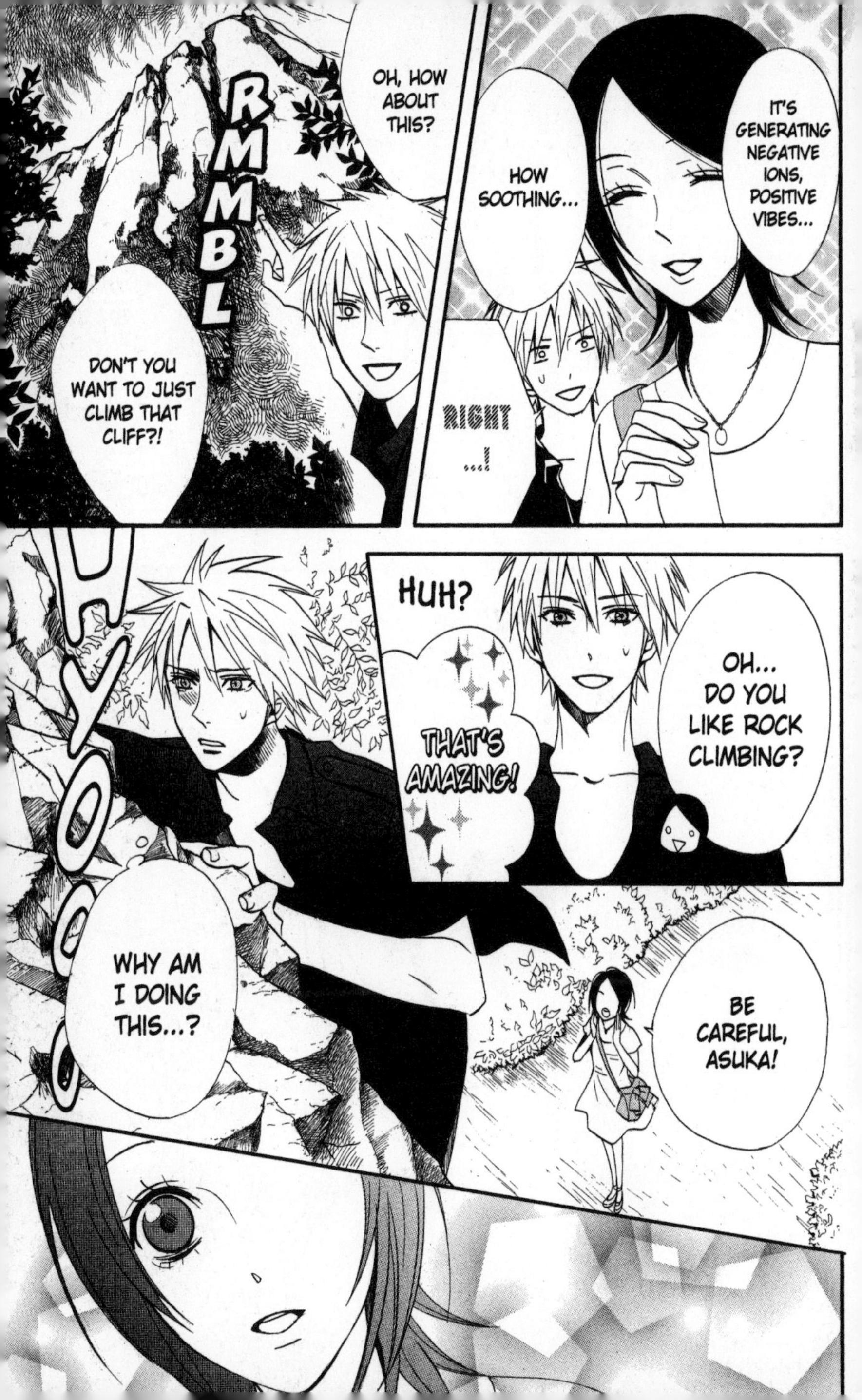
IT'S GENERATING NEGATIVE IONS, POSITIVE VIBES...
HOW SOOTHING...
RIGHT ...!
OH, HOW ABOUT THIS?
RMMBL
DON'T YOU WANT TO JUST CLIMB THAT CLIFF?!
OH... DO YOU LIKE ROCK CLIMBING?
HUH?
THAT'S AMAZING!
BE CAREFUL, ASUKA!
HYOOO
WHY AM I DOING THIS...?

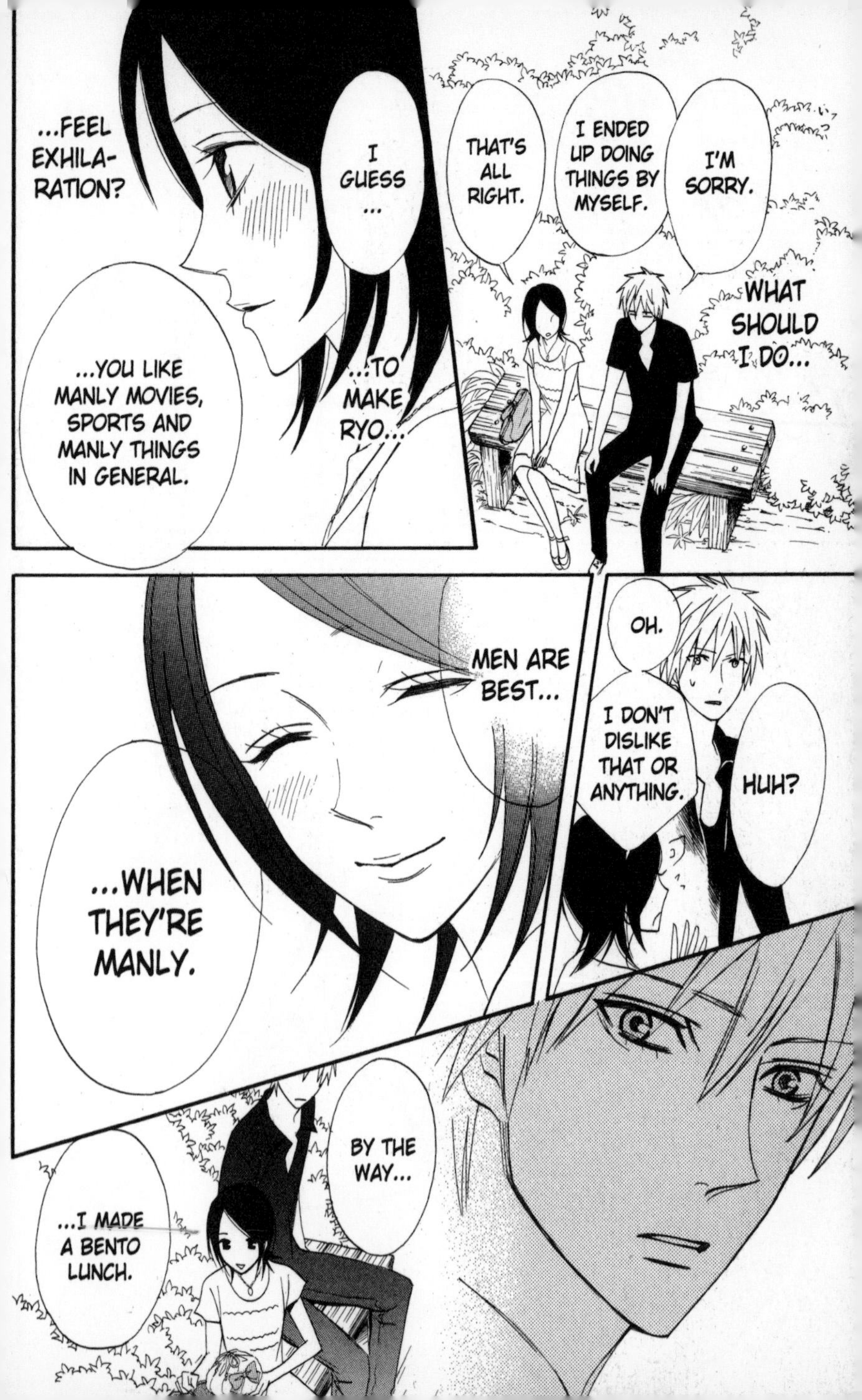
I'M SORRY.
I ENDED UP DOING THINGS BY MYSELF.
THAT'S ALL RIGHT.
WHAT SHOULD I DO...
I GUESS...
...TO MAKE RYO...
...FEEL EXHILARATION?
...YOU LIKE MANLY MOVIES, SPORTS AND MANLY THINGS IN GENERAL.
OH.
HUH?
I DON'T DISLIKE THAT OR ANYTHING.
MEN ARE BEST...
...WHEN THEY'RE MANLY.
BY THE WAY...
...I MADE A BENTO LUNCH.

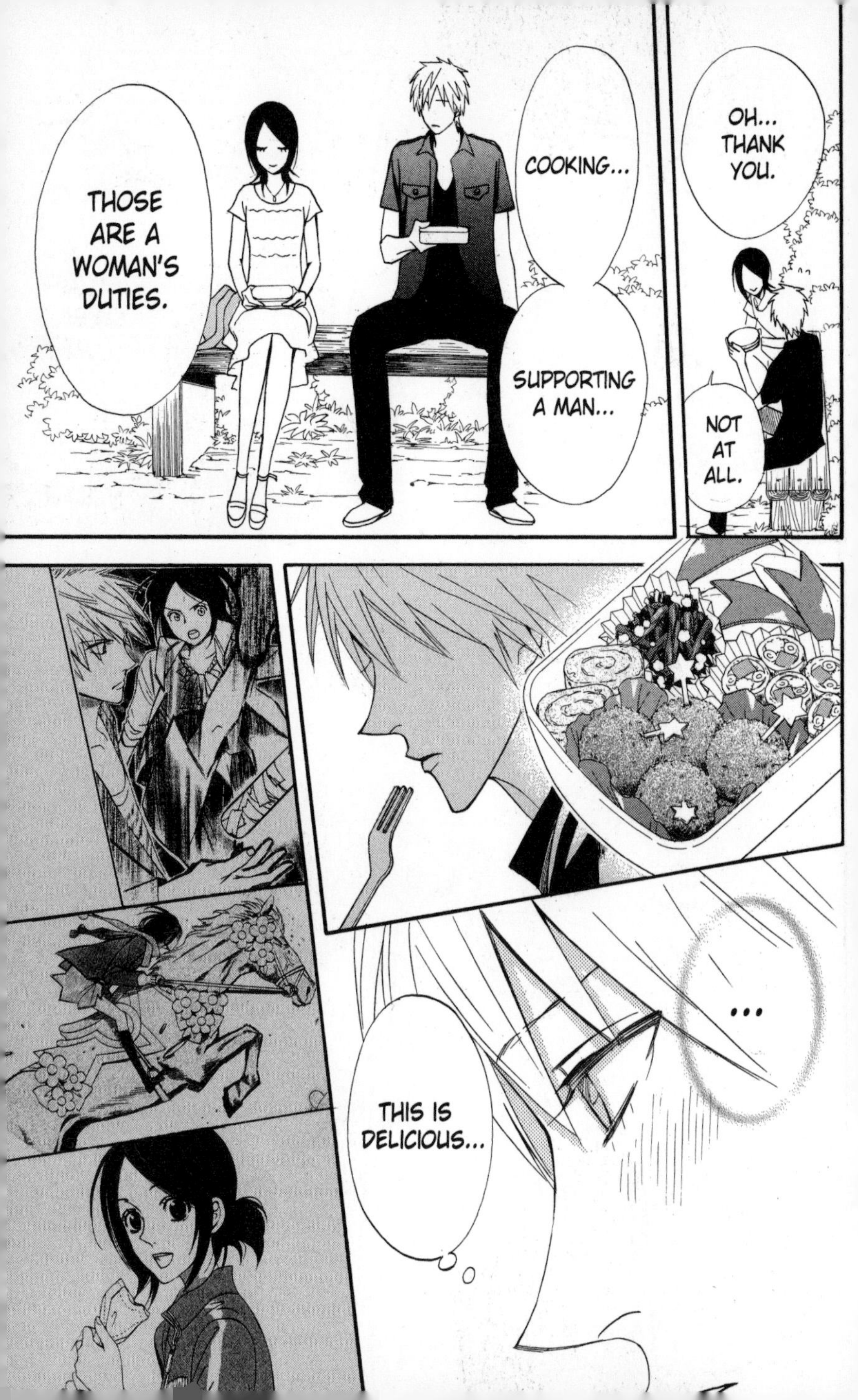
OH... THANK YOU.
NOT AT ALL.
COOKING...
SUPPORTING A MAN...
THOSE ARE A WOMAN'S DUTIES.
...
THIS IS DELICIOUS...

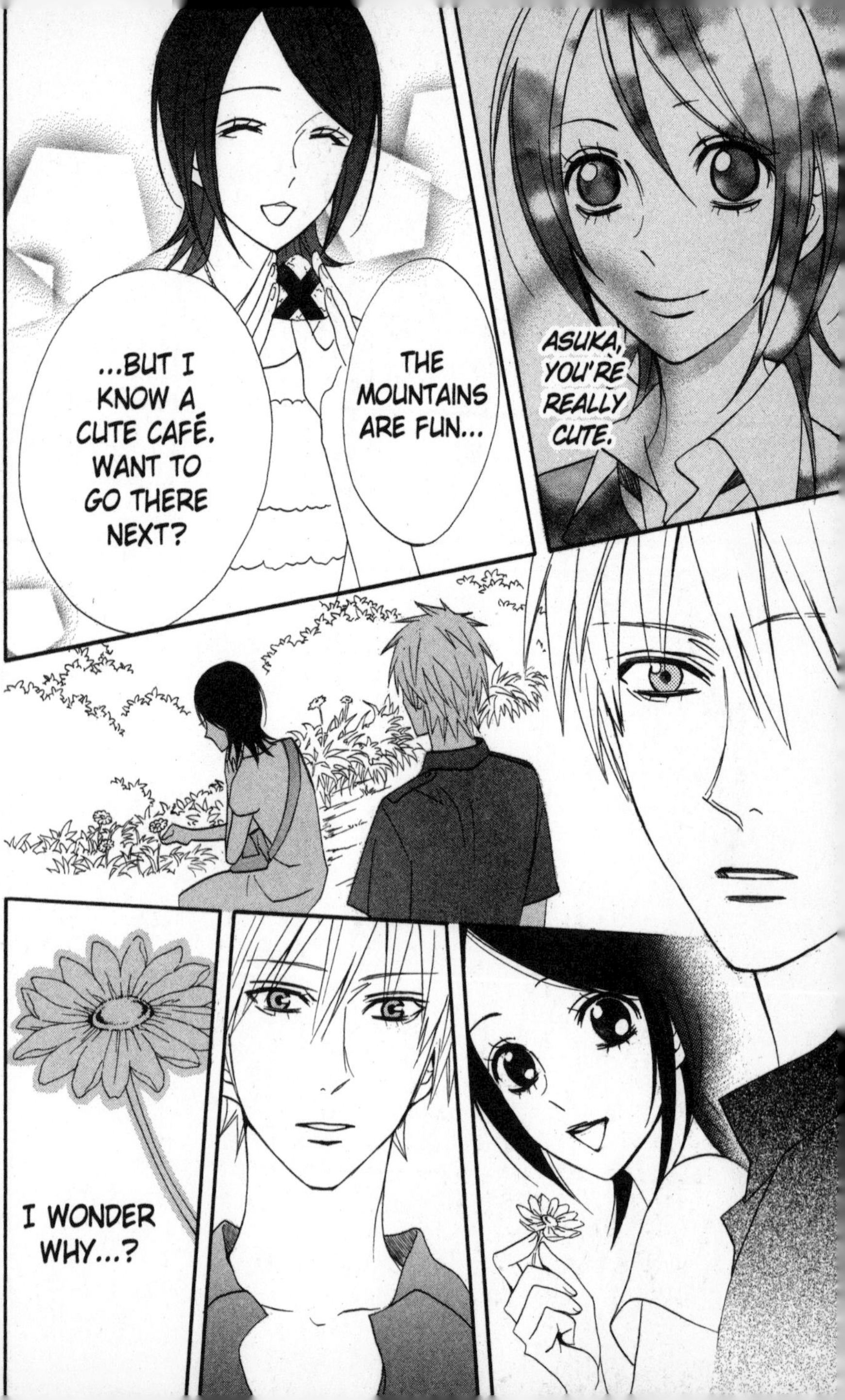
ASUKA, YOU'RE REALLY CUTE.
THE MOUNTAINS ARE FUN...
...BUT I KNOW A CUTE CAFÉ. WANT TO GO THERE NEXT?
I WONDER WHY...?

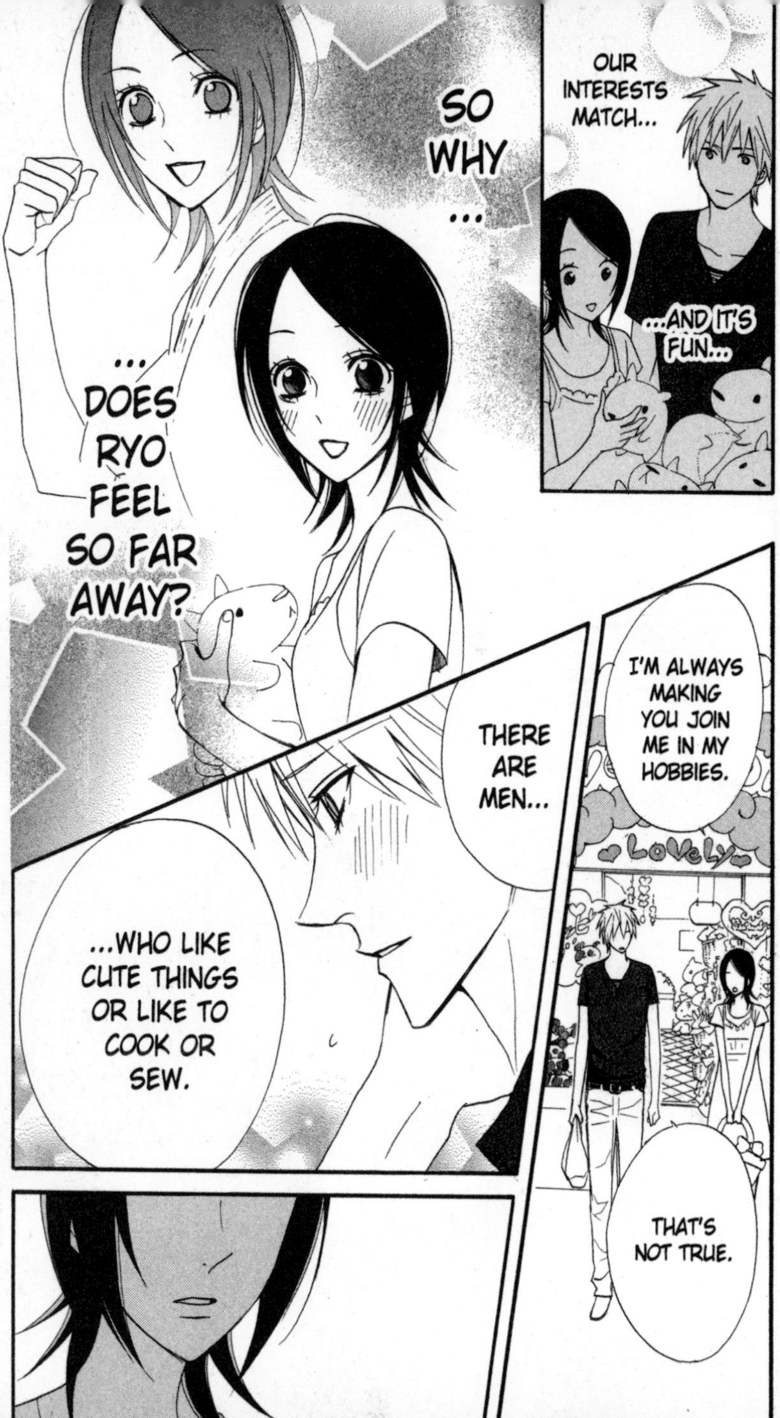
OUR INTERESTS MATCH...
...AND IT'S FUN...
SO WHY...
...DOES RYO FEEL SO FAR AWAY?
I'M ALWAYS MAKING YOU JOIN ME IN MY HOBBIES.
LoVeLy
THAT'S NOT TRUE.
THERE ARE MEN...
...WHO LIKE CUTE THINGS OR LIKE TO COOK OR SEW.

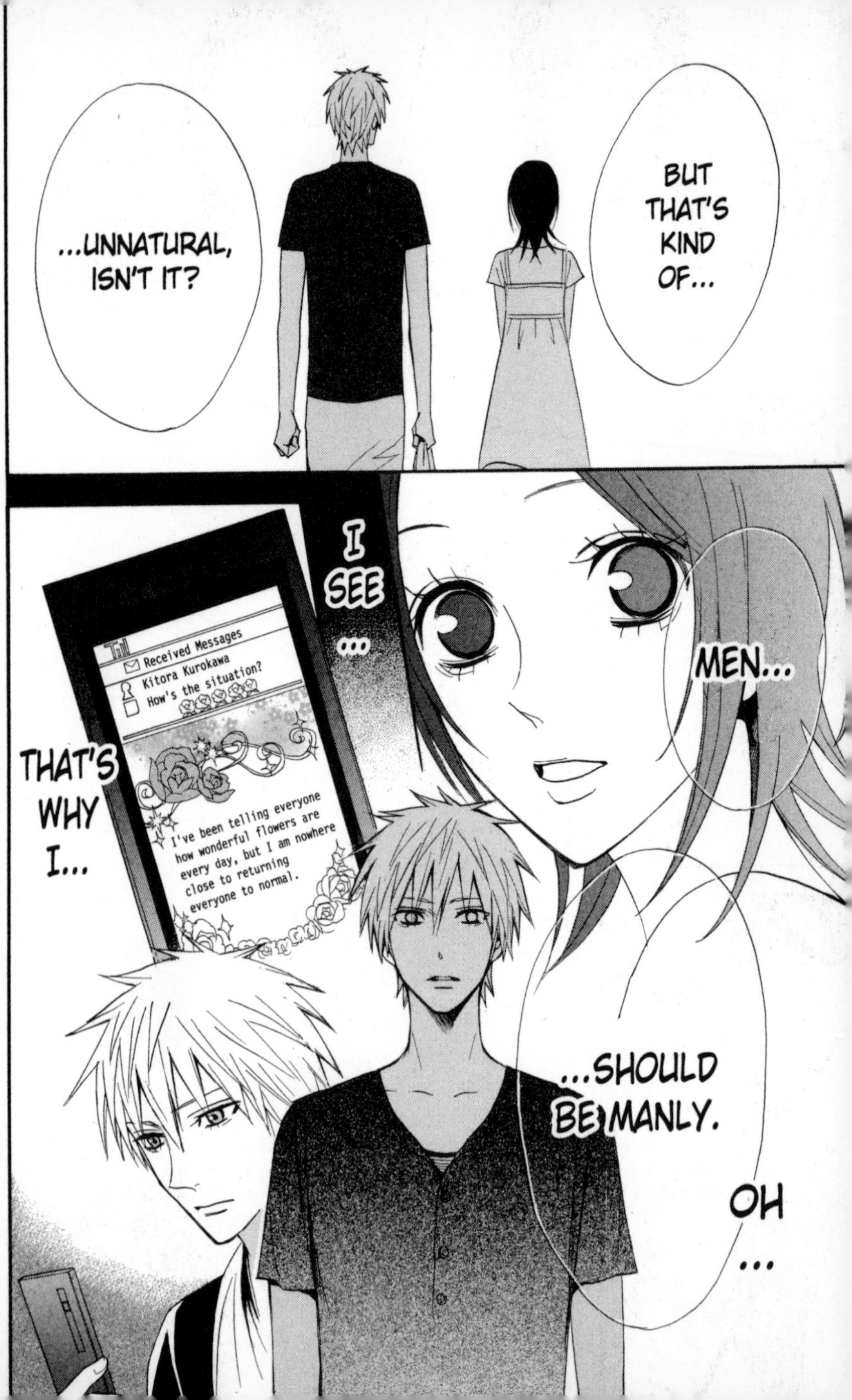
BUT THAT'S KIND OF...
...UNNATURAL, ISN'T IT?
I SEE...
MEN...
Received Messages
Kitora Kurokawa
How's the situation?
I've been telling everyone how wonderful flowers are every day, but I am nowhere close to returning everyone to normal.
THAT'S WHY I...
...SHOULD BE MANLY.
OH...

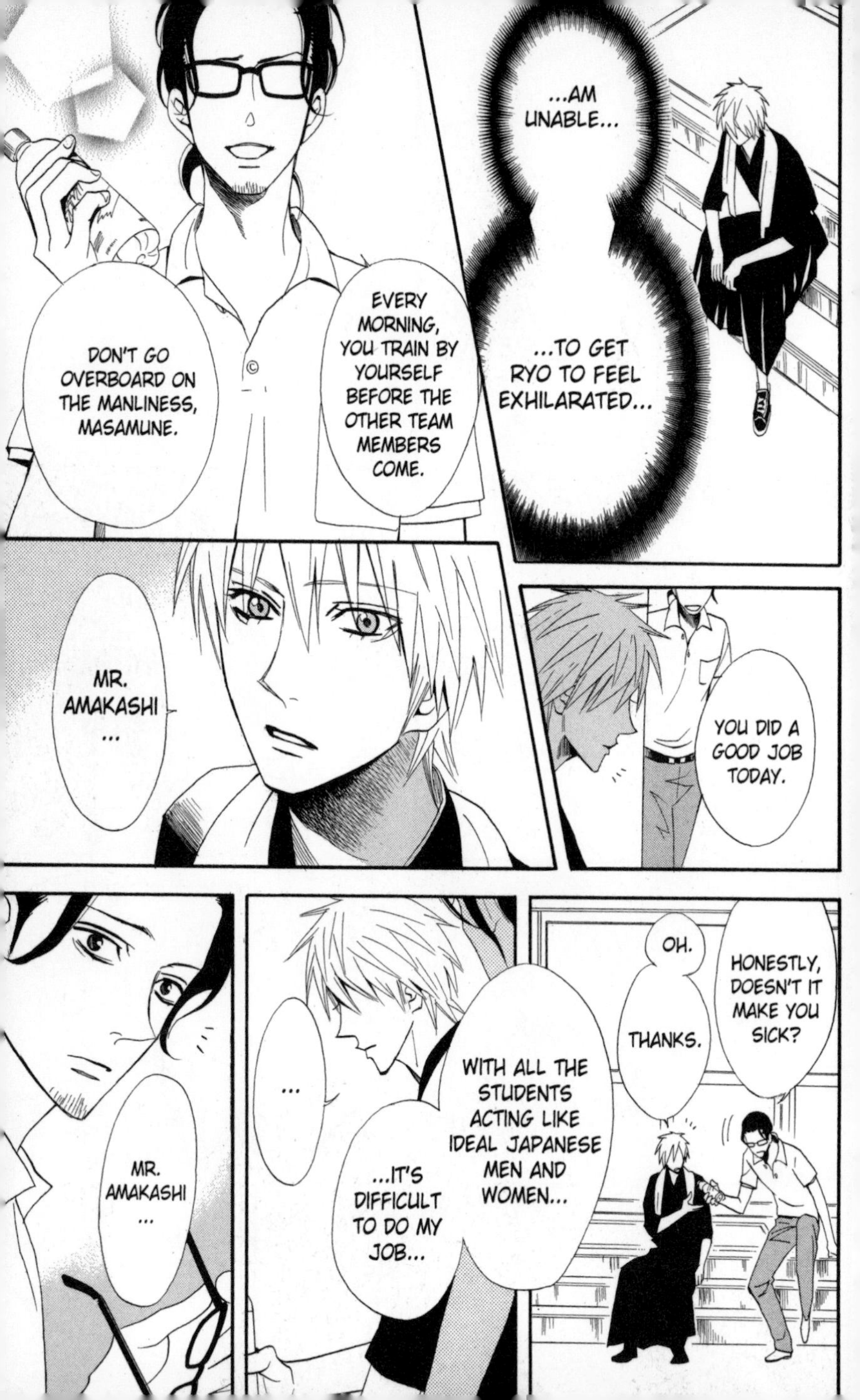
...AM UNABLE...
...TO GET RYO TO FEEL EXHILARATED...
EVERY MORNING, YOU TRAIN BY YOURSELF BEFORE THE OTHER TEAM MEMBERS COME.
DON'T GO OVERBOARD ON THE MANLINESS, MASAMUNE.
YOU DID A GOOD JOB TODAY.
MR. AMAKASHI...
HONESTLY, DOESN'T IT MAKE YOU SICK?
OH.
THANKS.
WITH ALL THE STUDENTS ACTING LIKE IDEAL JAPANESE MEN AND WOMEN...
...IT'S DIFFICULT TO DO MY JOB...
...
MR. AMAKASHI...

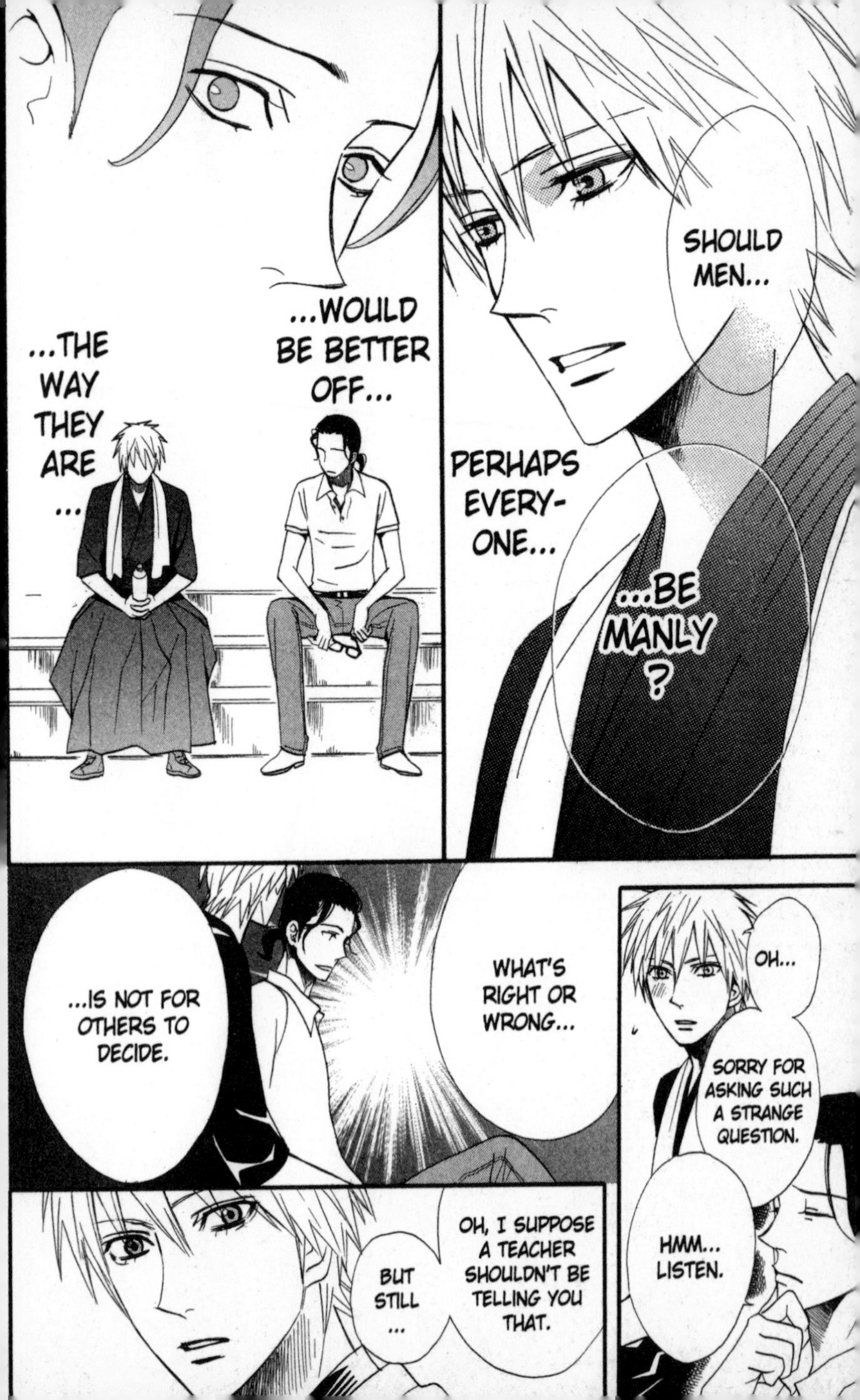
SHOULD MEN...
...BE MANLY?
PERHAPS EVERY-ONE...
...WOULD BE BETTER OFF...
...THE WAY THEY ARE...
OH...
SORRY FOR ASKING SUCH A STRANGE QUESTION.
HMM... LISTEN.
WHAT'S RIGHT OR WRONG...
...IS NOT FOR OTHERS TO DECIDE.
OH, I SUPPOSE A TEACHER SHOULDN'T BE TELLING YOU THAT.
BUT STILL...

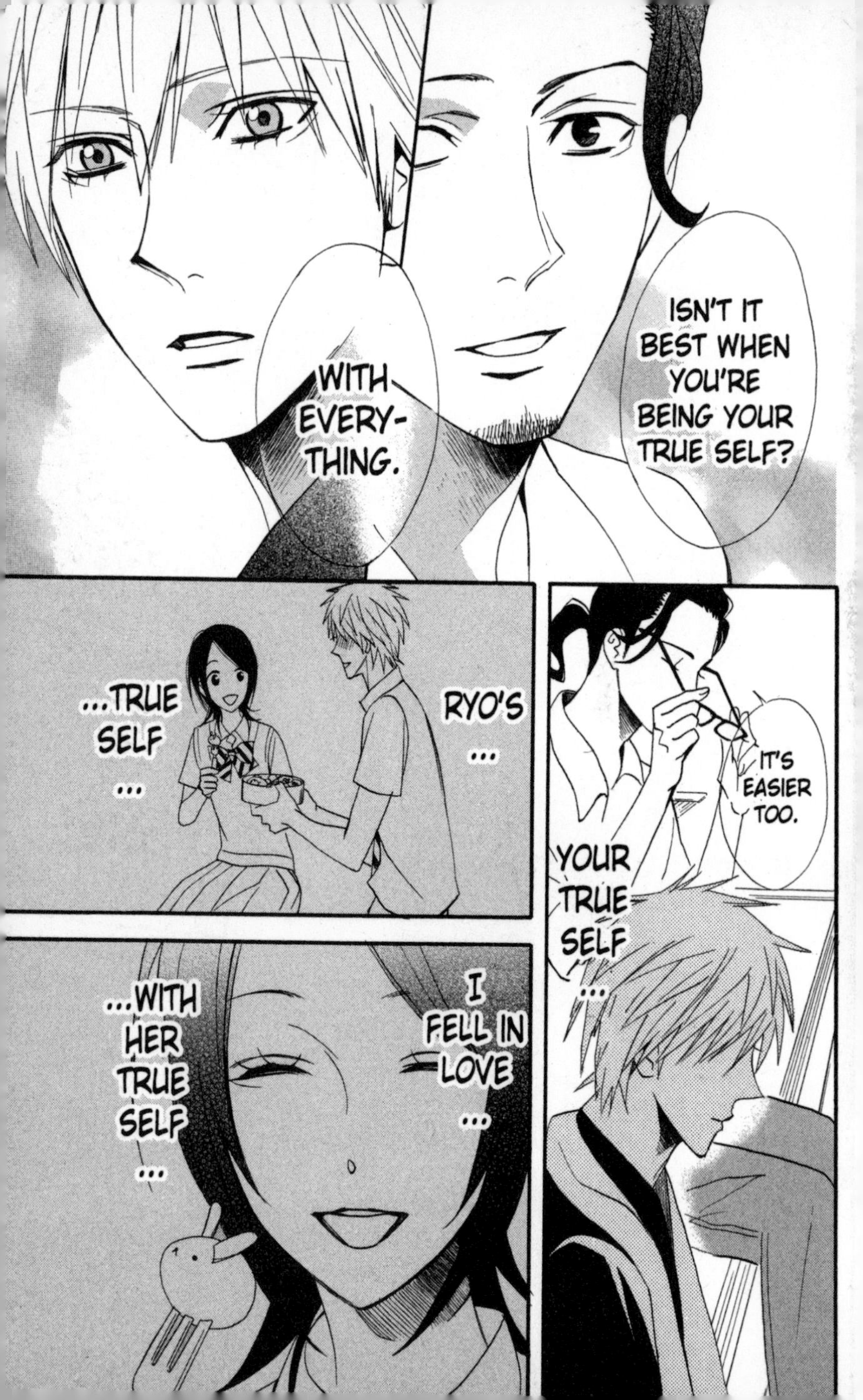
ISN'T IT BEST WHEN YOU'RE BEING YOUR TRUE SELF?
WITH EVERY-THING.
IT'S EASIER TOO.
YOUR TRUE SELF...
RYO'S...
...TRUE SELF...
I FELL IN LOVE...
...WITH HER TRUE SELF...

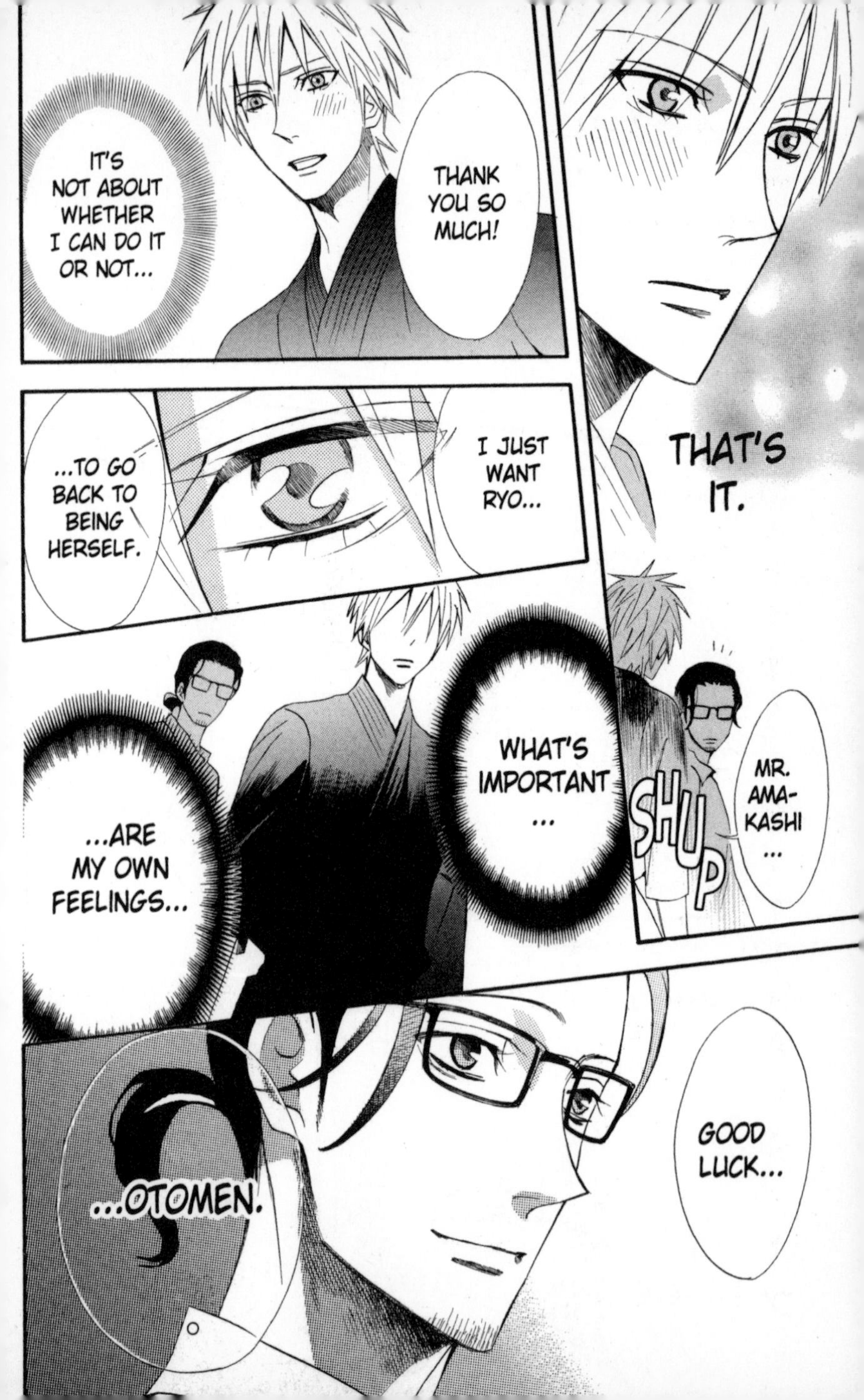
THAT'S IT.
THANK YOU SO MUCH!
IT'S NOT ABOUT WHETHER I CAN DO IT OR NOT...
I JUST WANT RYO...
...TO GO BACK TO BEING HERSELF.
MR. AMA-KASHI...
SHUP
WHAT'S IMPORTANT...
...ARE MY OWN FEELINGS...
GOOD LUCK...
...OTOMEN.

Production Assistance:

Shimada-san
Takowa-san
Kuwana-san
Kaneko-san
Sakurai-san
Nakazawa-san
Tanaka-san
Kawashima-san
Sayaka-san
Yone-yan

Special Thanks:

Abe-san
Babiccho-san
All My Readers

I hope you'll stick around for the next volume.

By the way, there's another column left.

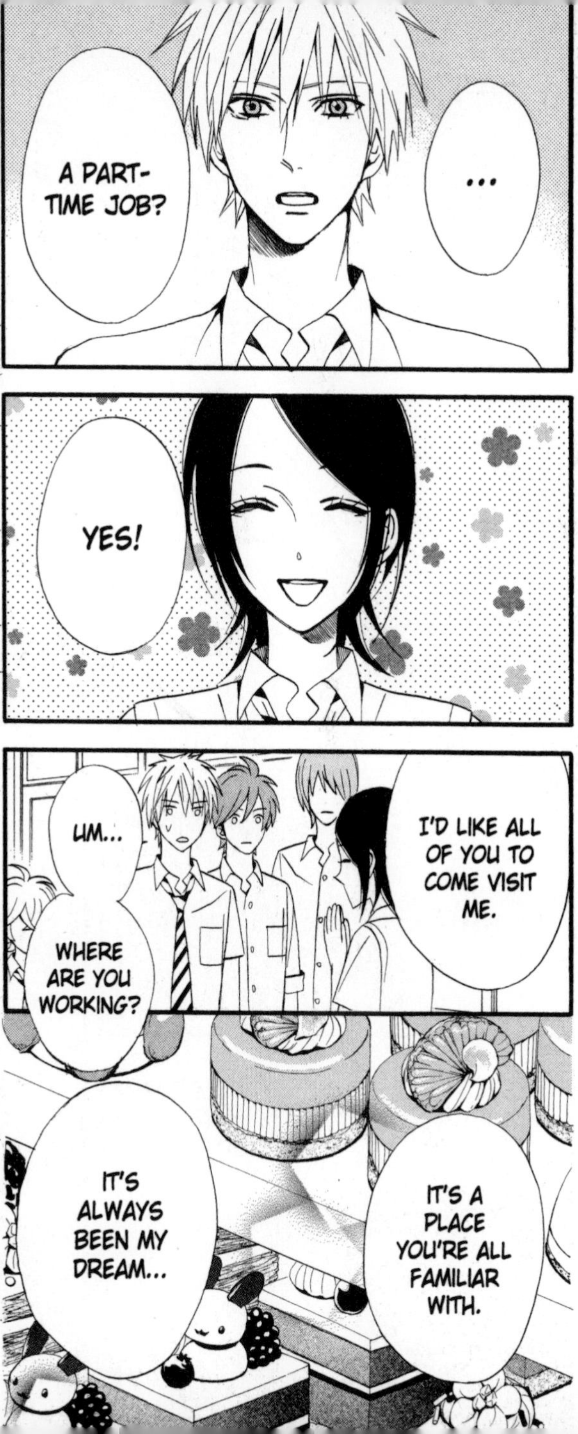
...
A PART-TIME JOB?
YES!
I'D LIKE ALL OF YOU TO COME VISIT ME.
UM...
WHERE ARE YOU WORKING?
IT'S A PLACE YOU'RE ALL FAMILIAR WITH.
IT'S ALWAYS BEEN MY DREAM...

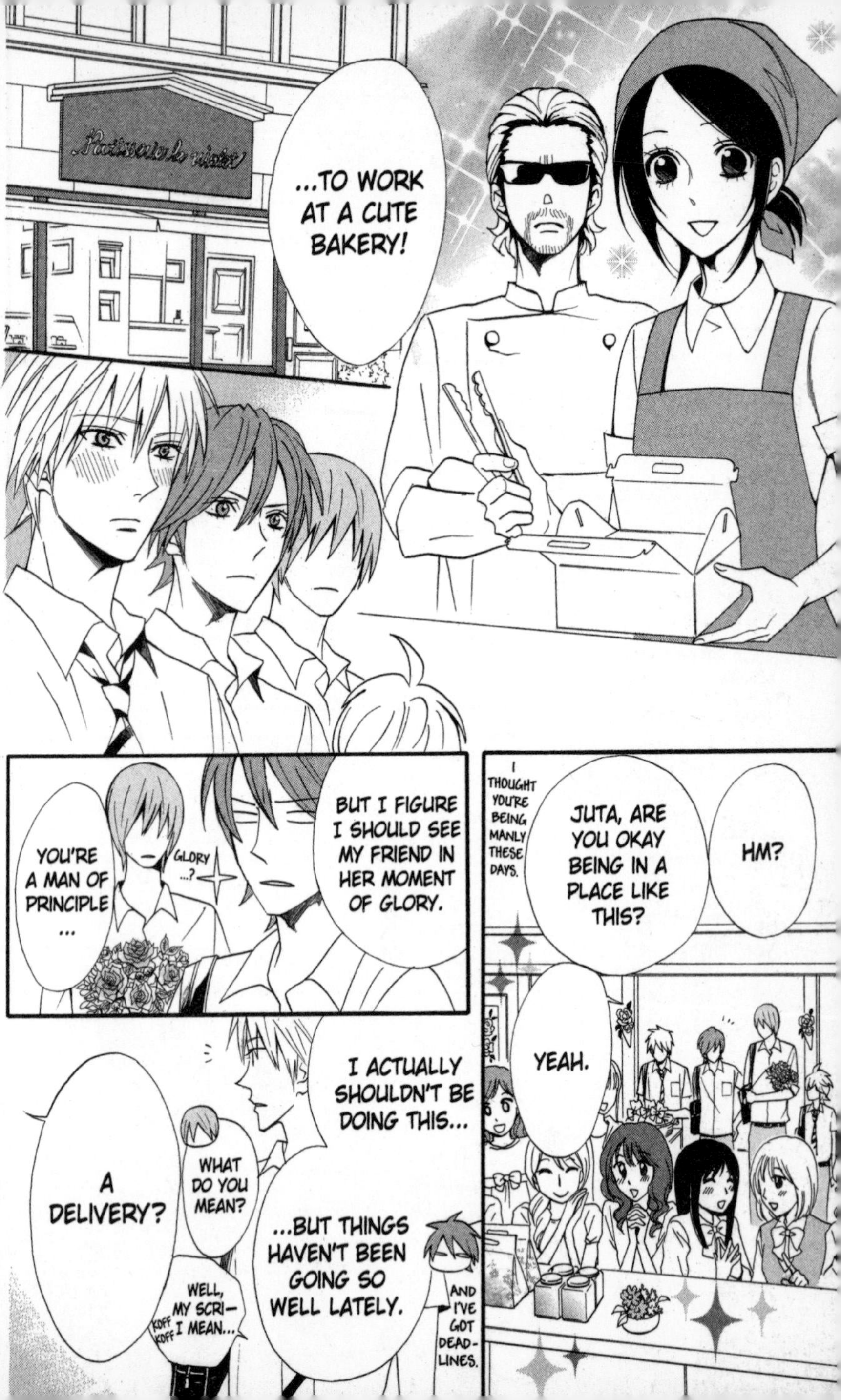
...TO WORK AT A CUTE BAKERY!
HM?
JUTA, ARE YOU OKAY BEING IN A PLACE LIKE THIS?
I THOUGHT YOU'RE BEING MANLY THESE DAYS.
YEAH.
BUT I FIGURE I SHOULD SEE MY FRIEND IN HER MOMENT OF GLORY.
GLORY ...?
YOU'RE A MAN OF PRINCIPLE ...
I ACTUALLY SHOULDN'T BE DOING THIS...
...BUT THINGS HAVEN'T BEEN GOING SO WELL LATELY.
AND I'VE GOT DEAD-LINES.
WHAT DO YOU MEAN?
WELL, MY SCRI— I MEAN...
KOFF KOFF
A DELIVERY?

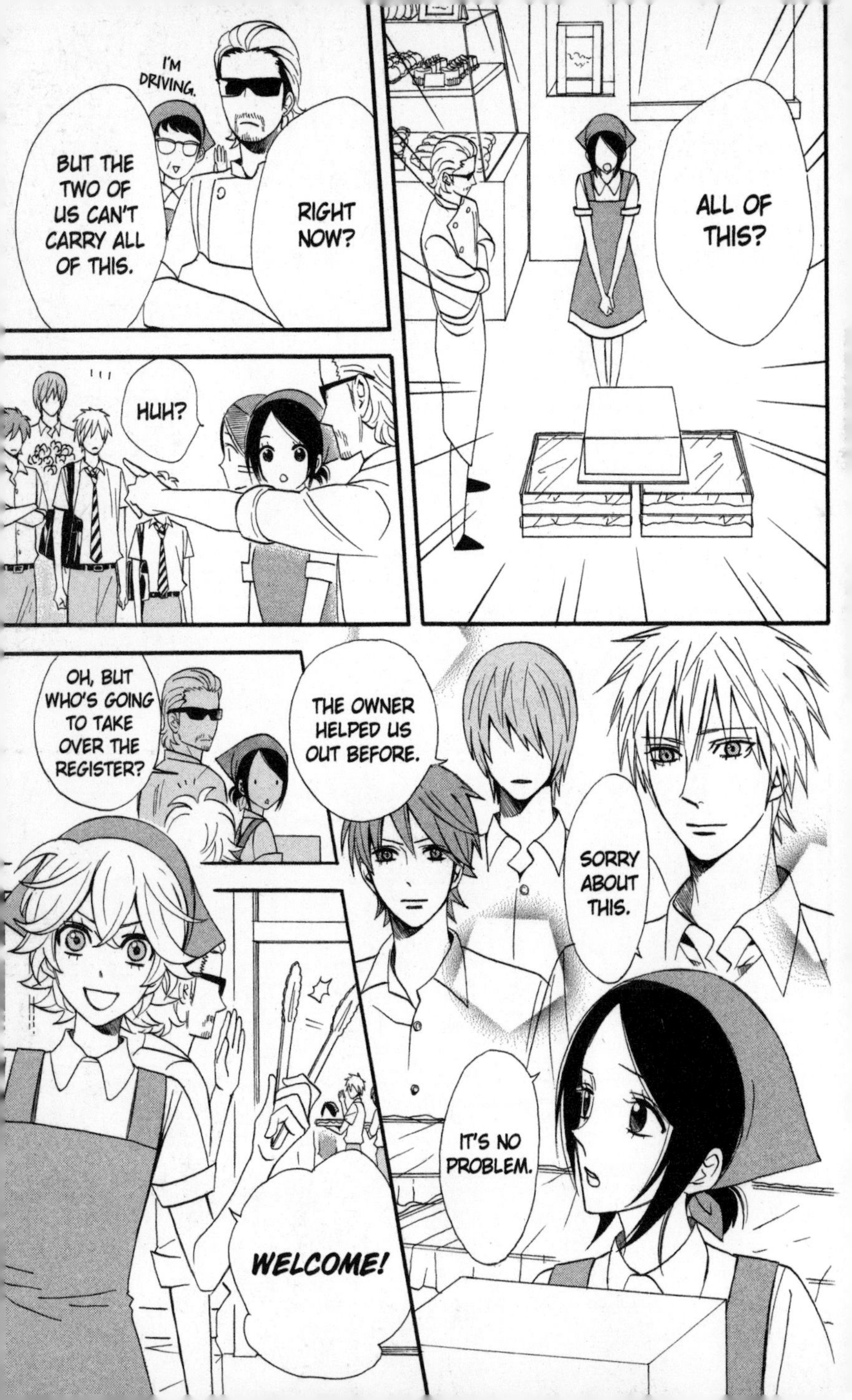
ALL OF THIS?
RIGHT NOW?
I'M DRIVING.
BUT THE TWO OF US CAN'T CARRY ALL OF THIS.
HUH?
SORRY ABOUT THIS.
THE OWNER HELPED US OUT BEFORE.
OH, BUT WHO'S GOING TO TAKE OVER THE REGISTER?
IT'S NO PROBLEM.
WELCOME!

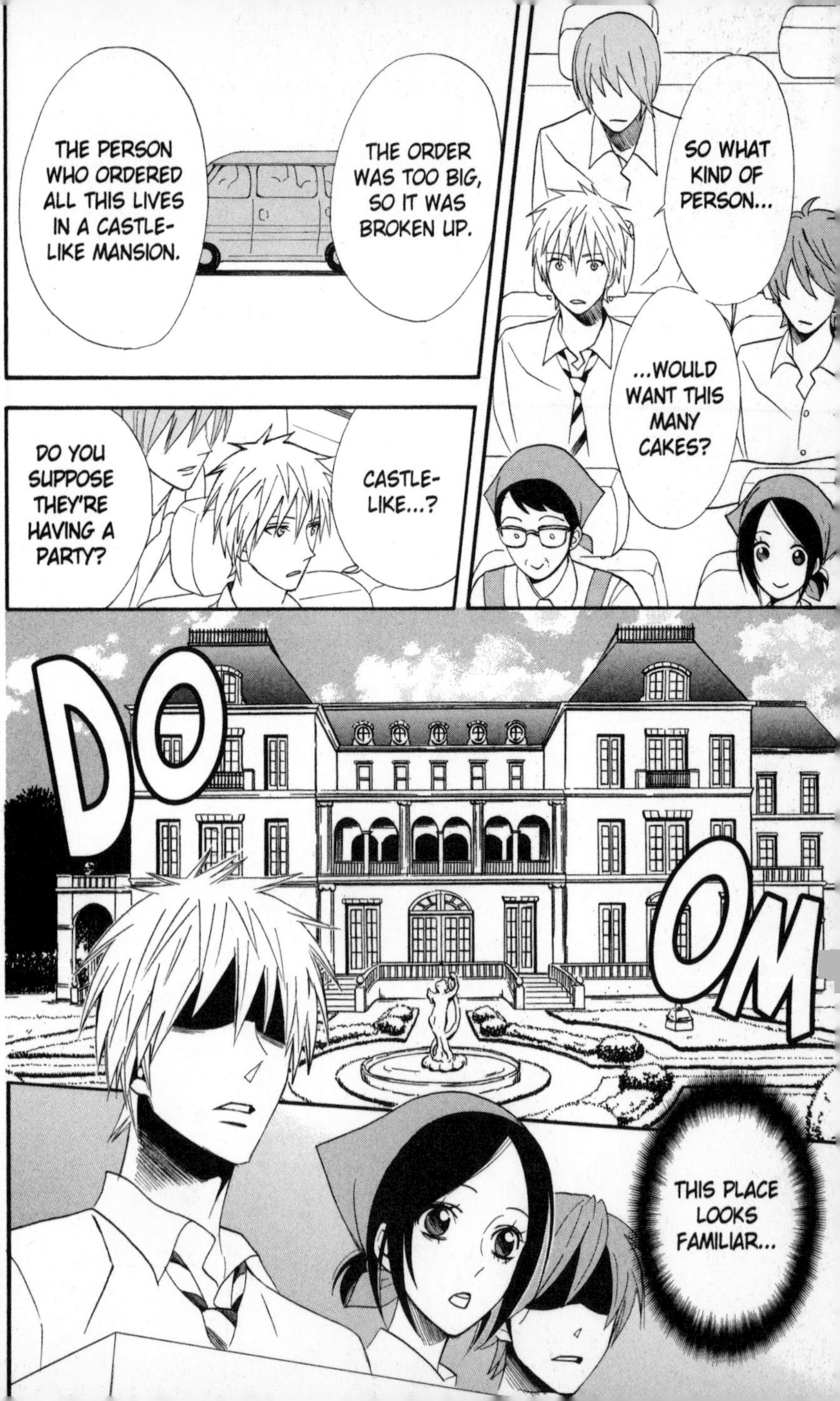
SO WHAT KIND OF PERSON...
...WOULD WANT THIS MANY CAKES?
THE ORDER WAS TOO BIG, SO IT WAS BROKEN UP.
THE PERSON WHO ORDERED ALL THIS LIVES IN A CASTLE-LIKE MANSION.
CASTLE-LIKE...?
DO YOU SUPPOSE THEY'RE HAVING A PARTY?
DOOM
THIS PLACE LOOKS FAMILIAR...

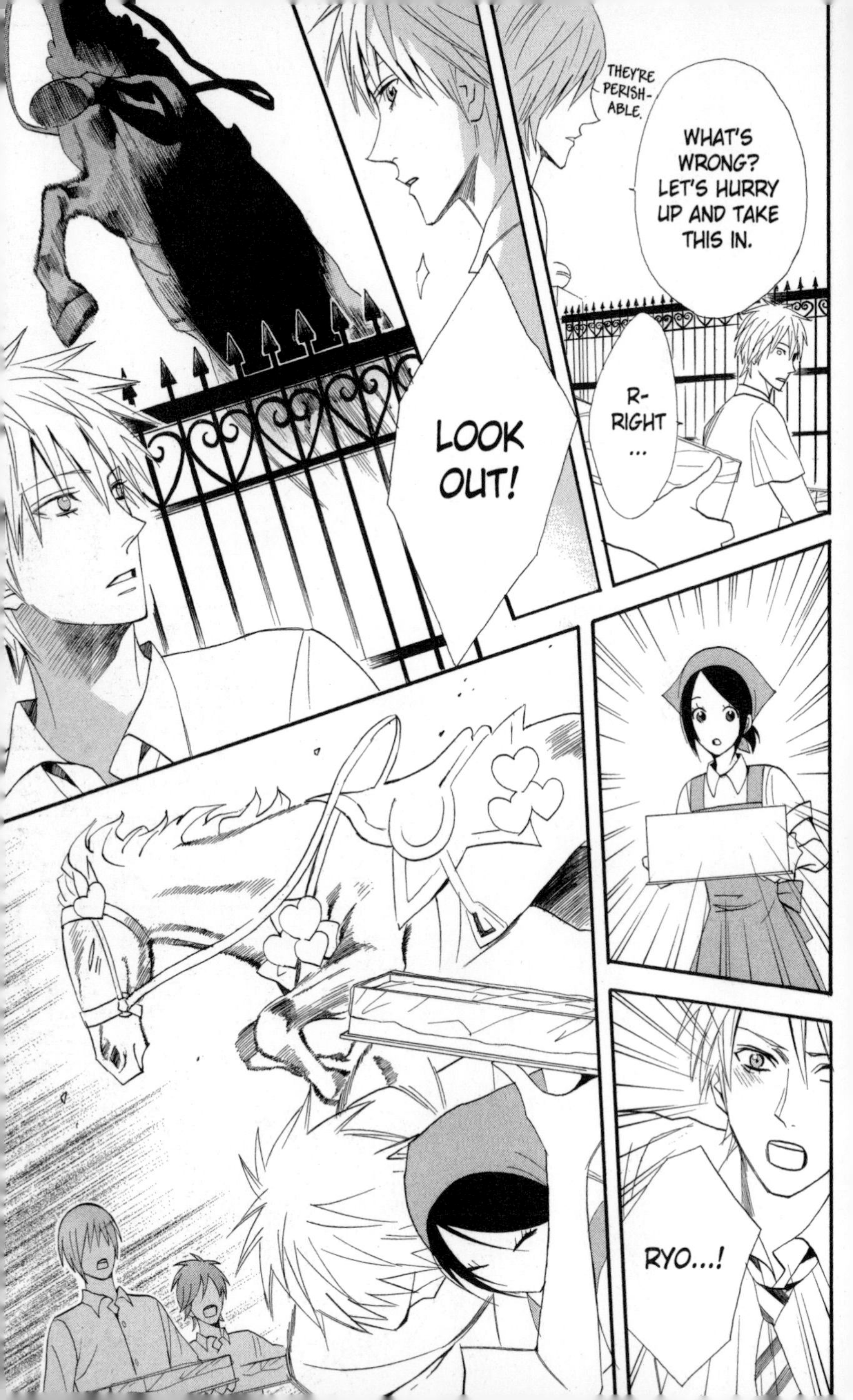
WHAT'S WRONG? LET'S HURRY UP AND TAKE THIS IN.
THEY'RE PERISH-ABLE.
R-RIGHT...
LOOK OUT!
RYO...!

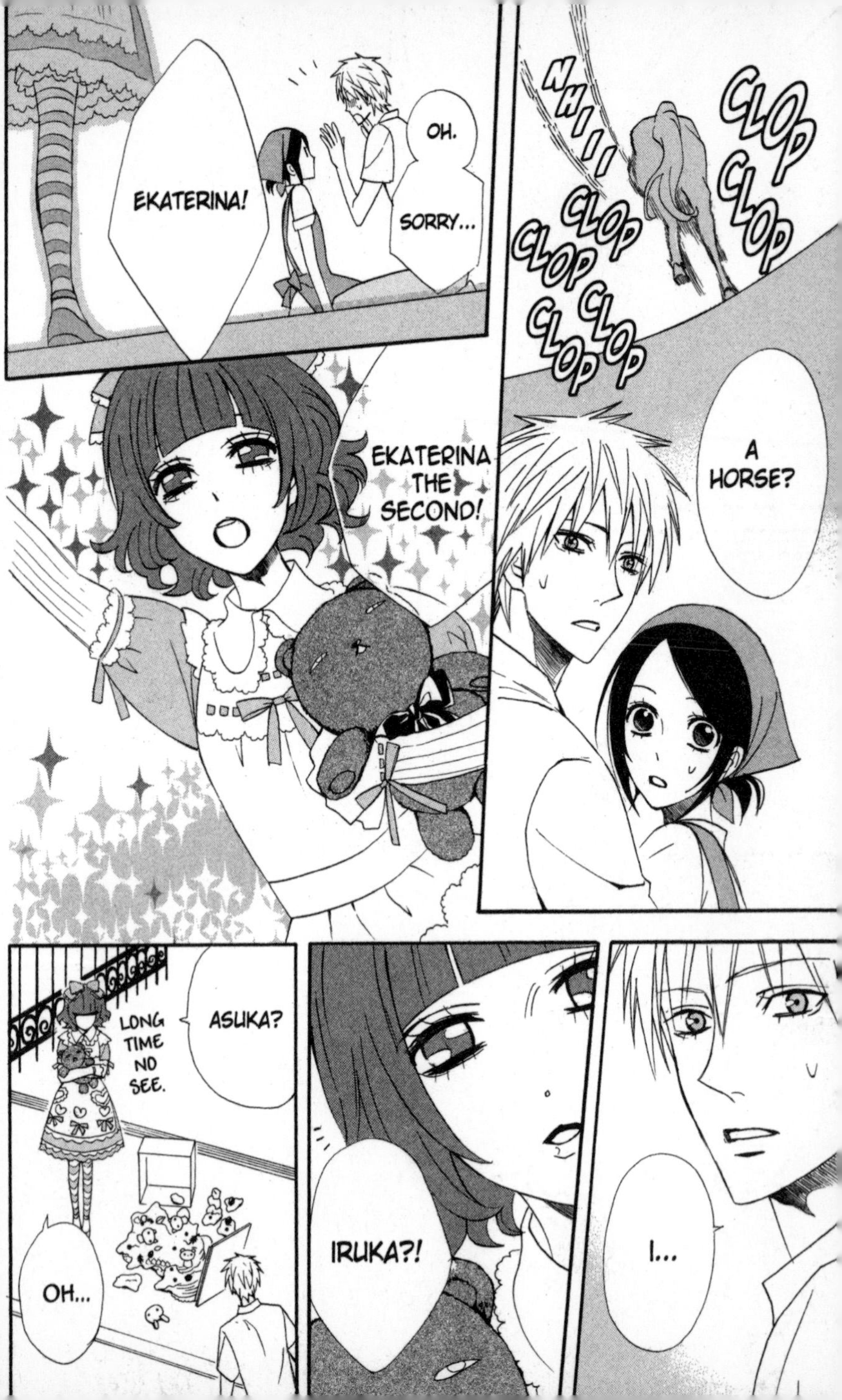

NHIII
CLOP CLOP
CLOP CLOP
CLOP CLOP
CLOP CLOP
A HORSE?
OH.
SORRY...
EKATERINA!
EKATERINA THE SECOND!
I...
IRUKA?!
ASUKA?
LONG TIME NO SEE.
OH...

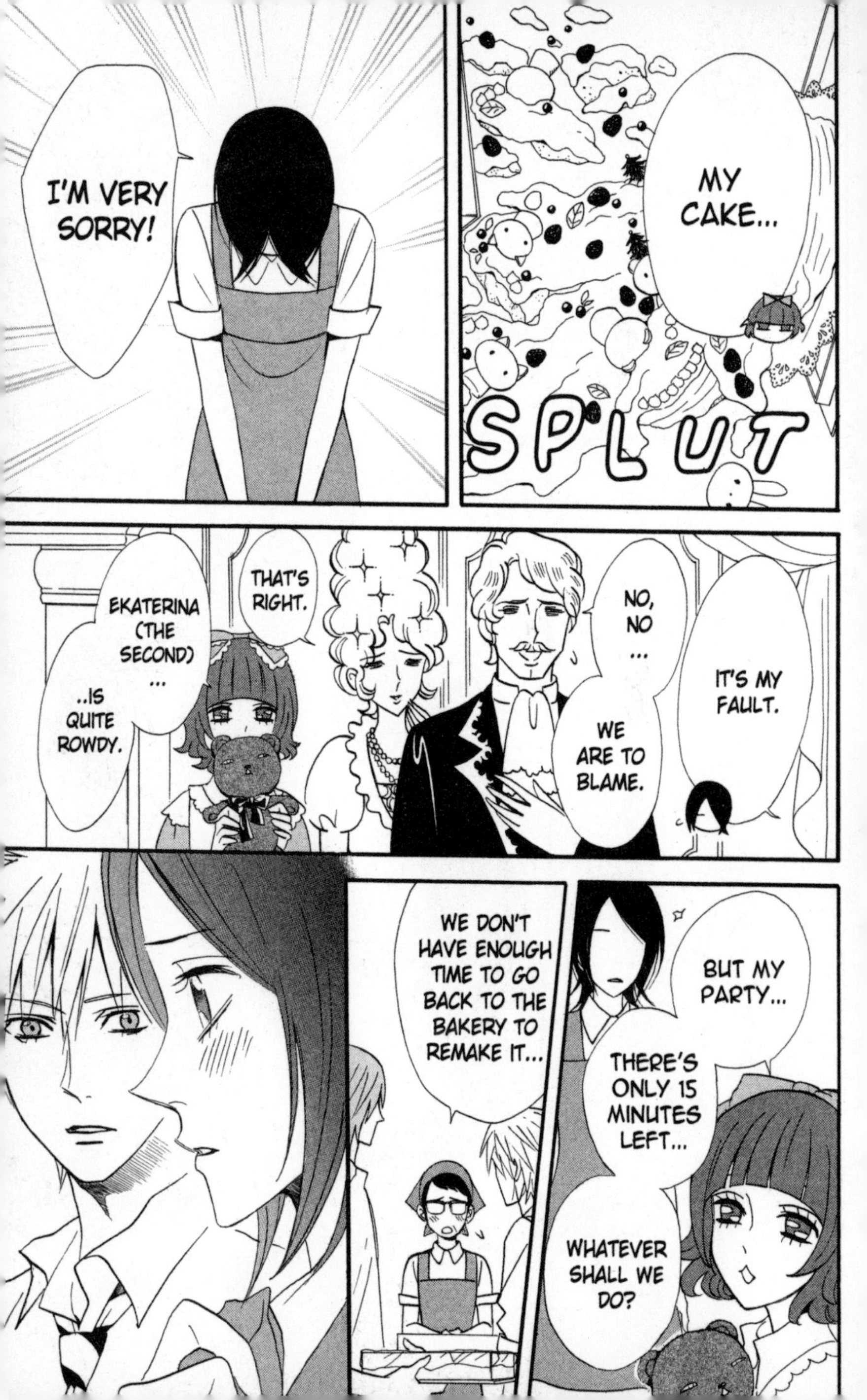
MY CAKE...
SPLUT
I'M VERY SORRY!
IT'S MY FAULT.
NO, NO ...
WE ARE TO BLAME.
THAT'S RIGHT.
EKATERINA (THE SECOND) ...
..IS QUITE ROWDY.
BUT MY PARTY...
THERE'S ONLY 15 MINUTES LEFT...
WHATEVER SHALL WE DO?
WE DON'T HAVE ENOUGH TIME TO GO BACK TO THE BAKERY TO REMAKE IT...

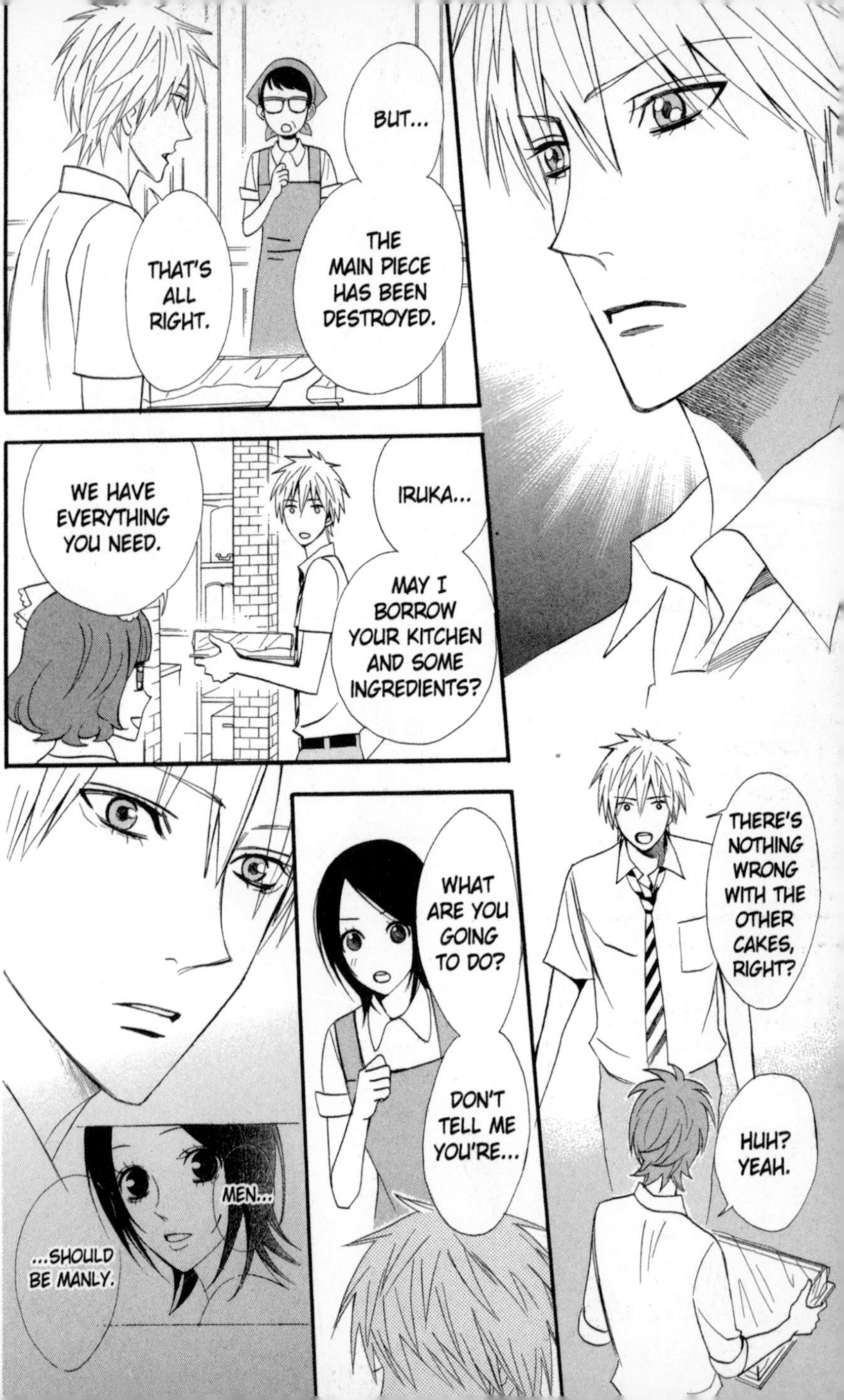
BUT...
THE MAIN PIECE HAS BEEN DESTROYED.
THAT'S ALL RIGHT.
IRUKA...
MAY I BORROW YOUR KITCHEN AND SOME INGREDIENTS?
WE HAVE EVERYTHING YOU NEED.
THERE'S NOTHING WRONG WITH THE OTHER CAKES, RIGHT?
HUH? YEAH.
WHAT ARE YOU GOING TO DO?
DON'T TELL ME YOU'RE...
MEN...
...SHOULD BE MANLY.

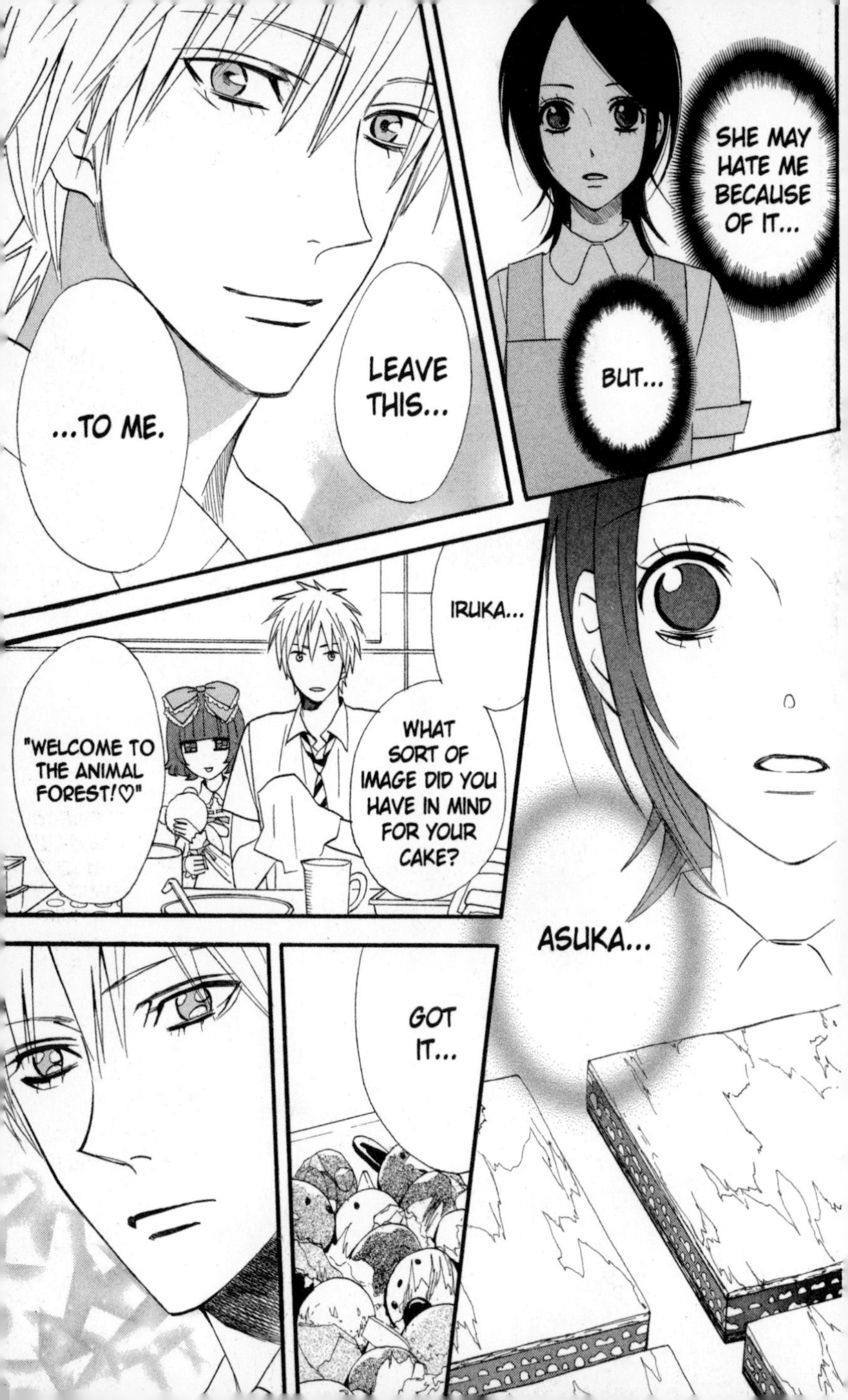
SHE MAY HATE ME BECAUSE OF IT...
BUT...
LEAVE THIS...
...TO ME.
ASUKA...
IRUKA...
WHAT SORT OF IMAGE DID YOU HAVE IN MIND FOR YOUR CAKE?
"WELCOME TO THE ANIMAL FOREST!♡"
GOT IT...

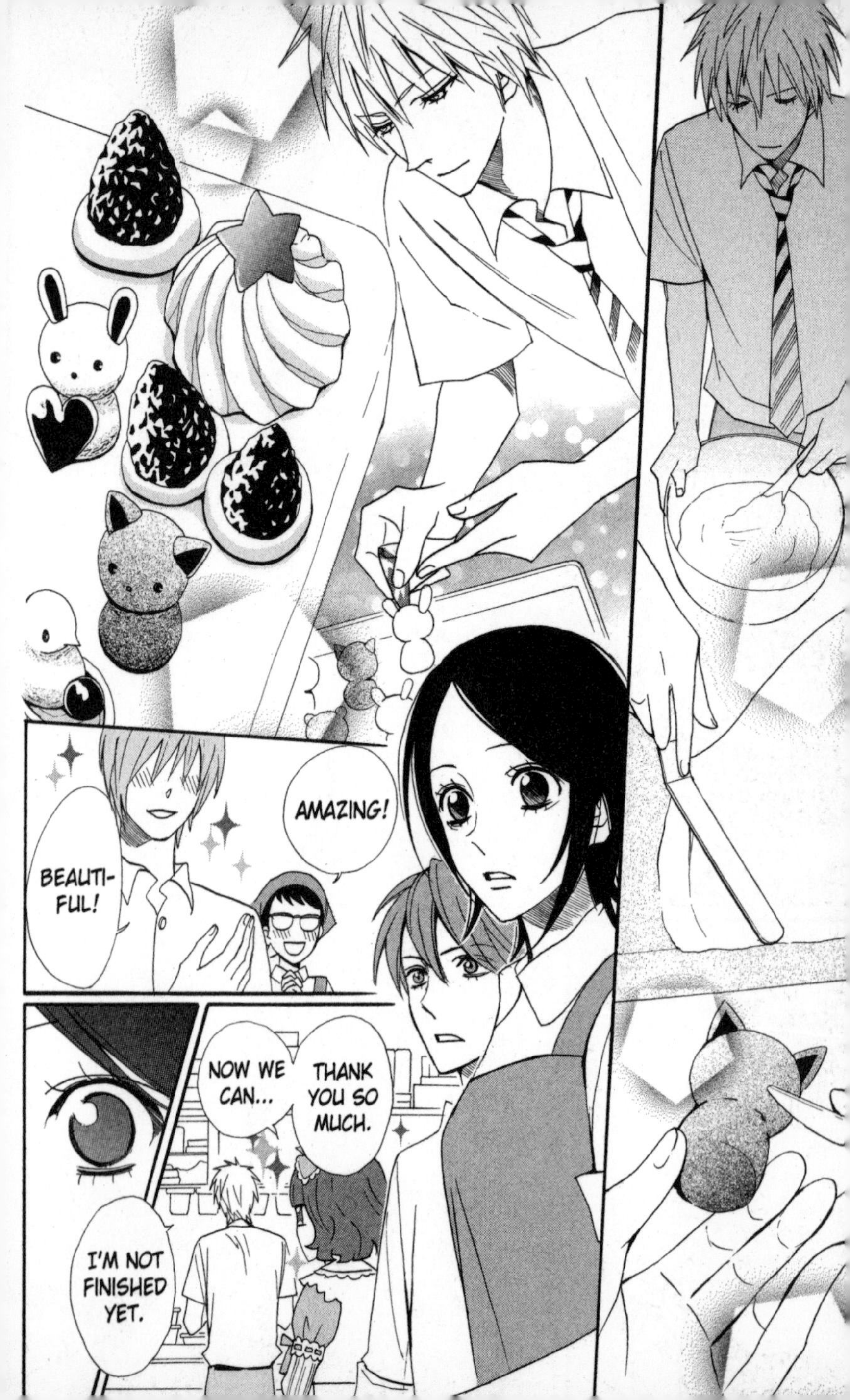
AMAZING!
BEAUTI-FUL!
THANK YOU SO MUCH.
NOW WE CAN...
I'M NOT FINISHED YET.

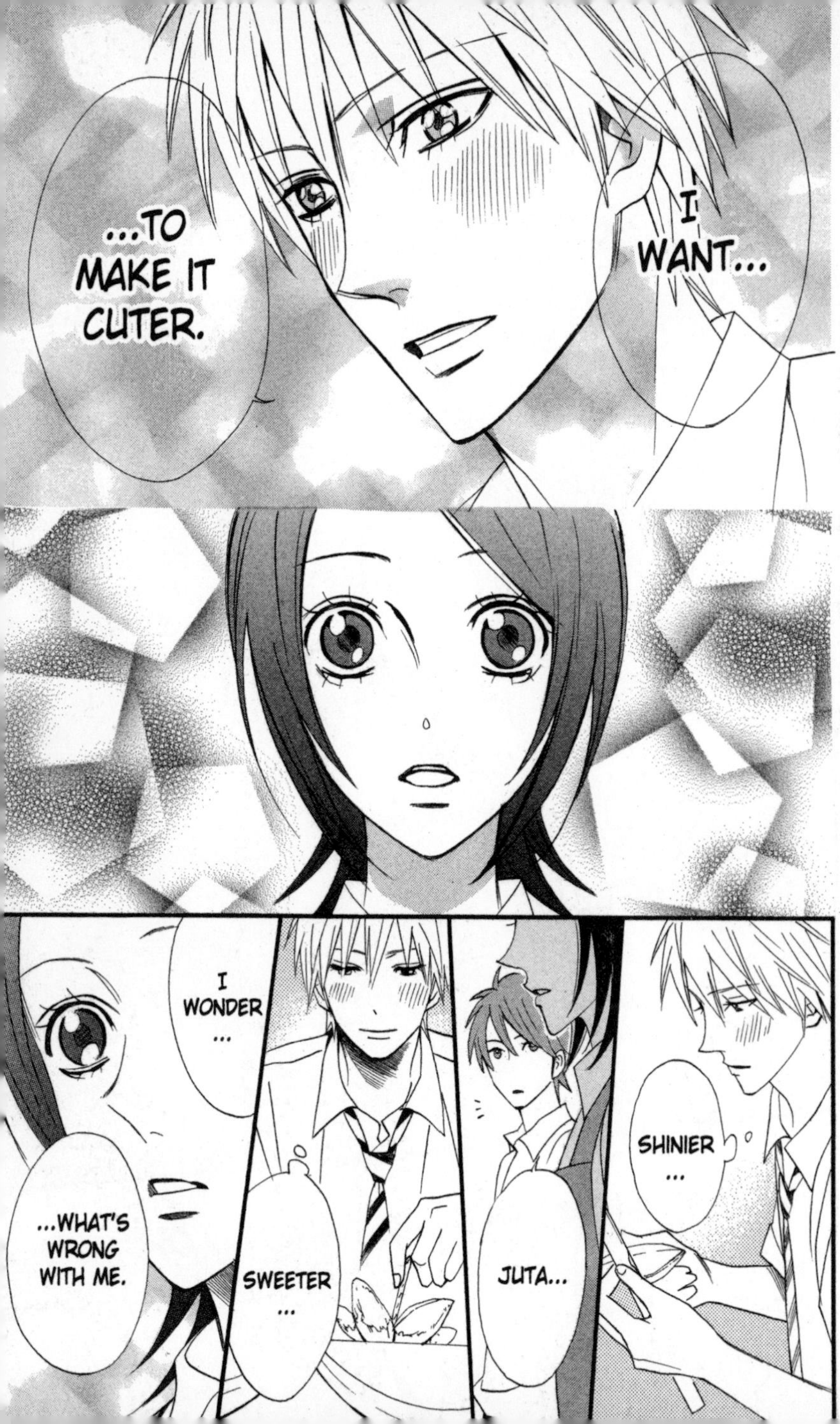
I WANT...
...TO MAKE IT CUTER.
SHINIER...
JUTA...
SWEETER...
I WONDER...
...WHAT'S WRONG WITH ME.

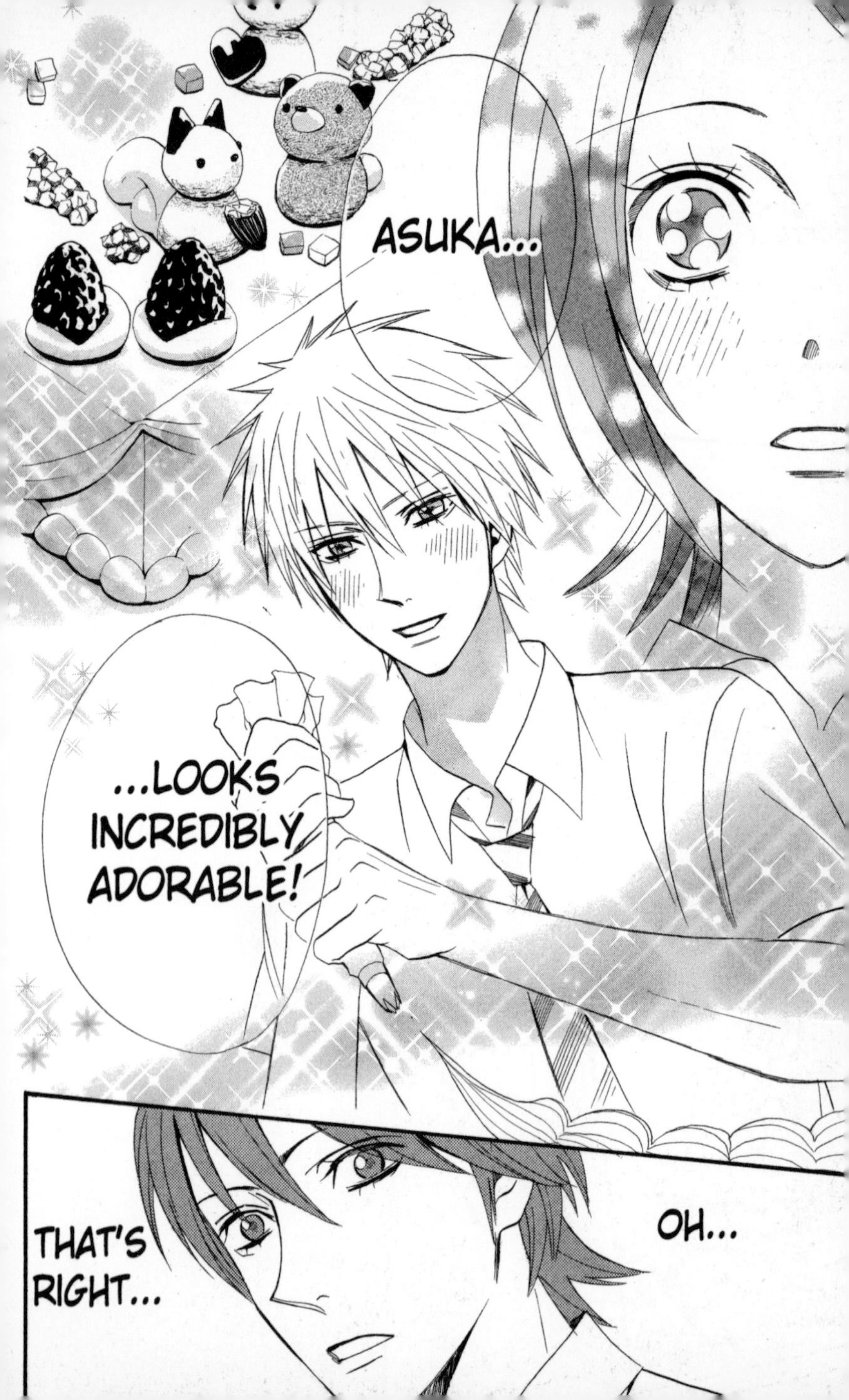
ASUKA...
...LOOKS INCREDIBLY ADORABLE!
OH...
THAT'S RIGHT...

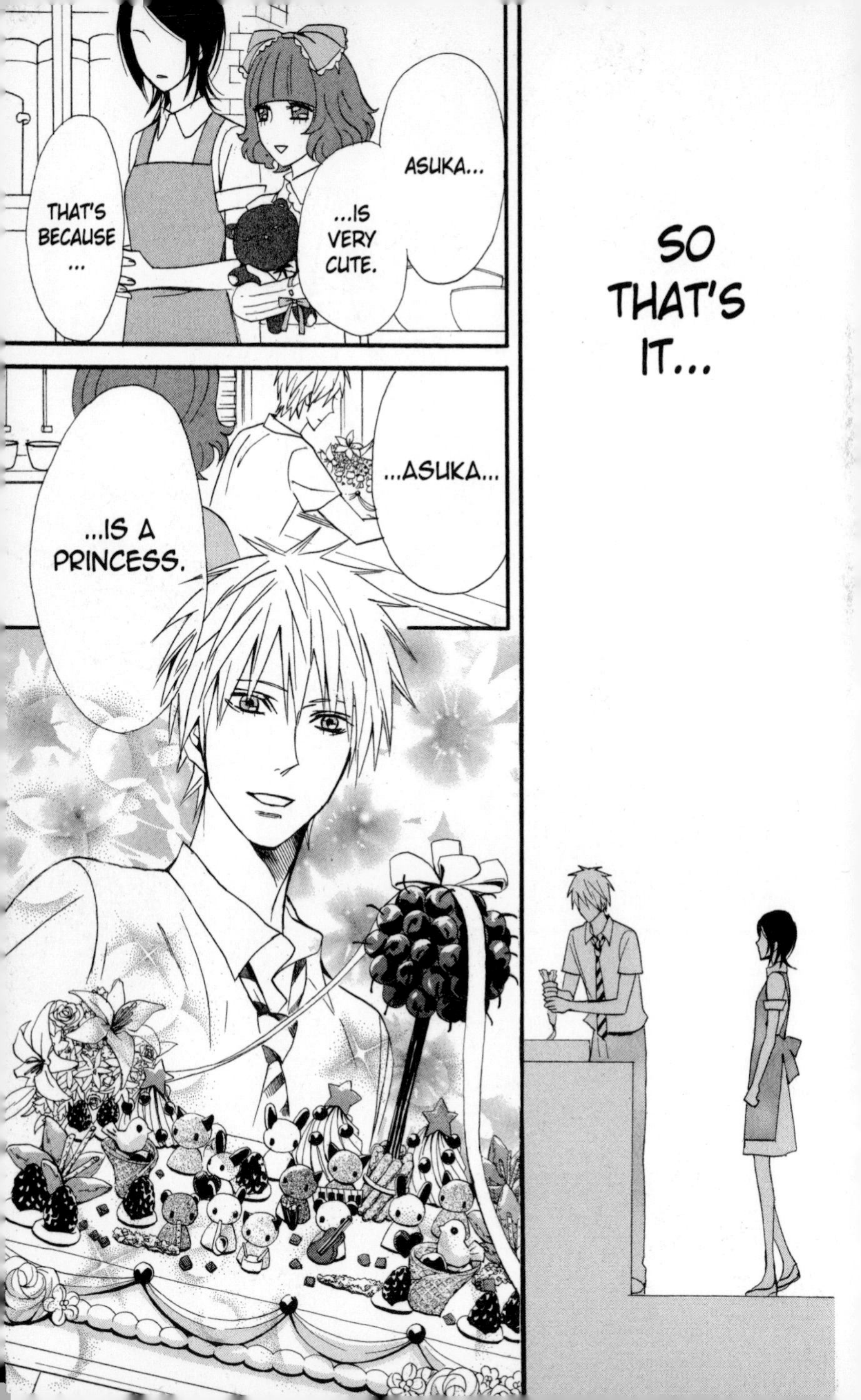
SO THAT'S IT...
ASUKA...
...IS VERY CUTE.
THAT'S BECAUSE ...
...ASUKA...
...IS A PRINCESS.

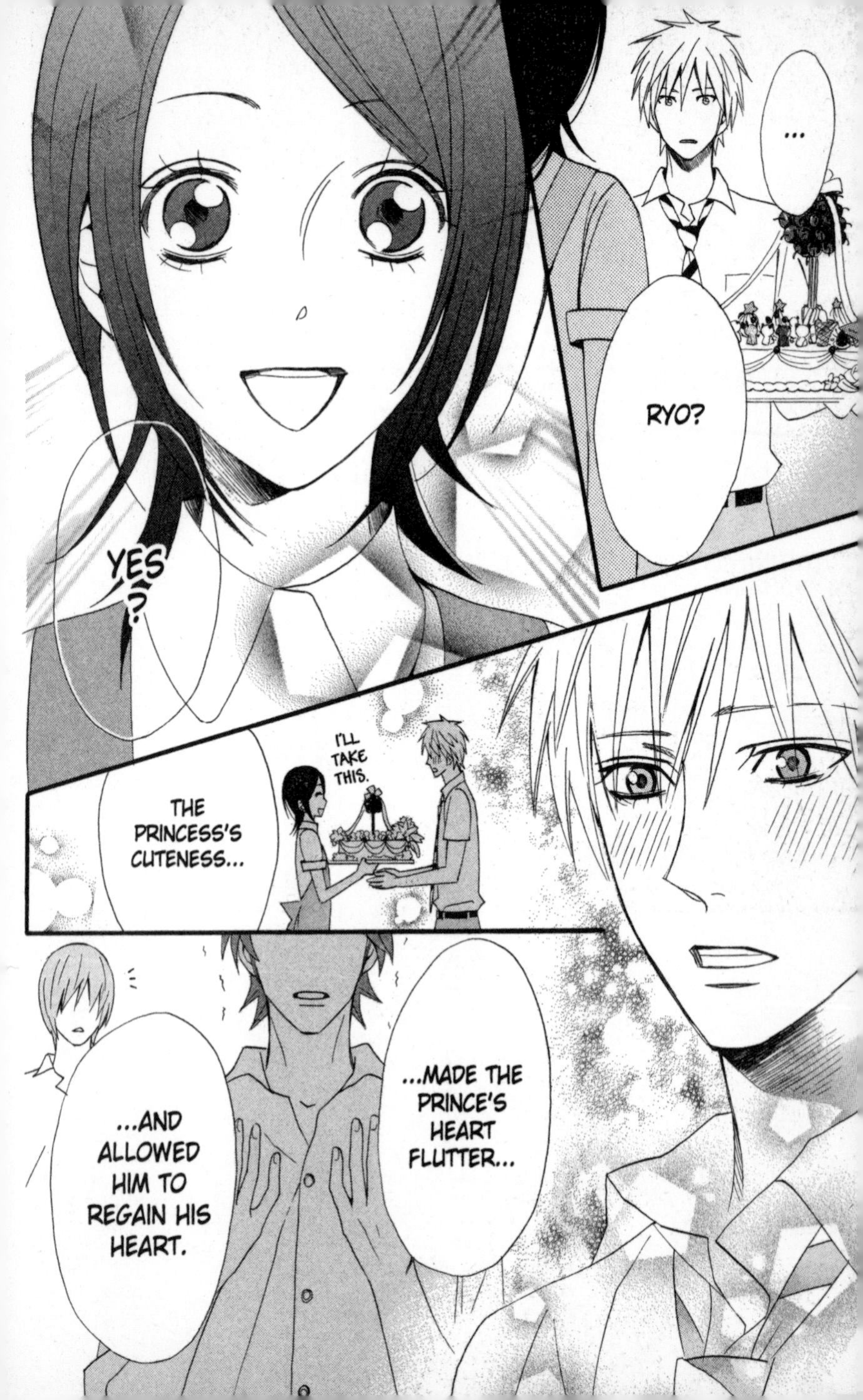
...
RYO?
YES?
I'LL TAKE THIS.
THE PRINCESS'S CUTENESS...
...MADE THE PRINCE'S HEART FLUTTER...
...AND ALLOWED HIM TO REGAIN HIS HEART.

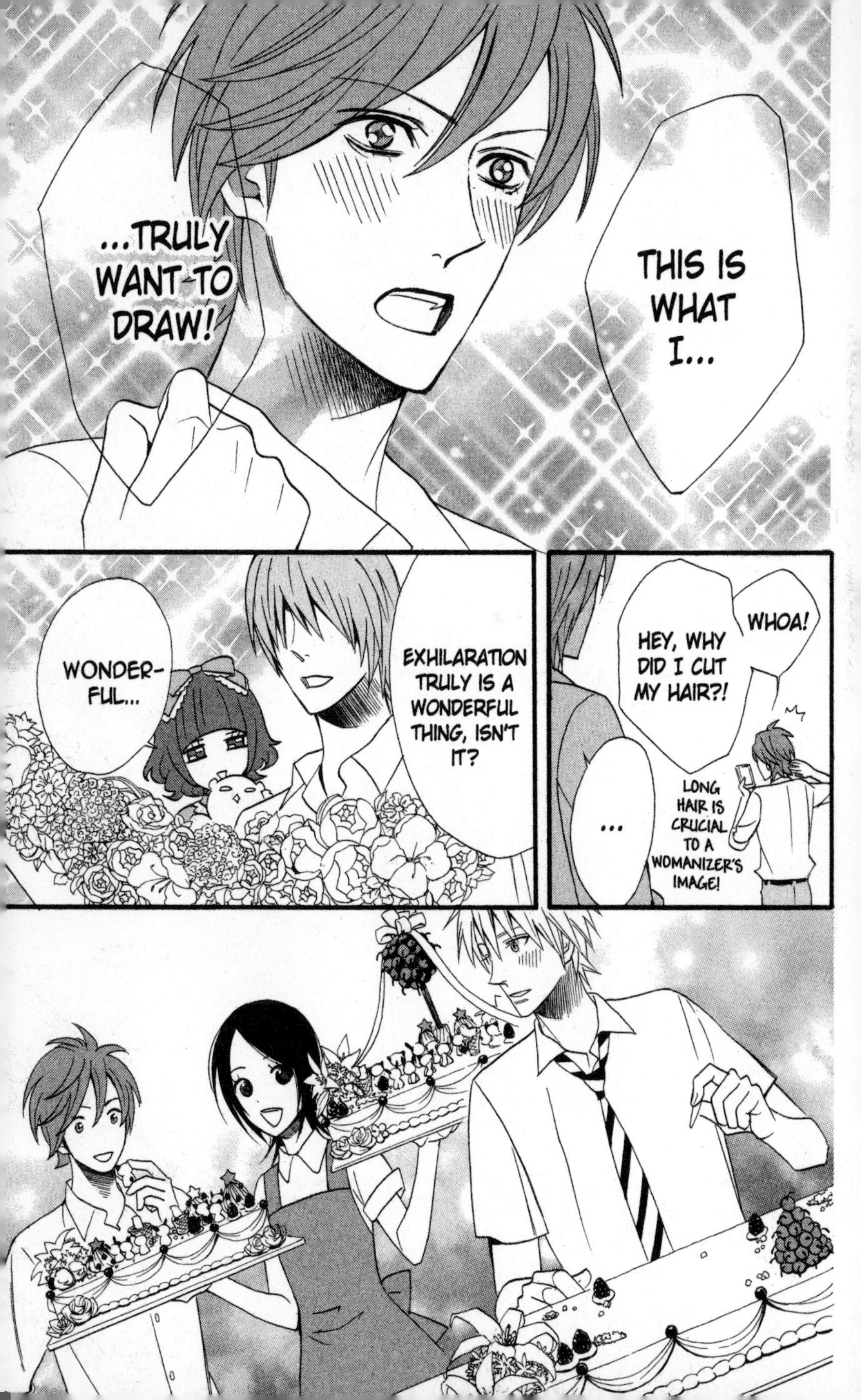
THIS IS WHAT I...
...TRULY WANT TO DRAW!
WHOA!
HEY, WHY DID I CUT MY HAIR?!
LONG HAIR IS CRUCIAL TO A WOMANIZER'S IMAGE!
...
EXHILARATION TRULY IS A WONDERFUL THING, ISN'T IT?
WONDER-FUL...

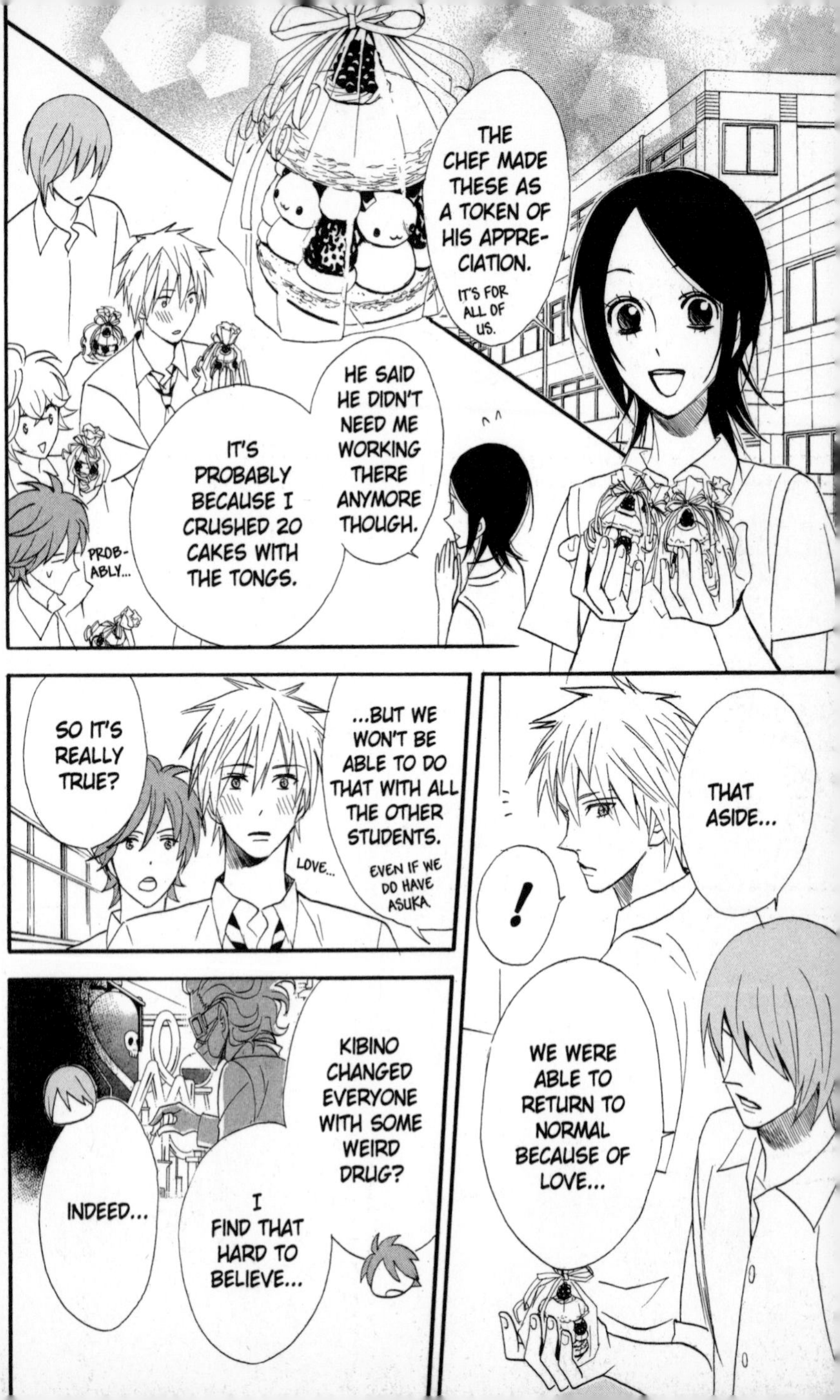
THE CHEF MADE THESE AS A TOKEN OF HIS APPRECIATION.
IT'S FOR ALL OF US.
HE SAID HE DIDN'T NEED ME WORKING THERE ANYMORE THOUGH.
IT'S PROBABLY BECAUSE I CRUSHED 20 CAKES WITH THE TONGS.
PROB-ABLY...
THAT ASIDE...
!
WE WERE ABLE TO RETURN TO NORMAL BECAUSE OF LOVE...
...BUT WE WON'T BE ABLE TO DO THAT WITH ALL THE OTHER STUDENTS.
EVEN IF WE DO HAVE ASUKA.
LOVE...
SO IT'S REALLY TRUE?
KIBINO CHANGED EVERYONE WITH SOME WEIRD DRUG?
I FIND THAT HARD TO BELIEVE...
INDEED...

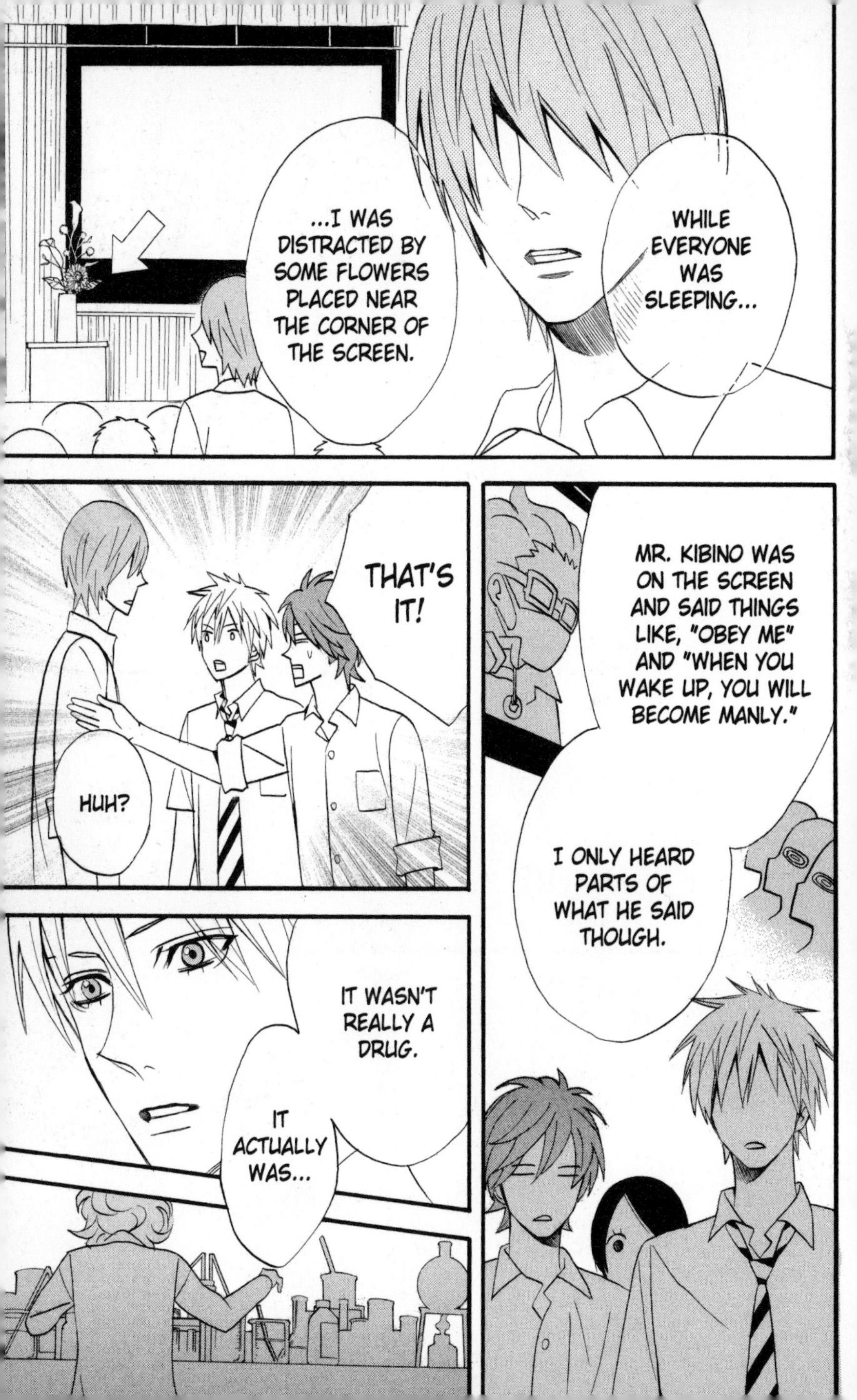
WHILE EVERYONE WAS SLEEPING...
...I WAS DISTRACTED BY SOME FLOWERS PLACED NEAR THE CORNER OF THE SCREEN.
MR. KIBINO WAS ON THE SCREEN AND SAID THINGS LIKE, "OBEY ME" AND "WHEN YOU WAKE UP, YOU WILL BECOME MANLY."
I ONLY HEARD PARTS OF WHAT HE SAID THOUGH.
THAT'S IT!
HUH?
IT WASN'T REALLY A DRUG.
IT ACTUALLY WAS...

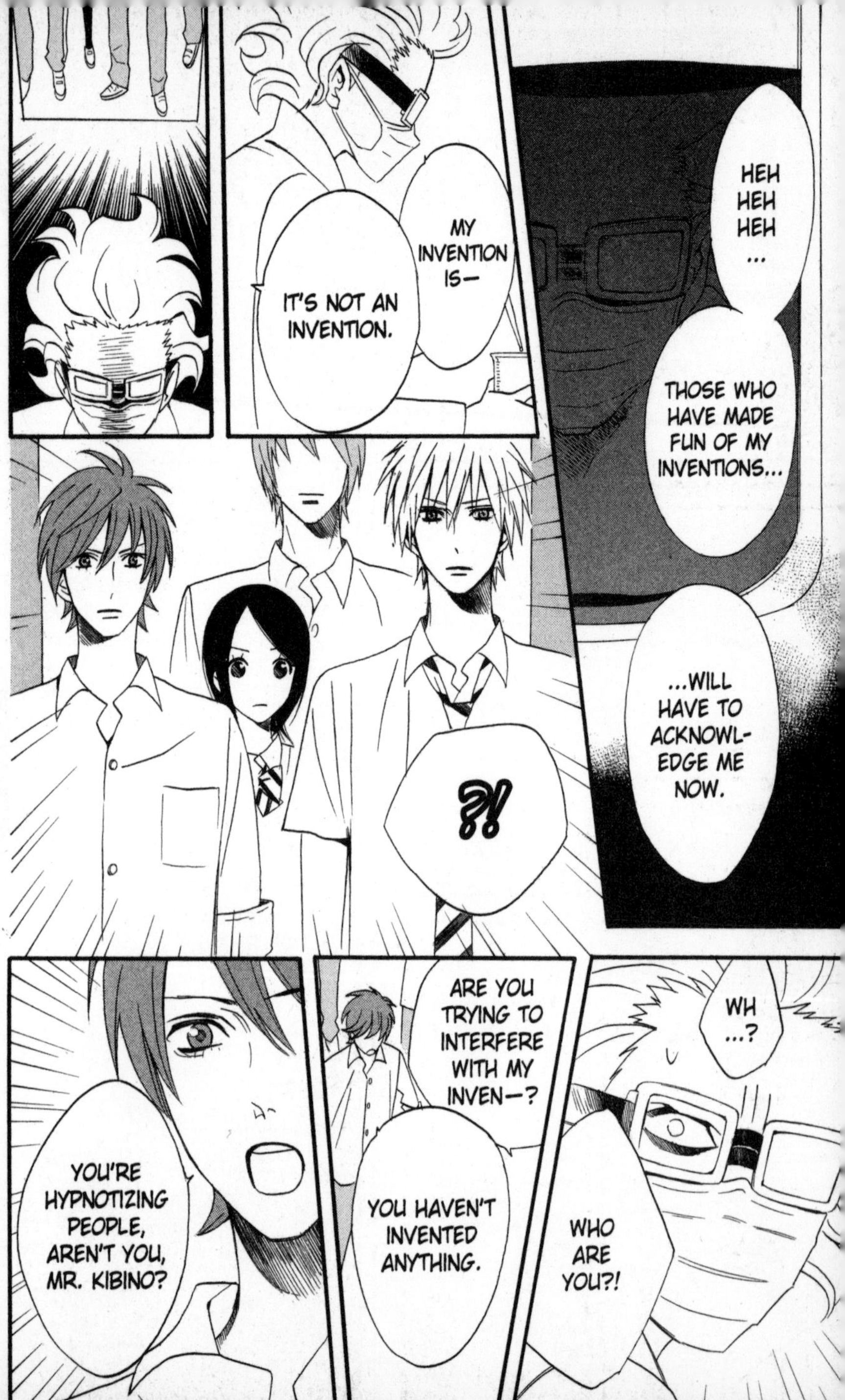
HEH HEH HEH ...
THOSE WHO HAVE MADE FUN OF MY INVENTIONS...
...WILL HAVE TO ACKNOWL-EDGE ME NOW.
MY INVENTION IS—
IT'S NOT AN INVENTION.
?!
WH ...?
WHO ARE YOU?!
ARE YOU TRYING TO INTERFERE WITH MY INVEN—?
YOU HAVEN'T INVENTED ANYTHING.
YOU'RE HYPNOTIZING PEOPLE, AREN'T YOU, MR. KIBINO?

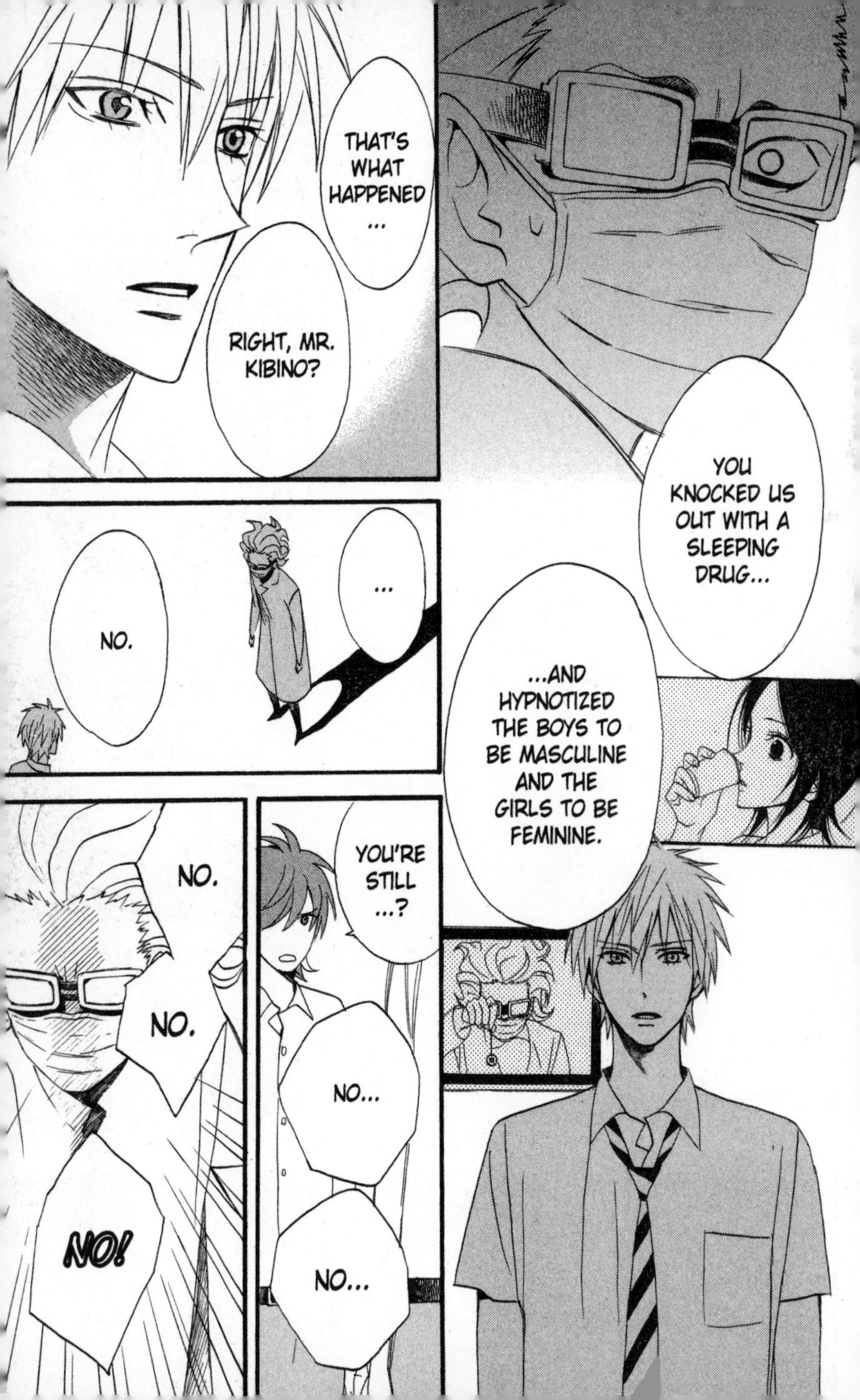
YOU KNOCKED US OUT WITH A SLEEPING DRUG...
...AND HYPNOTIZED THE BOYS TO BE MASCULINE AND THE GIRLS TO BE FEMININE.
THAT'S WHAT HAPPENED...
RIGHT, MR. KIBINO?
...
NO.
YOU'RE STILL ...?
NO...
NO...
NO.
NO.
NO!

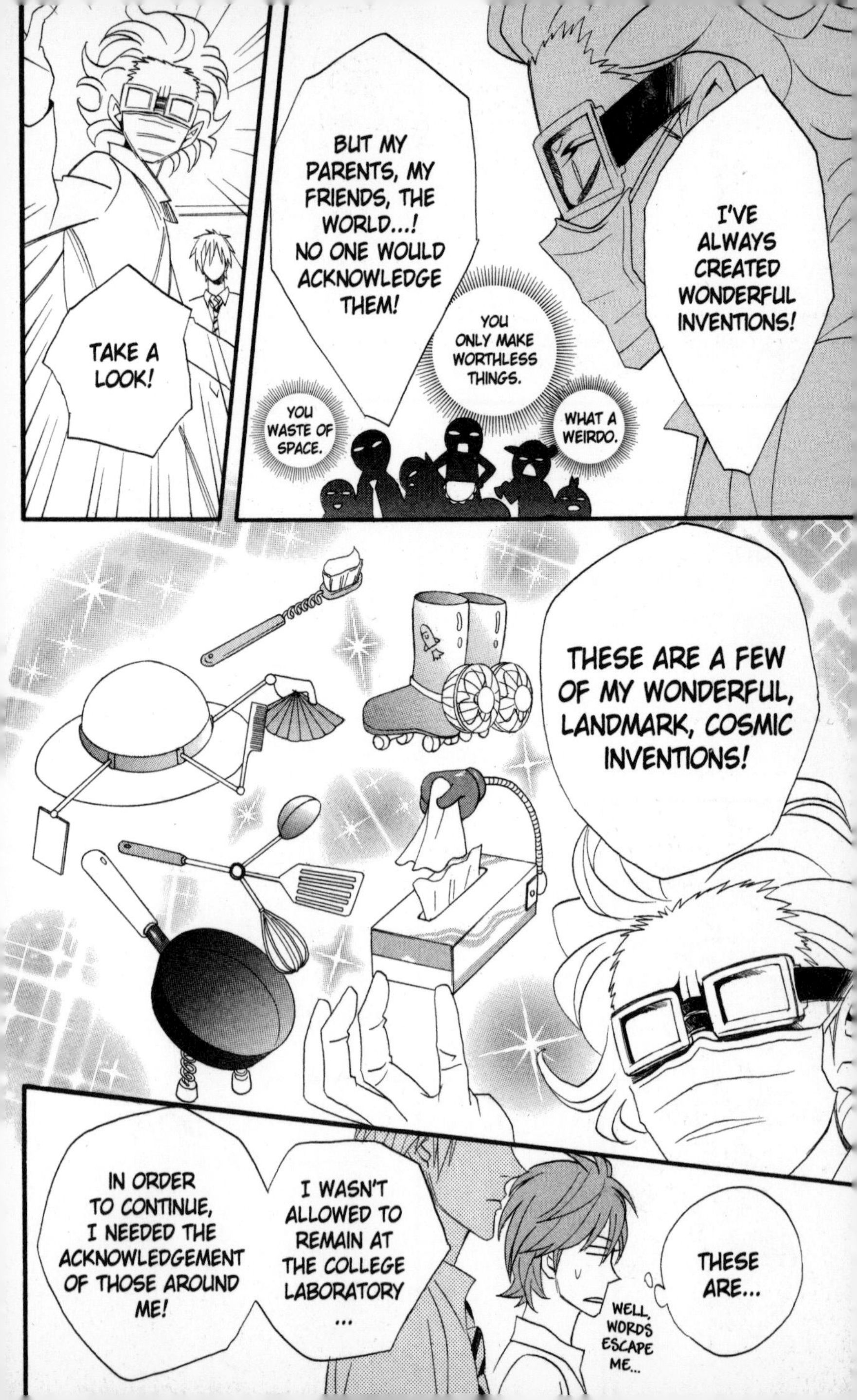
I'VE ALWAYS CREATED WONDERFUL INVENTIONS!
BUT MY PARENTS, MY FRIENDS, THE WORLD...! NO ONE WOULD ACKNOWLEDGE THEM!
YOU ONLY MAKE WORTHLESS THINGS.
WHAT A WEIRDO.
YOU WASTE OF SPACE.
TAKE A LOOK!
THESE ARE A FEW OF MY WONDERFUL, LANDMARK, COSMIC INVENTIONS!
THESE ARE...
WELL, WORDS ESCAPE ME...
I WASN'T ALLOWED TO REMAIN AT THE COLLEGE LABORATORY ...
IN ORDER TO CONTINUE, I NEEDED THE ACKNOWLEDGEMENT OF THOSE AROUND ME!

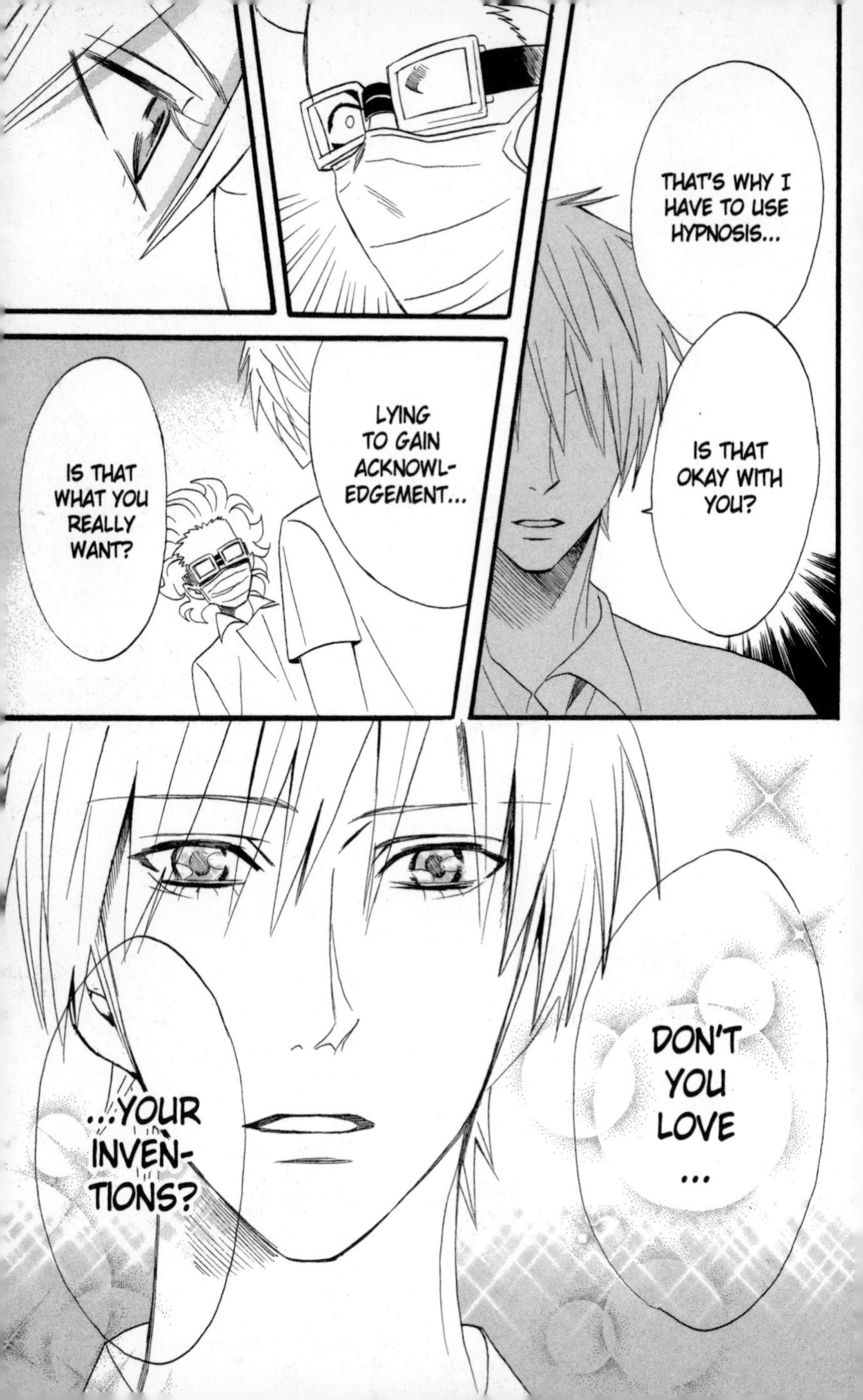
THAT'S WHY I HAVE TO USE HYPNOSIS...
IS THAT OKAY WITH YOU?
LYING TO GAIN ACKNOWL-EDGEMENT...
IS THAT WHAT YOU REALLY WANT?
DON'T YOU LOVE ...
...YOUR INVEN-TIONS?

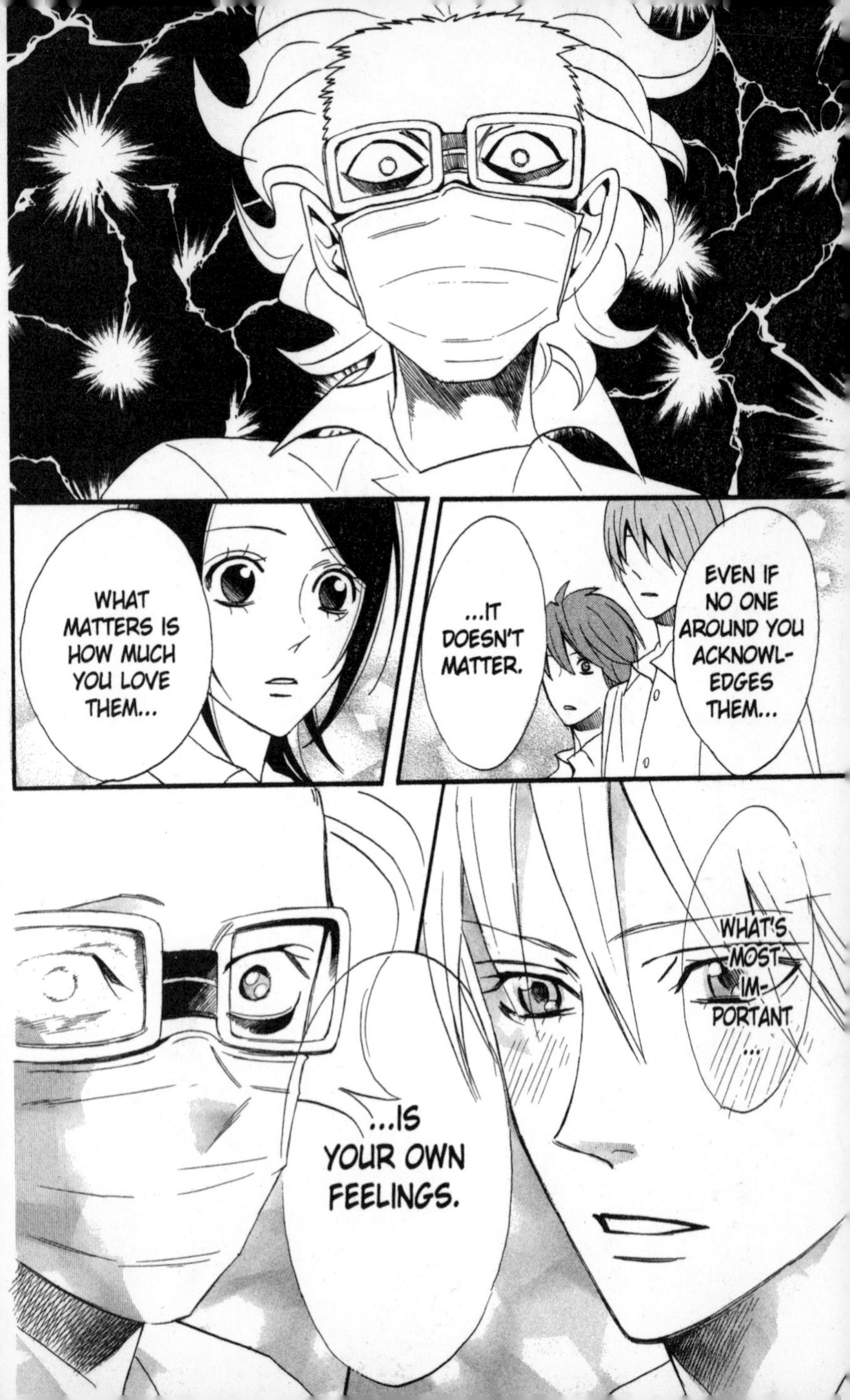
EVEN IF NO ONE AROUND YOU ACKNOWLEDGES THEM...
...IT DOESN'T MATTER.
WHAT MATTERS IS HOW MUCH YOU LOVE THEM...
WHAT'S MOST IMPORTANT...
...IS YOUR OWN FEELINGS.

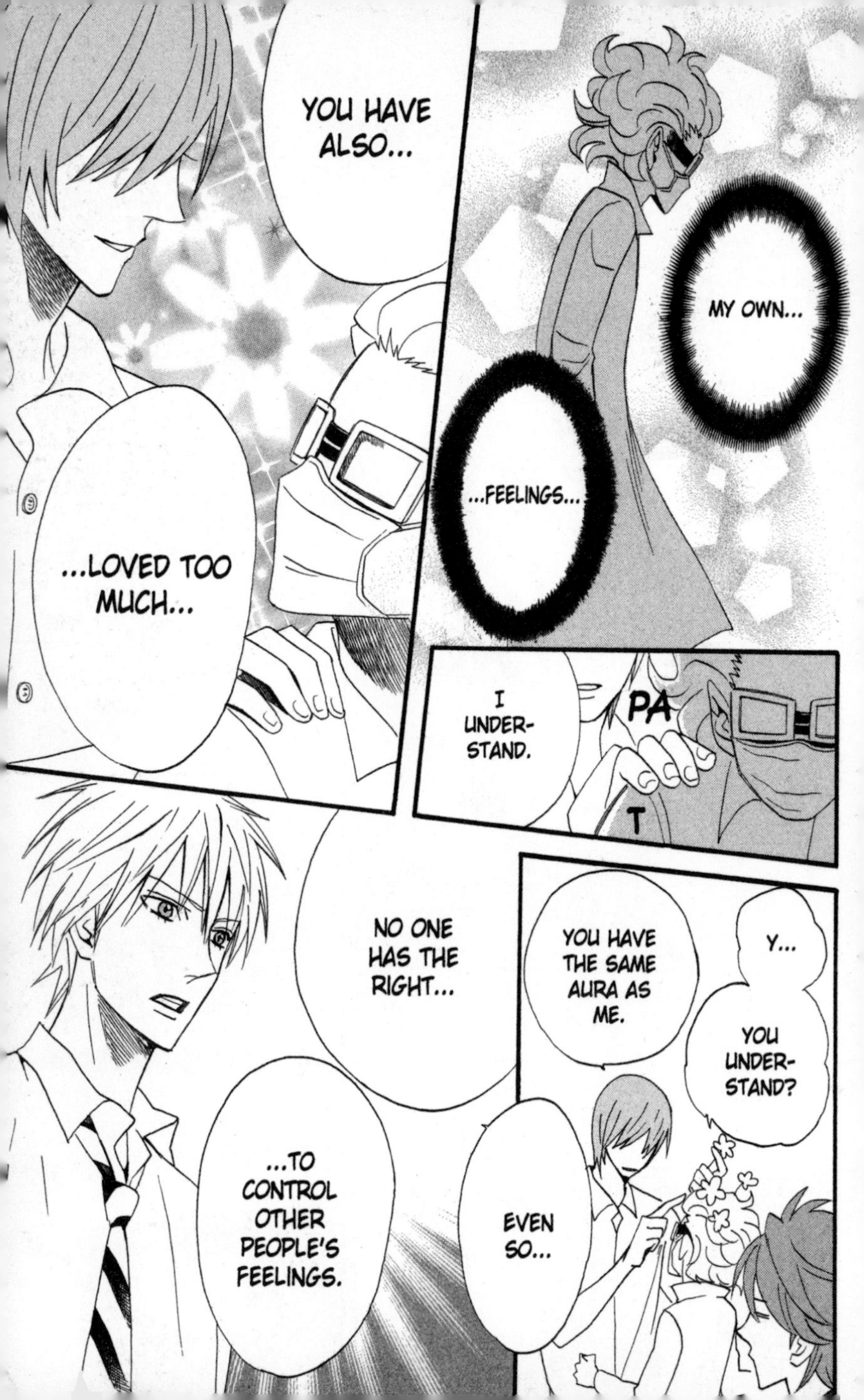
MY OWN...
...FEELINGS...
I UNDERSTAND.
PAT
YOU HAVE ALSO...
...LOVED TOO MUCH...
Y...
YOU UNDERSTAND?
YOU HAVE THE SAME AURA AS ME.
EVEN SO...
NO ONE HAS THE RIGHT...
...TO CONTROL OTHER PEOPLE'S FEELINGS.

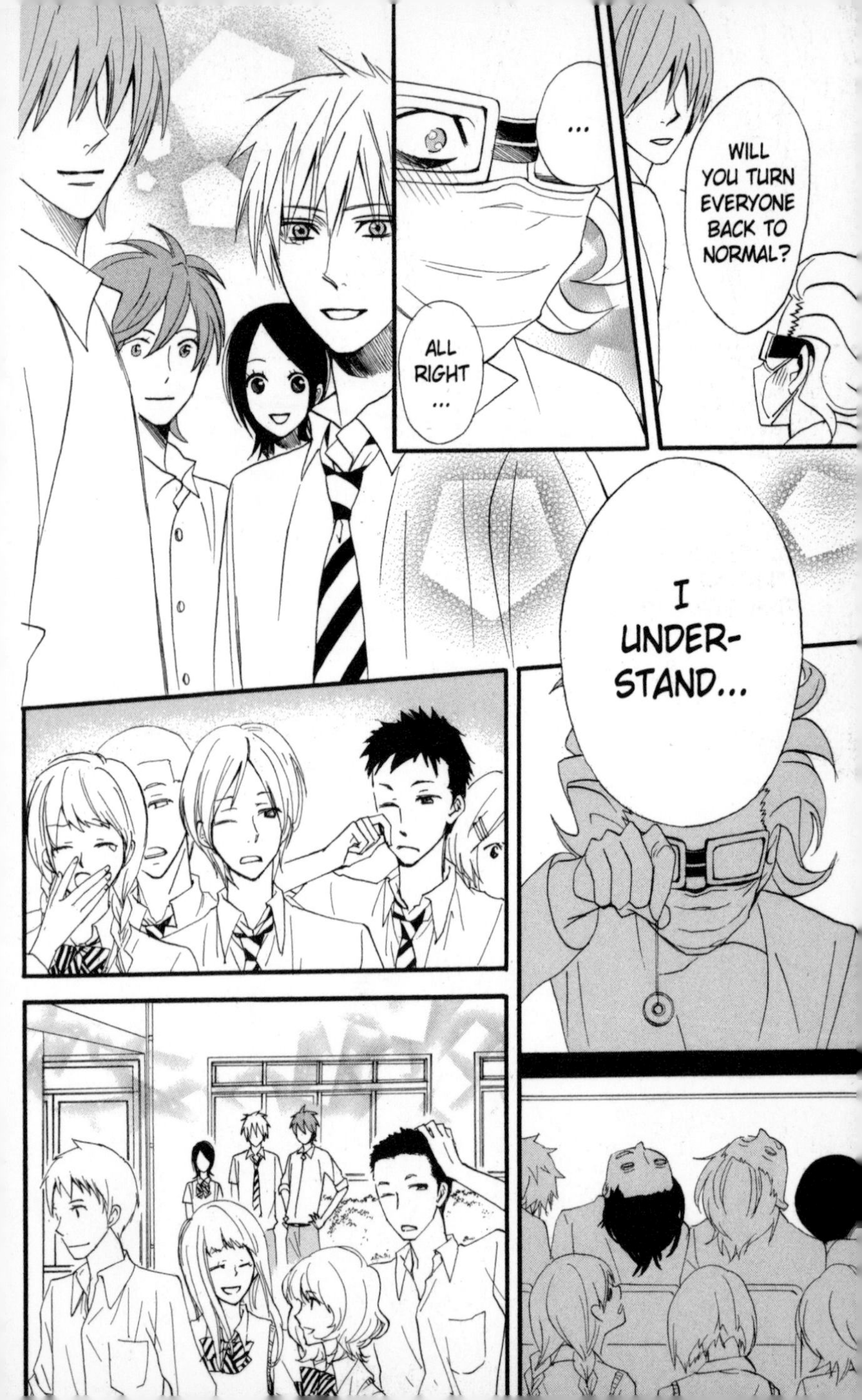
WILL YOU TURN EVERYONE BACK TO NORMAL?
...
ALL RIGHT ...
I UNDER-STAND...

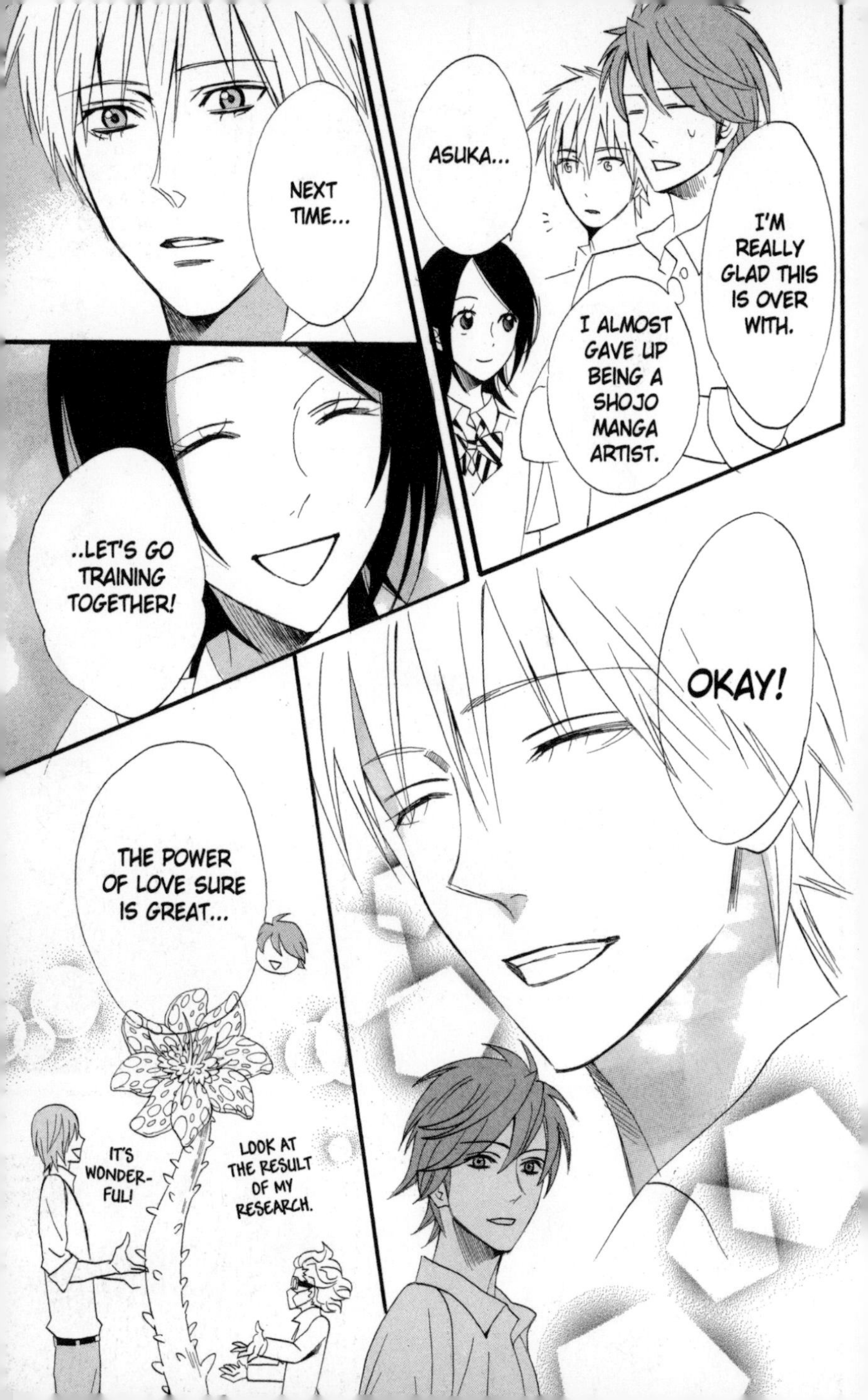
ASUKA...
I'M REALLY GLAD THIS IS OVER WITH.
I ALMOST GAVE UP BEING A SHOJO MANGA ARTIST.
NEXT TIME...
..LET'S GO TRAINING TOGETHER!
OKAY!
THE POWER OF LOVE SURE IS GREAT...
LOOK AT THE RESULT OF MY RESEARCH.
IT'S WONDER-FUL!

OTOMEN

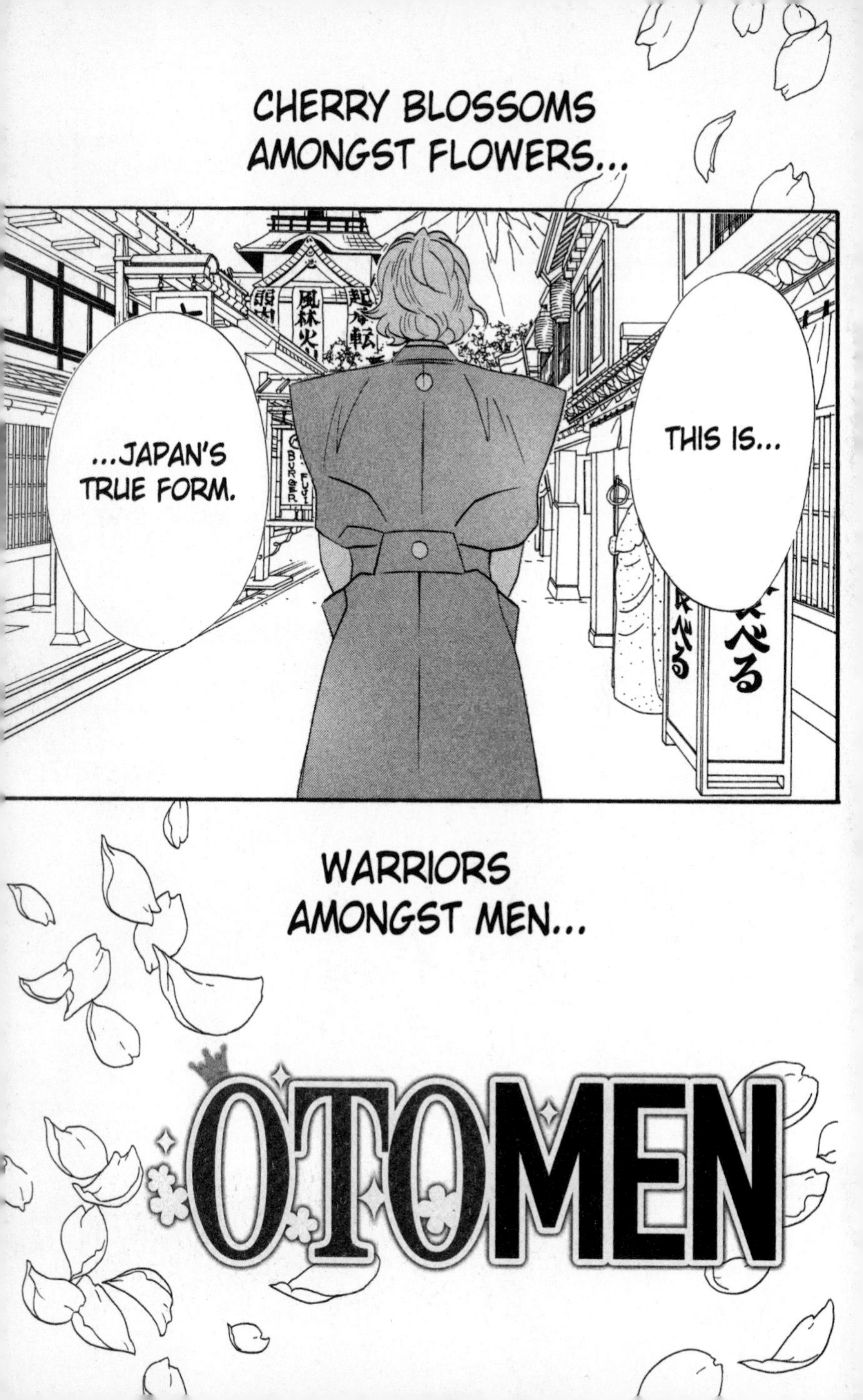
CHERRY BLOSSOMS AMONGST FLOWERS...
THIS IS...
...JAPAN'S TRUE FORM.
WARRIORS AMONGST MEN...
OTOMEN

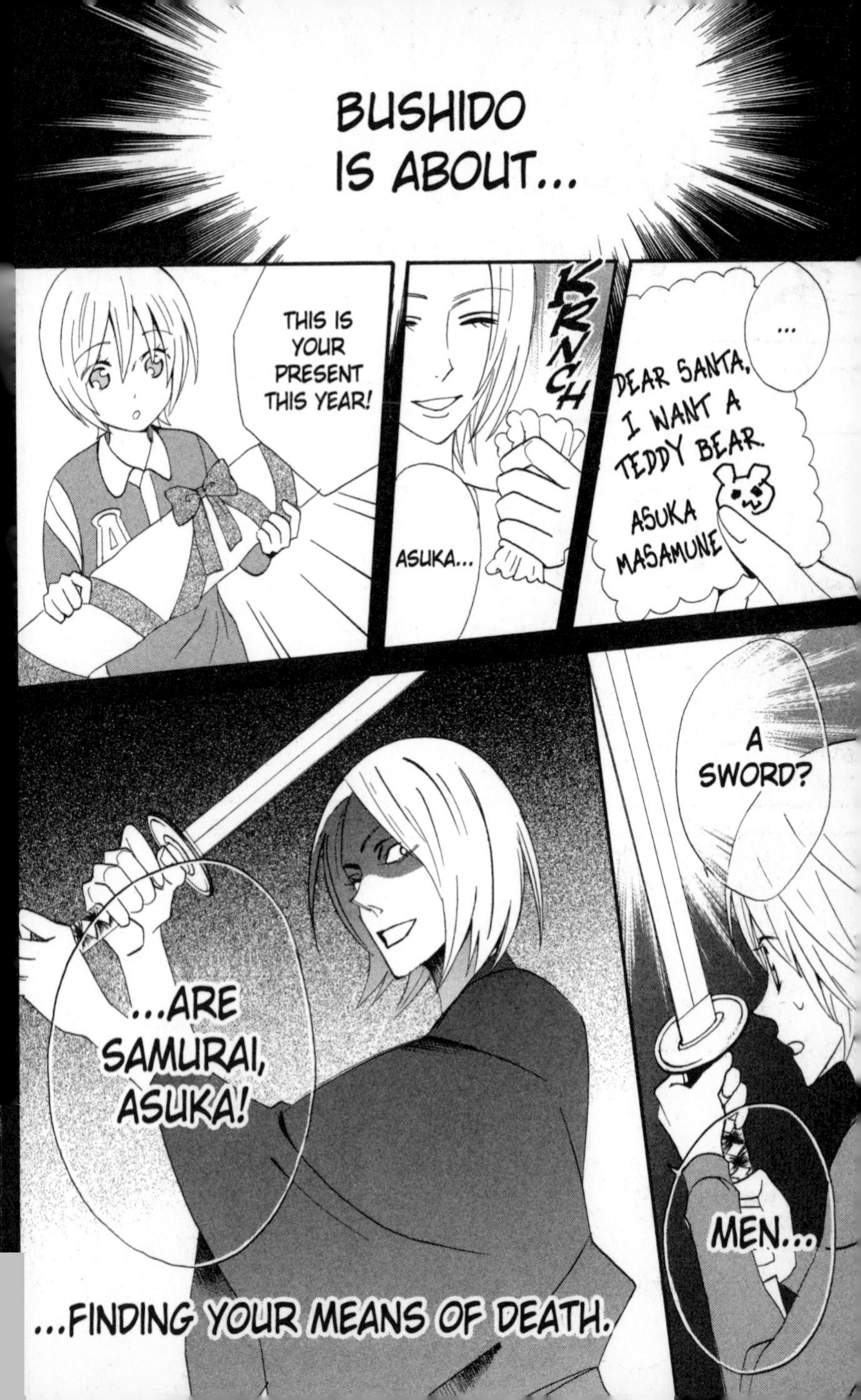
BUSHIDO IS ABOUT...
...
DEAR SANTA, I WANT A TEDDY BEAR.
ASUKA MASAMUNE
KRNCH
ASUKA...
THIS IS YOUR PRESENT THIS YEAR!
A SWORD?
MEN...
...ARE SAMURAI, ASUKA!
...FINDING YOUR MEANS OF DEATH.

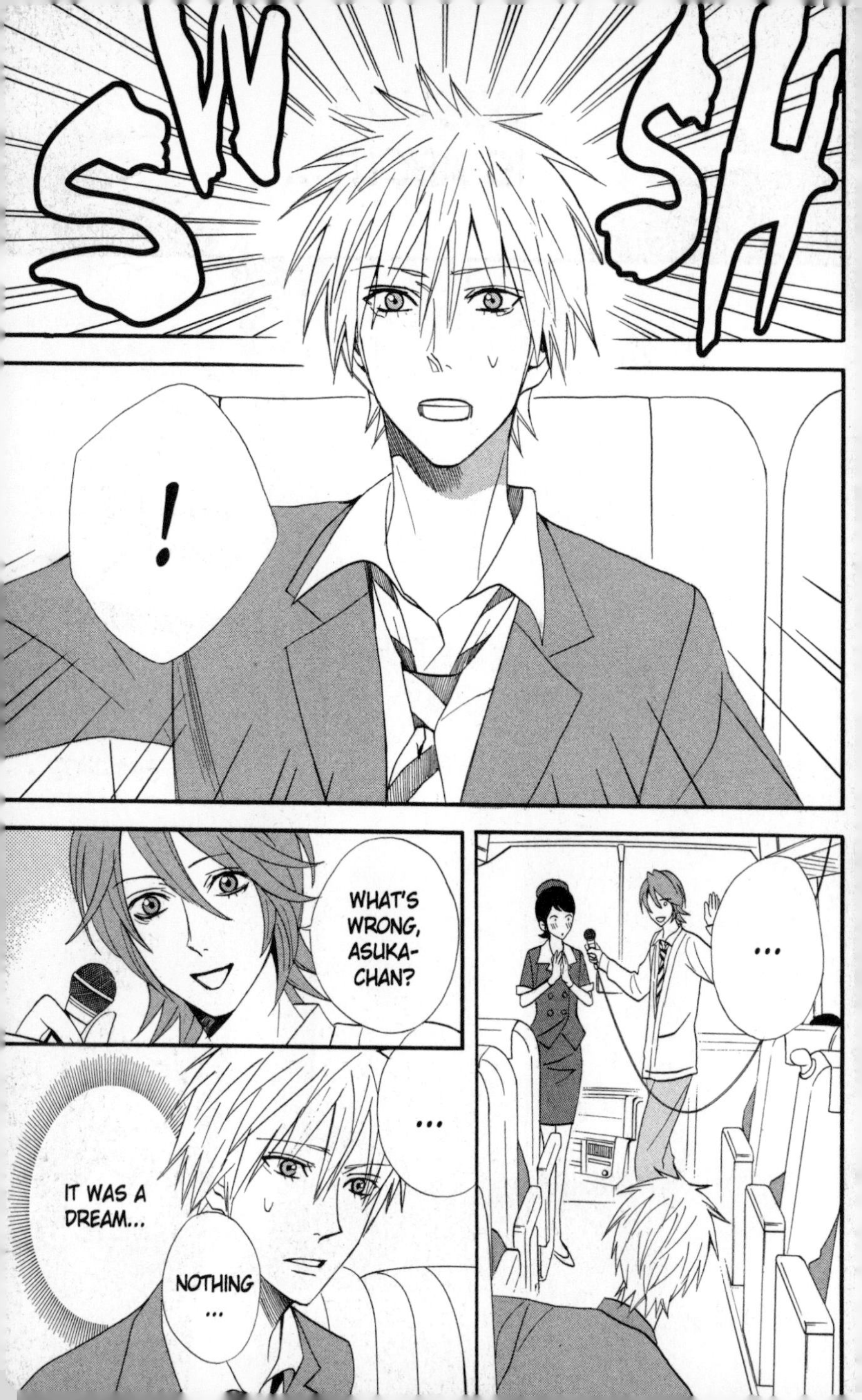
SWSH
!
...
WHAT'S WRONG, ASUKA-CHAN?
...
NOTHING ...
IT WAS A DREAM...

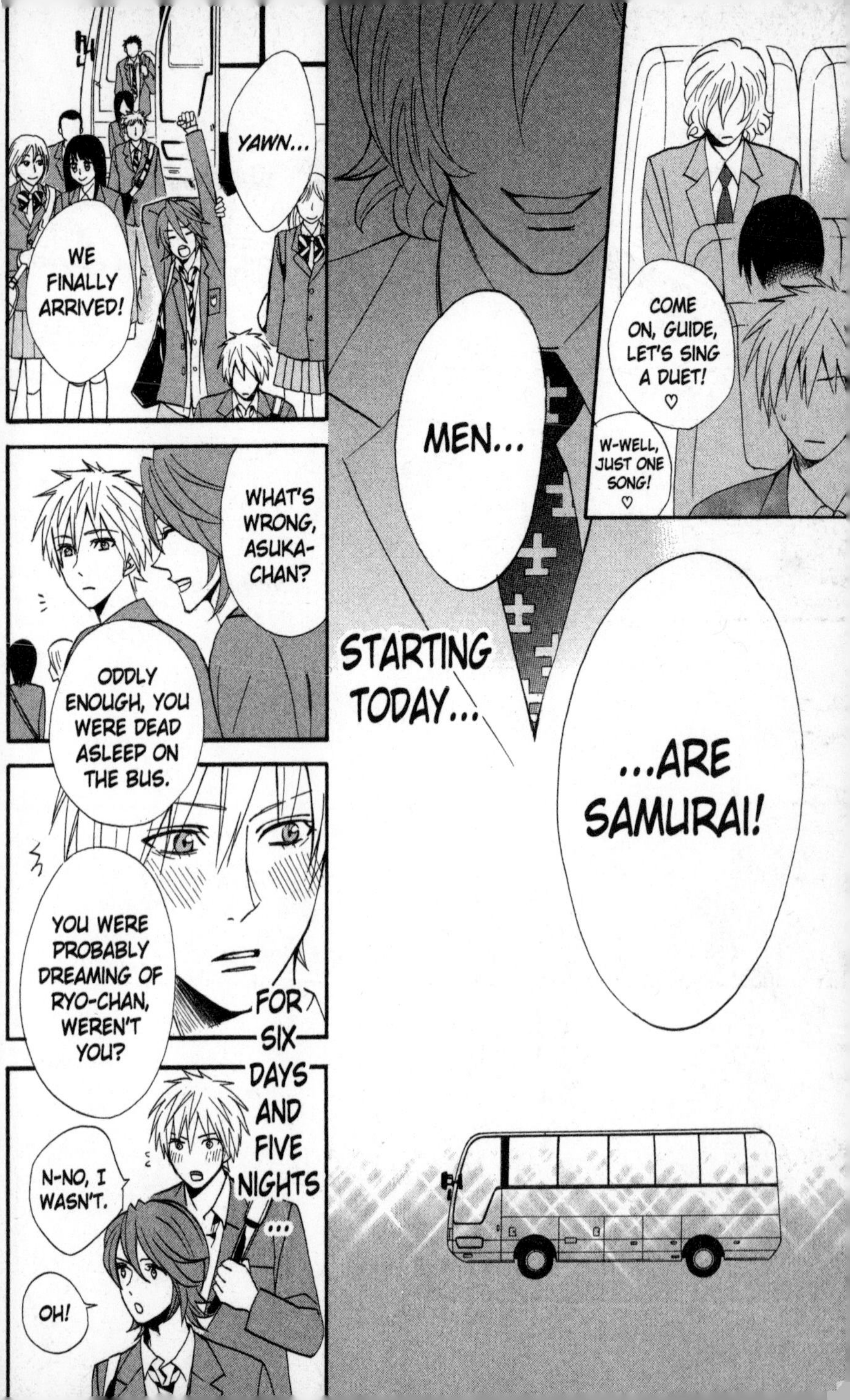
COME ON, GUIDE, LET'S SING A DUET! ♡
W-WELL, JUST ONE SONG! ♡
MEN...
STARTING TODAY...
...ARE SAMURAI!
YAWN...
WE FINALLY ARRIVED!
WHAT'S WRONG, ASUKA-CHAN?
ODDLY ENOUGH, YOU WERE DEAD ASLEEP ON THE BUS.
YOU WERE PROBABLY DREAMING OF RYO-CHAN, WEREN'T YOU?
FOR SIX DAYS AND FIVE NIGHTS...
N-NO, I WASN'T.
OH!

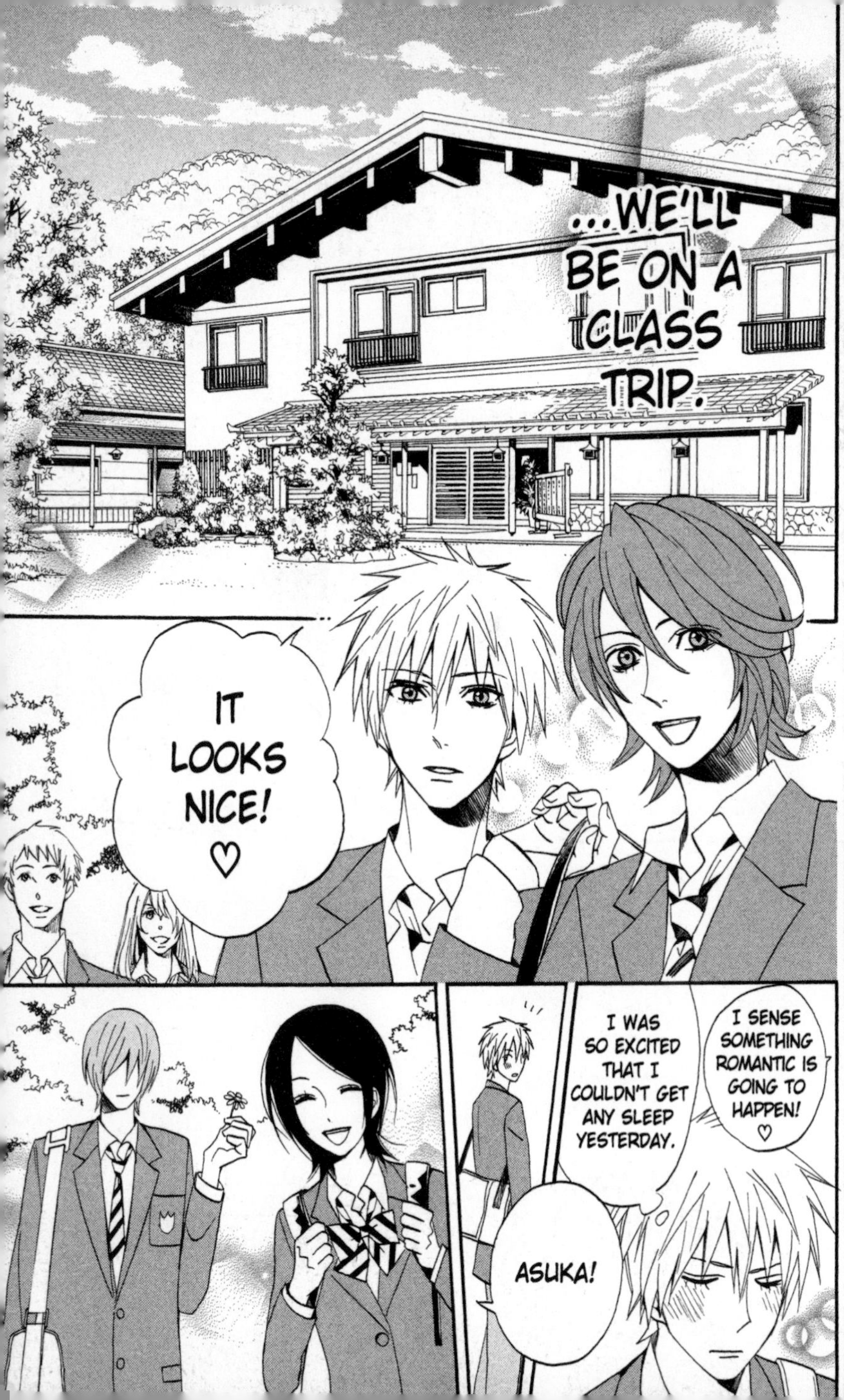
...WE'LL BE ON A CLASS TRIP.
IT LOOKS NICE! ♡
I SENSE SOMETHING ROMANTIC IS GOING TO HAPPEN! ♡
I WAS SO EXCITED THAT I COULDN'T GET ANY SLEEP YESTERDAY.
ASUKA!

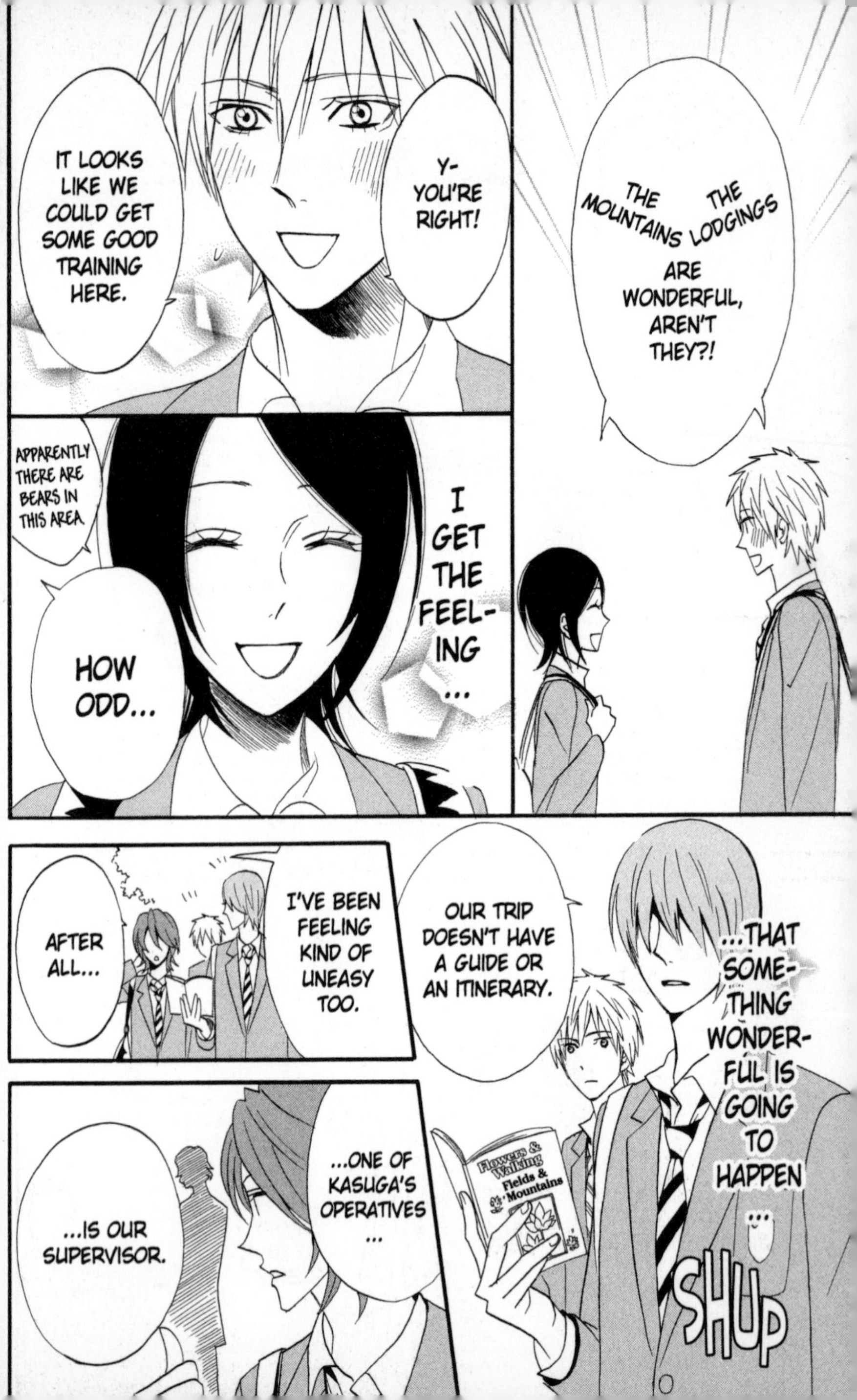
THE MOUNTAINS THE LODGINGS ARE WONDERFUL, AREN'T THEY?!
Y-YOU'RE RIGHT!
IT LOOKS LIKE WE COULD GET SOME GOOD TRAINING HERE.
I GET THE FEEL-ING...
APPARENTLY THERE ARE BEARS IN THIS AREA.
HOW ODD...
...THAT SOME-THING WONDER-FUL IS GOING TO HAPPEN...
SHUP
OUR TRIP DOESN'T HAVE A GUIDE OR AN ITINERARY.
Flowers & Walking
Fields & Mountains
I'VE BEEN FEELING KIND OF UNEASY TOO.
AFTER ALL...
...ONE OF KASUGA'S OPERATIVES...
...IS OUR SUPERVISOR.

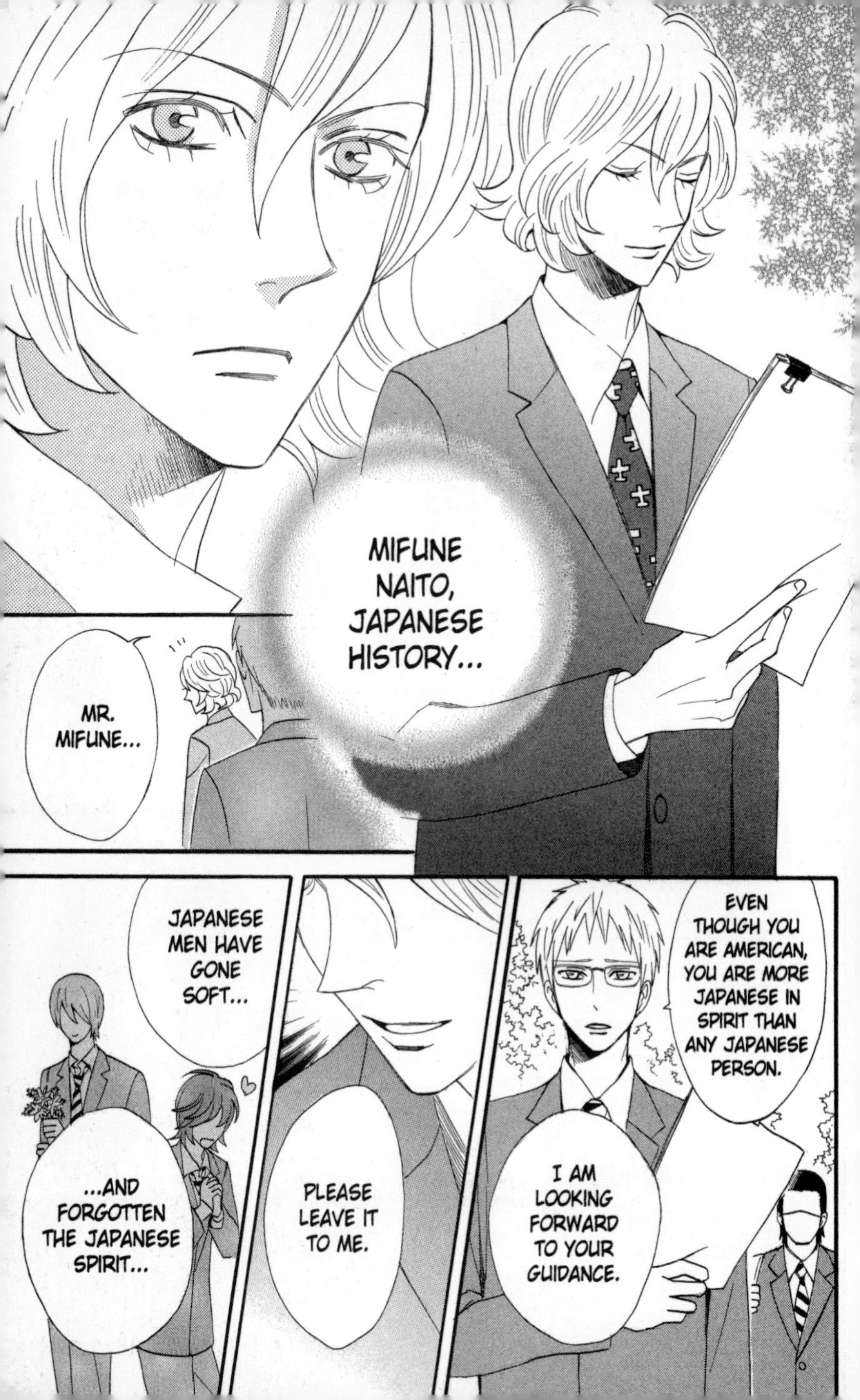
MIFUNE NAITO, JAPANESE HISTORY...
MR. MIFUNE...
EVEN THOUGH YOU ARE AMERICAN, YOU ARE MORE JAPANESE IN SPIRIT THAN ANY JAPANESE PERSON.
I AM LOOKING FORWARD TO YOUR GUIDANCE.
PLEASE LEAVE IT TO ME.
JAPANESE MEN HAVE GONE SOFT...
...AND FORGOTTEN THE JAPANESE SPIRIT...

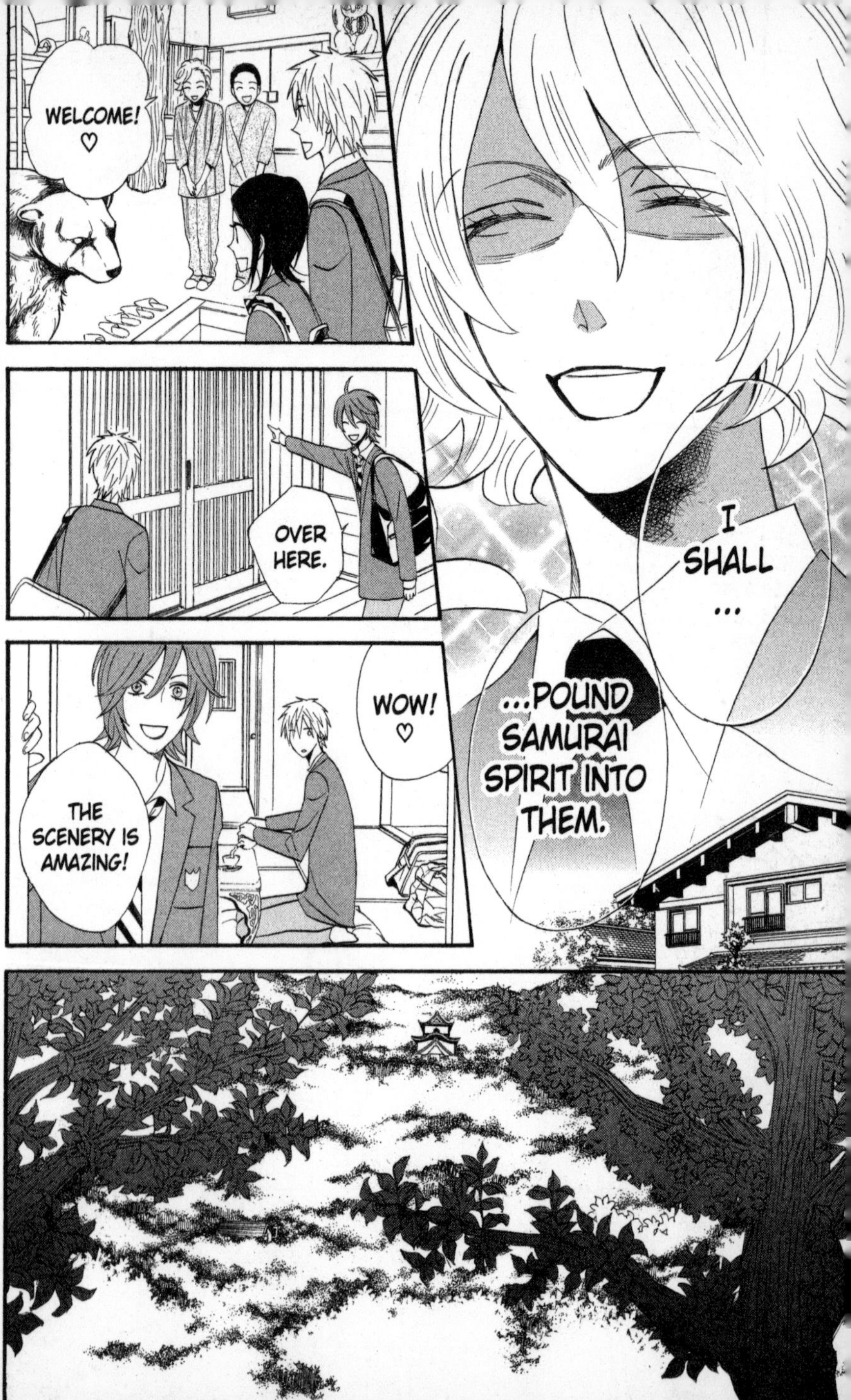
I SHALL ...
...POUND SAMURAI SPIRIT INTO THEM.
WELCOME! ♡
OVER HERE.
WOW! ♡
THE SCENERY IS AMAZING!

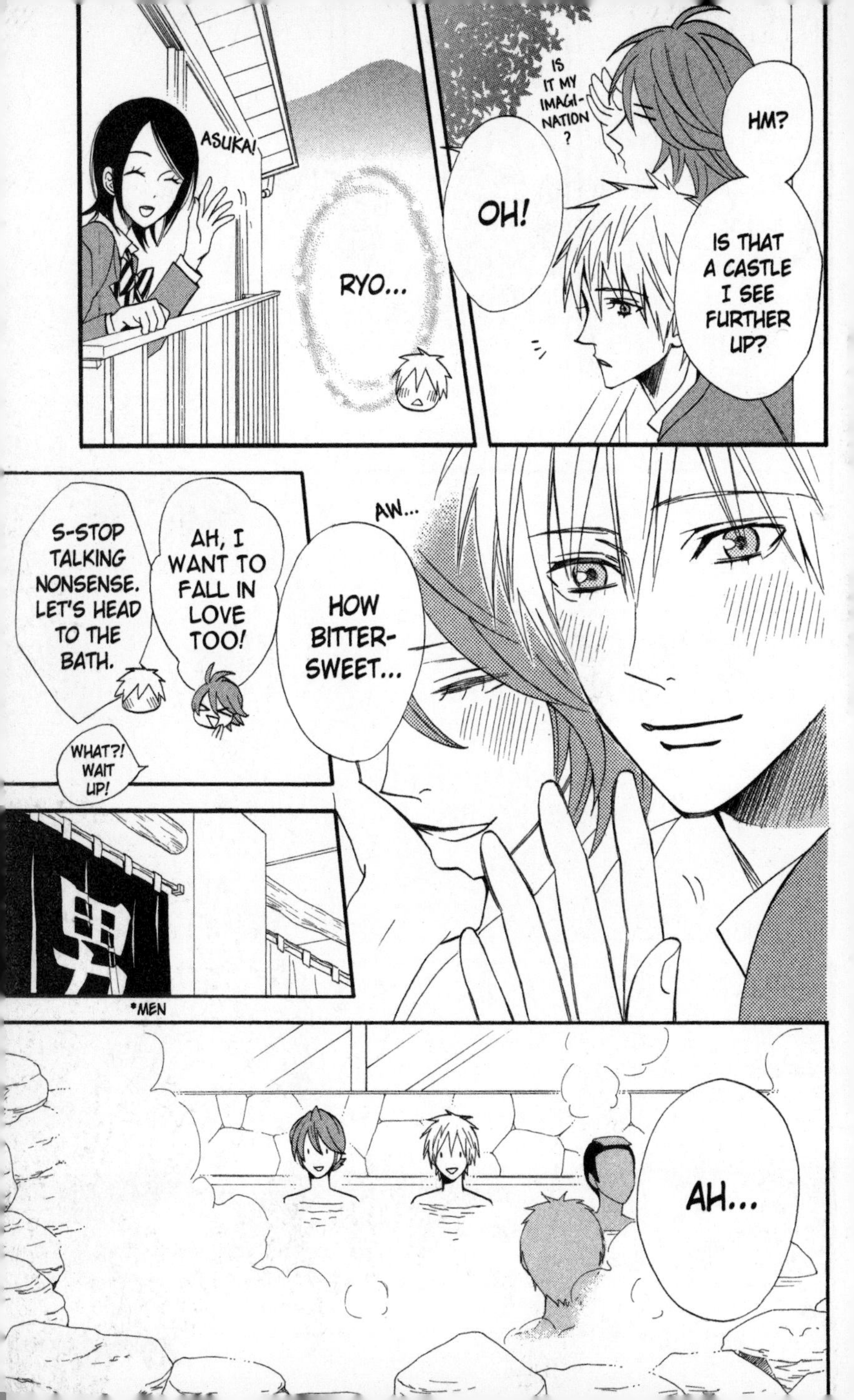
HM?
IS THAT A CASTLE I SEE FURTHER UP?
IS IT MY IMAGINATION?
OH!
ASUKA!
RYO...
AW...
HOW BITTER-SWEET...
AH, I WANT TO FALL IN LOVE TOO!
S-STOP TALKING NONSENSE. LET'S HEAD TO THE BATH.
WHAT?! WAIT UP!
男
*MEN
AH...

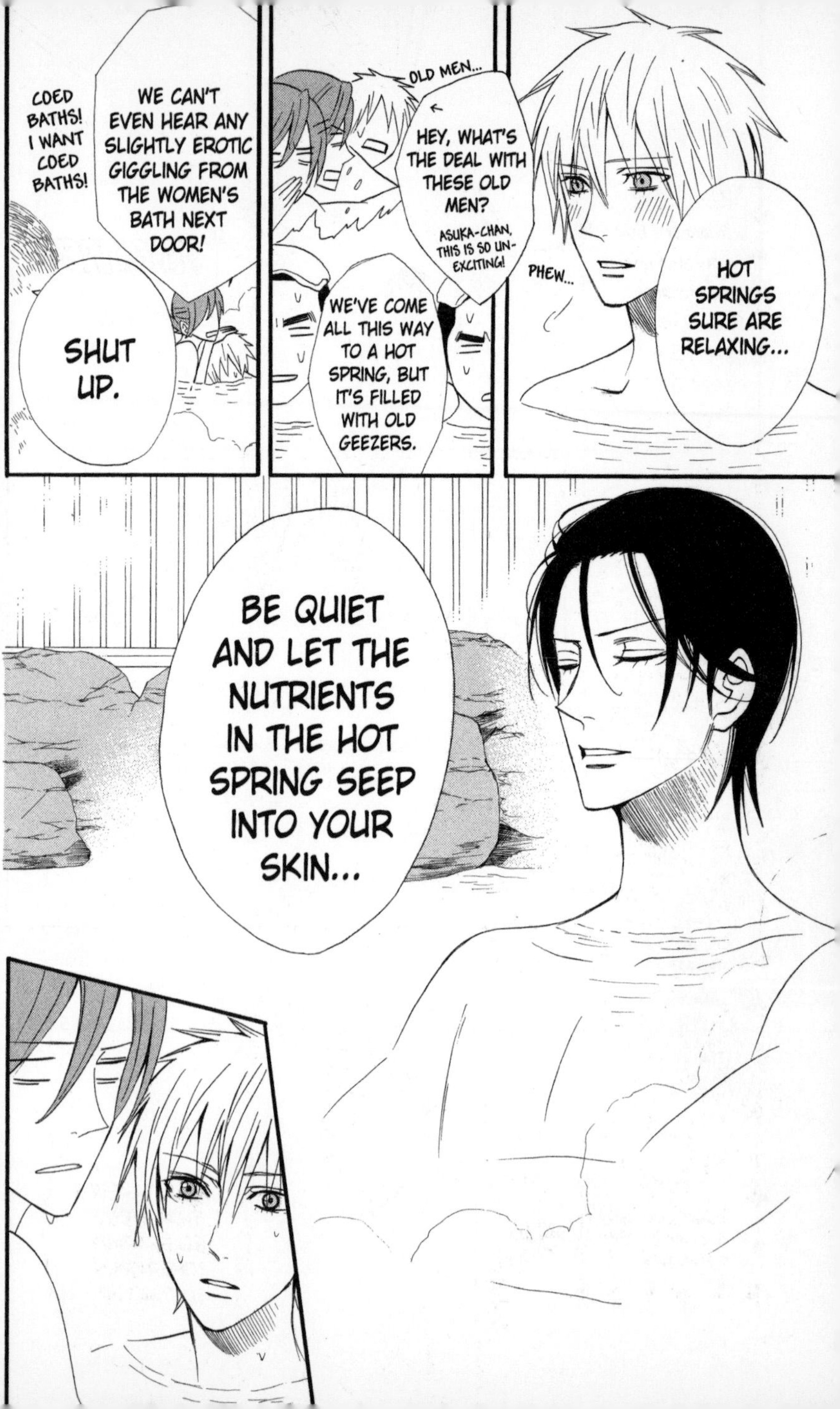
HOT SPRINGS SURE ARE RELAXING...
PHEW...
OLD MEN...
HEY, WHAT'S THE DEAL WITH THESE OLD MEN?
ASUKA-CHAN, THIS IS SO UN-EXCITING!
WE'VE COME ALL THIS WAY TO A HOT SPRING, BUT IT'S FILLED WITH OLD GEEZERS.
WE CAN'T EVEN HEAR ANY SLIGHTLY EROTIC GIGGLING FROM THE WOMEN'S BATH NEXT DOOR!
COED BATHS! I WANT COED BATHS!
SHUT UP.
BE QUIET AND LET THE NUTRIENTS IN THE HOT SPRING SEEP INTO YOUR SKIN...

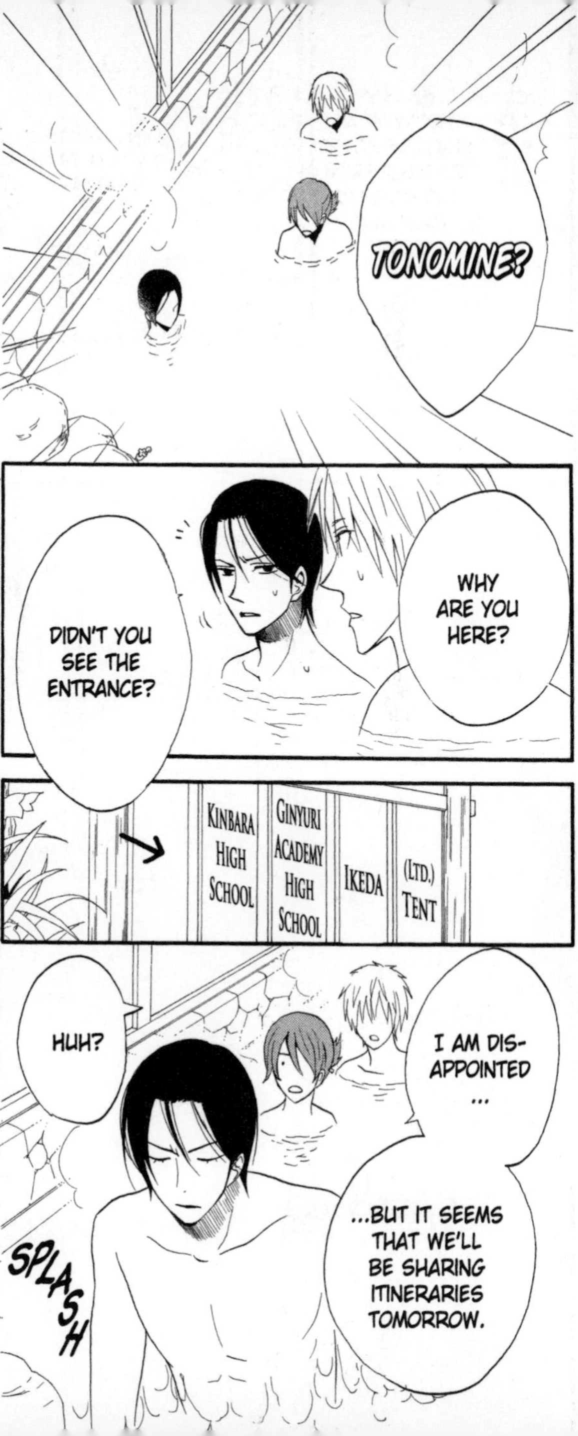
TONOMINE?
WHY ARE YOU HERE?
DIDN'T YOU SEE THE ENTRANCE?
KINBARA HIGH SCHOOL
GINYURI ACADEMY HIGH SCHOOL
IKEDA
(LTD.) TENT
I AM DIS-APPOINTED ...
HUH?
...BUT IT SEEMS THAT WE'LL BE SHARING ITINERARIES TOMORROW.
SPLASH

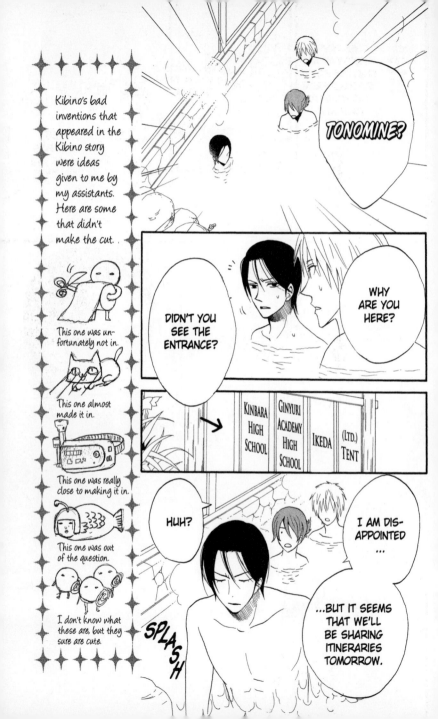

Kibino's bad inventions that appeared in the Kibino story were ideas given to me by my assistants. Here are some that didn't make the cut. .

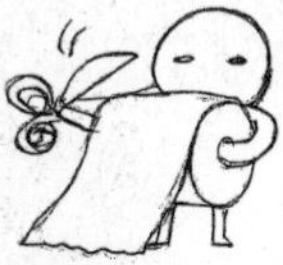

This one was unfortunately not in.

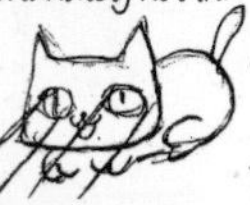

This one almost made it in.

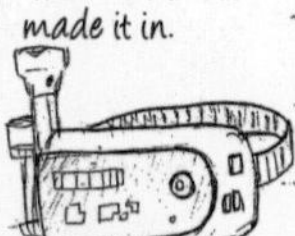

This one was really close to making it in.

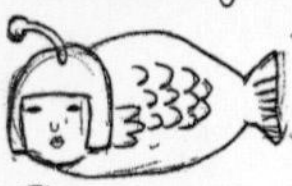

This one was out of the question.

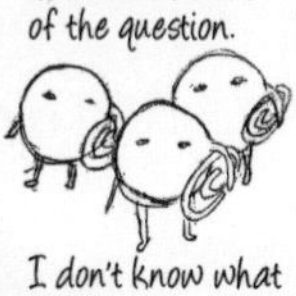

I don't know what these are, but they sure are cute.

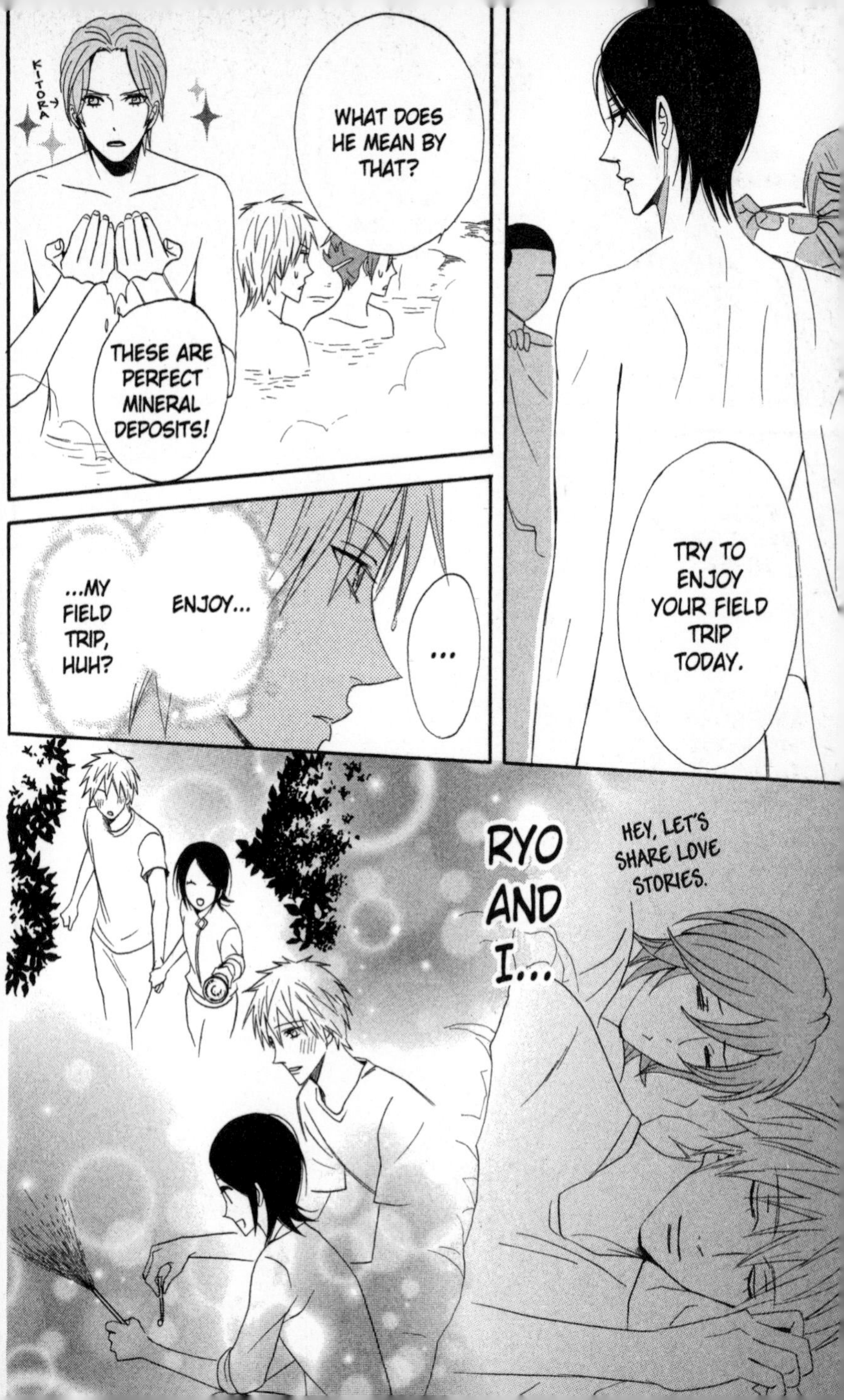
TRY TO ENJOY YOUR FIELD TRIP TODAY.
WHAT DOES HE MEAN BY THAT?
KITORA
THESE ARE PERFECT MINERAL DEPOSITS!
...
ENJOY...
...MY FIELD TRIP, HUH?
HEY, LET'S SHARE LOVE STORIES.
RYO AND I...

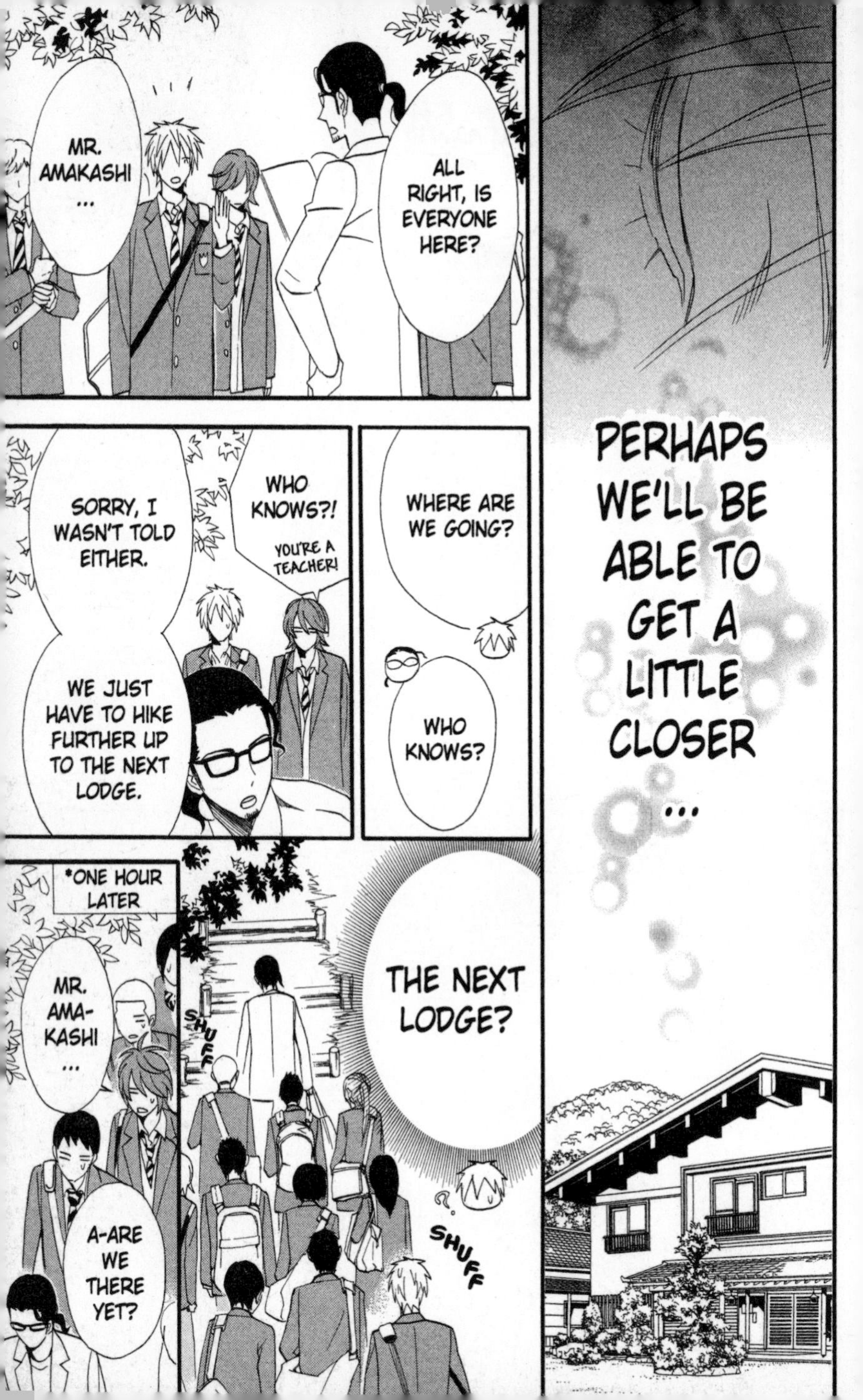
PERHAPS WE'LL BE ABLE TO GET A LITTLE CLOSER ...
ALL RIGHT, IS EVERYONE HERE?
MR. AMAKASHI ...
WHERE ARE WE GOING?
WHO KNOWS?
WHO KNOWS?!
YOU'RE A TEACHER!
SORRY, I WASN'T TOLD EITHER.
WE JUST HAVE TO HIKE FURTHER UP TO THE NEXT LODGE.
THE NEXT LODGE?
SHUFF
SHUFF
*ONE HOUR LATER
MR. AMA-KASHI ...
A-ARE WE THERE YET?

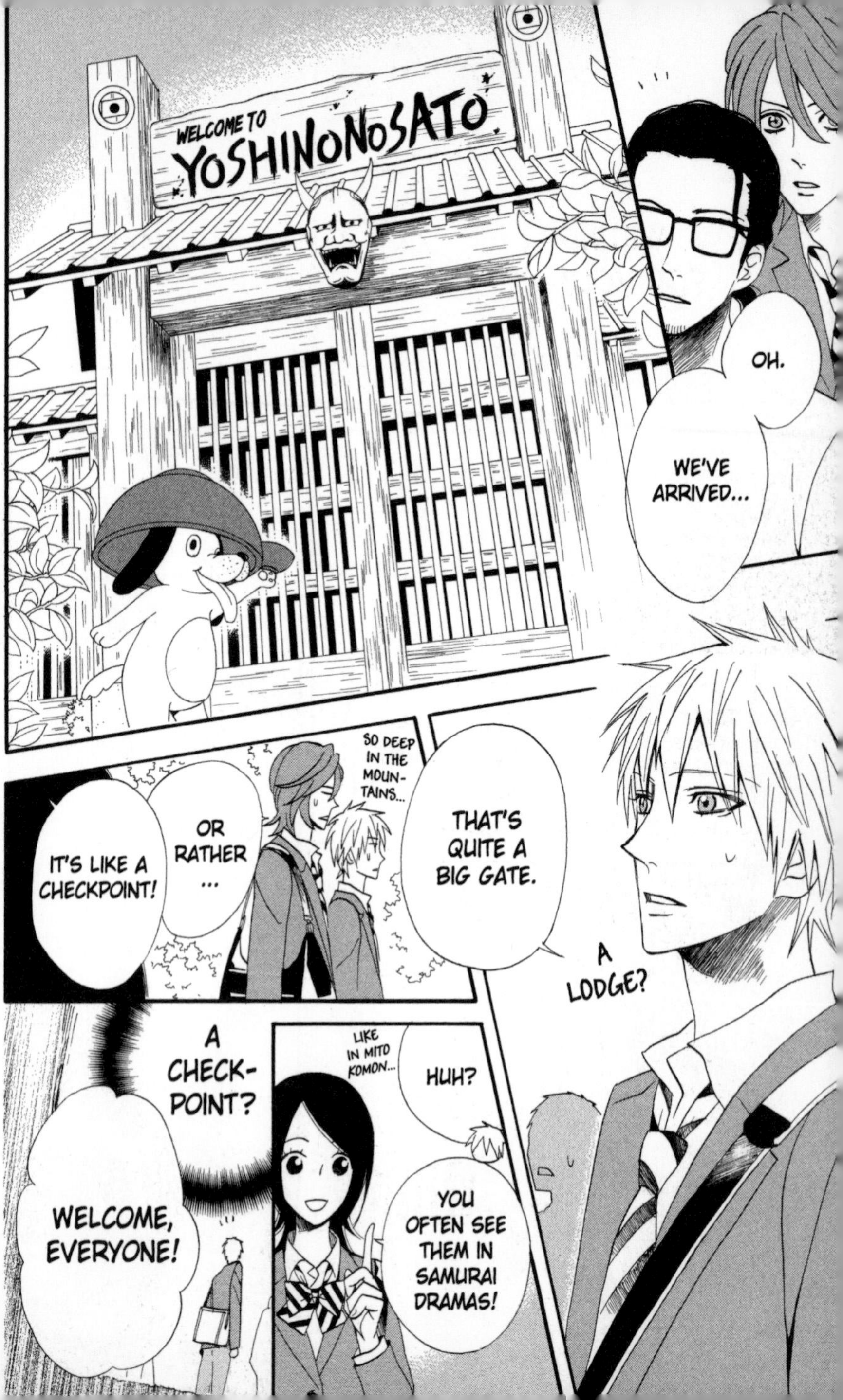
OH.
WE'VE ARRIVED...
WELCOME TO
YOSHINONOSATO
THAT'S QUITE A BIG GATE.
A LODGE?
SO DEEP IN THE MOUNTAINS...
OR RATHER...
IT'S LIKE A CHECKPOINT!
HUH?
LIKE IN MITO KOMON...
YOU OFTEN SEE THEM IN SAMURAI DRAMAS!
A CHECKPOINT?
WELCOME, EVERYONE!

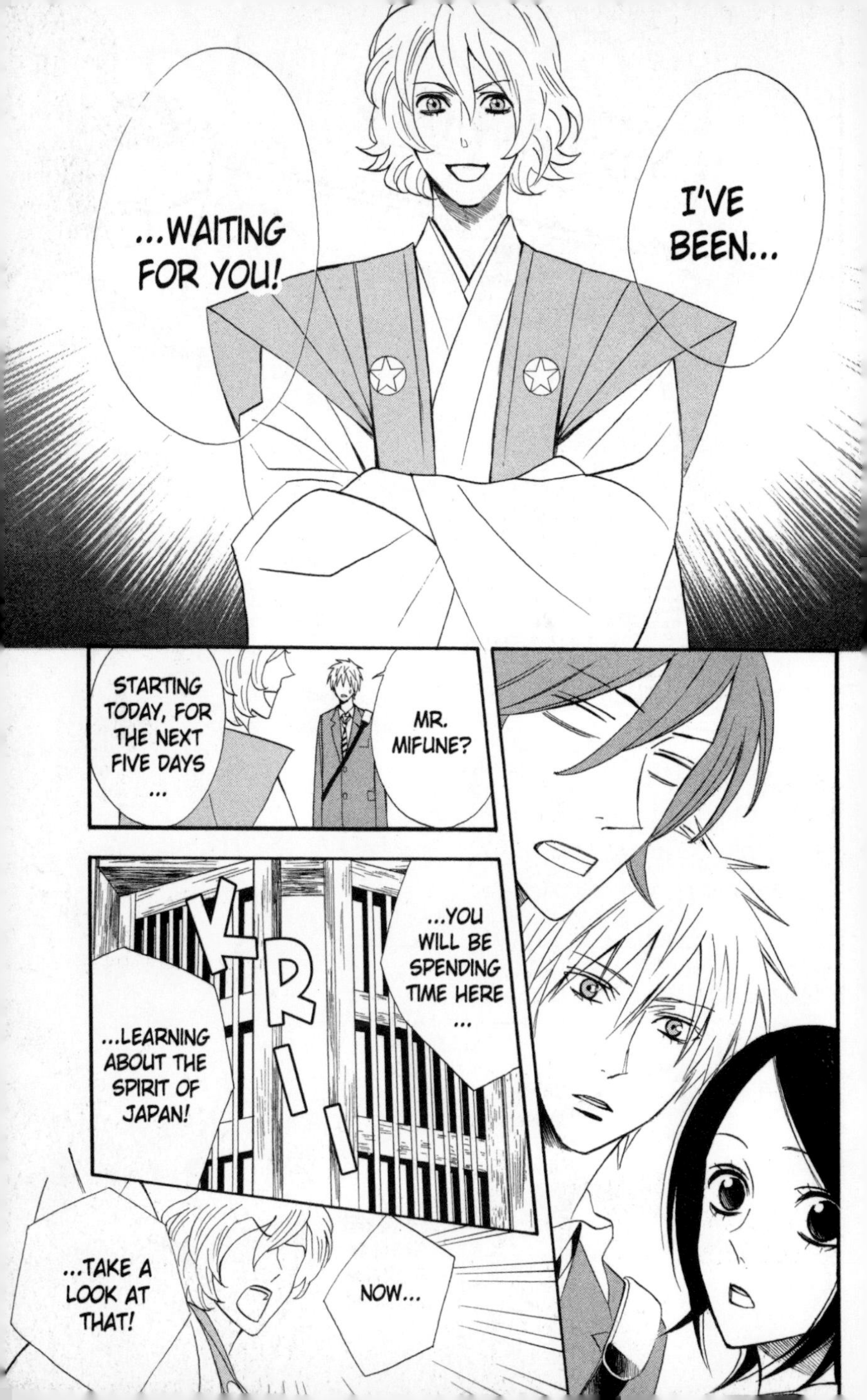
I'VE BEEN...
...WAITING FOR YOU!
MR. MIFUNE?
STARTING TODAY, FOR THE NEXT FIVE DAYS ...
...YOU WILL BE SPENDING TIME HERE ...
KRII
...LEARNING ABOUT THE SPIRIT OF JAPAN!
NOW...
...TAKE A LOOK AT THAT!

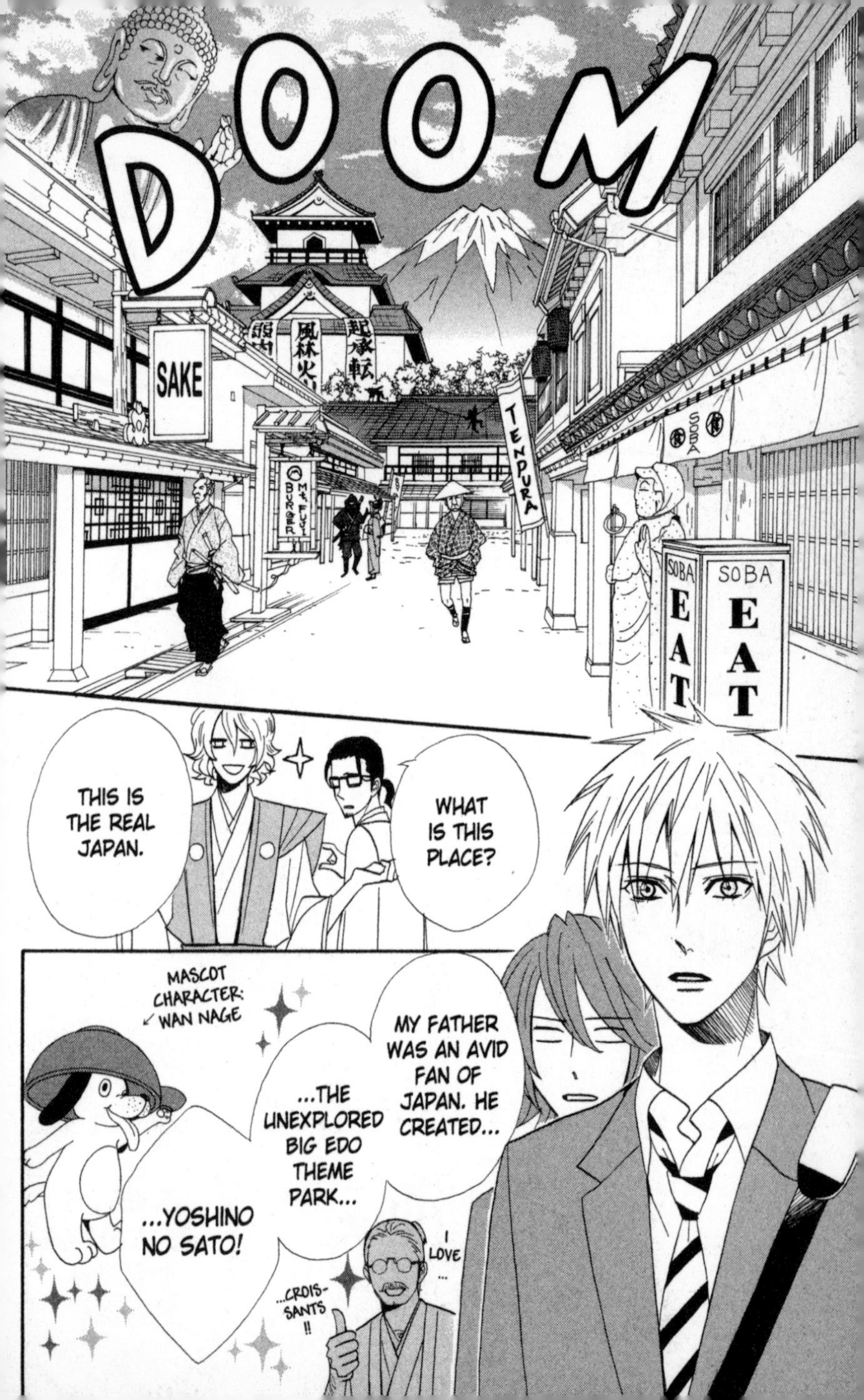
DOOM
SAKE
TENPURA
SOBA
Mt. FUJI BURGER
SOBA EAT
SOBA EAT
WHAT IS THIS PLACE?
THIS IS THE REAL JAPAN.
MY FATHER WAS AN AVID FAN OF JAPAN. HE CREATED...
...THE UNEXPLORED BIG EDO THEME PARK...
...YOSHINO NO SATO!
I LOVE...
...CROIS-SANTS!!
MASCOT CHARACTER: WAN NAGE

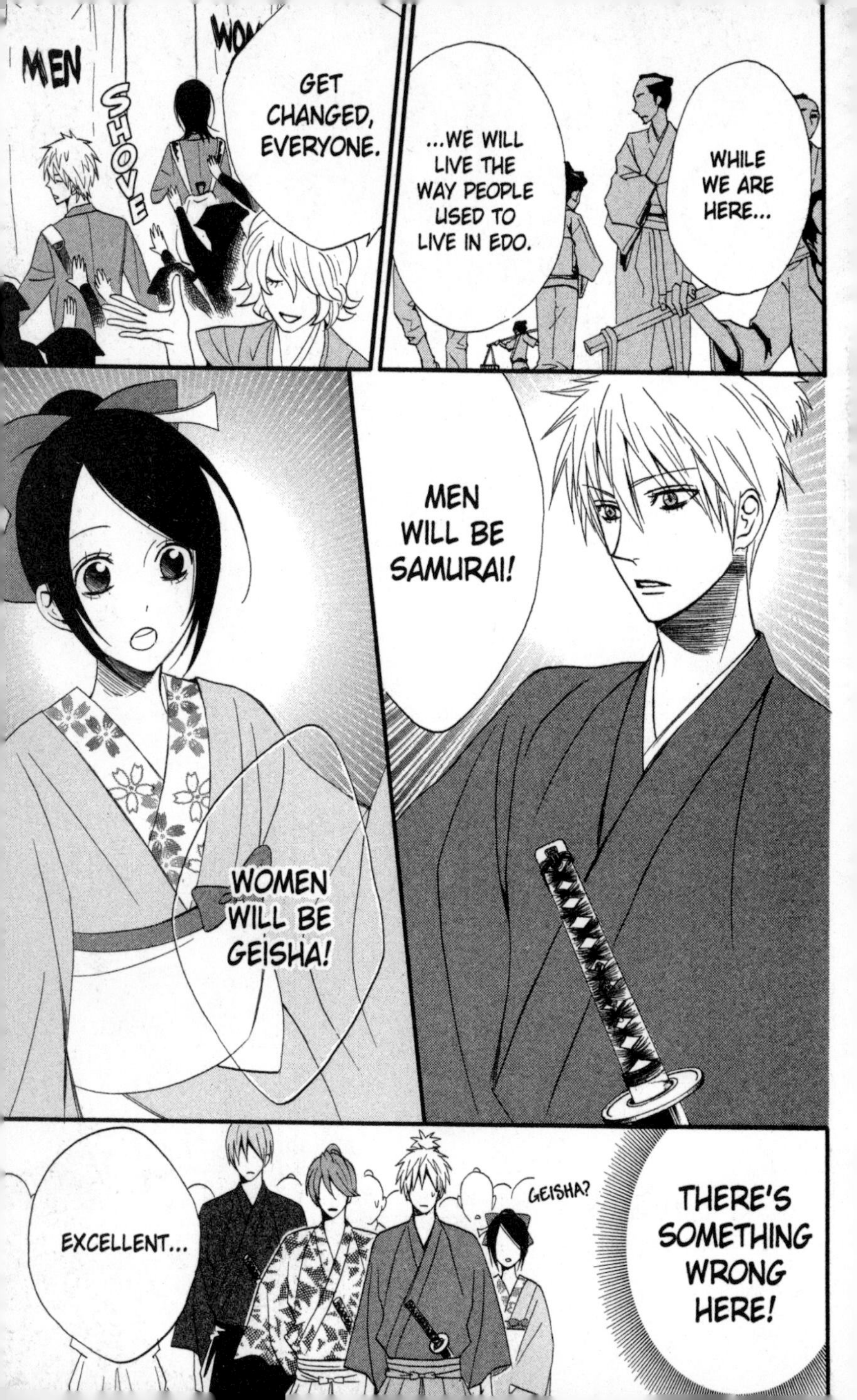
WHILE WE ARE HERE...
...WE WILL LIVE THE WAY PEOPLE USED TO LIVE IN EDO.
GET CHANGED, EVERYONE.
SHOVE
MEN
MEN WILL BE SAMURAI!
WOMEN WILL BE GEISHA!
THERE'S SOMETHING WRONG HERE!
GEISHA?
EXCELLENT...

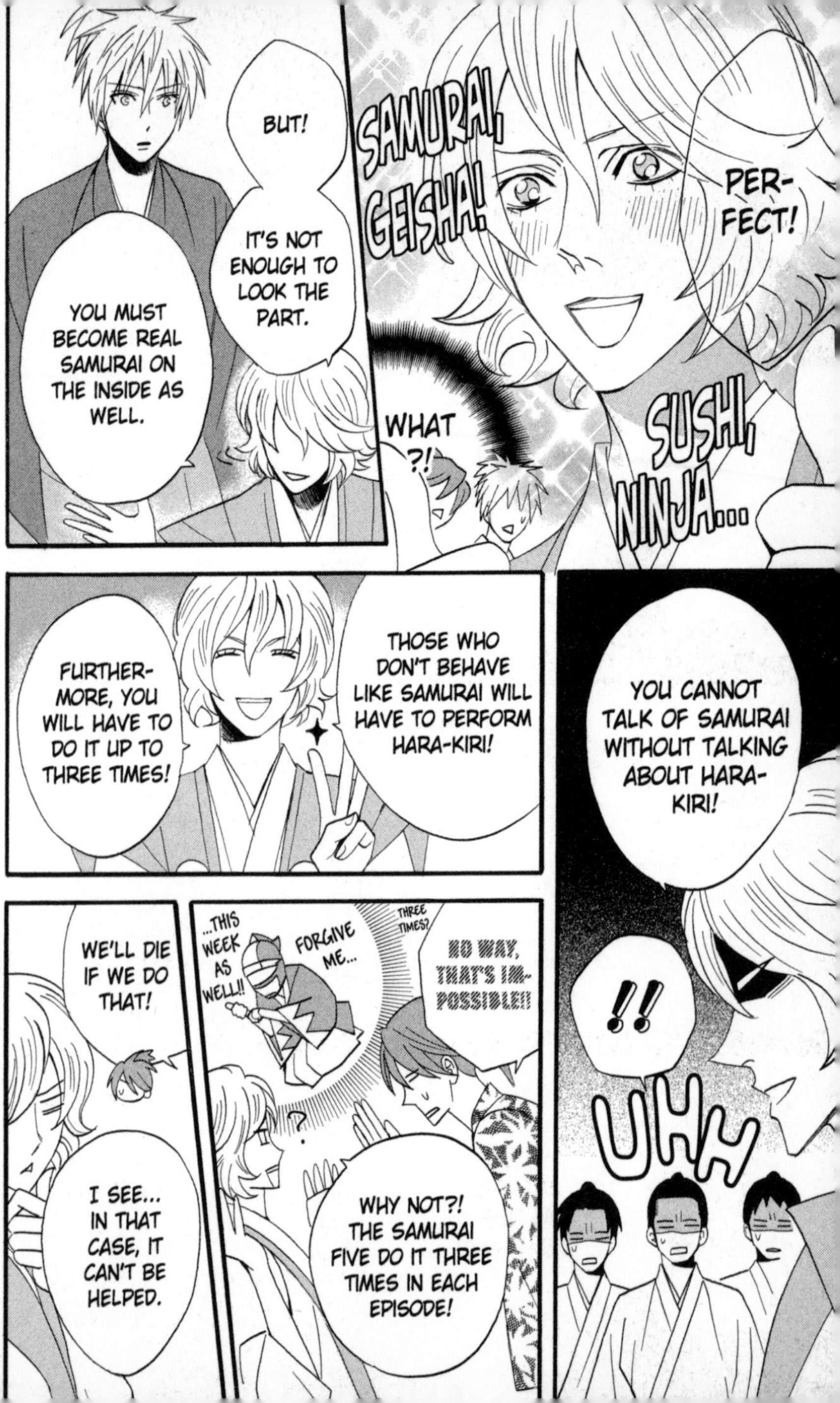

SAMURAI, GEISHA!
PER-FECT!
SUSHI, NINJA...
WHAT?!
BUT!
IT'S NOT ENOUGH TO LOOK THE PART.
YOU MUST BECOME REAL SAMURAI ON THE INSIDE AS WELL.
YOU CANNOT TALK OF SAMURAI WITHOUT TALKING ABOUT HARA-KIRI!
!!
UHH
THOSE WHO DON'T BEHAVE LIKE SAMURAI WILL HAVE TO PERFORM HARA-KIRI!
FURTHER-MORE, YOU WILL HAVE TO DO IT UP TO THREE TIMES!
NO WAY, THAT'S IM-POSSIBLE!!
THREE TIMES?
FORGIVE ME...
...THIS WEEK AS WELL!!
?
WHY NOT?! THE SAMURAI FIVE DO IT THREE TIMES IN EACH EPISODE!
WE'LL DIE IF WE DO THAT!
I SEE... IN THAT CASE, IT CAN'T BE HELPED.

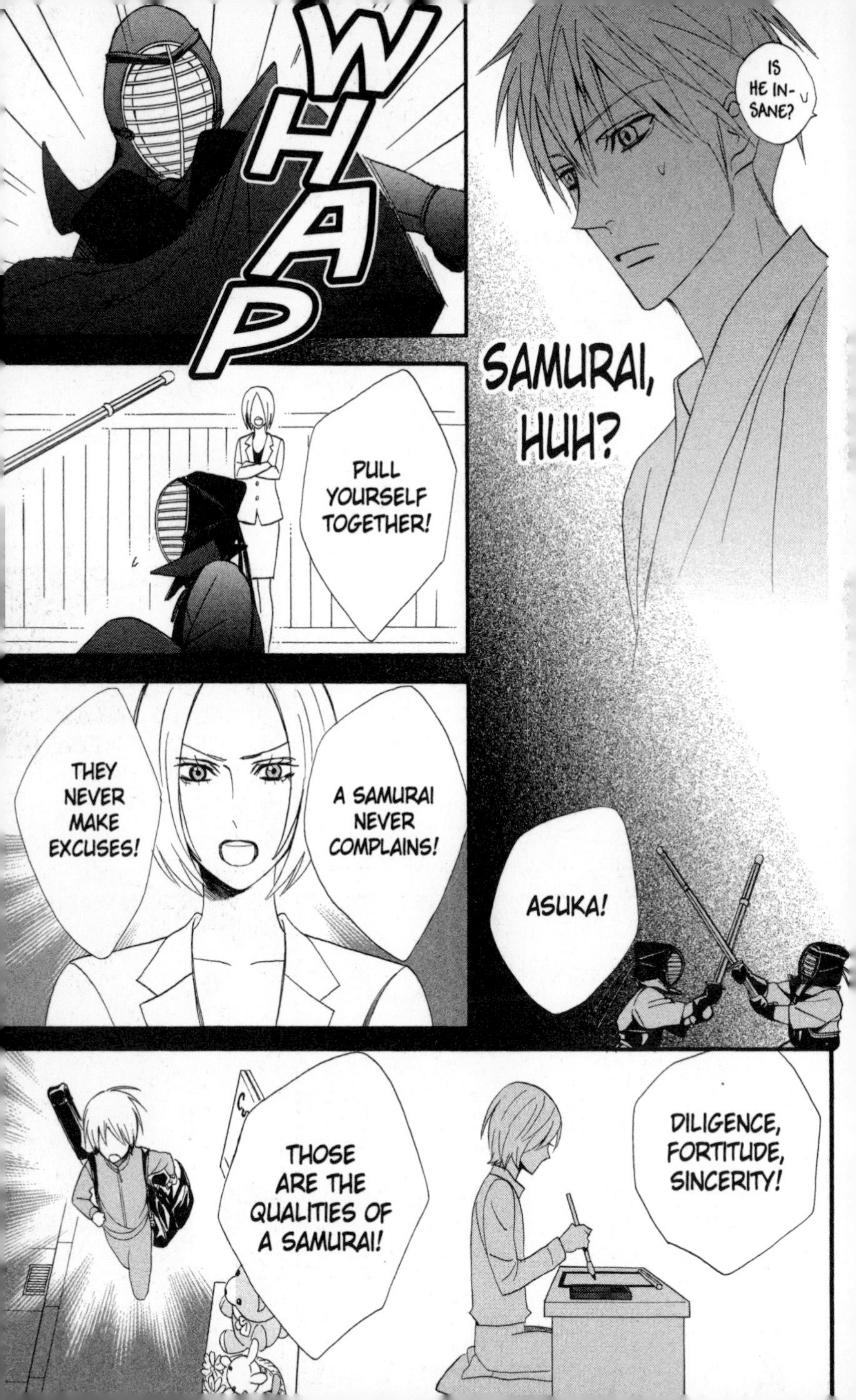
IS HE IN-SANE?
SAMURAI, HUH?
ASUKA!
WHAP
PULL YOURSELF TOGETHER!
A SAMURAI NEVER COMPLAINS!
THEY NEVER MAKE EXCUSES!
DILIGENCE, FORTITUDE, SINCERITY!
THOSE ARE THE QUALITIES OF A SAMURAI!

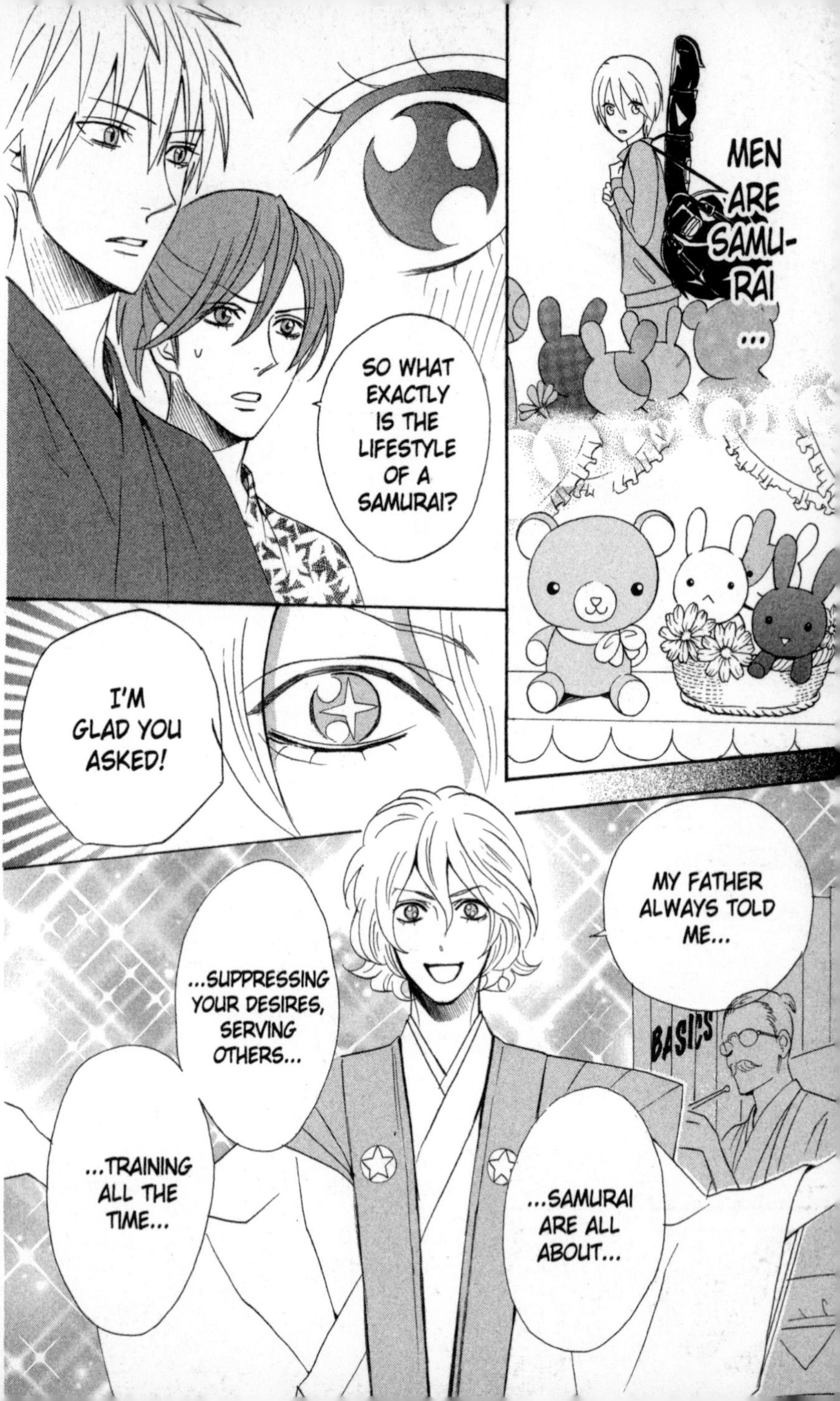
MEN ARE SAMU-RAI ...
SO WHAT EXACTLY IS THE LIFESTYLE OF A SAMURAI?
I'M GLAD YOU ASKED!
MY FATHER ALWAYS TOLD ME...
BASICS
...SAMURAI ARE ALL ABOUT...
...SUPPRESSING YOUR DESIRES, SERVING OTHERS...
...TRAINING ALL THE TIME...

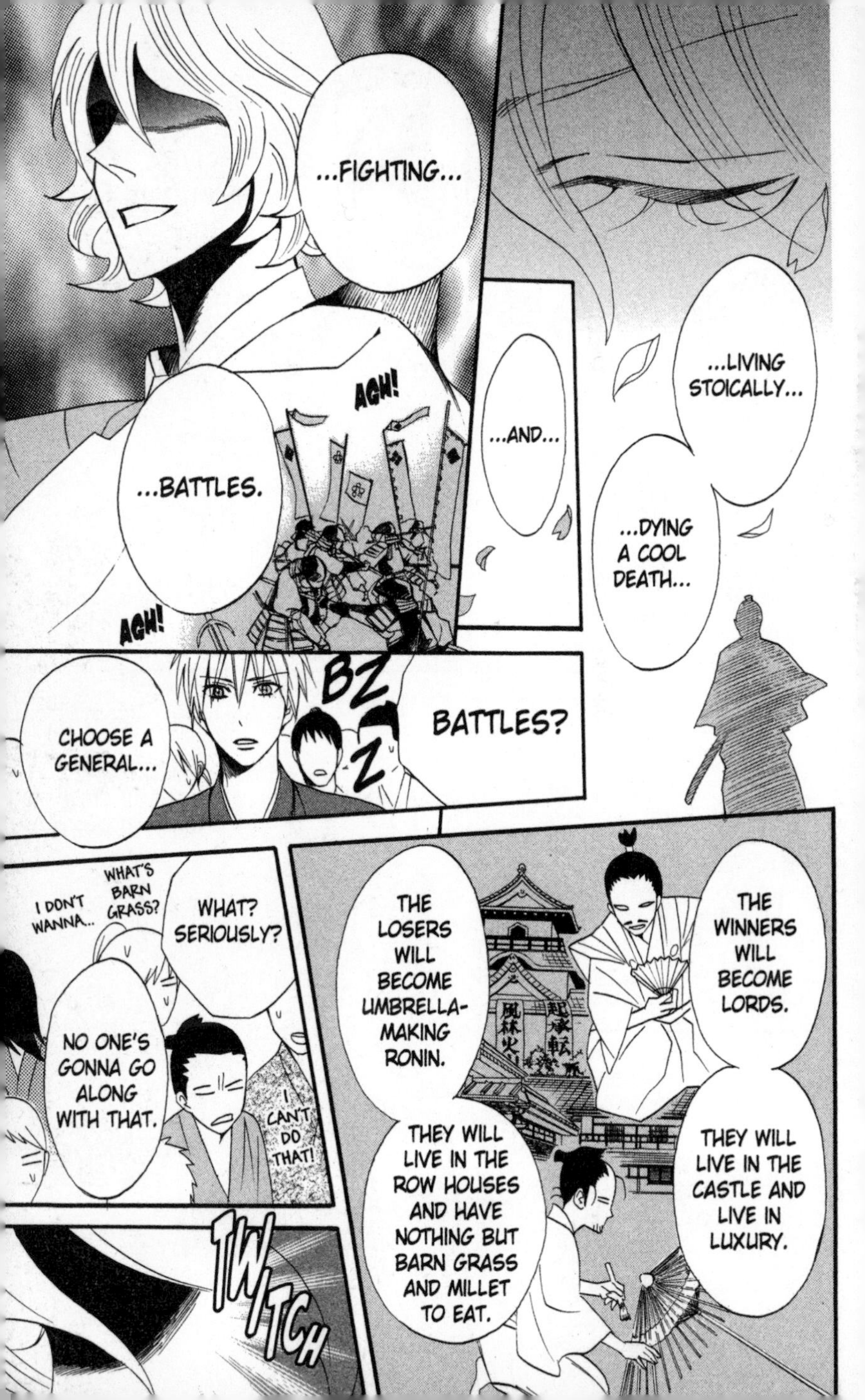
...LIVING STOICALLY...
...DYING A COOL DEATH...
...AND...
...FIGHTING...
...BATTLES.
AGH!
AGH!
BATTLES?
BZZ
CHOOSE A GENERAL...
THE WINNERS WILL BECOME LORDS.
THEY WILL LIVE IN THE CASTLE AND LIVE IN LUXURY.
THE LOSERS WILL BECOME UMBRELLA-MAKING RONIN.
THEY WILL LIVE IN THE ROW HOUSES AND HAVE NOTHING BUT BARN GRASS AND MILLET TO EAT.
WHAT? SERIOUSLY?
WHAT'S BARN GRASS?
I DON'T WANNA...
NO ONE'S GONNA GO ALONG WITH THAT.
I CAN'T DO THAT!
TWITCH

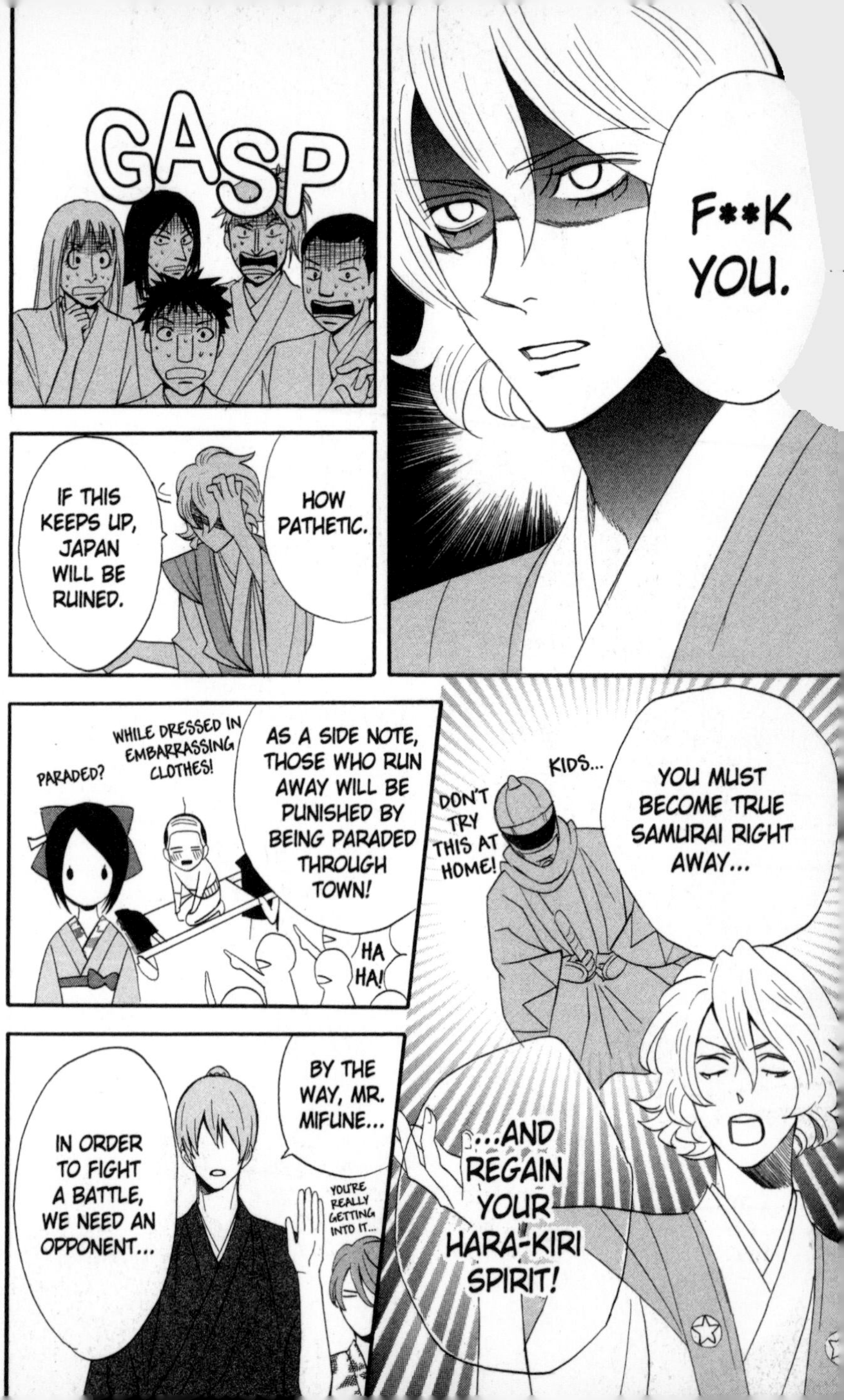
F**K YOU.
GASP
HOW PATHETIC.
IF THIS KEEPS UP, JAPAN WILL BE RUINED.
YOU MUST BECOME TRUE SAMURAI RIGHT AWAY...
KIDS... DON'T TRY THIS AT HOME!
...AND REGAIN YOUR HARA-KIRI SPIRIT!
AS A SIDE NOTE, THOSE WHO RUN AWAY WILL BE PUNISHED BY BEING PARADED THROUGH TOWN!
WHILE DRESSED IN EMBARRASSING CLOTHES!
PARADED?
HA HA!
BY THE WAY, MR. MIFUNE...
IN ORDER TO FIGHT A BATTLE, WE NEED AN OPPONENT...
YOU'RE REALLY GETTING INTO IT...

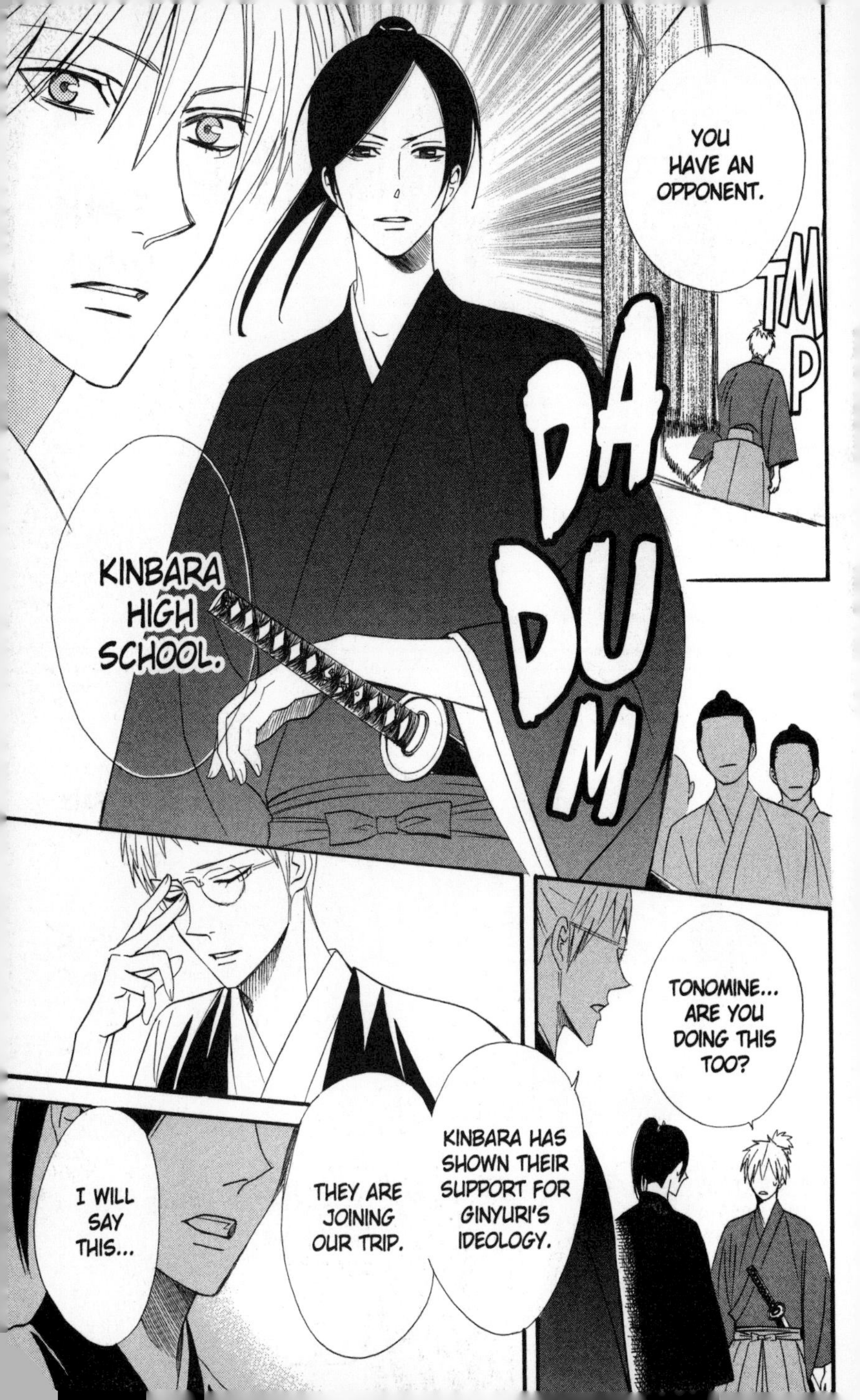

YOU HAVE AN OPPONENT.
TMP
DA DUM
KINBARA HIGH SCHOOL.
TONOMINE... ARE YOU DOING THIS TOO?
KINBARA HAS SHOWN THEIR SUPPORT FOR GINYURI'S IDEOLOGY.
THEY ARE JOINING OUR TRIP.
I WILL SAY THIS...

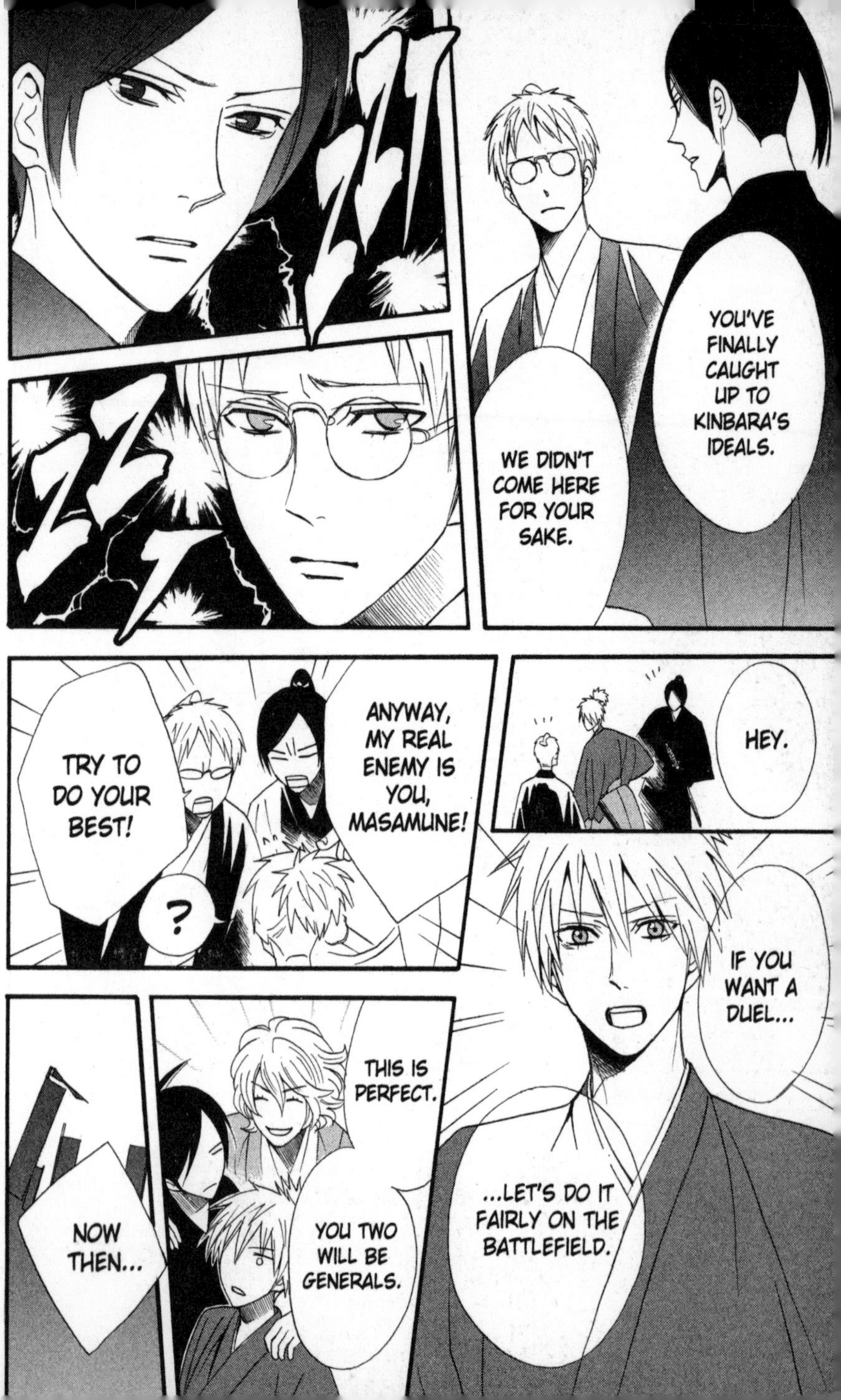
YOU'VE FINALLY CAUGHT UP TO KINBARA'S IDEALS.
WE DIDN'T COME HERE FOR YOUR SAKE.
HEY.
ANYWAY, MY REAL ENEMY IS YOU, MASAMUNE!
TRY TO DO YOUR BEST!
?
IF YOU WANT A DUEL...
...LET'S DO IT FAIRLY ON THE BATTLEFIELD.
THIS IS PERFECT.
YOU TWO WILL BE GENERALS.
NOW THEN...

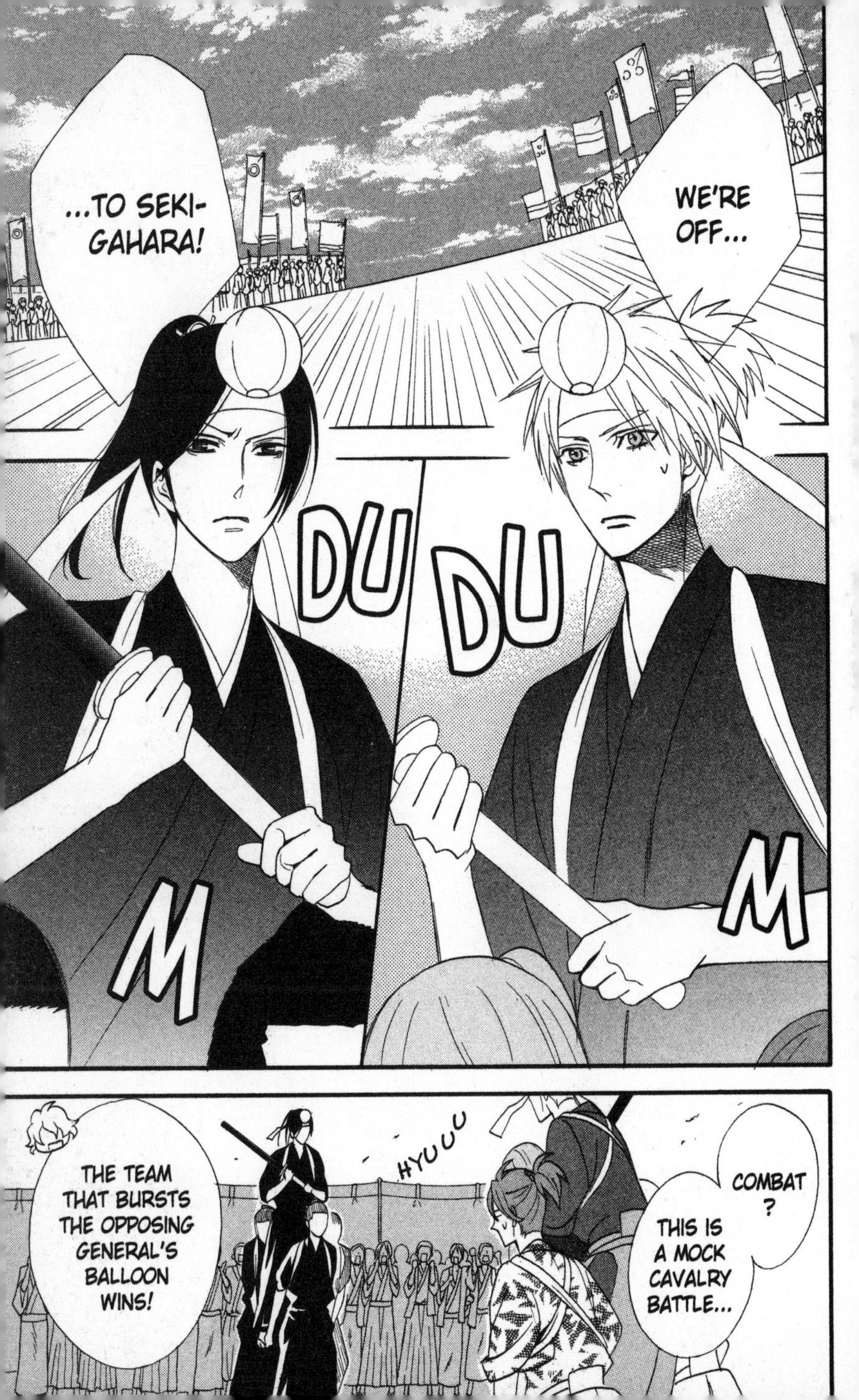
WE'RE OFF...
...TO SEKI-GAHARA!
DU
DU
M
M
COMBAT?
THIS IS A MOCK CAVALRY BATTLE...
HYUUU
THE TEAM THAT BURSTS THE OPPOSING GENERAL'S BALLOON WINS!

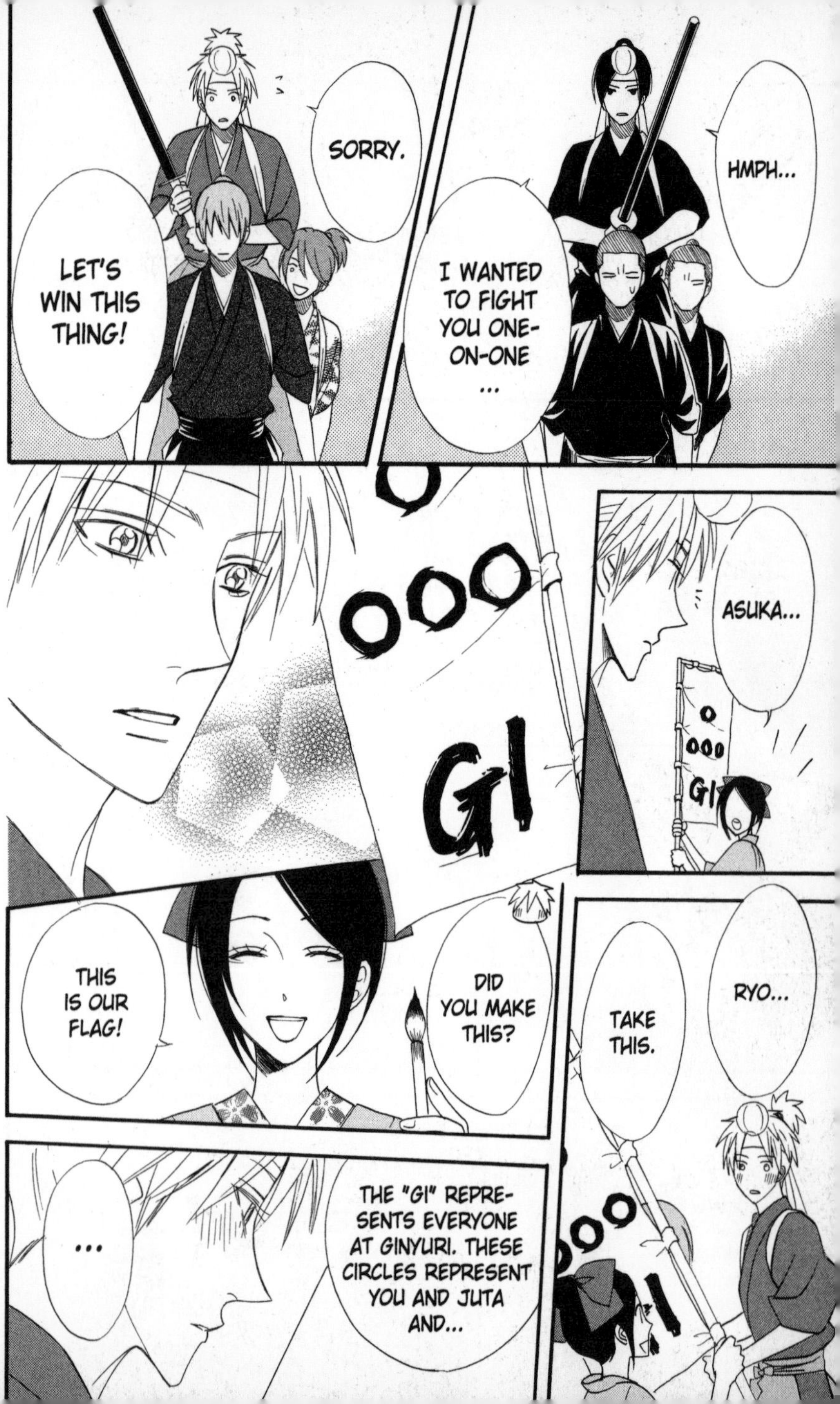
HMPH...
I WANTED TO FIGHT YOU ONE-ON-ONE...
SORRY.
LET'S WIN THIS THING!
ASUKA...
GI
RYO...
TAKE THIS.
DID YOU MAKE THIS?
THIS IS OUR FLAG!
THE "GI" REPRESENTS EVERYONE AT GINYURI. THESE CIRCLES REPRESENT YOU AND JUTA AND...
...

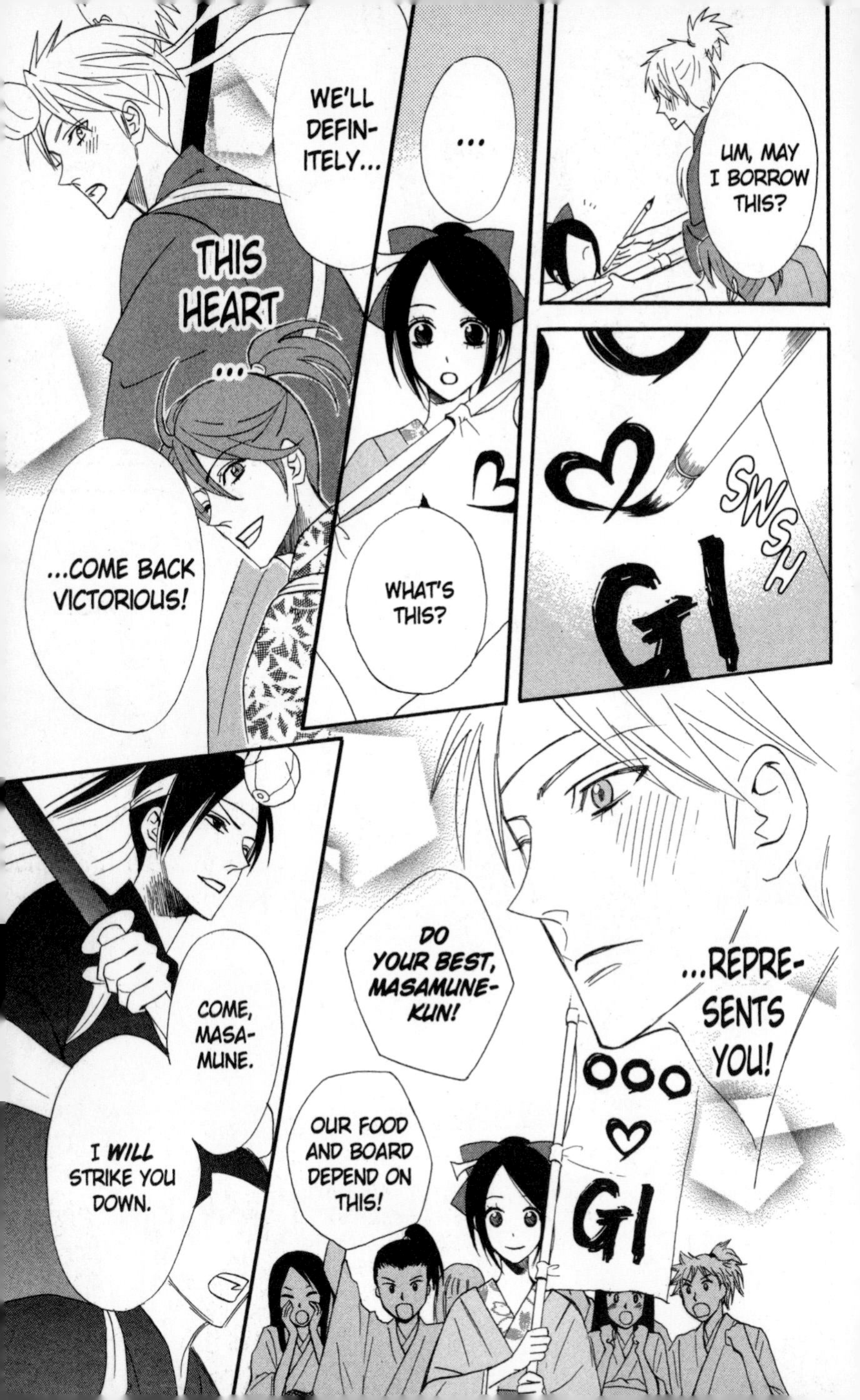
UM, MAY I BORROW THIS?
SWSH
GI
...
WHAT'S THIS?
WE'LL DEFINITELY...
THIS HEART...
...COME BACK VICTORIOUS!
...REPRESENTS YOU!
OOO ♡ GI
DO YOUR BEST, MASAMUNE-KUN!
OUR FOOD AND BOARD DEPEND ON THIS!
COME, MASAMUNE.
I *WILL* STRIKE YOU DOWN.

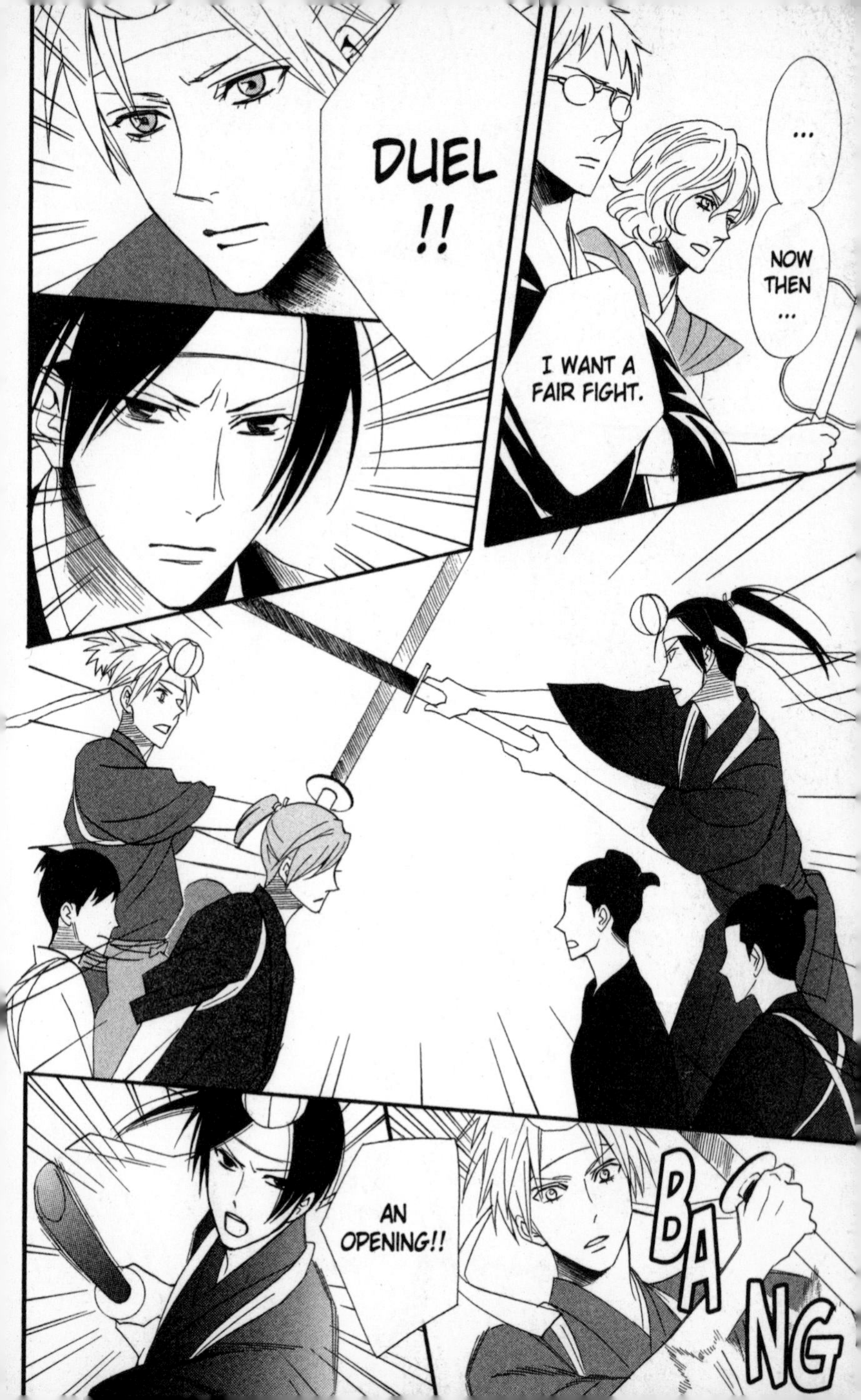
...
NOW THEN ...
I WANT A FAIR FIGHT.
DUEL !!
BANG
AN OPENING!!

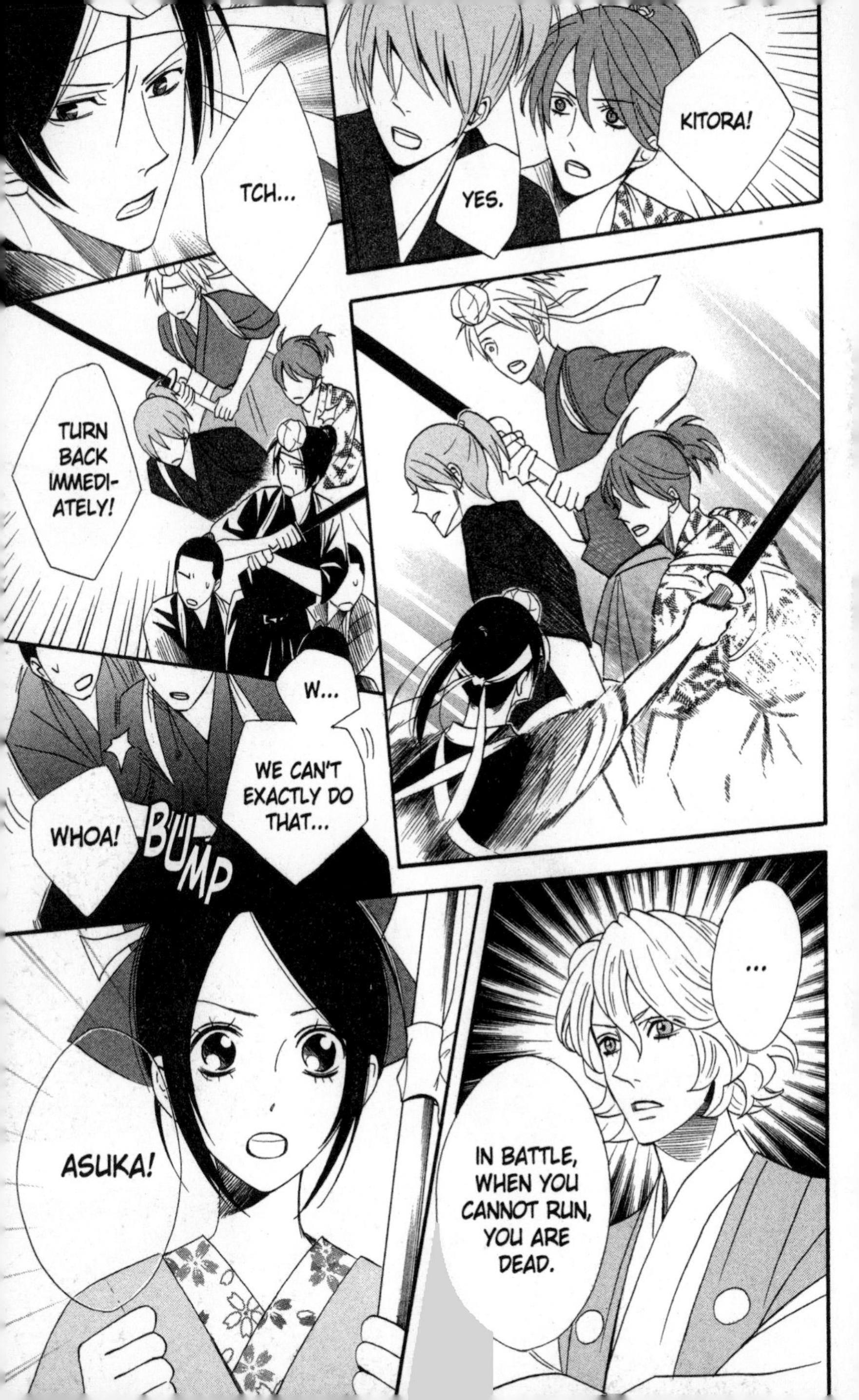
KITORA!
YES.
TCH...
TURN BACK IMMEDI-ATELY!
W...
WE CAN'T EXACTLY DO THAT...
BUMP
WHOA!
...
IN BATTLE, WHEN YOU CANNOT RUN, YOU ARE DEAD.
ASUKA!

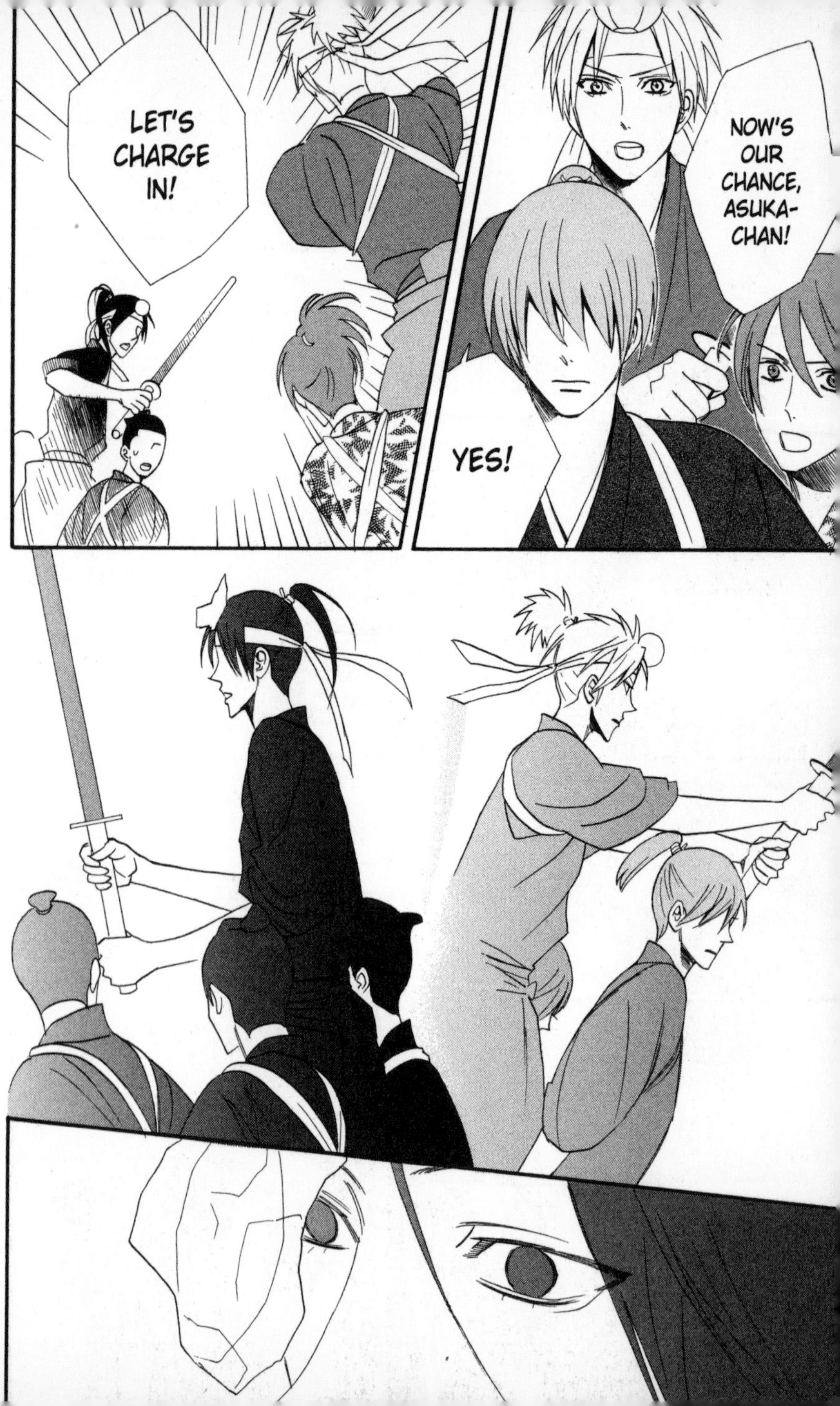
NOW'S OUR CHANCE, ASUKA-CHAN!
YES!
LET'S CHARGE IN!

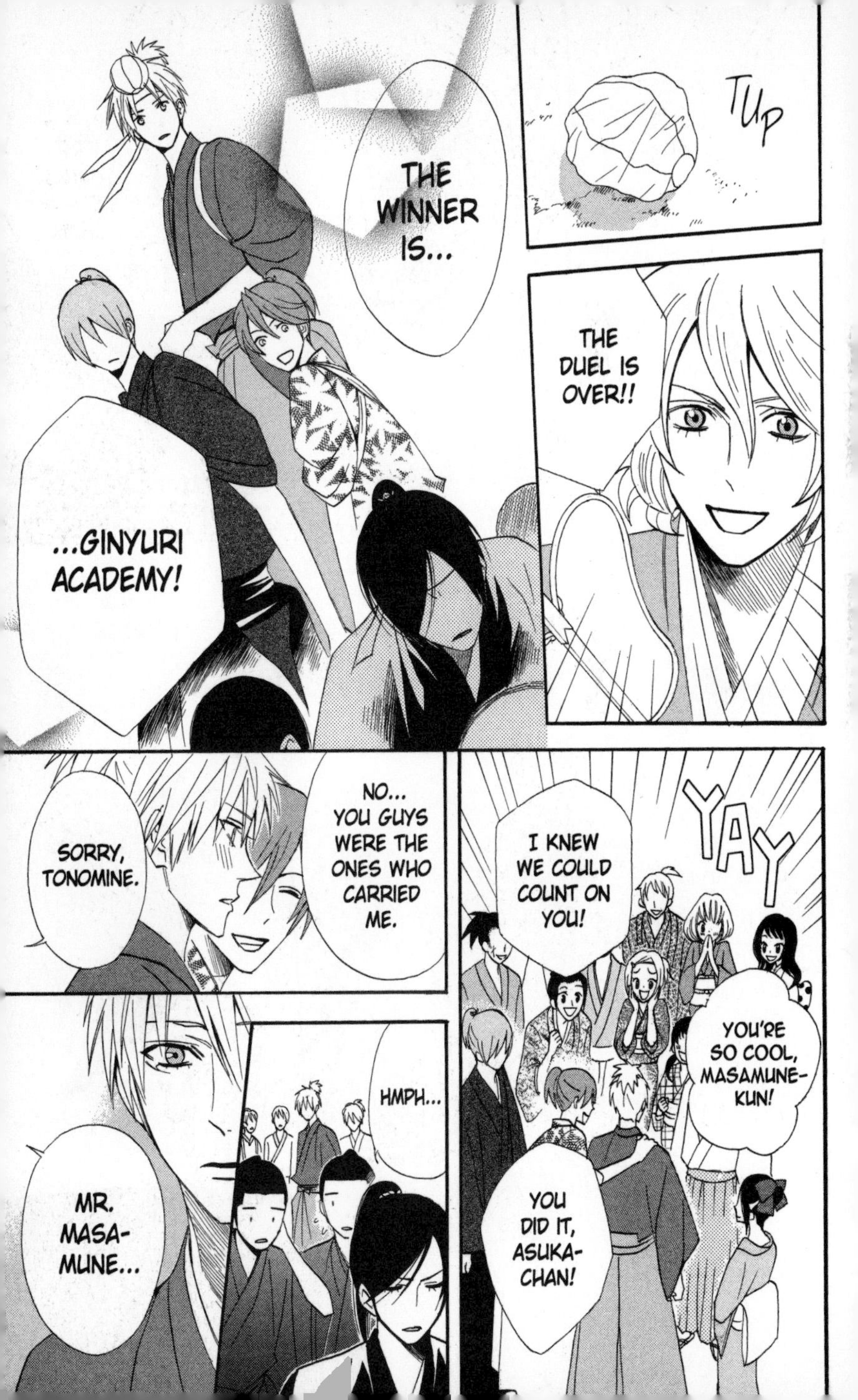
TUP
THE DUEL IS OVER!!
THE WINNER IS...
...GINYURI ACADEMY!
YAY
I KNEW WE COULD COUNT ON YOU!
YOU'RE SO COOL, MASAMUNE-KUN!
YOU DID IT, ASUKA-CHAN!
NO... YOU GUYS WERE THE ONES WHO CARRIED ME.
SORRY, TONOMINE.
HMPH...
MR. MASA-MUNE...

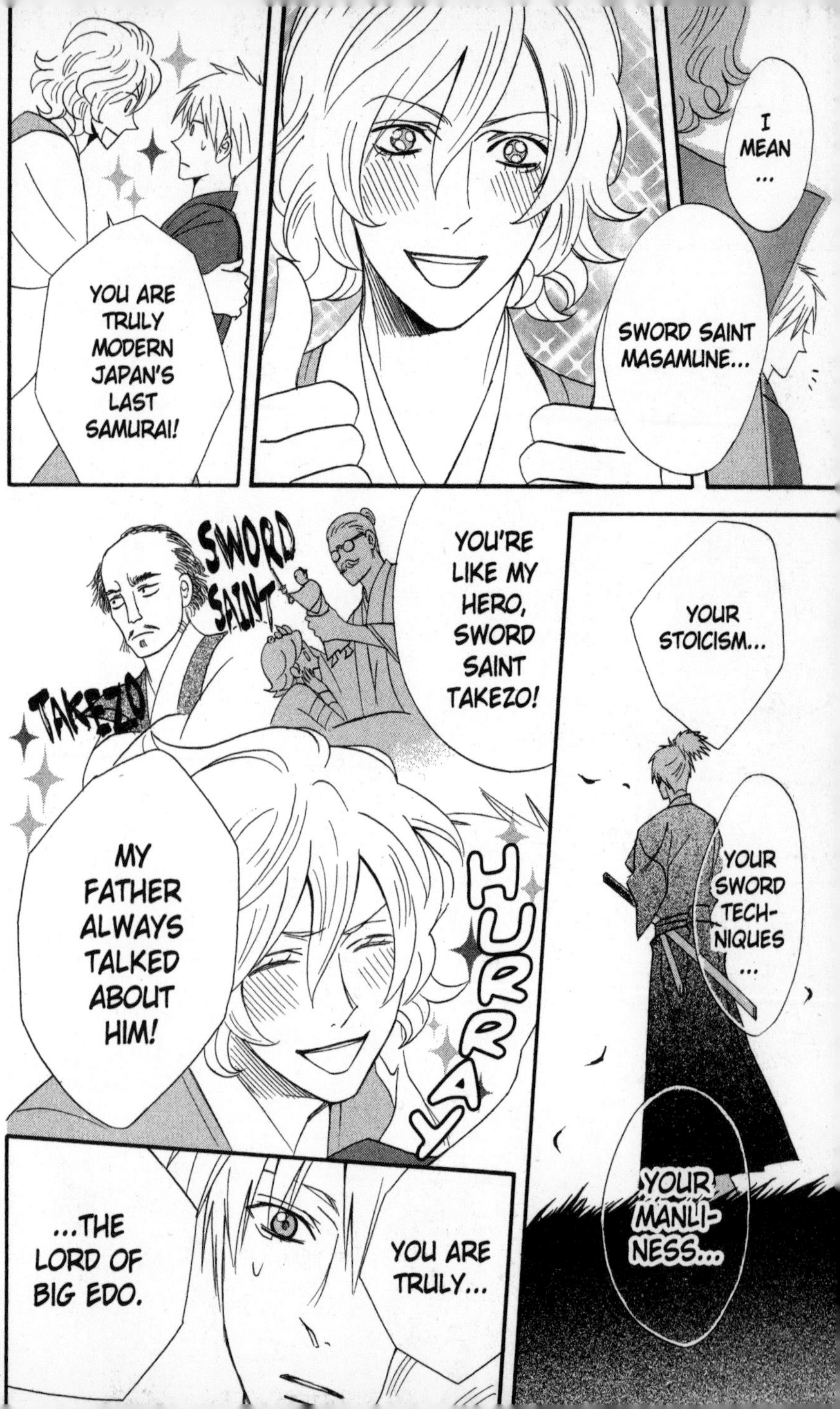
I MEAN ...
SWORD SAINT MASAMUNE...
YOU ARE TRULY MODERN JAPAN'S LAST SAMURAI!
YOUR STOICISM...
YOUR SWORD TECH-NIQUES ...
YOUR MANLI-NESS...
YOU'RE LIKE MY HERO, SWORD SAINT TAKEZO!
SWORD SAINT
TAKEZO
MY FATHER ALWAYS TALKED ABOUT HIM!
HURRAY
YOU ARE TRULY...
...THE LORD OF BIG EDO.

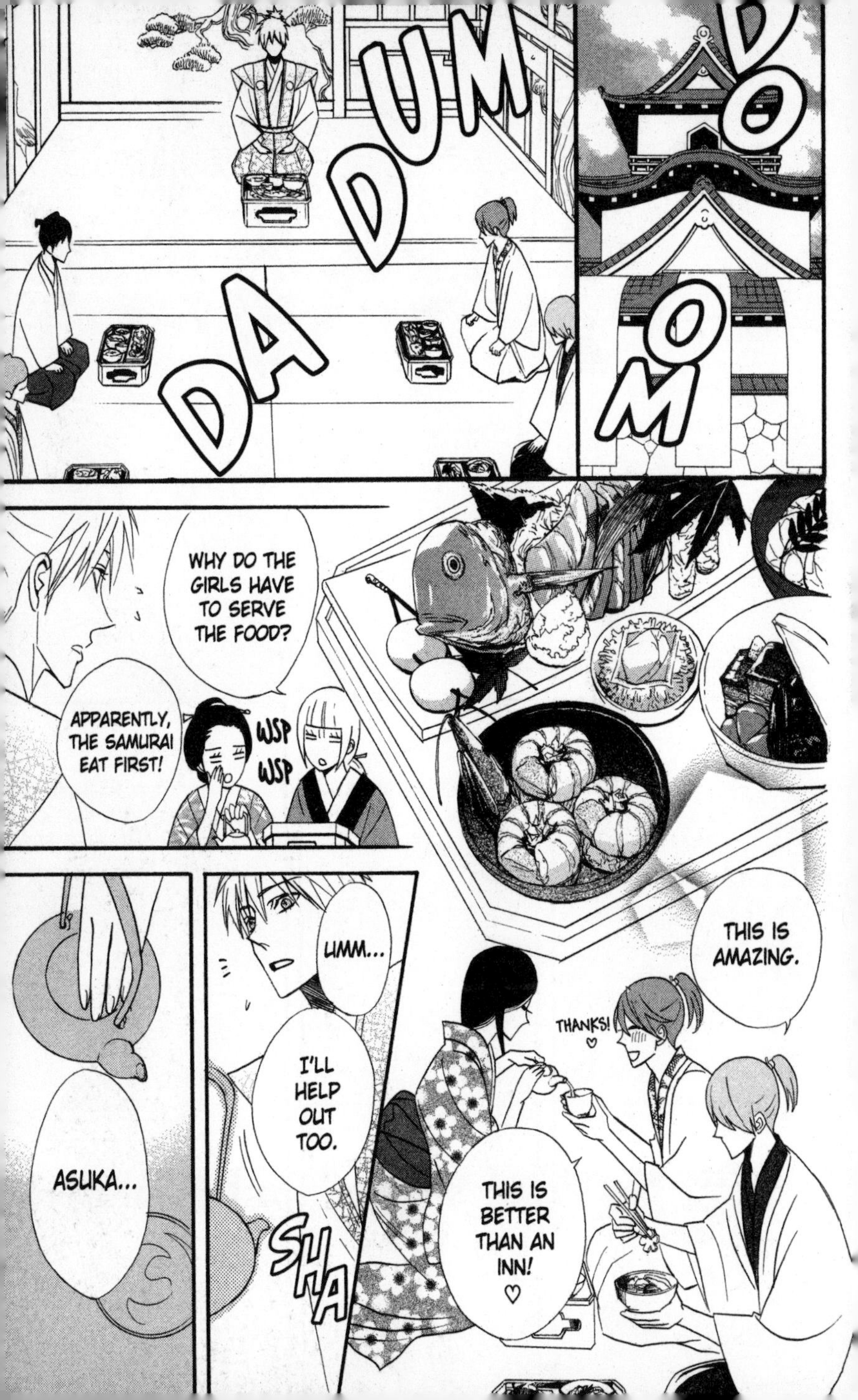
DOOM
DA DUM
WHY DO THE GIRLS HAVE TO SERVE THE FOOD?
APPARENTLY, THE SAMURAI EAT FIRST!
WSP WSP
THIS IS AMAZING.
THANKS! ♡
THIS IS BETTER THAN AN INN! ♡
UMM...
I'LL HELP OUT TOO.
SHA
ASUKA...

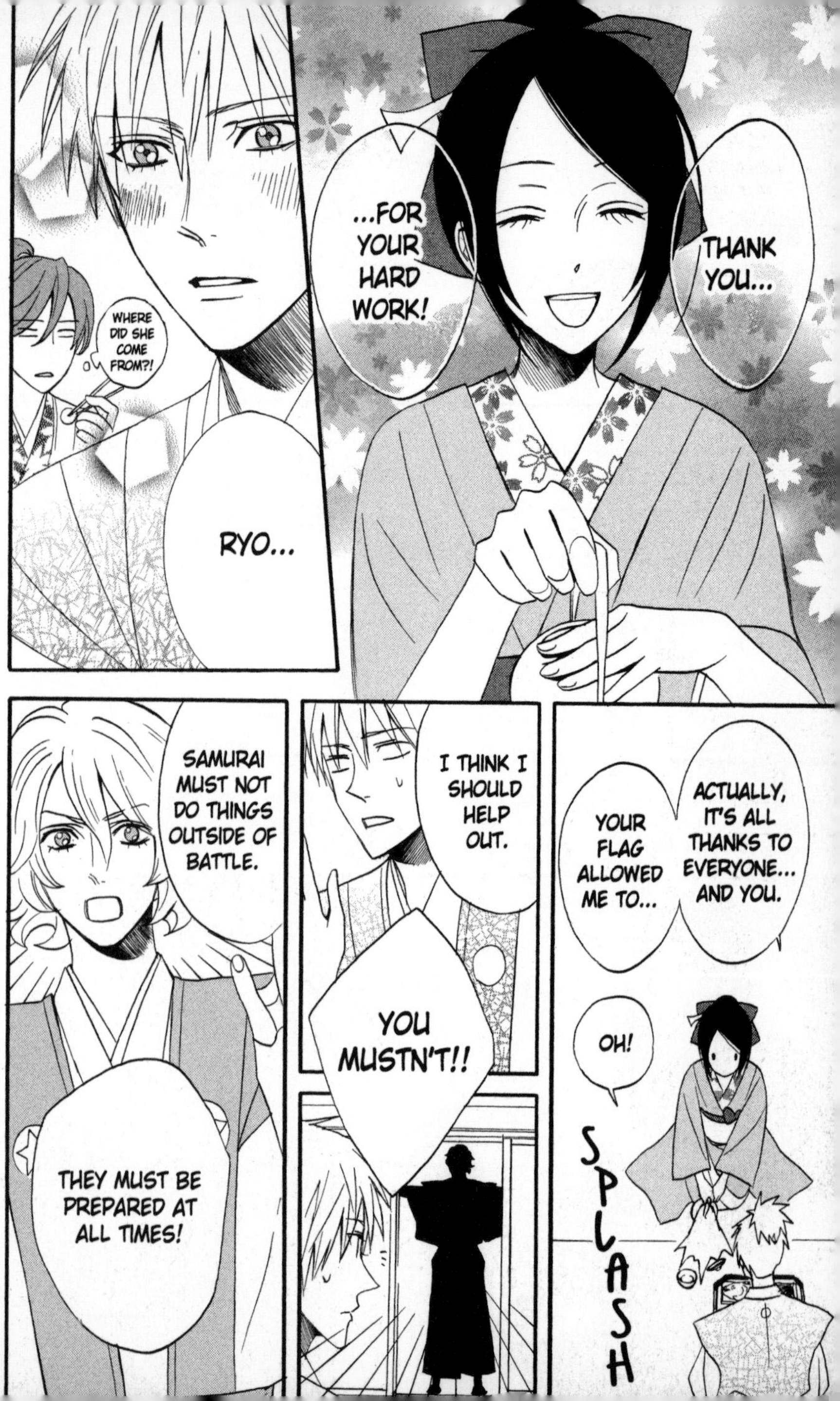
THANK YOU...
...FOR YOUR HARD WORK!
RYO...
WHERE DID SHE COME FROM?!
ACTUALLY, IT'S ALL THANKS TO EVERYONE... AND YOU.
YOUR FLAG ALLOWED ME TO...
OH!
SPLASH
I THINK I SHOULD HELP OUT.
YOU MUSTN'T!!
SAMURAI MUST NOT DO THINGS OUTSIDE OF BATTLE.
THEY MUST BE PREPARED AT ALL TIMES!

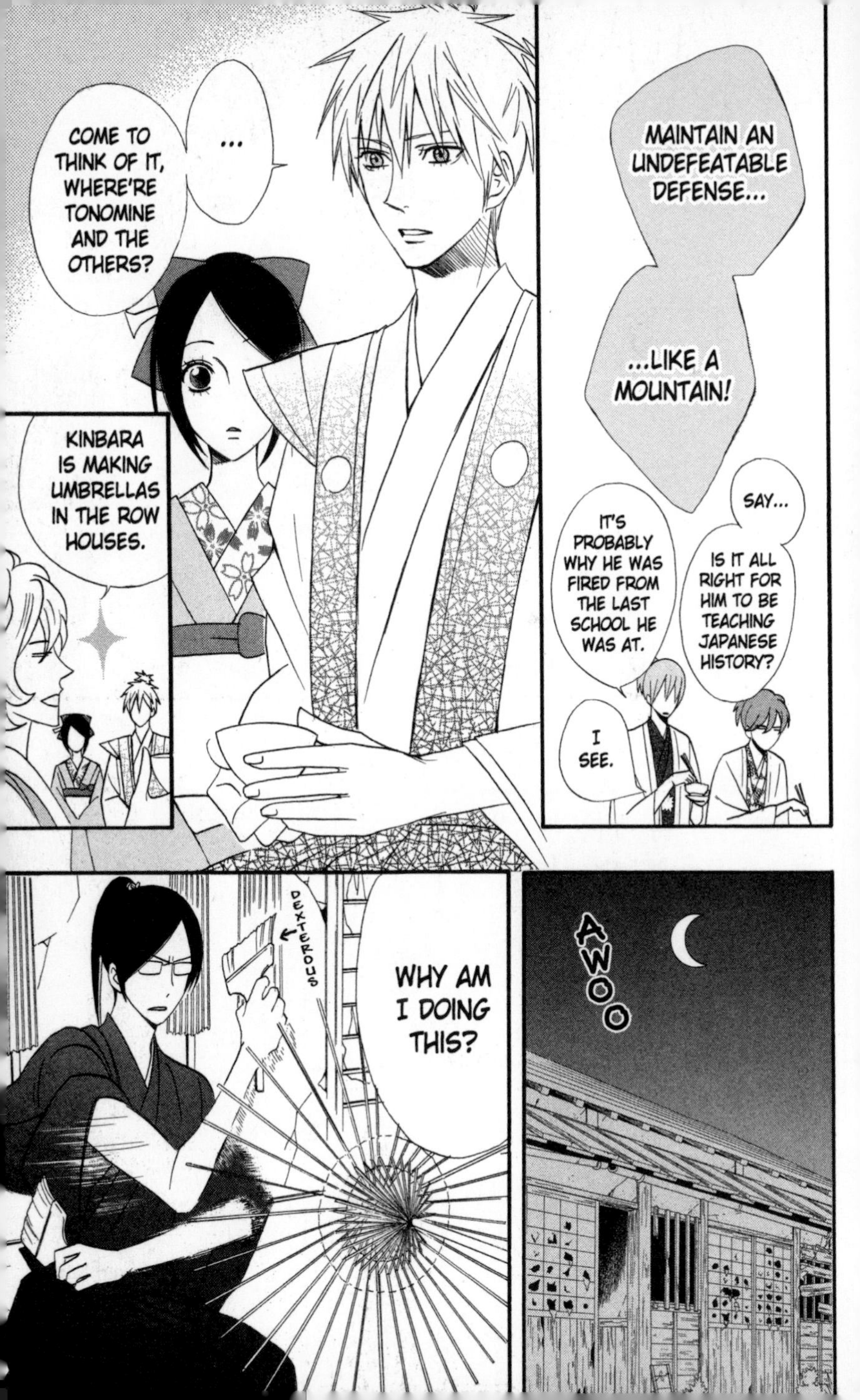
MAINTAIN AN UNDEFEATABLE DEFENSE...
...LIKE A MOUNTAIN!
SAY...
IS IT ALL RIGHT FOR HIM TO BE TEACHING JAPANESE HISTORY?
IT'S PROBABLY WHY HE WAS FIRED FROM THE LAST SCHOOL HE WAS AT.
I SEE.
...
COME TO THINK OF IT, WHERE'RE TONOMINE AND THE OTHERS?
KINBARA IS MAKING UMBRELLAS IN THE ROW HOUSES.
AWOO
WHY AM I DOING THIS?
DEXTEROUS

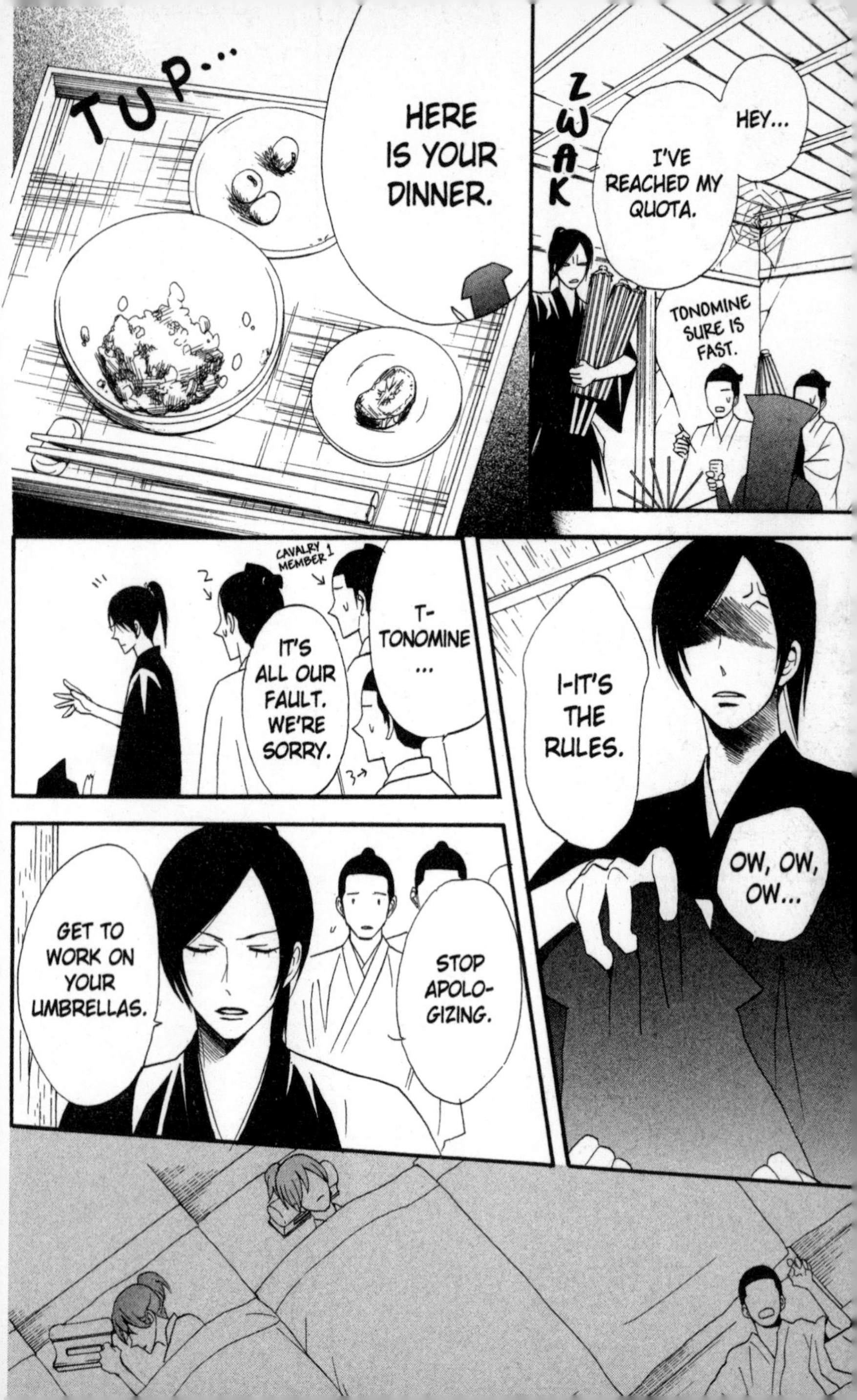
ZWAK
HEY...
I'VE REACHED MY QUOTA.
TONOMINE SURE IS FAST.
TUP...
HERE IS YOUR DINNER.
I-IT'S THE RULES.
OW, OW, OW...
CAVALRY MEMBER 1
T-TONOMINE...
IT'S ALL OUR FAULT. WE'RE SORRY.
STOP APOLOGIZING.
GET TO WORK ON YOUR UMBRELLAS.

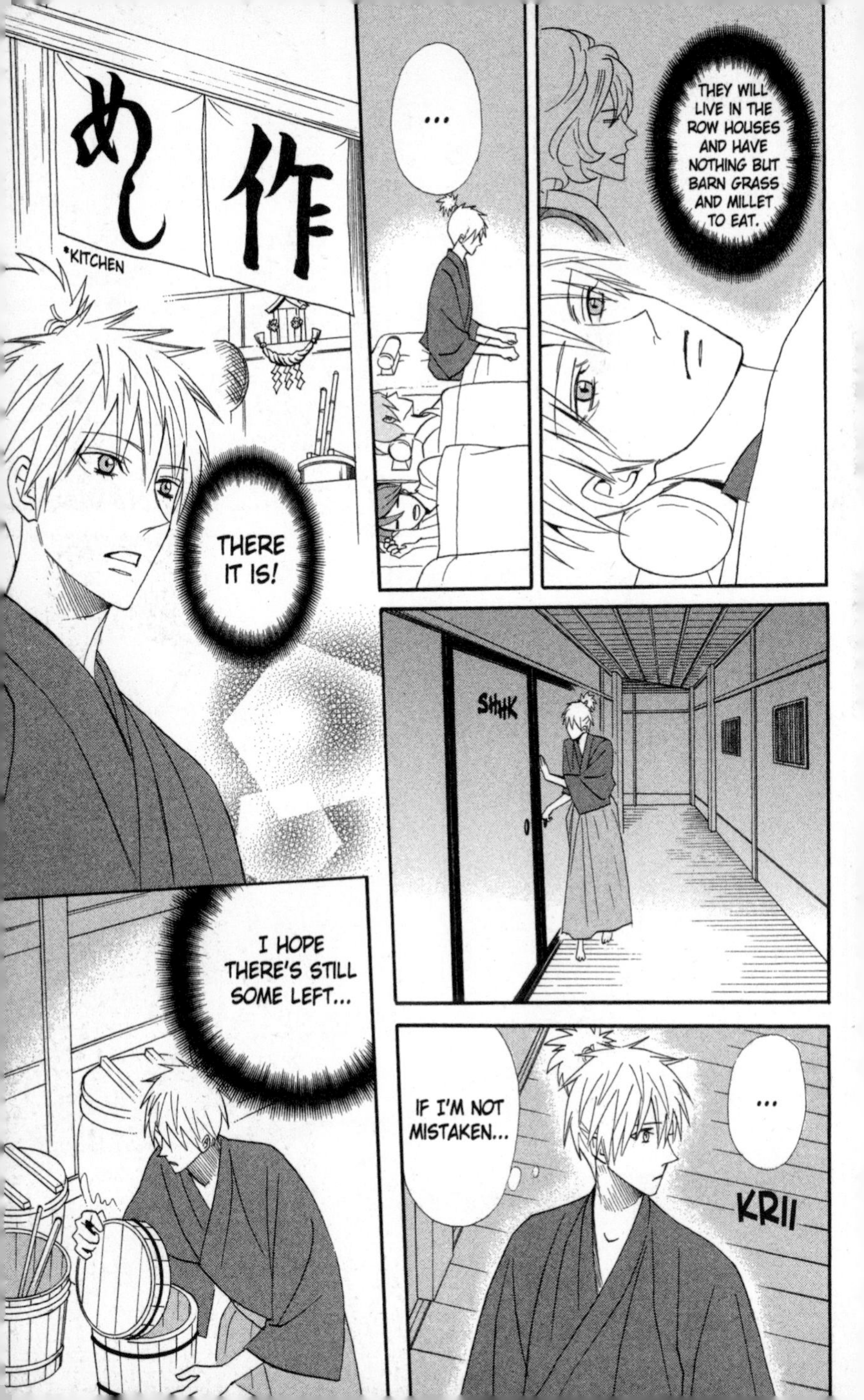
THEY WILL LIVE IN THE ROW HOUSES AND HAVE NOTHING BUT BARN GRASS AND MILLET TO EAT.
...
SHHK
...
IF I'M NOT MISTAKEN...
KRII
作
めし
*KITCHEN
THERE IT IS!
I HOPE THERE'S STILL SOME LEFT...

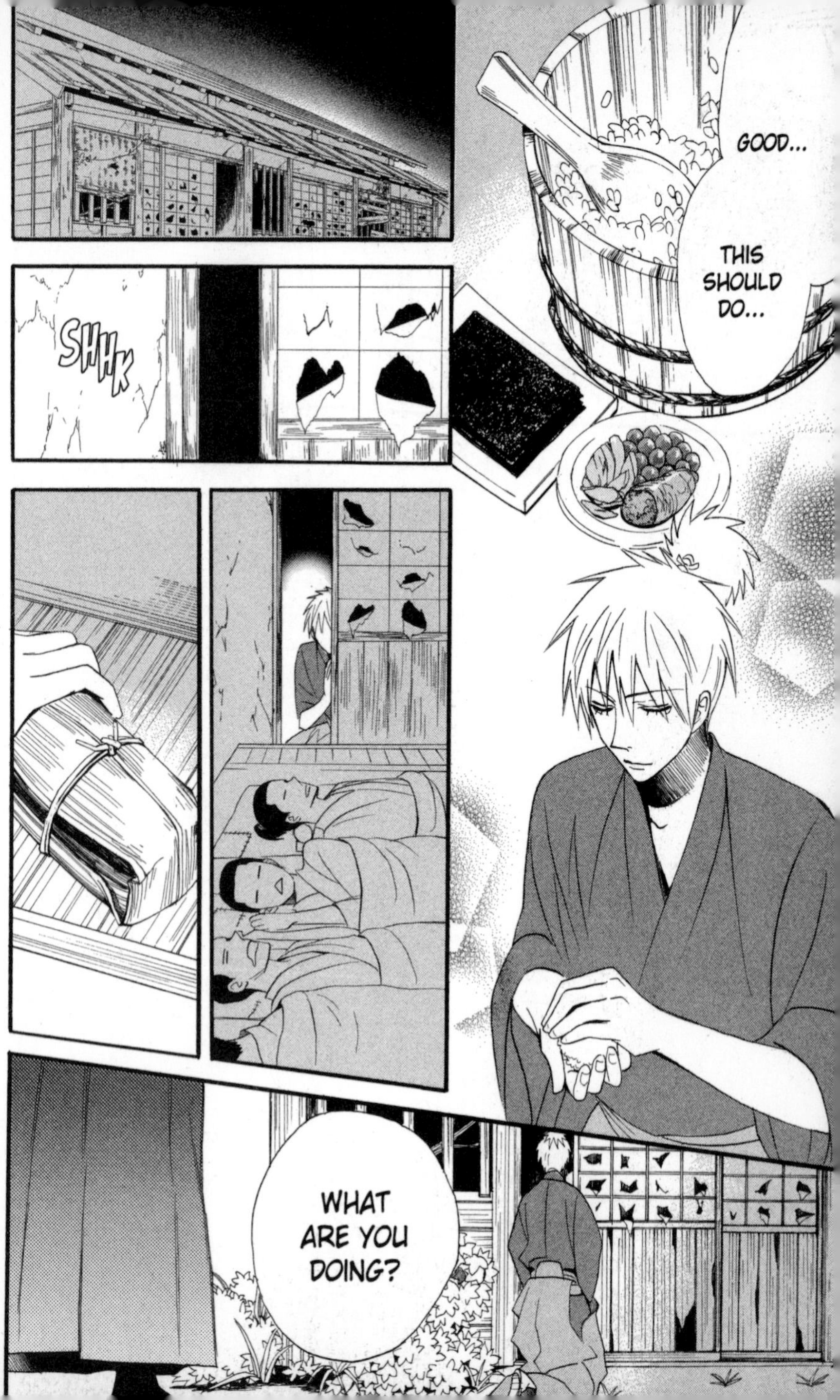
GOOD...
THIS SHOULD DO...
SHHK
WHAT ARE YOU DOING?

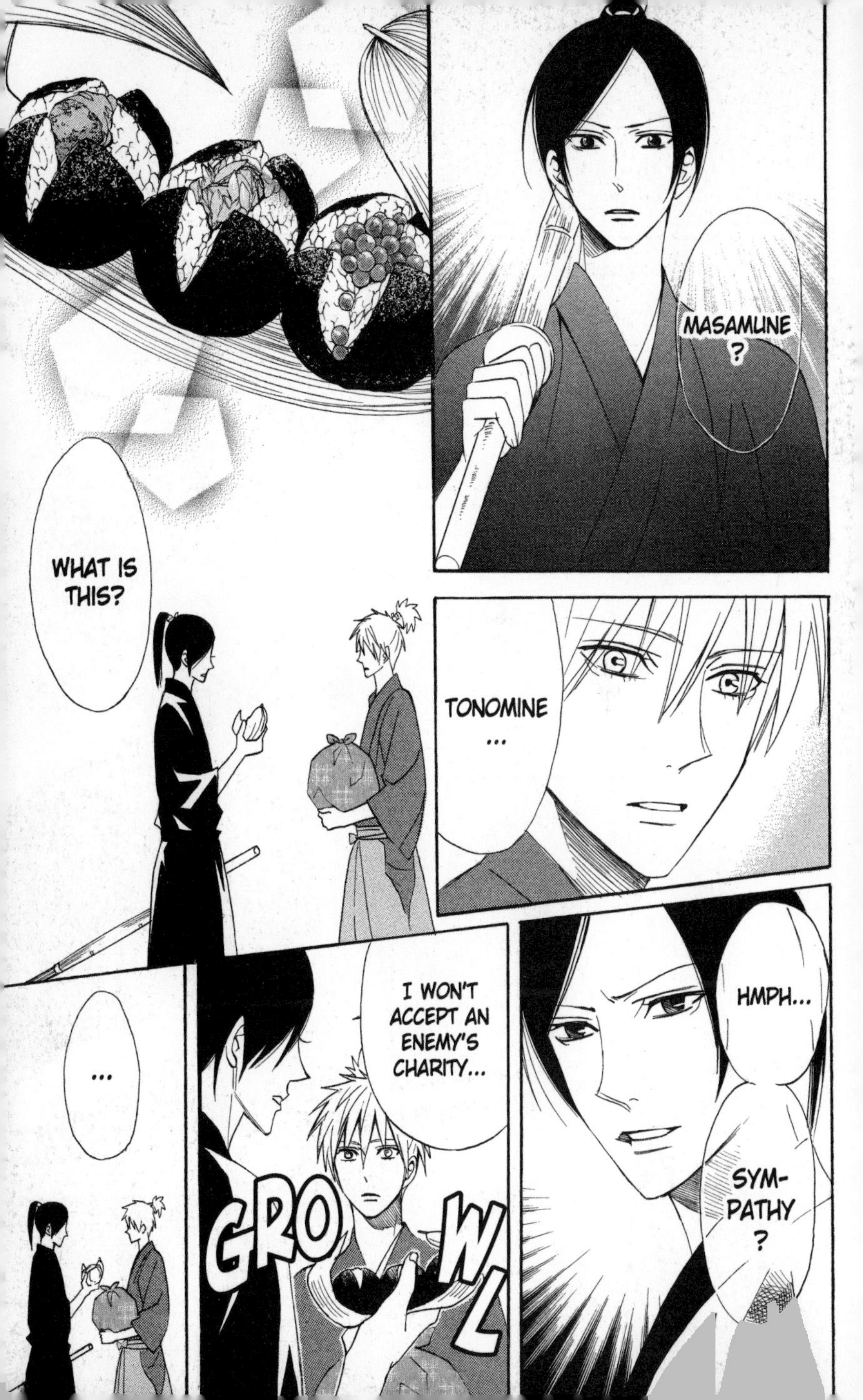
MASAMUNE ?
TONOMINE ...
WHAT IS THIS?
HMPH...
SYM-PATHY ?
I WON'T ACCEPT AN ENEMY'S CHARITY...
GROWL
...

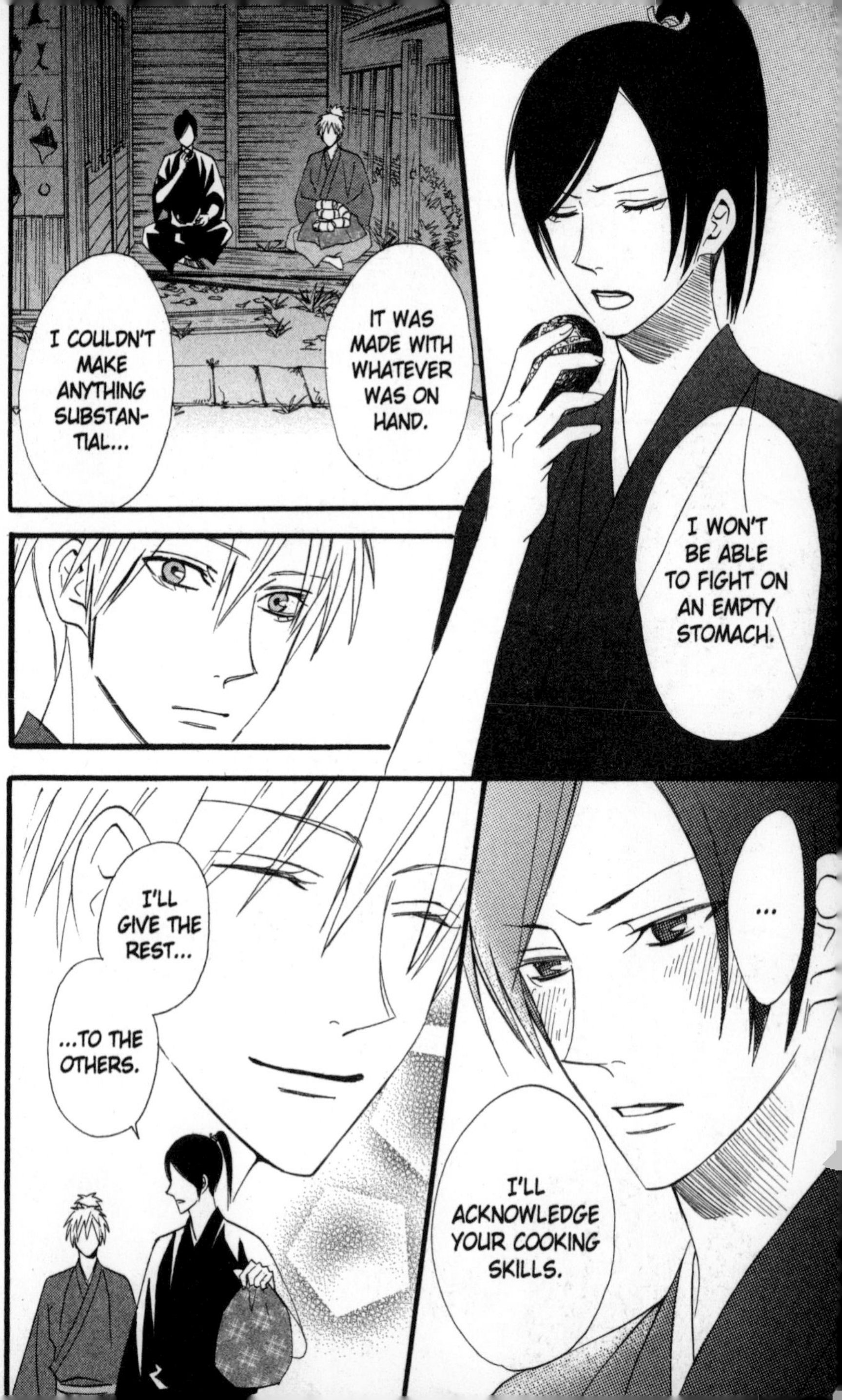
I WON'T BE ABLE TO FIGHT ON AN EMPTY STOMACH.
IT WAS MADE WITH WHATEVER WAS ON HAND.
I COULDN'T MAKE ANYTHING SUBSTAN-TIAL...
...
I'LL ACKNOWLEDGE YOUR COOKING SKILLS.
I'LL GIVE THE REST...
...TO THE OTHERS.

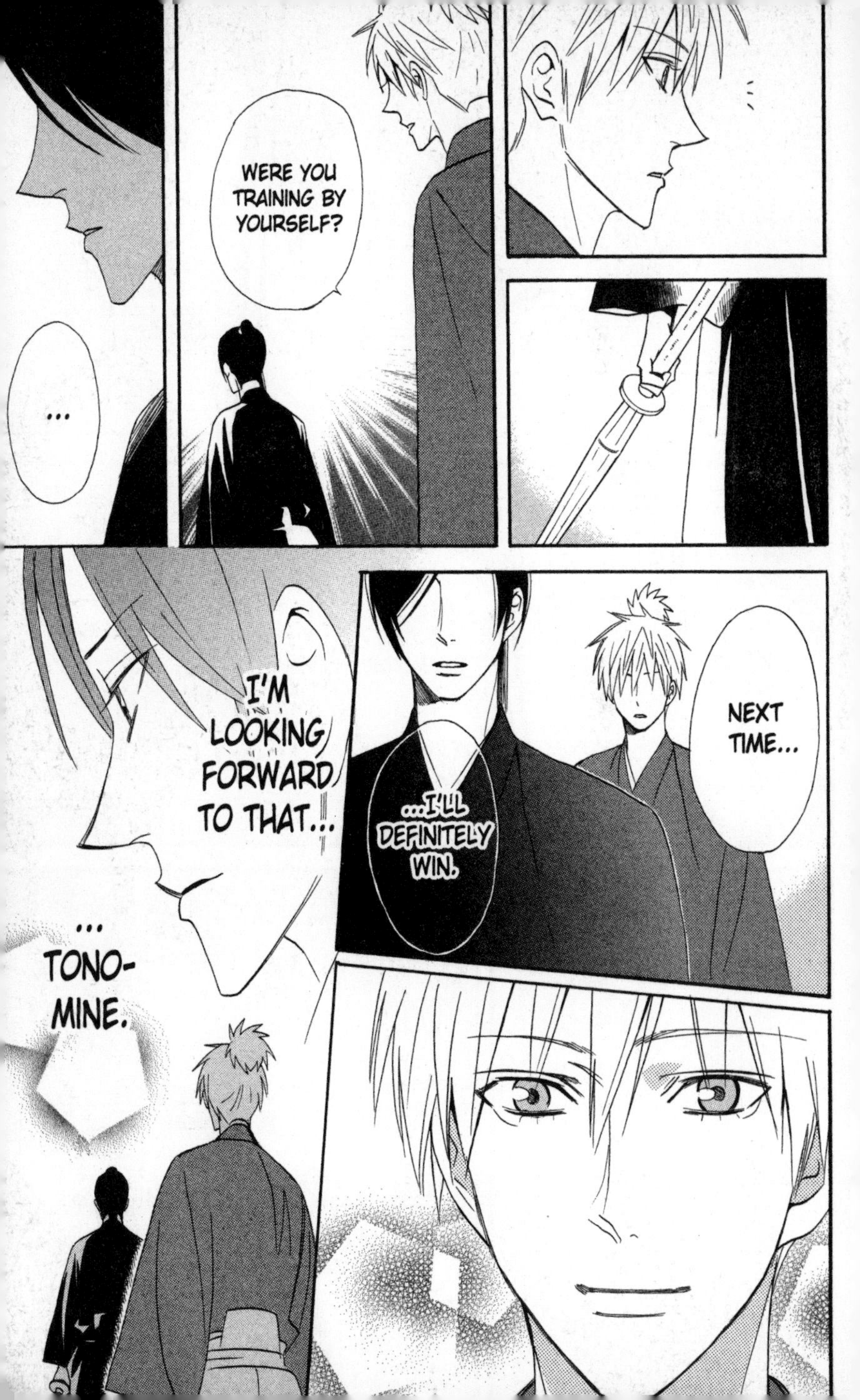
WERE YOU TRAINING BY YOURSELF?
...
NEXT TIME...
...I'LL DEFINITELY WIN.
I'M LOOKING FORWARD TO THAT...!
...TONO-MINE.

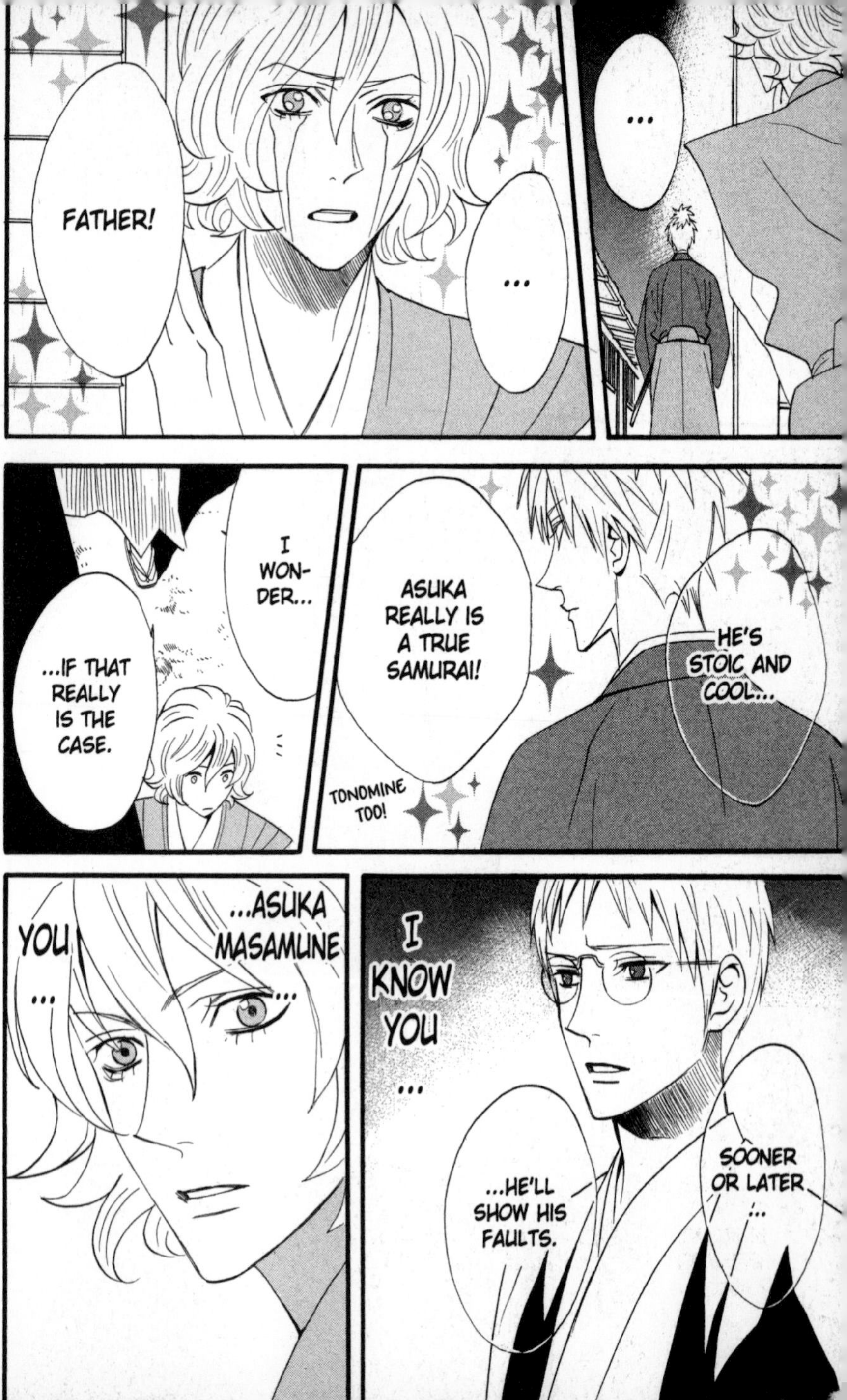
...
...
FATHER!
HE'S STOIC AND COOL...
ASUKA REALLY IS A TRUE SAMURAI!
TONOMINE TOO!
I WONDER...
...IF THAT REALLY IS THE CASE.
I KNOW YOU ...
SOONER OR LATER ...
...HE'LL SHOW HIS FAULTS.
...ASUKA MASAMUNE ...
YOU ...

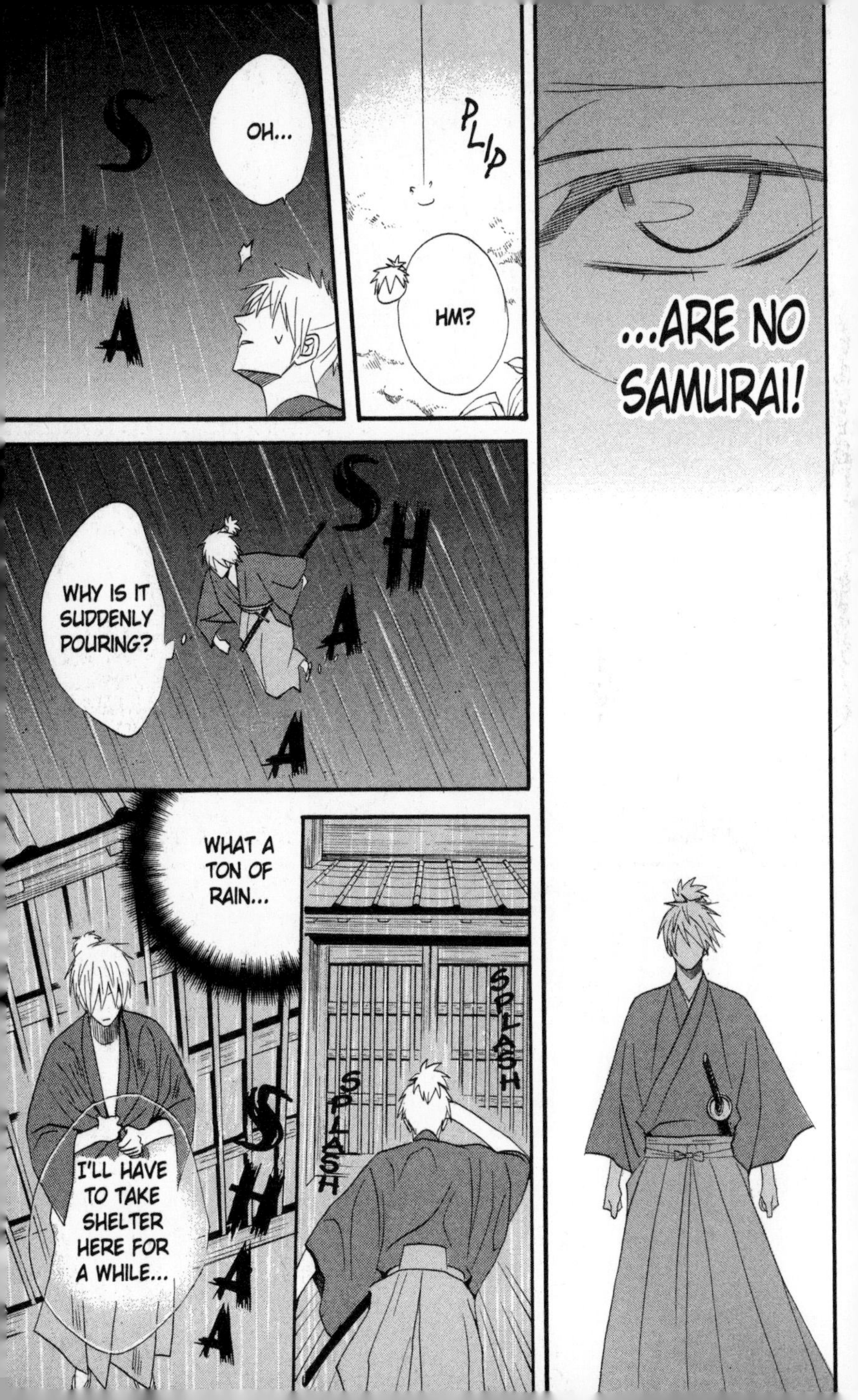
...ARE NO SAMURAI!
PLIP
HM?
SHA
OH...
SHAA
WHY IS IT SUDDENLY POURING?
SPLASH
SPLASH
WHAT A TON OF RAIN...
SHAA
I'LL HAVE TO TAKE SHELTER HERE FOR A WHILE...

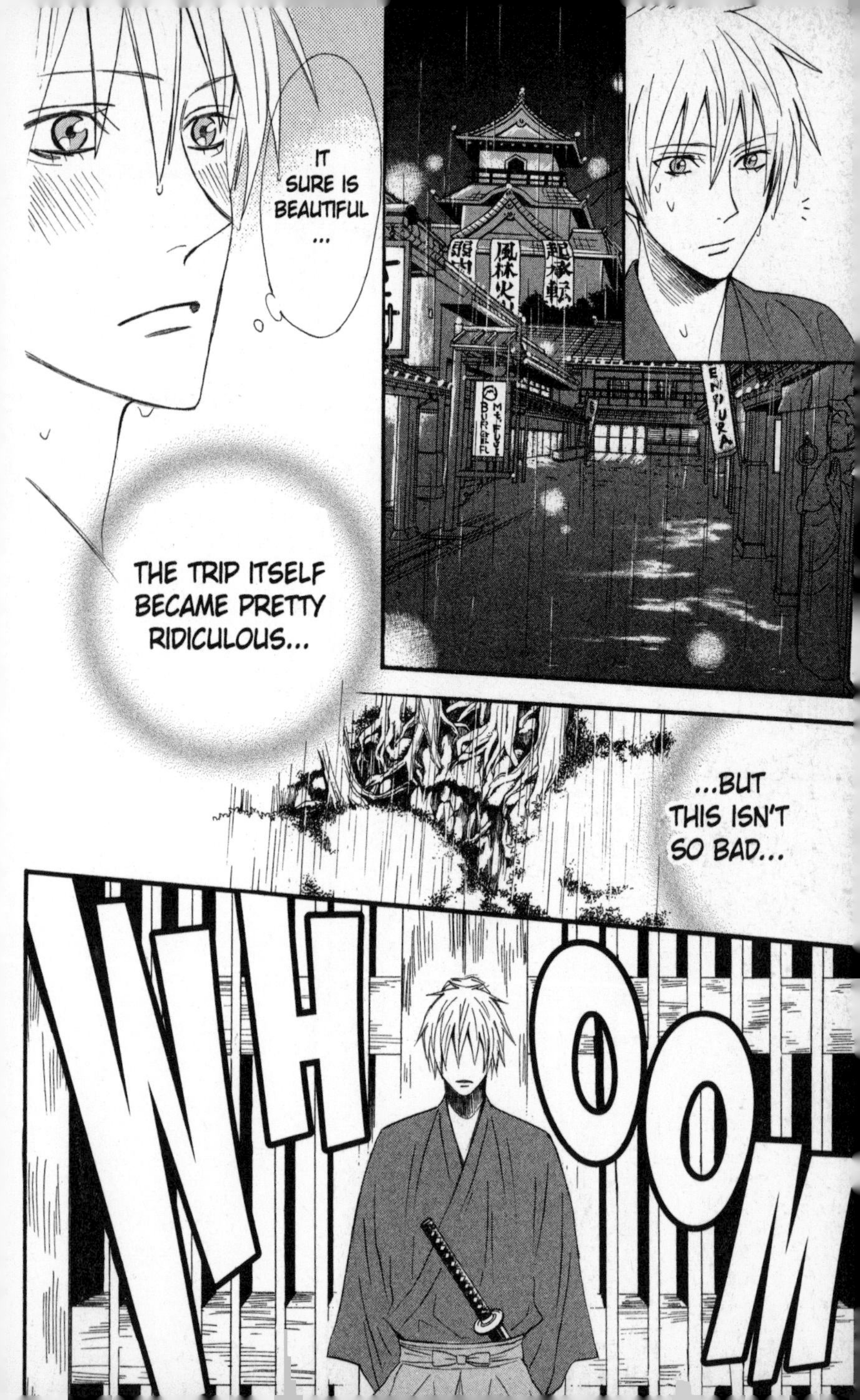
IT SURE IS BEAUTIFUL ...
THE TRIP ITSELF BECAME PRETTY RIDICULOUS...
...BUT THIS ISN'T SO BAD...
WHOOM

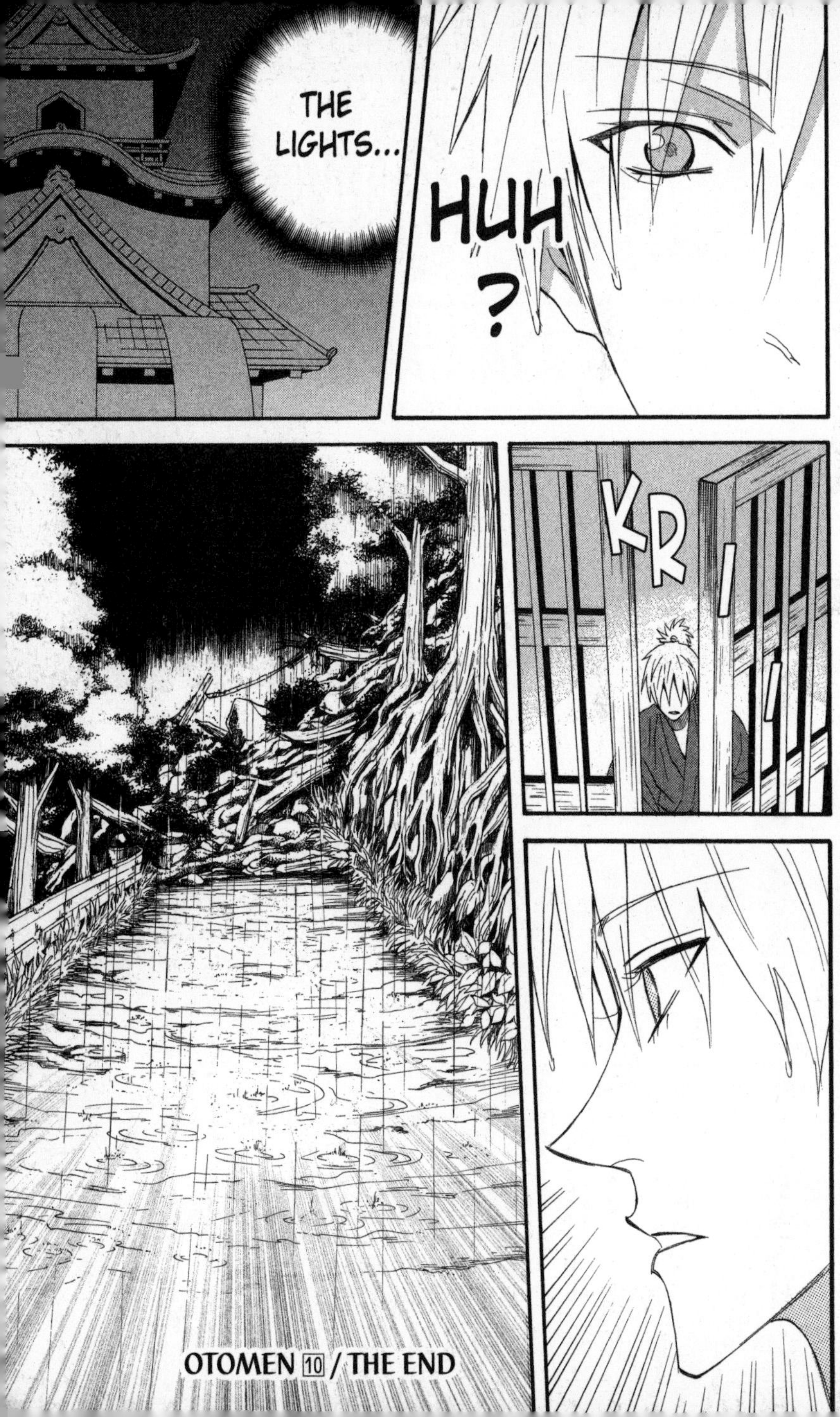
HUH ?
THE LIGHTS...
KRI I
OTOMEN 10 / THE END

TRIBUTE COMICS

GLASS OTOMEN

AYA KANNO

*This work was drawn to commemorate *Glass Mask*'s return to publication.

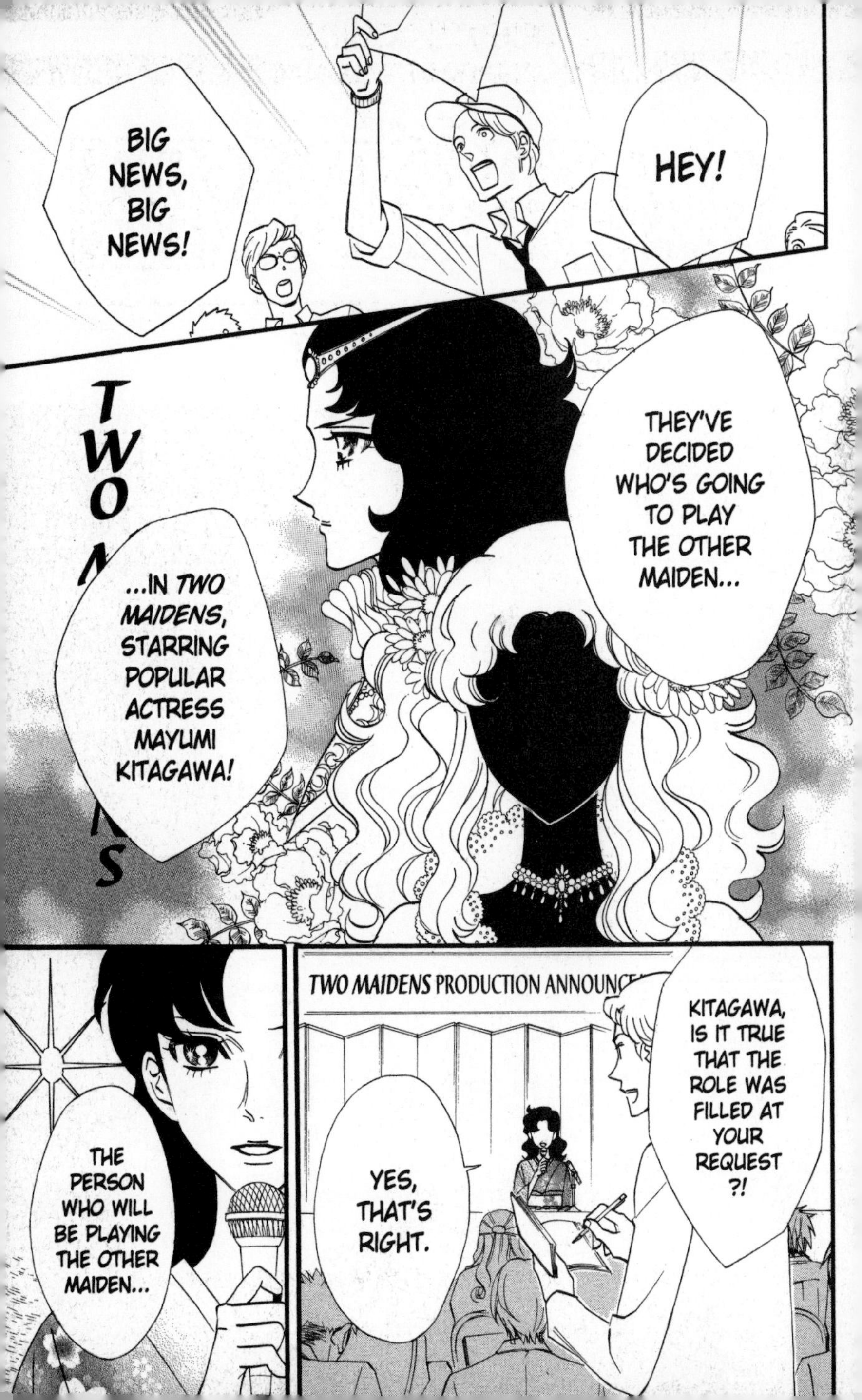
HEY!
BIG NEWS, BIG NEWS!
THEY'VE DECIDED WHO'S GOING TO PLAY THE OTHER MAIDEN...
...IN *TWO MAIDENS*, STARRING POPULAR ACTRESS MAYUMI KITAGAWA!
TWO MAIDENS PRODUCTION ANNOUNC
KITAGAWA, IS IT TRUE THAT THE ROLE WAS FILLED AT YOUR REQUEST?!
YES, THAT'S RIGHT.
THE PERSON WHO WILL BE PLAYING THE OTHER MAIDEN...

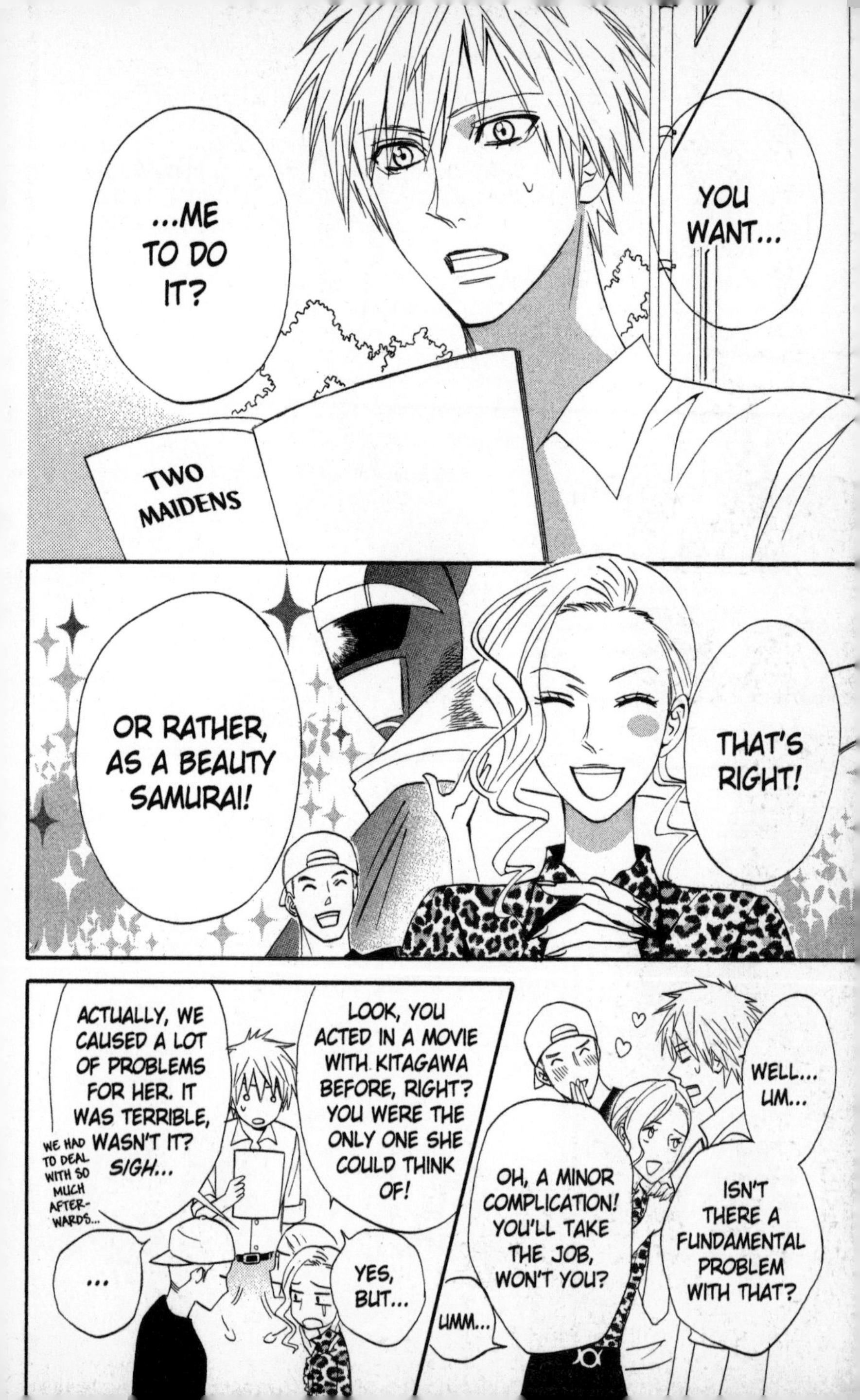
YOU WANT...
...ME TO DO IT?
TWO MAIDENS
THAT'S RIGHT!
OR RATHER, AS A BEAUTY SAMURAI!
WELL... UM...
ISN'T THERE A FUNDAMENTAL PROBLEM WITH THAT?
OH, A MINOR COMPLICATION! YOU'LL TAKE THE JOB, WON'T YOU?
UMM...
LOOK, YOU ACTED IN A MOVIE WITH KITAGAWA BEFORE, RIGHT? YOU WERE THE ONLY ONE SHE COULD THINK OF!
YES, BUT...
ACTUALLY, WE CAUSED A LOT OF PROBLEMS FOR HER. IT WAS TERRIBLE, WASN'T IT? SIGH...
WE HAD TO DEAL WITH SO MUCH AFTER-WARDS...
...

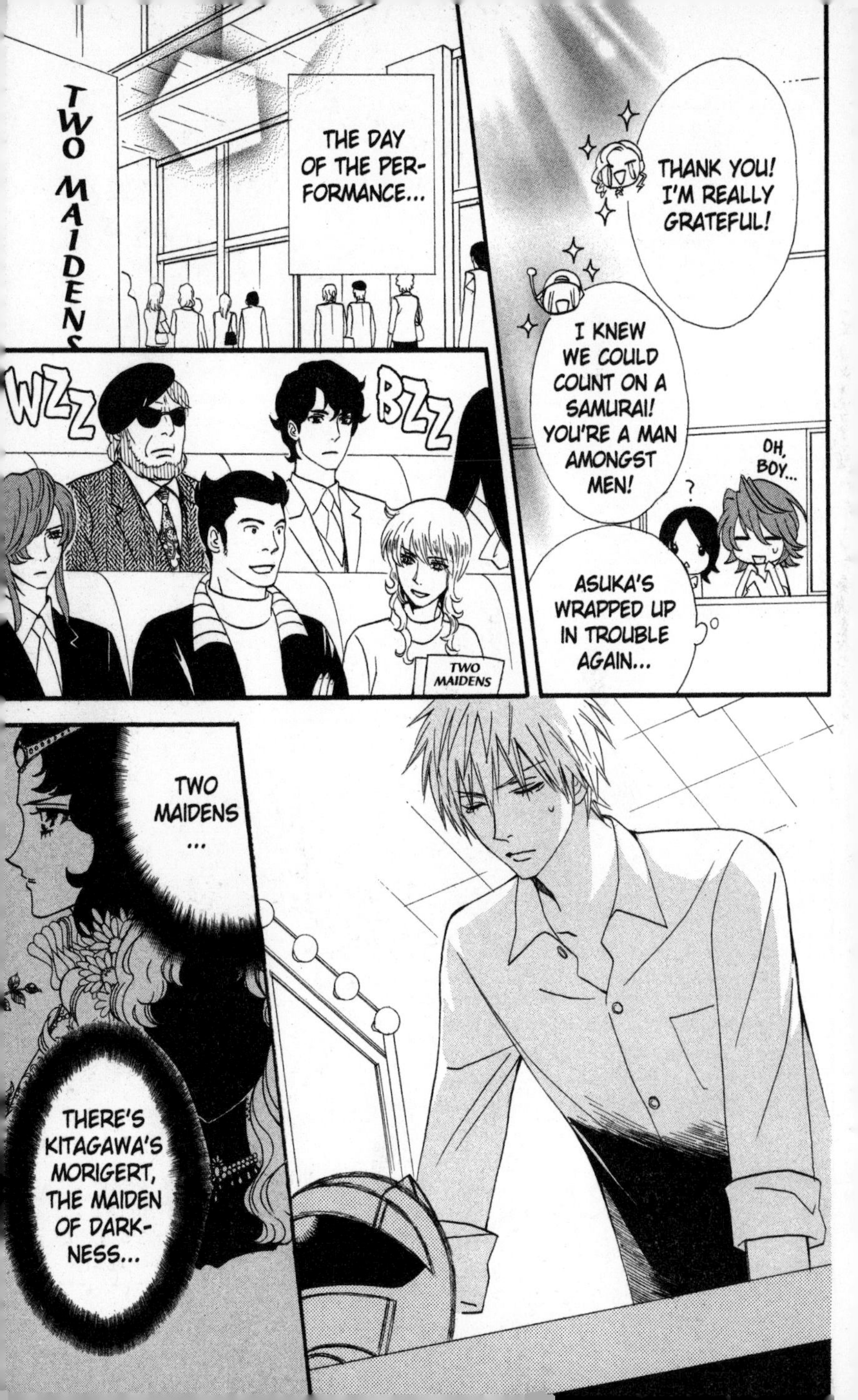
THANK YOU! I'M REALLY GRATEFUL!
I KNEW WE COULD COUNT ON A SAMURAI! YOU'RE A MAN AMONGST MEN!
OH, BOY...
?
ASUKA'S WRAPPED UP IN TROUBLE AGAIN...
THE DAY OF THE PER-FORMANCE...
TWO MAIDENS
BZZ
WZZ
TWO MAIDENS
TWO MAIDENS ...
THERE'S KITAGAWA'S MORIGERT, THE MAIDEN OF DARK-NESS...

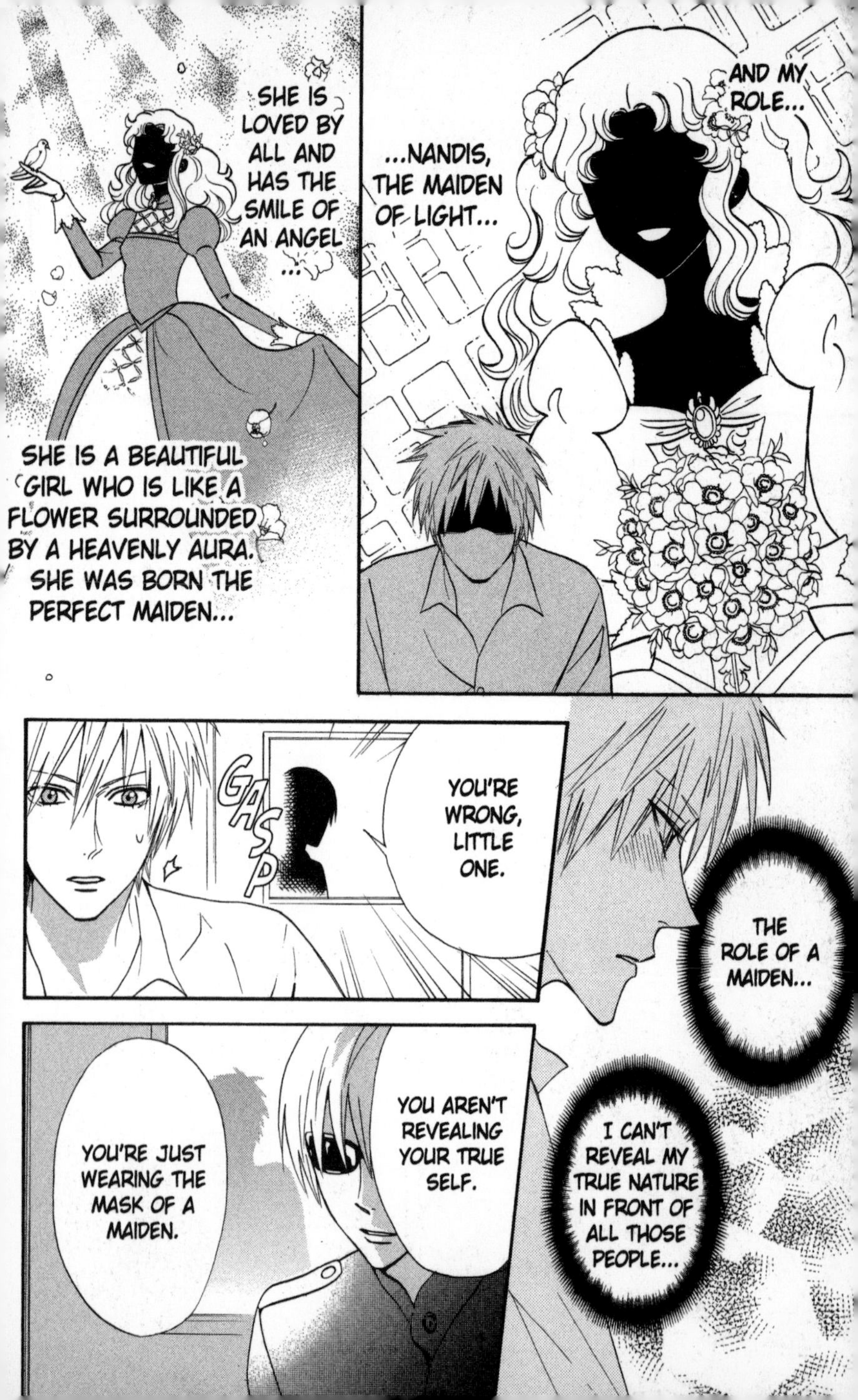
AND MY ROLE...
...NANDIS, THE MAIDEN OF LIGHT...
SHE IS LOVED BY ALL AND HAS THE SMILE OF AN ANGEL...
SHE IS A BEAUTIFUL GIRL WHO IS LIKE A FLOWER SURROUNDED BY A HEAVENLY AURA. SHE WAS BORN THE PERFECT MAIDEN...
THE ROLE OF A MAIDEN...
I CAN'T REVEAL MY TRUE NATURE IN FRONT OF ALL THOSE PEOPLE...
YOU'RE WRONG, LITTLE ONE.
GASP
YOU AREN'T REVEALING YOUR TRUE SELF.
YOU'RE JUST WEARING THE MASK OF A MAIDEN.

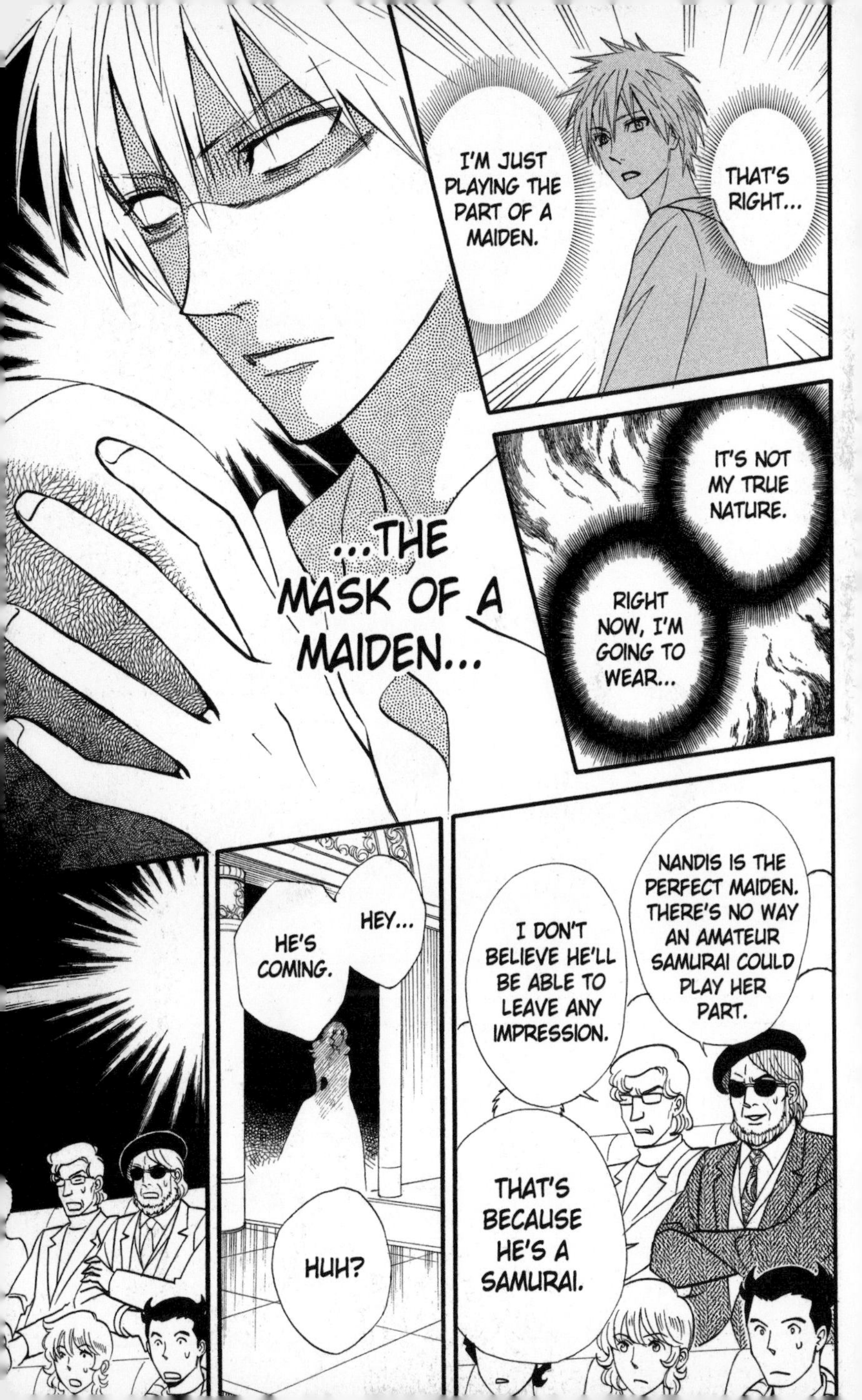
THAT'S RIGHT...
I'M JUST PLAYING THE PART OF A MAIDEN.
IT'S NOT MY TRUE NATURE.
RIGHT NOW, I'M GOING TO WEAR...
...THE MASK OF A MAIDEN...
NANDIS IS THE PERFECT MAIDEN. THERE'S NO WAY AN AMATEUR SAMURAI COULD PLAY HER PART.
I DON'T BELIEVE HE'LL BE ABLE TO LEAVE ANY IMPRESSION.
THAT'S BECAUSE HE'S A SAMURAI.
HEY...
HE'S COMING.
HUH?

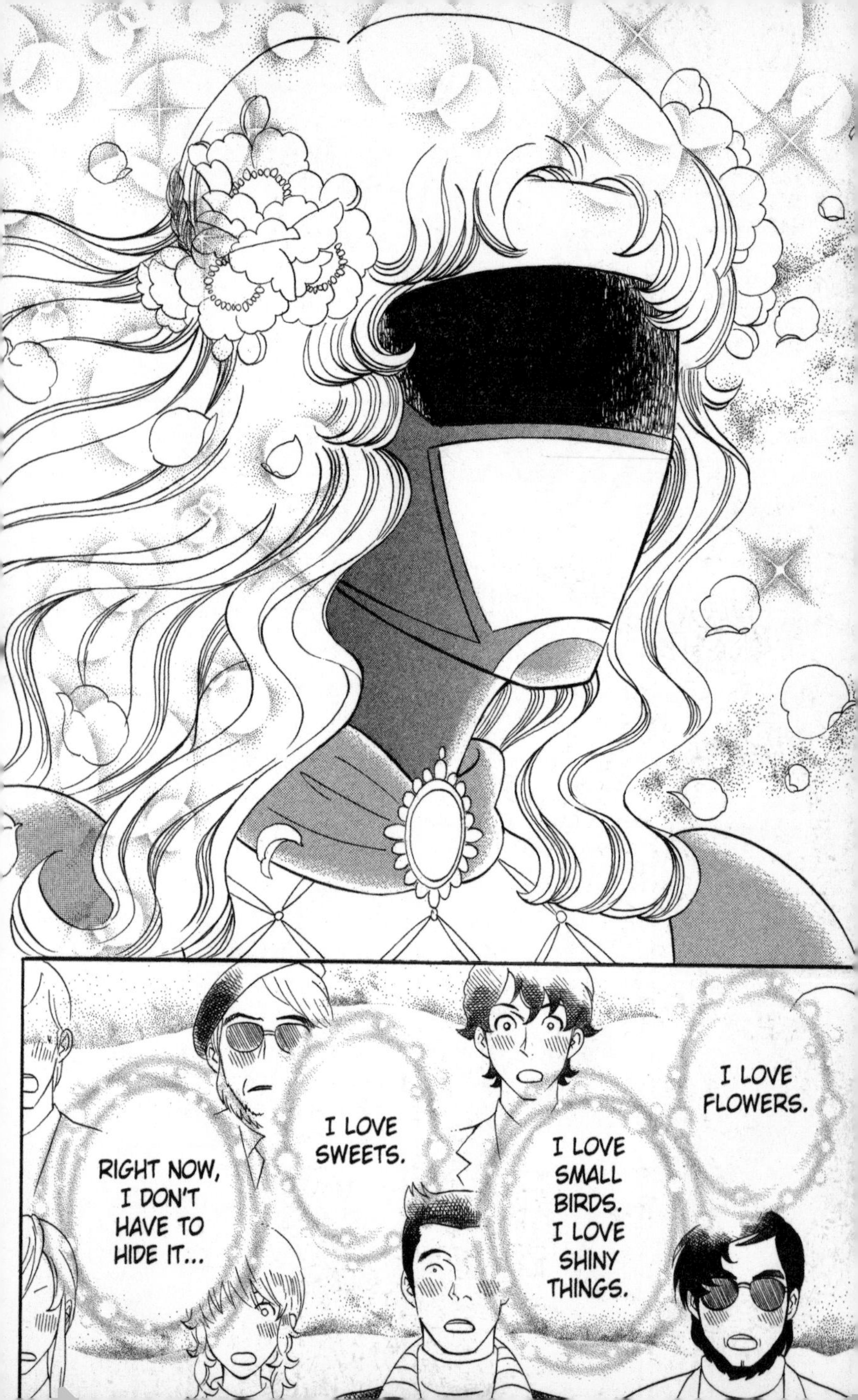
I LOVE FLOWERS.
I LOVE SMALL BIRDS. I LOVE SHINY THINGS.
I LOVE SWEETS.
RIGHT NOW, I DON'T HAVE TO HIDE IT...

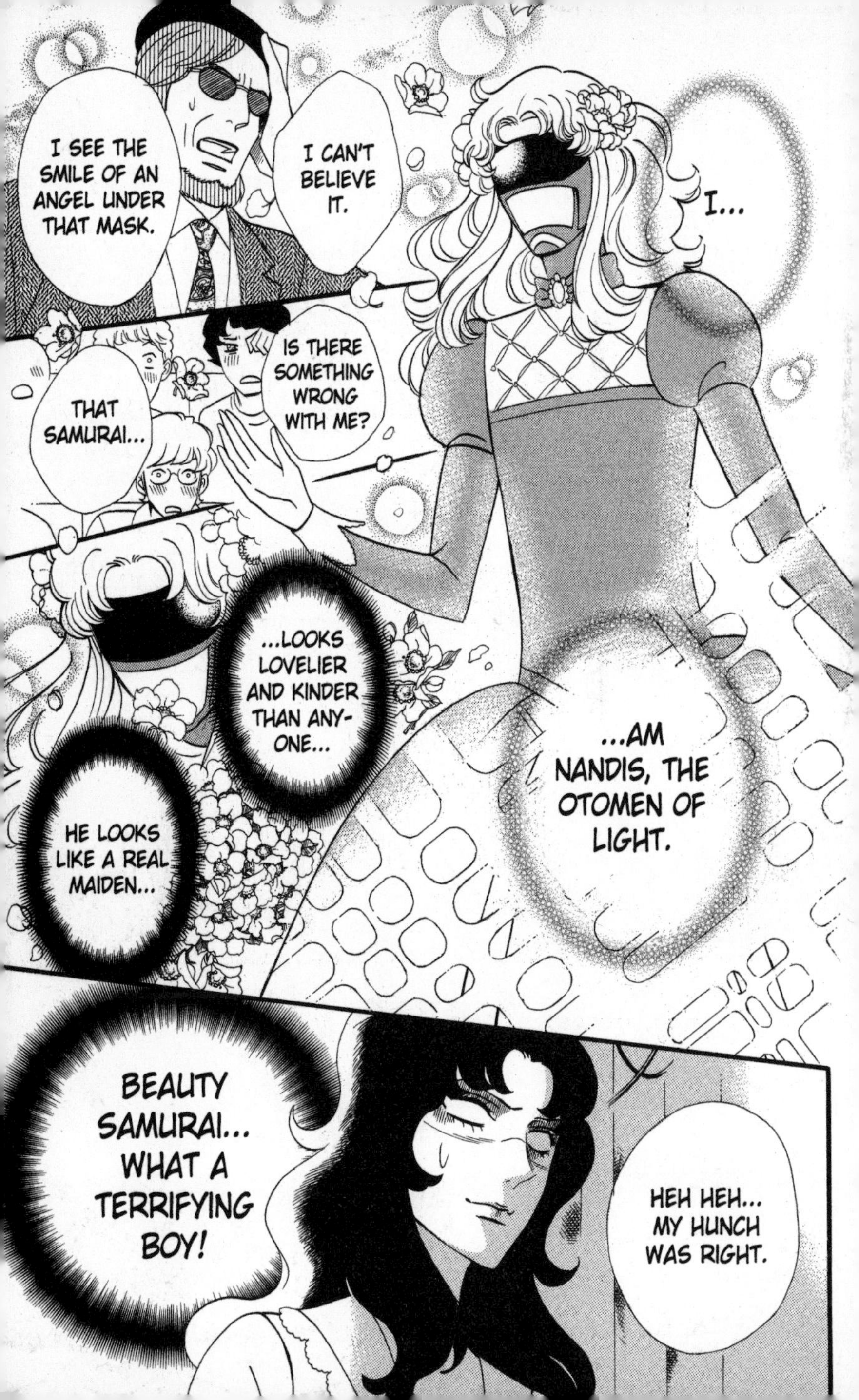
I...
...AM NANDIS, THE OTOMEN OF LIGHT.
I CAN'T BELIEVE IT.
I SEE THE SMILE OF AN ANGEL UNDER THAT MASK.
IS THERE SOMETHING WRONG WITH ME?
THAT SAMURAI...
...LOOKS LOVELIER AND KINDER THAN ANY-ONE...
HE LOOKS LIKE A REAL MAIDEN...
HEH HEH... MY HUNCH WAS RIGHT.
BEAUTY SAMURAI... WHAT A TERRIFYING BOY!

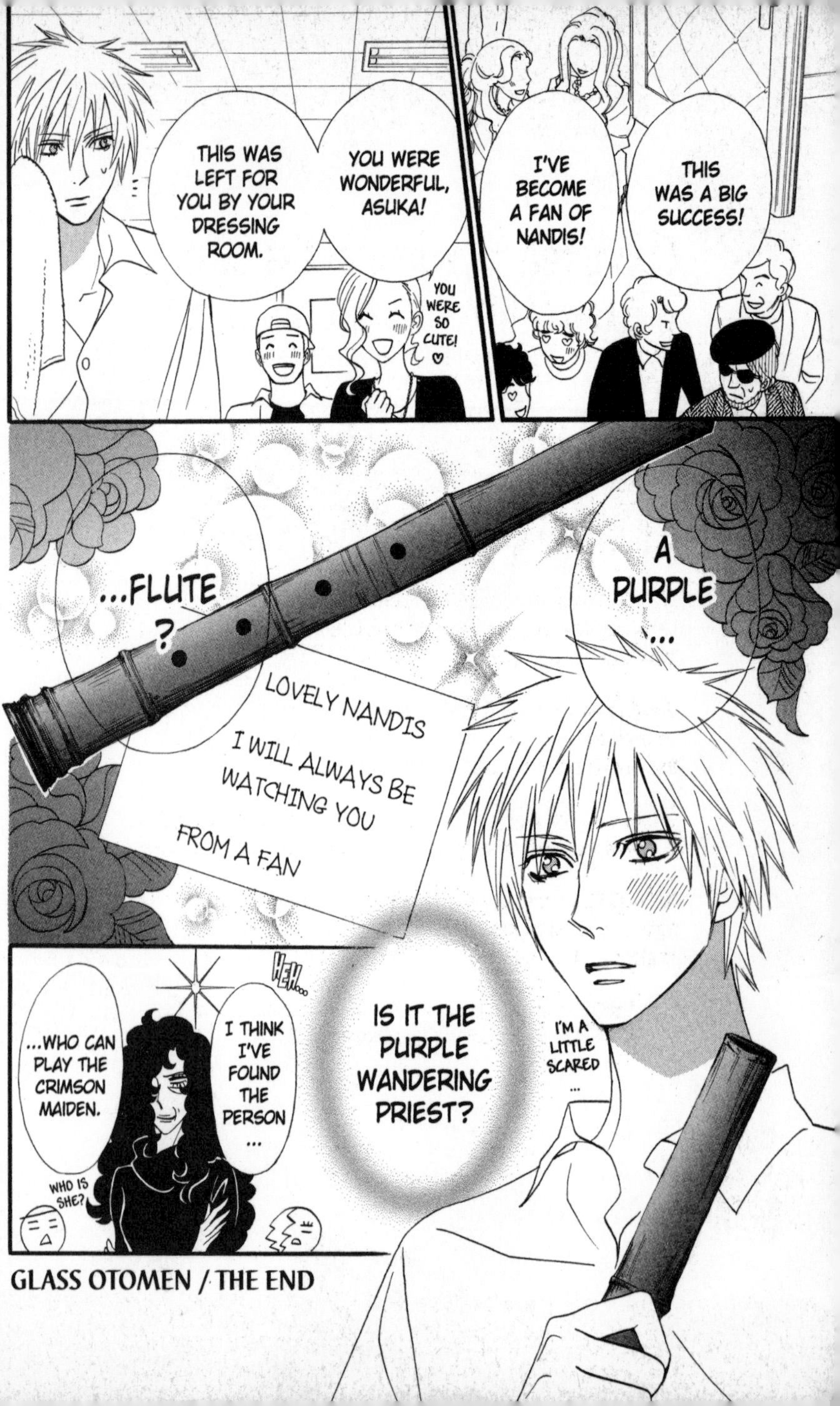
THIS WAS A BIG SUCCESS!
I'VE BECOME A FAN OF NANDIS!
YOU WERE WONDERFUL, ASUKA!
YOU WERE SO CUTE! ♡
THIS WAS LEFT FOR YOU BY YOUR DRESSING ROOM.
A PURPLE...
...FLUTE?
LOVELY NANDIS
I WILL ALWAYS BE WATCHING YOU
FROM A FAN
IS IT THE PURPLE WANDERING PRIEST?
I'M A LITTLE SCARED...
HEH...
I THINK I'VE FOUND THE PERSON...
...WHO CAN PLAY THE CRIMSON MAIDEN.
WHO IS SHE?

GLASS OTOMEN / THE END

Confused by some of the terms, but too MANLY to ask for help?

Here are some **cultural notes** to assist you!

HONORIFICS

Chan – an informal honorific used to address children and females. *Chan* can also be used toward animals, lovers, intimate friends and people whom one has known since childhood.

Kun – an informal honorific used primarily toward males; it can be used by people of more senior status addressing those junior to them or by anyone addressing male children.

San – the most common honorific title. It is used to address people outside one's immediate family and close circle of friends.

Senpai – used to address one's senior colleagues or mentor figures; it is used when students refer to or address more senior students in their school.

Sensei – honorific title used to address teachers as well as professionals such as doctors, lawyers and artists.

NOTES

Page 10, panel 4 | Ujikintoki
Ujikintoki is a shaved ice dessert that is topped with green tea syrup and red beans.

Page 23, panel 3 | Visual Kei
Similar to glam rock, visual kei is a branch of Japanese rock in which the musicians' hairstyles, makeup and costumes convey an outrageous and sometimes androgynous look.

Page 81, panel 4 | Love Chick
Love Chick is a very popular shojo manga that Juta Tachibana secretly writes and draws (under the pen name Jewel Sachihana), and it is serialized in the manga magazine *Hana to Mame*. Asuka is normally a big fan of this series.

Page 99, panel 4 | Hana to Mame
The name *Hana to Mame* (Flowers and Beans) is a play on the real shojo manga magazine *Hana to Yume* (Flowers and Dreams) published by Hakusensha.

Page 110, panel 5 | Bento
A lunch box that may contain rice, meat, pickles and an assortment of side dishes. Sometimes the food is arranged in such a way as to resemble objects like animals, flowers, leaves, and so forth.

Page 124, panel 5 | Iruka Sakiyama
Asuka's former fiancée who loves cute things. For more information, see *Otomen* volume 2.

Page 146, panel 1 | Bushido
Bushido means "the way of the warrior" and is a code of conduct that emphasizes loyalty, martial arts mastery and honor unto death.

Page 158, panel 5 | Mito Komon
Mito Komon is a Japanese samurai drama about the fictionalized travels of Mitsukuni Tokugawa, the former vice-shogun of the Mito province.

Page 162, panel 3 | Hara-kiri
Ritual suicide by disembowelment practiced by the Japanese samurai or formerly decreed by a court instead of the death penalty.

Page 169, panel 1 | Sekigahara
Sekigahara was the site of one of the largest battles in Japanese history.

Page 176, panel 5 | Takezo
Shinmen Takezo is also known as Miyamoto Musashi, a famous Japanese swordsman.

Page 191, panel 2 | Mayumi Kitagawa
An actress who starred in the *Beauty Samurai* movie with Asuka. For more information, see *Otomen* volume 6.

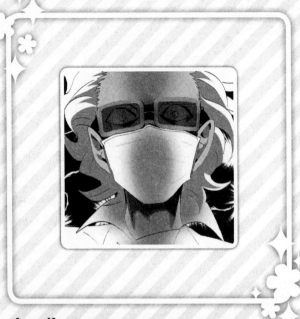

Aya Kanno was born in Tokyo, Japan.
She is the creator of *Soul Rescue* and *Blank Slate*
(originally published as *Akusaga* in Japan's
BetsuHana magazine). Her latest work, *Otomen*,
is currently being serialized in *BetsuHana*.

OTOMEN

Vol. 10
Shojo Beat Edition

Story and Art by | **AYA KANNO**

Translation & Adaptation | **JN Productions**
Touch-up Art & Lettering | **Mark McMurray**
Design | **Fawn Lau**
Editor | **Amy Yu**

Otomen by Aya Kanno © Aya Kanno 2010
All rights reserved. First published in Japan in 2010 by HAKUSENSHA, Inc., Tokyo.
English language translation rights arranged with HAKUSENSHA, Inc., Tokyo.

The rights of the author(s) of the work(s) in this publication to be so identified
have been asserted in accordance with the Copyright, Designs and Patents Act 1988.
A CIP catalogue record for this book is available from the British Library.

Printed in the U.S.A.

Published by VIZ Media, LLC
P.O. Box 77010
San Francisco, CA 94107

10 9 8 7 6 5 4 3 2 1
First printing, May 2011

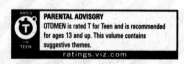

PARENTAL ADVISORY
OTOMEN is rated T for Teen and is recommended
for ages 13 and up. This volume contains
suggestive themes.
ratings.viz.com

www.viz.com

www.shojobeat.com

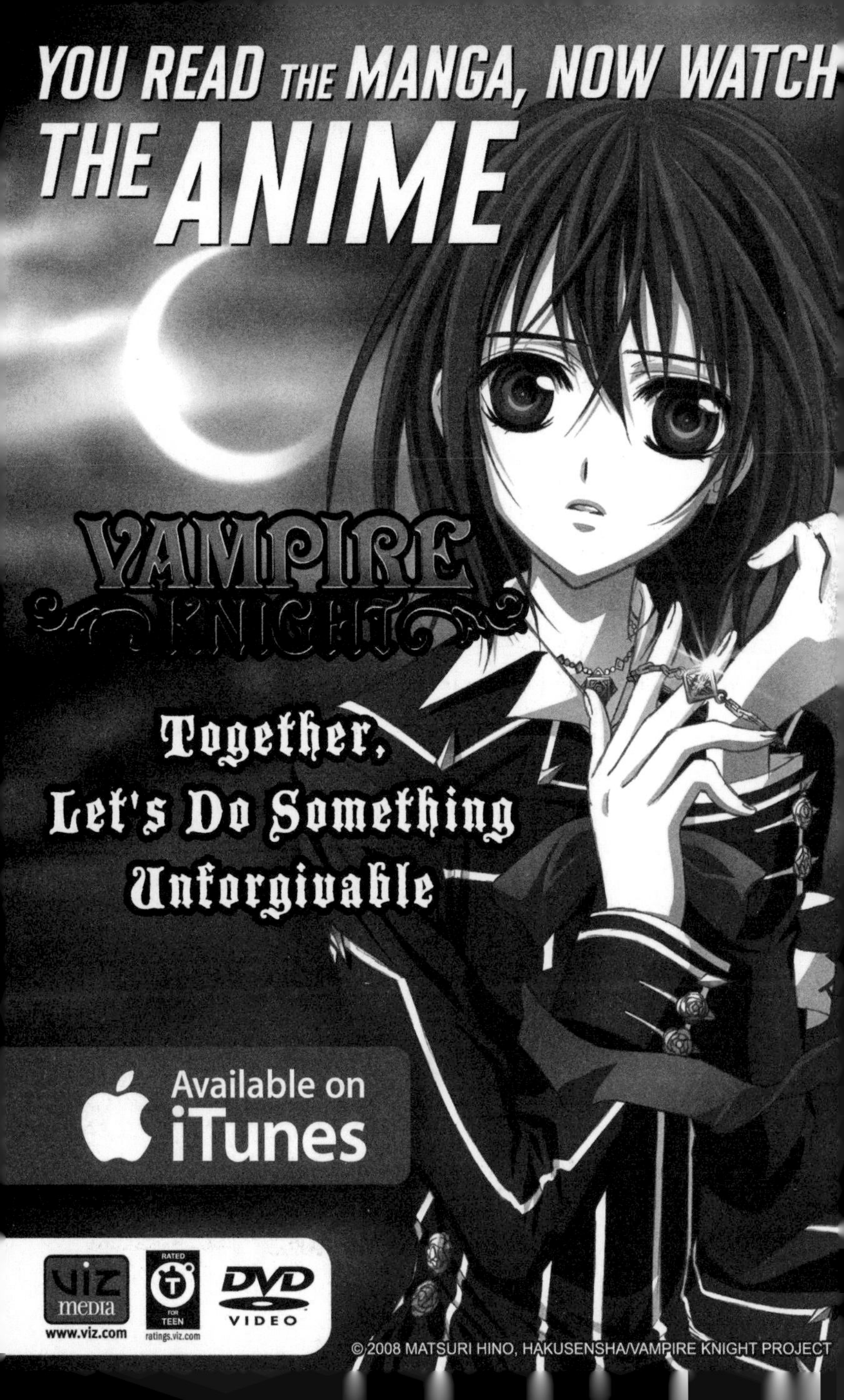
YOU READ THE MANGA, NOW WATCH THE ANIME
VAMPIRE KNIGHT
Together, Let's Do Something Unforgivable
Available on iTunes
VIZ media
www.viz.com
RATED T FOR TEEN
ratings.viz.com
DVD VIDEO
© 2008 MATSURI HINO, HAKUSENSHA/VAMPIRE KNIGHT PROJECT

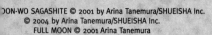

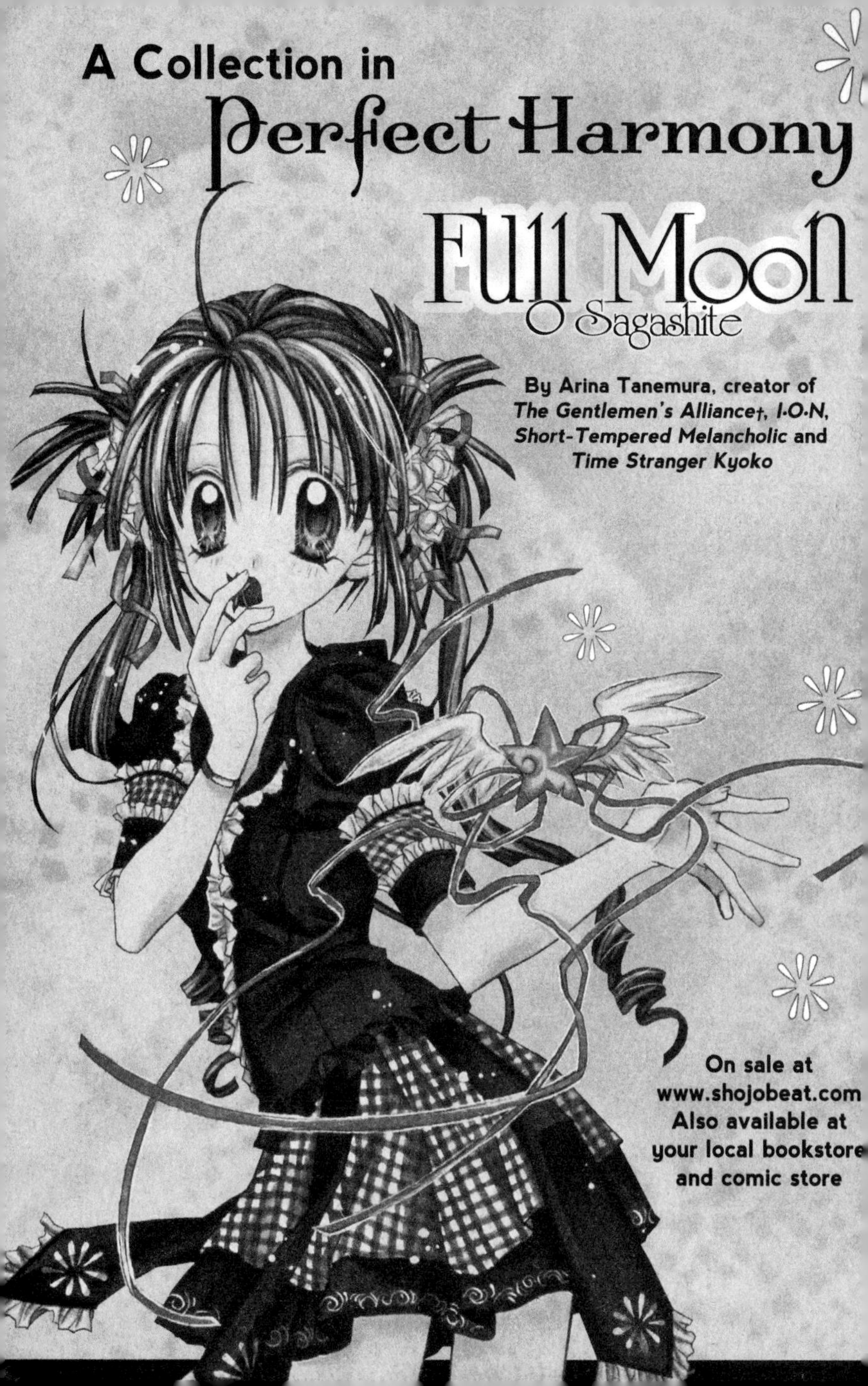
A Collection in
Perfect Harmony
Full Moon
O Sagashite
By Arina Tanemura, creator of
The Gentlemen's Alliance†, *I·O·N*,
Short-Tempered Melancholic and
Time Stranger Kyoko
On sale at
www.shojobeat.com
Also available at
your local bookstore
and comic store